Les Ca

Heaven Can Wait
I'm Busy

The Ultimate Challenge

To Ryon with Best wishes Les

Leslie Carvall Publishing

Published in Great Britain in 2016 by Leslie Carvall Publishing

This edition first published in May 2016

Copyright 2016 © Leslie Carvall Publishing
The moral rights of the author have been asserted

A CIP catalogue record of this book is
available from the British Library

ISBN 978-0-9935937-0-3

All maps supplied by FreeVectorMaps.com

Typeset by Hilite Design and Reprographics Limited
Print Managed by Jellyfish Print Solutions

Leslie Carvall Publishing
lescarvall@hotmail.co.uk

www. heavencanwaitimbusy.org

Someone's watching over me

Content to follow the truck ahead of me, I was driving close behind and being sucked along at 55 mph, fatigued and tired from driving long hours day after day with no proper sleep. I just sat there thinking about what I had to do the following day, how my wife was coping at home on her own and anything else that came into my head. Realising that I had been behind the lorry long enough, I decided to overtake. Normally it's not a problem, first talk to the car nicely to get it excited, change down to 4th or 3rd gear, then wind up the little 1328cc engine by hitting the floor with the accelerator and away you go. I checked my rear mirror; there was one car behind but a long way back. I then let the lorry move forward so I could have a look to see if I could overtake. I moved out to the oncoming traffic lane, the road ahead was clear apart from a white van coming towards me but there was plenty of time to overtake. Already travelling at 55 mph, I was short of additional power, I was already heavy on the accelerator, my overloaded, low-powered little Jimny struggled to respond. I changed down to 4th and wound her up.

I was slowly moving forward, the white van ahead was closer now but I still had time. The car behind had followed me to overtake, I looked ahead, the shock when I realised that there were two lorries and not one, driving nose to tail, I still could make it. I coaxed my little car along the side of the first lorry at about 60 mph, my mouth had dried and beads of sweat formed on my forehead. "Make a decision," a voice resonated in my head. At this point I was level with the driver of the first lorry, he could see the accident about to happen and he looked down at me, our eyes met momentarily but I was still overtaking. "Make a decision, look for a way out," I said to myself as

I glanced at the rear view mirror and seeing, to my horror, the car behind was now on my rear bumper. At the same time, I noticed that my forward momentum was slowing and engine rpm was dropping, why, why, why? Desperately, I scanned the panel trying to find what was wrong, I changed down to 3rd gear, the little engine was screaming, I then realised it was not the engine, I'm going up an incline, I won't make it. I looked ahead to see where the white van was, the shock that followed was a heart stopper, it wasn't a slow moving van it was a fast moving white Toyota truck, lights flashing and horn screaming, coming straight at me. The alarm bell ringing in my head was deafening, there was nothing I could do, the Toyota kept coming, braking wheels and smoking tyres as it skidded towards me, no hard shoulder at the road edge to offer either of us sanctuary, the outcome was unavoidable.

My first contact with Les Carvall was during 2011 when I received a management plan relating to a major project he was bringing together. I read about his proposal to drive around the world in a Suzuki Jimny in aid of charity, at the time I thought it a bit ambitious but certainly interesting enough to agree to a meeting with him. I met Les mainly to discuss details of the project and at the same time meet the person who was to undertake such a daunting task - and without any additional support. I was surprised when Les said he would be 73 years old when he set off on his epic journey but he convinced me that Suzuki should assist in some way, not solely because he chose a Suzuki Jimny to drive around the world but also his will and sheer determination to succeed.

During the period leading up to the departure day of 31st March 2013 the one man one vehicle project had become a two vehicle eight man team effort with one new car donated by Suzuki. As a representative of Suzuki GB PLC, I remained in contact with Les providing support both at the beginning through Newmans Suzuki Southampton and then later with our global dealer network as he travelled. I was confident that both Suzuki Jimny cars would perform as required and eventually return Les and his crew back to the UK with a glowing testimonial. My confidence in Les to succeed was never in doubt and my colleagues and I at Suzuki GB would like to congratulate Les and the whole team for a job well done. They certainly reinforced the outstanding durability reputation of the Jimny too.

Alun Parry
Head of Press and PR Automobile Division
Suzuki GB PLC

The Crew

I would like to offer my sincere thanks and appreciation to the guys who took part as road crew at various stages. With their approval I have been able to write about the journey the way it happened, the trials and tribulations as we travelled, clashes of personalities, and tension at times, as a result of people being confined together for long periods of time. The journey in the format as described in the book would not have been possible without their participation.

Les Carvell
Author and project director

Crew at the welcome home reception at the Novotel Southampton.
From left front Roland Spencer, middle left Keith Twyford, back left Les Carvall,
right front Glyn Maher, middle right Mike Bailey, back right Graham Higgins

Author's notes

 What I have written is a personal narrative of the situations and issues that I experienced, and the decisions that I made during the preparation period up to departure day and the journey around the world, also how it affected me personally. The events all happened as described, although on occasion I have used a little creative writing to reflect my personal mood at the time. The chronology and geography is correct to the best of my knowledge and according to my notes I made as I travelled. It is all about what I personally saw, heard and experienced, therefore, so as not to be restricted or compromised in any way, I have decided to tell the story the way it happened. I have not excluded myself from personal criticism or credit for the way I conducted myself or for the way I held everything together as we travelled. I will be open and to the point when explaining some of the situations and clashes of personalities caused when people are confined together for long periods and travelling to a strict schedule. However, I would like to take this opportunity to thank those who took part and accompanied me at various times as road crew, Roland Spencer, Keith Twyford, Graham Higgins, Mike Bailey, Glyn Maher and Roger Winkworth for their support throughout the preparation and the journey itself, particularly when compromises had to be made to keep us on track or when the going got difficult. I would like to give a special thank you to Alan Butler and Charles Scott who, due to health issues, could not participate as originally planned.

To help guide you through the story I have divided it into three parts.

1. My history and what makes me tick, the motivation to drive around the world

2. Conception, Preparation and Departure, March 31st 2013

3. No turning back, the journey around the world

I am indebted to my wife, Vi, and our family for their support, particularly my daughter Carole who comforted and supported Vi in my absence. I apologise to everyone for any distress caused as a result of my quest to drive around the world. In memory of our son Lee, who passed away and left us for another place on 4th June 2008, his memory was my constant travelling companion.

I would like to thank my very good friend, Keith Rimmer, he made sure we had the best website and was always there when I needed a chat. Very special thanks to David Ellery, Viewpoint Productions and Maureen Wycherley for her support and who managed to keep me pointing in the right direction. Also Alun Parry, Suzuki G.B. for believing in me and for the support I received from Suzuki worldwide. To Guy Foster, Newmans Suzuki, Glen Findley and Claire Smith, Novotel Southampton, and my friends, Robert Rickman, Anu Overseas India, Trevor Strickland, Brian Shearsby, Richard Austin Alloys, Julian Clegg of Julian's People B.B.C. Radio Solent and many others who helped me, I would like to say a very big thank you.

Les Carvall

Contents

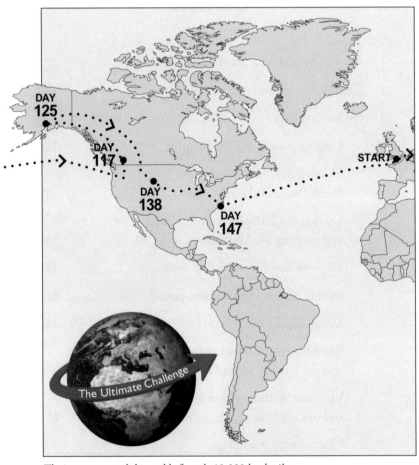

The journey around the world of nearly 19,000 land miles

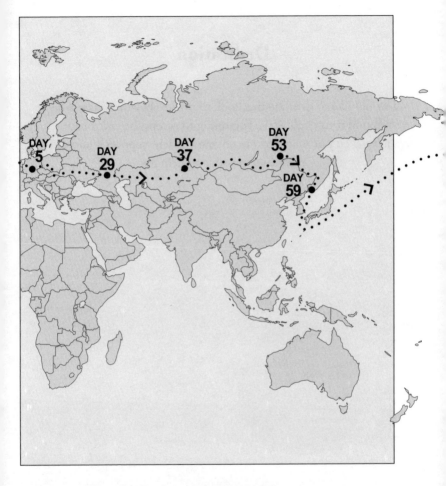

Approximate route with some of the stopping points:

Day 5	Leipzig, Germany
Day 29	Volgograd, Russia
Day 37	Semey, Kazakhstan
Day 53	Mogocha, Russia
Day 59	Vladivostok, Russia
Day 117	Vancouver, Canada
Day 125	Anchorage, USA
Day 138	Cody, USA
Day 147	New York, USA

Dedication

I would like to dedicate this book to my lovely wife Violet, who found it difficult at the beginning to accept the task I had undertaken but soon became my most ardent supporter and did everything possible to help me

Part One

My history and what makes me tick

To get some idea why I decided to take on The Ultimate Challenge and personally drive a standard Suzuki Jimny, a small four wheel drive car around the world, you first need to understand what has motivated and fuelled my determination to succeed. In my younger days, I wasn't exactly a saint, more like a bit of a rascal. Compassionate and understanding I have been, but I have a long memory when it comes to those who didn't help me or my family when we needed it. If I did something wrong or upset someone in one way or another I would probably admit I was wrong and apologise. There is a point when I will say no and other times I will look for the simplest solution and deal with the problem or situation quickly. Don't worry, I have had my share of problems and made a lot of mistakes but it worked out in the end. This is important to me; I have always been considerate towards people less fortunate than myself and would help if I could. Throughout my business career I have created employment for a lot of people who I respected and in the main became my friends. I have always referred to them as working with me and never for me. If I came up with an idea that was successful or made a decision that was right, I would always refer to it as our idea or our decision. I never asked, expected, or received any special thanks for what I achieved and other people benefited from, when things didn't turn out right I alone accepted the blame. I am not an accomplished author so I'm afraid what you read is who I am. It will also give me an opportunity to put the record straight relating to a number of things that happened in the past and for the first time in my life talk about the decisions I made, and what I achieved rather than we made and we

1

achieved. Please bear with me if my East London vocabulary or the odd naughty word slips out now and again, put it down to old age.

My lovely long-suffering wife Vi, the other half for 52 years will be checking my spelling, so to keep her happy I had better say something complimentary at the beginning. We have been together since 1957 and married in 1961, we first met when Vi was 16 and I was 17 years old opposite the Quality Fish and Chip shop on Mare Street, Hackney (good fish and chips in those days). Something special happened when we met that day because we have been together ever since. Apart from being the love of my life I found out later that she had bookkeeping experience which came in handy as we struggled to build a business. We have worked together pretty well all that time, me driving the business forward and Vi trying to keep me out of trouble and managing the finances. We had our fight on occasion, the making up afterwards wasn't too bad either. Vi worked as hard as me in addition to bringing up our two children, on reflection, she never complained. I have always decided what to do and made the decisions but that never stopped Vi from having her say. Sometimes it was like having a parrot on my shoulder that needed throttling, but that to one side I still love her to bits.

As for me, I entered this world at 8.30am on the 3rd of July 1940, christened Leslie George Carvall. Born at 315, Chirnside Road, Glasgow, I arrived as a newborn to take my place in a loving English family temporarily residing at Glasgow due to my dad's work. I must say, it was a fine way to start my life, my birth certificate confirms that I am a Scot but our family is English, I guess you can say that we were working class. Our home address in London was 876a Romford Road, Manor Park, London; I was second in the pecking order.

When Mum and Dad took a breather from expanding the family, we consisted of my dad Robert George, and my mum

Doris Winifred, my elder brother Robert Douglas, myself, and my younger brother Daniel James, then some years later and out of the blue my little sister Nita turned up. Mum had her hands full bringing up three boys and a girl and it became more difficult as we got older.

1944-1948. My earliest recollection as to what was going on in the world was when I was about four years old, the period up to 1944 Dad finished the work at Glasgow and the family moved back to Manor Park, London. During that time the bombs were being dropped on London, particularly around the docks area close to Manor Park. Mum and Dad must have decided to move away from the bombs and relocated the family to 17 Aspland Grove, Hackney E8, around the corner from the boarded up Hackney train station, our new address was to be my home until I got married. Like all the kids in the Grove at that time, when you heard the siren sounding you walked or were carried to the air raid shelter and stayed there until the all clear was sounded. I remember looking up and seeing the vapour trails in the sky not knowing it was our boys flying overhead, the bangs in the distance at night, the search lights, the sound of fire engines, bells clanging as they passed the end of the Grove, are all vague memories. The particular day I remember, it was a bright sunny day, the sun's rays brightening the dark corners of the kitchen, Mum was at home, brother Bob and I were not allowed out because flying bombs were dropping on London so we stayed inside getting in the way as Mum tried to get the housework done. My younger brother Danny was a baby and in his cot. What happened next has remained with me all my life, for some reason Mum went to the street door opened it and went out to see what the commotion was, brother Bob and myself not wishing to miss an opportunity to get outside followed her out to the street. We didn't get past the door, Mum turned, scooped us up, shouldered the door shut screaming at us to get under the kitchen table; I was slow to react so I waited by the table not knowing what to do, the next thing I knew was Mum, with the baby under her arm, grabbed hold of me and pushed me under the table, my forehead striking something hard in the process. My head hurt as we crouched under the table but I was too frightened to cry, then there was an almighty bang, the house shook, the sound of breaking glass and dust everywhere, the bomb dropped on the next street. I found out some years later what had happened, Mum reacted to a shout of alarm and ran for cover, a flying bomb, or doodlebug as we used to call them, was heading in our direction. The rocket motor had stopped and it looked like it was going to drop onto Aspland Grove, our road. As it closed onto its target it veered to the right and ended up dropping on Spurstow Road, the next road along killing a lot of people, we were lucky that day.

I was about six years old, the war had ended, the street parties a fading memory, it was a time when kids could be left playing in the street unmolested, while the parents were at work. School summer holidays when the sun shone all day, and warm breezes at night, they were good days. We used to make up our games, such as Tin-Can Tommy, other times I was like a kid from hell. One of the tricks I did was to get the hosepipe from the garden, connect it to the tap in the scullery and stand my little brother on a box by the tap to wait for my signal. The remainder of the hosepipe I would drag along the passage to the street door and signal to my brother to turn on the tap. I would then hold the pressure back with my thumb and wait for a victim. When I saw someone coming along I would close the street door and give them a squirt of water through the letterbox, you should have seen their faces as they looked around to see where the water was coming from.

On one occasion I did it to a lady who was walking past but Mum saw the water squirting out of the letterbox and soaking the lady in front of her. Mum apologised for what had happened then

4

entered the house like a raging bull gave us both a good hiding and sent us to our room. It's only now that I am older, I have got around to thinking about my Mum and how she managed to cope during those hard times. Mum worked as a home help, today's equivalent of a care worker, looking after old people, cleaning, feeding and doing jobs for them that they couldn't do for themselves. Even as a youngster I used to wonder why her knees were red sometimes, I found out later that every day she washed floors on her hands and knees. Every day Mum would arrive home really tired, then have to start cooking the dinner, occasionally there would be a knock on the door, someone complaining about me fighting or throwing stones. It didn't really matter whether I did it or not, I seemed to get the blame. It continued like that for the next few years, everything I touched would break or not work if I had been near it, I couldn't do anything right.

1948 Mum and Dad looked after us as well as they could, they made sure that we were properly fed and clothed; we also received presents at Christmas and birthdays like most other kids. It was the custom at that time for the whole family to come and stay at our house over Christmas, us kids were turfed out of our beds to make way for the older folks and it was normally like that for four days. Sometimes there would be an argument and we would get our beds back sooner than expected. Mum paid five shillings a week to the local tallyman all through the year, so that at Christmas time she could take us three boys to the tallyman's shop to get a new suit and boots. Regardless of my protest I wasn't old enough for long trousers, next was a pair of boots, we always had to have a size larger, they had to last a year, Dad would hammer steel studs into the soles and heels too so that they would last longer, walking to school they felt like lead weights on my feet.

Growing up at that time was a bit like the survival of the fittest, you learned to fight if you had to or run like hell if you needed to. Scrapping was a regular occurrence, a number of times I went home with a fat lip and bruises, if I had torn my clothes as well Mum would show no mercy and give me another good hiding. Too much happened to me during those early years for me to talk about it individually now, so I have selected a few instances to give you some idea what growing up was like at that time. I was about ten, a bit big for my age, there were four of us kids who lived at Aspland Grove, all about the same age, we were always together. Other kids from different streets on occasion clashed with us and we would slog it out, I found myself top dog and soon after we got ourselves a bit more organised especially when we locked horns with other kids. If we decided to go somewhere we would wait for each other then walk along the Grove together, the reason was a much bigger boy named Jimmy, who lived at No 10, every time we passed his house he would run after us, if you got caught you would be on the receiving end of a punch. This went on for a long time, one day we decided that we'd had enough so the next time he chased us we would turn and jump on him. A day or two later he came after us, but this time we didn't run, I stopped and turned to face him ready to have a go, I looked behind me expecting support but they had run. Accepting that I would get hurt I stood there as he came towards me shouting what he was going to do to me. He tried to grab me but I side stepped and kicked him in the shin, turned and ran. I looked back and saw he was hopping on one leg calling for his mum crying his eyes out, reminding myself of the times he had punched me, I ran back and kicked his other shin, it must have hurt he was howling like a baby. He never bothered us again.

We were always short of money, so as to earn a few shillings I would follow the horse drawn milk cart, also coal and scrap iron carts that visited the Grove on occasion to collect the horse manure, then sell it to the people who had allotments to help them grow their vegetables. One other source of quick money was, at the far side of Amhurst Road, the road that crossed the end of the Grove, there was an off-licence, equivalent to today's liquor store, from the end of the Grove you could look across the road and see if the gate at the back of the off-licence was open, if it was two of us would go into the shop to keep the old boy busy, while the other two went around the back and grabbed as many empty screw top beer bottles as they could carry then took them into the shop at the front. The man behind the counter would give us 3 pence for each bottle. I will always remember the four of us with contorted faces, trying to hold back from laughing when he handed over the money. We kept this little scam going for ages, until being caught in the act by the local bobby who gave us a clout and a warning then took us home and handed us over to our parents who gave each of us another good hiding.

From a young age I attended two schools then ended up at the Hackney Free and Parochial School, Paragon Road. During the school holidays we were out terrorising the neighbourhood at every opportunity, when we were hungry we would buy bread rolls with the few pence we would scrape together, but Friday was pork pie day. We looked forward to paying Sainsbury's a visit every Friday to nick one of their pork pies from the delivery yard at the back of the shop. Sixty or so years ago there were no supermarkets like there are today selling the old folks items they don't want or need, or buy one you get one free! Back then people would go to Sainsbury's to buy what they could afford, half a pound of sugar, two ounces of butter, one small piece of cheese or a slice of bacon cut off a side as you looked on, spotless marble counters and the people who served you had time to chat to you, it's all gone forever unfortunately. Back then, every Friday morning at 10 o'clock the lorry would turn up with the stock for the day. It was unloaded by hand off the back of the lorry onto wheeled trolleys with shelves, we would be waiting, looking over the wall that divided the church graveyard and Sainsbury's unloading area. The wall was about 9 feet (2.7 metres in new money), there were trees on the graveyard side and a car, a Riley Pathfinder, nice car, against the wall on the other side. When the lorry was unloaded, the Sainsbury's man would check and sign for the load and the lorry would leave. The trolleys were then wheeled into the shop one at a time. When the man pushed a trolley inside, I would jump down from the wall onto the top of the car, run to the trolleys and relieve them of a 14 inch pork pie and throw it over the wall then climb back over the wall. We did this for a long time, until one day, I guess I got too clever, too cocky if you like. This particular Friday we looked over the wall there was no lorry but it had been unloaded onto the trolleys and it was just sitting there, there was nobody about so over I went to nick a pie, but they were waiting for me. Two big guys came running out of the shop to grab me but I was on the car and over the wall real quick, we ran through the graveyard laughing our heads off. No more Friday pork pie. These days I still go to Sainsbury's on a Friday, but now I use the front door and push the trolley for my wife, providing that she treats me to a bacon sandwich and coffee at the café.

Another caper we used to get up to was bunking into the pictures; we were proper film buffs in those days, there were about twelve cinemas in our area we always knew what films were showing and when we had decided which film we wanted to see, we tried to get in without paying. We would be at the cinema just before the film ended and the second showing, we would wait outside the exit door usually located at the side of the building, when the doors burst open and the people came out we held the doors open until the last person had come out then stepped inside and closed the doors behind us. We would then stand there sandwiched between a black curtain on the inside and the doors to the outside behind us. When the lights dimmed we would crawl on our hands and knees from behind the curtain and hopefully find some vacant seats. We didn't always get away with it, on most occasions nobody checked the doors, but other times we would be standing behind the curtain, the usherettes opened them to check that the door was closed and find us four standing there like zombies, she would scream as we frightened the life out of her. One other time we were caught by a security man appointed to stop people like us getting in for free. On that occasion we were standing behind the curtain waiting for the lights to go dim when somebody on the inside opened the curtains, that time we screamed, standing in front of us was a man who looked like a man mountain all-in wrestler, he gave the four of us a good hiding and threw us out the way we had come in. We picked ourselves up nursing our cuts and bruises, the big guy was still standing there as we began to run and at the same time shouted that we had decided to take our business elsewhere in future.

1952. Twelve years old and a bit wiser, I got a part time job with a local fruit and vegetable stall holder, their pitch was a gap made by a bomb dropped sometime during the war which landed between The Railway Tavern and Marks and Spencer's on the corner of Mare Street and Amhurst Road. Every morning Monday to Saturday I had to be at Millers coal yard, opposite Hackney Station at 7am to meet George, the boss, and to help push three fruit and veg four wheel barrows along the coal yard, then across Mare Street, bounce up the curb at the zebra road crossing, along the pavement and position the barrows ready for the day. There was a 4th barrow that sold fish, it had to be positioned at the other side of the road, I didn't like the fish barrow, when we finished positioning the barrow I had to unload the boxes containing fish that had been iced overnight. Consequently I got splashed, resulting in my clothes not exactly smelling of roses and I wasn't too popular with the other kids, especially when the weather was hot, but it was a job. After everything had been set up for the day I would go to school. At the end of the school day I would do the whole thing in reverse,

I learnt a lot from George. Apart from pushing barrows every morning I worked all day Saturday, I had to keep all the displays topped up with produce, this meant lifting heavy boxes and sacks of potatoes, it was a long time before I could lift a hundred weight sack of potatoes (about 54 kilos) on my own and carry it on my shoulder. One day we received a consignment of bananas, I had heard of them but never actually seen one, so naturally I showed some interest, George gave me a banana to try, it was green and yellow and a bit on the hard side, I ate the banana, it was the most foul thing I have ever eaten, difficult to swallow and leaving a bitter taste in my mouth, I told George that it was horrible. Laughing, he said, "I'm not surprised, you are supposed to take the skin off before you eat it." It was a memorable time in my life. I had to work hard but got paid every week. Learning quickly, I was left on my own to get on with the work, I loved it. What was nice, for the first time, I didn't have to ask my mum for pocket money and I was able to give some money to her each week to help out.

I attended the Hackney Free and Parochial School, I saw less of my friends because I was working and I wasn't getting into so much trouble after school. At school I couldn't do anything right, it seemed that I got the cane every day for one thing or another, if something happened and I was nearby I would be caned for it. The floors at the school were tiled and highly polished, the long corridors had swing doors at intervals and a coconut mat at the base of each set of doors. When no one was looking, two of the boys would hold the doors open and we would take turns at running at the mat and jump on it to see how far we could slide, we had been sliding up and down the corridor for some time, but that particular day I thought that I would try and break the record for the longest slide. I took an extra-long run and jumped on the mat. As I did I lost my balance, I went one way ending up in a heap, the mat became airborne and exited through a plate glass window.

The following morning I had to report to Mr Anckerson, the headmaster, after assembly. I was concerned, not knowing if I was getting the cane on my hand or my backside. It wasn't so bad on my hand but across my arse I knew it would hurt. To prepare for the worst I put a comic down the back of my trousers. I knocked on the headmaster's door and stepped inside. I tried to explain to Mr Anckerson that I tripped but he wasn't having any of it, he produced the punishment register and read out all my entries. I didn't realise that I had been caned so much. I thought that he'd had enough and was going to expel me but he didn't, he gave me my last warning and six of the best. He picked up the cane and said "Drop your trousers and bend over," I thought for a second whether to walk out of the door and never come back, or take the punishment. I dropped my trousers and the comic fell out onto the floor, I was stark naked from the waist down, money didn't stretch to underpants at that time. After the caning I went to the toilet and stood inside a cubicle for a while. Normally when I was caned I accepted the punishment and suffered in silence, but this time I cried, the pain of those six strokes I will remember as long as I live. I got over the caning and was looking forward to the summer holiday, two weeks before the school broke up they organised a field trip for the whole school (900 children). We would be bundled into London buses and taken to Epping Forest for the day, another excuse to have some fun. The morning before the day of the field trip everybody was in the assembly hall to hear what the arrangements were for the trip the following day. I was at the back of the hall not taking much notice of what was being said, the teacher in charge had finished what he had to say, then said "I have a special announcement to make," pausing so as to have everyone's attention, then continued by saying "one person, Leslie Carvall, will not be going on the trip tomorrow, he will be attending school as normal."

The next day I arrived at the school at the normal time, I tried to avoid eye contact as I discreetly walked past all the other kids who were being loaded onto the waiting buses. I was met by a teacher who had been assigned to look after me for the day and taken to an empty classroom, I was asked to sit at a desk and was given a times table card to memorise. I had no idea how it worked so to make it look like I was doing something, I started to write down simple sums and added up using my fingers. The teacher sometimes left me alone in the classroom so I had plenty of time to think. Sitting alone in the empty classroom, there was a kind of eerie silence, no noise or chattering you get when thirty-five boys and girls are packed into one room for any length of time. I accepted that I was a bit of a dunce; I couldn't add up or understand arithmetic and could hardly read or write. For the first time in my life I felt scared, even frightened about what was going to happen if I left school and couldn't read or write, or handle basic arithmetic.

To make matters worse, and as if I wasn't in enough trouble, the week after the school trip I was given a letter to hand to my mother asking if she would come to the school for a meeting. Mum attended as requested, when I asked what it was all about, she told me what they had said to her. I felt so sorry for her and ashamed of myself for putting her through the ordeal of being told how bad I was at school, the condition of my clothes, I didn't wash as often as I should and fell asleep during lessons. In a few days I would be thirteen, I made up my mind to try harder when school started after the summer holiday, as for the last days before the end of term, I still had to go to school, I decided from now on I would bath twice a week, instead of only once a week, also I would pay more attention when I wash myself. Mum gave me a pair of Dad's one-piece overalls (too big for me really but who cares) for me to wear when pulling out the barrows and unloading the fish boxes from the fish barrow every morning, so my clothes wouldn't get splashed with the fishy ice water. All the kids at school knew through the school telegraph what had happened to me over the past week or so, I knew they would be looking and pointing at me but I still had to go to school. The next morning I got up earlier than usual, ran to Millers coal yard, helped pull the fruit and veg barrows across the road and position them, then slipped on my overalls and positioned the fish barrow and unloaded the fishy boxes without getting soaked for a change. When I had finished my work I ran back home to have another wash, to be on the safe side, polished my boots to a mirror finish, had a good sniff all around to make sure I was pong-free, then walked to school head held high.

1953. The summer holiday was a time to think about what had happened over the past months, and what I would do when I went back to school after the holiday. The headmaster and teachers knew how to get to me, they taught me a lesson by excluding me from the trip and it worried the life out of me. Knowing that I was disruptive in class as well as being an academic dunce, I decided to do something about it, I made my mind up to try harder and keep out of trouble. Throughout the holiday I still pulled the barrows out in the morning and back in the evening, sometimes I would work all day if they were busy. When school started after the holiday, I carried on with my early morning job, but somehow felt eager to start learning, my routine of doing things now included making sure I always looked and smelt sweet ready for the classroom. I got into the habit of getting to school early and getting organised for the lesson. Because I didn't pay much attention during my previous years I struggled to understand what they were trying to tell me, but after a week or so I started to get the hang of it and everything seemed to become much clearer. I looked forward to the lessons so as to learn as much as I could. The rest of that year I worked as hard as my ability would let me, I was slow to learn but I persevered, particularly with arithmetic. I kept the times table card they gave me to memorise that day when I sat alone in the classroom so that I could continue memorising the times tables after school, by the end of the year I could pretty well recite from memory the whole card. The memorised contents of that white card has served me well and remained with me throughout my working life. Who needs calculators?

1954. I felt more confident at the start of the New Year, I kept out of trouble so I didn't get the cane anymore, my school work was improving but I was still bottom of the class. It was about that time I was handed another one of those heart stopping notes for my mum.

The teacher who gave me the note didn't say what it was about but Mum came to the school for a meeting with Mr Ankerson, the headmaster, as requested. The day of the meeting, when school finished, I ran all the way home to see Mum before going to work, desperate to find out why I was in trouble. I asked Mum what the meeting was about, with a bit of a smile she said "You're not in trouble for once, Mr Ankerson said he was pleased to say that you are improving, he asked why you didn't wear a school blazer, I had to explain that I have three boys to clothe so couldn't afford to buy a school uniform." "Is that all?" I said, with relief. "No," Mum said, "you have to wear a school uniform, Mr Ankerson has given me a voucher to go to the school shop to collect a free uniform." All the kids at school would know soon enough through the school telegraph that I had a charity uniform, but what mattered to me was I would have a school uniform. The first day I put on my uniform I was excited, I woke a little earlier than usual, pulled and positioned the barrows ready for the day and completed the other jobs I had to do, then ran home, had a good wash (I smelt lovely), put on my new grey long trousers, new white shirt and blue tie, dark blue jersey and my new dark blue blazer. I stood there for a few minutes taking it all in, my boots buffed up to a mirror finish; I looked and felt the business. A few months later I was appointed milk monitor. I soon got things organised, orderly queuing, no skylarking about, no nicking extra bottles of milk to drink later. I also resisted my natural instinct to set up some sort of under-the-counter trading, was I getting soft, or was it poacher turned gamekeeper? I was learning fast, and seemed to be sorting myself out, if I saw a problem coming my way I would avoid it if I could, I was still pulling the barrows out every morning and was strong enough to do it on my own, plus I had a bit of help from the local bobby at the crossing. He would watch for me coming from Millers coal yard, stop the traffic so that I could cross the road and then gave me a push when I bumped up the curb on to the pavement. George, the boss, didn't need me in the evenings anymore and that suited me as I started to get interested in girls and motorbikes anyway. Just before the break for the summer holiday, I was appointed Prefect, I told Mum and she was so proud of me, after the holiday, I was appointed Head Prefect, when I told Mum and Dad they both said how proud they were. I carried out my duties responsibly and had enough confidence to talk to the teaching staff if there was an issue that needed to be dealt with.

1955. It was my last year at school, the first day back after the Christmas break, everyone was packed into the assembly hall, prayers had been dealt with, next was the announcement for the appointment of two new Prefects, which I already knew about, there was a pause then the headmaster said, "I am pleased to announce that Leslie Carvall has been appointed Head Boy of the school." I was overwhelmed, speechless, I couldn't take in what the headmaster had just said, I was on cloud nine for the rest of the day, when I told Mum and Dad of my appointment they looked at me with amazement, congratulated me and I think they were mystified how I managed it. I took the position and my duties as Head Boy seriously, I already knew there was some bullying going on, and it was always the smaller kids on the receiving end. If I caught a boy picking on someone smaller I would tell him to pick on someone his own size, and at the same time tell the little fella, "If it happens again, kick him in the shins as hard as you can, he won't expect you to do that and he will think twice before he picks on you again." I will never forget my time as Head Boy representing and looking after 900 pupils, I didn't let my position at the school slow my learning, I only had six months to go before I was to be let loose on the world.

Before my time at school came to an end, two things happened. Mike, my friend since I first attended school, well, somehow we had a bit of an argument about some trivial matter that got out of all proportion, there was a certain amount of mixing from other kids, you know the sort of thing going back and forth, telling me Mike said this about me, then telling Mike I said that about him, it got to a point where we were going to fight each other. It wasn't the fighting, I felt uneasy about having to fight my friend. The fight was to take place under the gym the following Friday at 4 o'clock. The whole school had been buzzing all week, the day and time had come for Mike and I to slog it out, I was finishing up a few things I had to attend to then, reluctantly, decided to get it over with. As I made my way through the school to the gym, I reminded myself that I was Head Boy and should prevent this sort of thing happening. I opened the door to the playground then stopped, virtually the whole school, boys and girls had stayed behind to watch the fight, it was like a scene from the film Tom Brown's School Days, everyone cheering as I walked to the gym. Mike was there waiting, we had avoided eye contact during the past few days but now we were facing each other from either side of a cleared circle, I felt real bad about what was about to happen, I removed my blazer and tie and gave them to someone to hold, I looked across at Mike, his face was snow white, not like the rosy cheeked friend he normally was. He needed an

Les, (Second from Left) became Head Boy at his school

out, we both did. I walked across to Mike and stood in front of him for a moment then said, "I don't know how we got into this mess and I don't want to fight you but if I have to I will." Mike said he didn't want to fight either, I said, "Lets shake hands and go home," which we did. I learnt something that day; I was going to fight my friend mainly because of what other people said that we said. I made a promise to myself, in future only listen to advice or what other people have to say, but decide for myself what is right, these days they call it being stubborn!

Something else happened that I would like to mention, my school days had a lasting effect on me, I arrived at the school when I was nine a complete dunce, my academic sheet of paper was blank. They got to me in the end though; they turned me around, turned poacher into game keeper, call it what you like, I was Head Boy from January to July 1955. It didn't end there, on the 24th of June the same year, I was awarded the Sedgwick Medal for Merit, one of ten medals awarded periodically, the schools highest honour. I have kept my cherished Head Boy's badge and Sedgwick Medal to this day. I left the comfort zone of my school at the end of the summer; I was fifteen years old and keen to get going. My brother Bob, who is six years older than me, got me a job as an apprentice rubber floor layer, working for the Harefield Rubber Company where he worked. Generally we worked together travelling from job to job in his van, we became closer and were always laughing and joking, I seemed to see the funny side of everything.

1956. I started my working life the way I wanted it to continue, working as much overtime as I could and earning as much money as I could. The work, the travelling to and from each job and sometimes having to stay away from home was all part of the deal, I loved it. I was too young to have a licence for a motorbike or car but Dad bought a car, it was a Standard Ten, I thought I was a bit of a mechanic and spent some of my time tinkering with the car. When Dad was away I taught myself to drive by driving up and down Aspland Grove, sometimes I parked near the main road to watch the traffic to understand what I had to do if I turned left onto Amhurst Road, I was getting bored with driving up and down the Grove in second gear. It was a funny thing, at that time other people in the Grove had cars and in the evenings it was very busy with people trying to teach themselves to drive, there were no driving schools in those days. I was outside the house tinkering with Dad's car on this particular day, a few houses along the family had acquired a Morris Ten, the son decided to teach his girlfriend to drive, they jerked up and down the road a few times and seemed to be getting the hang of it, so far so good. The fool then got out of the car insisting the girl have a go on her own, she was terrified, she didn't want to do it but he insisted. At this stage the number of people watching had increased, the boy got back into the car and drove it up to the end of the road and turned it around so that it was pointing in the opposite direction, the girl was frightened to death but got behind the wheel. The boy gave her last minute instructions, and from what I could see he was going to run alongside the car. The engine was running, he must have said put it into gear but for some reason she pressed the accelerator, the engine was screaming and the gearbox was making a terrible noise, everyone heard the boy shout press the clutch pedal, as she did there was an almighty thud followed by the car taking off and leap-frogging and zig-zagging along the road. Picture the scene unfolding before us, the car with the boy's legs protruding from the driver's side window as a result of him diving head first through the open window in a failed attempt to gain control and finally hitting a lamp post and wrecking the car. There was an eerie silence as those who had witnessed what had happened quietly returned to their homes to watch the continuing saga from behind the curtains. I still laugh to myself when I think of that day.

Not wishing to drag this out, but I finally plucked up courage to sneak a drive on the road in my dad's car. I know, under age, no licence or insurance, but I had to have a go. This particular Saturday morning, Dad was away, I was wearing mechanic type overalls and looked older than I was, feeling a little bit apprehensive as I taped on the battery leads onto the battery terminals, I then started the car and was off. I felt rather like a young bird leaving the nest and flying for the first time. I turned left into Amhurst Road and soon realised I had only driven using first and second gears and never above 15 mph causing me to panic a bit but I got it sorted out. I approached the roundabout, I didn't know what to do, cars appeared from all directions and those behind sounded their horns impatiently, waiting for me to do something. I rolled forward merging into the circulating flow of the traffic, sweating as I drove three times around the roundabout trying to work out how to get off. I finally I slipped off to the left hoping it was Dalston Lane. Confused and forgetting to change gear as I drove to the incline at the top of the road, my dilemma got worse due to people using the crossing forcing me to stop on the incline, I managed to keep the car in position and engine running, cursing at the people crossing as I waited for an opportunity to move forward. Finally and with unperfected brake and accelerator footwork I leapt forward and turned right into Mare Street, as I did the engine stopped, at that point I wanted to die. I got out of the car to start pushing and as I did, a policeman who I didn't recognise was walking towards me, I nearly pooed myself. I stood as tall as I could as he came towards me, then said to him in a deep voice, "Can you give me push mate?" As he did and before he could get a better look at me, I had the bonnet up and re-fixed the loose battery lead, started the car and was on my way again waving a thank you to the bobby at the same time. At the end of Mare Street I turned right into Amhurst Road then left and back home. As I turned right into Amhurst Road my friend, the local bobby, you know the one who helps me every morning with the barrows, he was holding up the traffic at the crossing to let people cross, he saw me waiting, I just smiled and waved he knew I didn't have a licence, but he let it go. 'Proper bobbies' in those days.

1957. I liked my work, I didn't get it right all the time, I got better with more experience. Just after Christmas I was told by the Contracts Manager that I would have to be laid off due to the lack of work, I was shattered having been told there was no job for me. At the first opportunity, I went to the labour exchange to sign on, I had in the past heard people talk about signing on but thought no more of it, until I walked through the door of the labour exchange. The place was dark and there were long queues of people waiting their turn at the counter, others looking at slips of paper pinned to a notice board, it was a run-down depressing place, I really felt uncomfortable being there. I finally reached the counter and was looking at a man, his head was the shape of a turnip, he had huge ears and false teeth two sizes bigger than his mouth. We looked at each other momentarily; I really struggled to keep a straight face. He then said speaking and whistling through his teeth at the same time, "Have you been here before?" Directing my contorted face to the floor, I said, "No." "Fill this in and bring it back to me," he said as he handed me a piece of paper. I sat down, tears streaming down my face. I just sat there for a few minutes, I looked at the form I had to fill in, the thought of another long wait in the queue, and then a glance at turnip head at the counter whistling Yankee Doodle Dandy through his teeth at another customer was just too much. That day I made a pact with myself to never ever let myself be in this situation again, and I never was. A few days later I applied and got a job working for the Runnymede Rubber Company as an apprentice floor layer. The site I was asked to go to was the new Lloyds building just off Fenchurch Street, London and I was to report to the Foreman on site. The next day, I arrived at the site early and was paired up with two nice old guys who taught me a lot during the next six months that I worked with them.

I knew that area pretty well, Whitechapel, Aldgate and the Tower of London, getting to the site was easy. Each day I would catch a 653 trolley bus from Hackney Station all the way to Aldgate and walk along Fenchurch Street to the site and a stone's throw from the River Thames. I'm not sure how it happened but ever since I was a youngster I have had an urge for me to be on, in or by the sea and a natural interest in anything that floats, strange coming from someone with no family ties with the sea. To break the monotony of the everyday routine of site work, at lunch time I would run to the River Thames to watch the comings and goings of people, boats and sometimes ships being unloaded on the south side. I would eat my lunch breathing in the salt air, it seemed so natural to be there, at 1.45pm I would then reluctantly run back to the site. The Thames was like a magnet, drawing me to its water's edge irrespective of the weather, there was something tranquil about being there. I remembered as a kid watching the paddle steamer dock and take on passengers who wanted to go down stream or as far as Southend-on-Sea. Mum and Dad took the family on a day trip to Southend, I wanted to die, I was sick all day, my face was green by the time we got back but once on dry land I soon recovered. On another occasion, when eating my lunch at the water's edge, my mind drifted back to eight years previously. At that time, the summer holidays always seemed to be hot, heatwaves even, all the kids went swimming sometimes in the River Lea not far from where we lived or on other occasions we would catch a number 653 bus to the Tower of London and swim in the Thames.

This particular day it was blistering hot so we decided to go to the Thames for a swim, the bus fare was three pence each, each way. This amount we could usually scrape together but we couldn't resist trying to get one over on the bus conductor.

We would wait for a bus to come along, if the conductor was at the front of the bus we would get on, two of us would walk towards the conductor and buy two tickets while the other two concealed themselves by squatting on the passenger platform at the back of the bus, the two with the tickets would ask the conductor where the bus stopped, to keep him busy, while the other two without tickets sneaked up stairs and hid by lying flat across the seats at the front. If it worked out as planned it meant that we got to share two ice-creams. If the ticket inspector got on the bus we would have to buy two more tickets which meant no ice-cream. The bus would take us as far as Aldgate; from there we would walk along the Minnories to the Tower of London and the paddle steamer jetty. When the tide was out it would expose a strip of sand and mud against the centuries-old stone wall either side of the jetty. When nobody was looking we would climb down the outside of the jetty and hide under the walkway and change into our costumes, we would then swim and generally get up to no good until the water started to rise. The water was dirty but always warm, bloated dead dogs, cats and rats were among the flotsam that littered the shoreline, our beach looked like a catchment area for old balloons, we had lots of fun blowing them up and sending them through the air like zeppelins. It wasn't until we were a bit older and wiser that we found out that we had been blowing up used condoms!!! This particular day, we had our swim and were sitting on the stone steps under the jetty, three of us were larking around as usual, we noticed that John, the youngest, was just sitting there looking upwards, pointing to the underside of the jetty public walkway. Interested to see what he was looking at, we moved closer and looked up to see what he was pointing at, we couldn't make it out at first then someone said, "I'm looking at some old granny's bloomers." We sat there dumbfounded. In reality we were only kids, it frightened the hell out of us, the novelty soon wore off when we realised that it only would take someone to look down as we were looking up so we decided to sit there still and quietly until the boat left. When there was nobody walking about above us, we started to talk about what had happened, laughing and joking, most of what was said is unprintable but the four of us were much wiser from that day on.

April 1957. I was walking along Mare Street with my mate Kenny when he suddenly saw two girls walking towards us, "I know one of them," he said and before I knew it the four of us were in conversation and paired off. A pretty little thing, I thought to myself, "I'm Les," I said, "what's your name?" "Vi, short for Violet," she replied. She couldn't resist me, I gave her my best come and get me eyes, flashed a set of diamond sparkling white teeth, she had no defence, that day was the beginning of forever. Fate brought us together that day but not wanting to be in a rush we stretched out our courting for four years before we got married, just to make sure that all the departments were working correctly. To be serious though, marrying Vi was the best thing I ever did in my life, but let's keep that to ourselves, if Vi finds out I said that I will never hear the end of it. I was very much looking forward to my seventeenth birthday on the 3rd of July so that I could apply for my motorbike and car licence and legally be allowed to drive on the road. The morning of my birthday I was awake early, eager to go to the dealer and collect the bike that was waiting for me, it was second-hand but it was my bike, that's what mattered. Clutching a set of learner plates, I hopped onto a bus and was standing outside the dealers when they opened. I rode the bike home experiencing the freedom of going where I wanted, when I wanted for the first time. After a while, and for some unknown reason, my bike and car test were to be taken during the same week, by this time I had become friendly with some other bike riders and on most occasions we rode together, eventually forming our own club.

I still had to display my learner plates so I was desperate to pass my bike test so Vi could officially ride pillion. The day arrived to take my bike test, hyped up to get it over with, I went through the test procedure as requested but failed for some reason, I was devastated. That's what you get for being too cocky I thought to myself. Two days later I was back at the test centre to take my car test, the examiner got into the car, asked a few questions then told me to drive giving me directions along the way, I had no heart for it, I was still smarting after failing my bike test. We arrived back at the office, we sat in silence for a minute or two then the instructor handed me a piece of paper and said that I had passed, I thanked him and sat there thinking to myself there must be a lesson there somewhere, I passed my bike test the following week. Vi and I went everywhere on our bike, unfortunately Vi's parents, her mum mainly, didn't like me at all, even more so when Vi rode on the bike, she made Vi's life a misery, she kept telling her not to be tied to a no-hoper like me. Perhaps they knew something I didn't, they tried to intimidate or humiliate me at every opportunity but generally I rose above it all, there were times when they got to me though, but for Vi's sake I didn't respond. Vi's family went on to become the in-laws from hell.

From here on and so as to give you some idea of what happened to me throughout my lifetime, I will have to be brief when describing what happened and select only some of the instances that shaped my life.

The situation with Vi's parents deteriorated over the four years we were courting, but I hung on in there for her sake. The job at the Lloyds building, working for the Runnymede Rubber Company, came to an end, at the same time my brother Bob got me a job working with him mainly, back at Harefield Rubber Company, where I remained more or less until we started our own business. Brother Bob was in charge and we travelled from job to job in his Austin van, I liked the work and enjoyed the daily travelling to and from each job. I was three years into my apprenticeship and had been thinking more and more over the previous months about the rubber tiles and materials left over after each job that were either left on site for collection, which rarely happened, or dumped. Sometimes there was hardly anything left, other times quite a lot. I said to Bob that if the surplus materials were going to be taken by somebody it might as well be us, explaining that if on each occasion we kept a proportion of the tiles that were of the same size and thickness irrespective of colour, we could do private jobs and call it Harlequin Flooring, choosing that name solved the colour problem. We soon tiled a kitchen floor for a taxi driver, it was a success and before long we were working evenings and weekends, when not working for the company, we laid harlequin floors for ourselves and in so doing laid, excuse the pun, the foundation for our own business. We worked every hour available, working for the company and ourselves. The Contracts Manager told me he had a lot of work and for that reason he split Bob and I up and sent me to work with someone else for the time being. I was to work with Polly Perkins, his last name was Perkins and so everybody called him Polly for short. Our first job together was at Rubery and Hollymoor mental hospitals, as they were known as in those days, situated near Birmingham. I met Polly and travelled to the site in Polly's old Morris Ten van. Arriving at Rubery, we parked outside the main entrance; I waited while Polly went inside to find the Site Engineer.

I got out of the van to stretch my legs and climbed the ten steps or so to the ground floor level and the ornate main entrance. I was by the entrance waiting for Polly to return, when I heard a scraping noise coming from somewhere above me, I looked up to see an old man hanging by his fingertips from a first floor window, his shoes scraping the brickwork as he tried to get back from where he had come from. Shocked, I shouted at the people just inside the building and at the same time pointed up at the old man, there was more shouting and people running in all directions, I said to the nearest man to me, "Lets catch him, break his fall," before I had finished what I was saying, I was pushed clear just as the old man made a bone breaking sound as he hit the ground where I had been standing moments before. Polly returned asking what all the commotion was all about, concerned, I told him what had happened, he looked up at the window then at me, thought for a moment, then said, "Why didn't he use the door like everyone else?"

We got ourselves organised, I talked the Maintenance Engineer into letting us sleep in a disused ward and I also scrounged blankets, sheets and pillows. The next thing was to have a word with the chef with the view to getting ourselves fed. When speaking to the chef he said that if there were any tiles over when the job was finished he would like some. We had two jobs to do, one in each Hospital. Rubery and Hollymoor were situated about half a mile apart, surrounded by farm land linked by a narrow lane, it was a Friday, both jobs had been completed and signed off by the engineer, all that was left to do before we made our way back to London was to hand over to the chef the tiles and other materials he wanted in exchange for the food he provided. The tiles were in the back of Polly's van and it was backed up to the kitchen door to unload. We completed the unloading and thanked the chef for his help then turned to go, he said, "Wait a moment, I have something for you." Polly and I waited by the van then the chef reappeared with a side of bacon over his shoulder and put it in the back of the van, saying, "Don't go yet," and once again came out holding two huge legs of smoked ham, one in each hand, followed by large tins containing all sorts of food. Finally, we were able to close the doors of the van but not before we covered our contraband over with an old blanket and put our tools and away bags on top, just in case. The old van was creaking a bit when we started to move, and we were pleased with ourselves that we had enough food to feed our families for a week. To start our journey back to London, we first had to drive along the narrow lane from Rubery to get to Hollymoor and the road to London, as we entered the lane we were laughing and joking about when the chef appeared at the door with the side of bacon, and how nice it would be if we could get a job like that every week. Still laughing, we made our way along the lane until it turned to the left, as we followed the road around the curve and had a clear view of the lane ahead of us, we stopped laughing. A short distance in front of us, standing in the middle of the road was the local police constable, his bike pointing across the road to prevent us passing and waving a hand indicating to us to stop. Parking his bike, he ambled around to the driver's side to have a word with Polly. I displayed a sickly grin that passed for a smile, concerned partly because he may ask us to open the back of the van, also I suddenly realised that I needed to go to the toilet. He looked at me and then at the contents in the back of the van, I swallowed, when he said, "What's in the bags?" Polly answered his questions; he looked satisfied as he made a note of the registration number and looked the van over once more, and then grumbled, "This is not a main road, watch your speed," followed by, "on your way." Both sweating, we rolled forward and continued our journey in silence. For some reason I never did work with Polly again.

Bob and I continued to work together, we were always laughing and joking at one thing or another, we got on together at work and socially, our private work outside working hours was increasing and it wouldn't be long before we would be running our own business.

Vi and I became engaged in 1958, so we had enough time to get to know each other, and we instinctively knew we would be together for the rest of our lives. During the latter part of 1960 we announced to our family and friends that we were getting married on March 11th 1961. The situation with Vi's parents regarding our relationship continued to get worse, until eventually, and with only two weeks to go before our wedding, Vi's mother told her that they, together with some of their family, would not be attending the wedding and told her to leave the house there and then. It upset Vi very much, she was crying when she arrived at our house with a bag containing the few possessions she could carry, and told me what had happened. I don't know why Vi's mother hated me, but we both got over it. We married as planned on March 11th at St John's Church, Hackney. My family turned out in force together with majority of Vi's family who didn't like what her mother had done, we must have been popular because there were about two hundred family and friends at the reception in the evening. It is comforting when people rally around you on these occasions, it all worked out in the end. Fortunately, a few weeks before our wedding, we were able to rent a house at No 41 Aspland grove, the opposite side of the road to where I used to live, which was helpful, in as much that my mum would be able to keep an eye on Vi when I had to go away to work. Things seemed to be settling down; I was twenty one on July 3rd, my five years as an apprentice had come to an end so I earned more money. Bob and I worked hard, weekdays and overtime for the company, all the other time including night work on occasion, was for us. Eventually we had to make a decision; we couldn't work for the company and expand our own business further so we amicably left the employment of Harefield Rubber Company, but made ourselves available to them on a subcontract basis. Bob wasn't too sure about taking the plunge and working to build our own company, but I convinced him we could make it work. He needn't have concerned himself, we made a few mistakes, but we really never looked back.

We were kept busy, initially by working as a subcontractor for the old company, also for General Asphalt, a new company to us at that time, but fairly big in the business so with the subcontracting work and our own work we were kept very busy. One day we received a phone call from Jim Green, Contracts Manager of General Asphalt, saying that he had a contract at the world famous London Palladium variety theatre, but it had to be finished within four days, did we want to do it. "What is the job?" we asked, "To renew the flooring on the stage," he replied. Work is work, so we said yes, provided we could have a look at the job beforehand. The job was to be carried out during a four day theatre closure in March that year. We visited the site and carried out a visual inspection but because the theatre ran daily performances, we weren't allowed to uplift any of the existing flooring to see what was underneath, so we had to assume there would be no problems when we remove the existing old flooring and lay the new floor, apart from that issue, the job itself was pretty straight forward. Or was it?

The day we started the job, Bob and I, together with two other floor layer friends of ours who worked with us on occasion, arrived very early to ensure that we could park close to the theatre (no parking meters in those days). We managed to park the van, containing the equipment we would need, close to the stage door then went inside to have a closer look at what we had to do. I remember it was a peculiar feeling standing on the stage, where so many world famous people have performed over the years. The theatre, normally packed with excited people, was now empty and silent. Jim Green, the Contracts Manager, arrived and together with the Theatre Manager discussed the job with us and everything seemed O.K. As they were about to leave and let us get on with the job, the Theatre Manager said, "Don't forget the revolving stage," Bob and I looked at him and said simultaneously, "What revolving stage?" The manager walked towards the centre of the stage and pointed to a thin line in the floor that was part of a circle 25 foot (7.5 metres) diameter. The revolving stage was where the long legged and feathered Tiller Girls, stars and performers wave to the audience as they rotate as the curtain goes up. The narrow joint dividing the main stage from the revolving stage went unnoticed when we first visited, I guess because nobody mentioned it so we didn't look for it, also it was fairly dark on the stage at the time. Finding out about this unwelcome addition to our workload would test our ability to complete the job within the four days allocated. There was now an element of concern about the job as we set about uplifting the old existing flooring. We expected to be able to uplift the existing flooring in large pieces, but it wasn't long before we realised we were looking at a very serious problem. The old flooring was stuck to the floor like poo to a blanket and resisted all our attempts to remove it, instead of it being removed in large pieces as we hoped, we only managed to remove very small pieces with the aid of a hammer and chisel. All four of us worked all day with hardly anything to show for our effort. I said to Bob that we were going to need more time, we would need six days based on the first day's rate of progress, he replied, "The theatre opens in another three days," "Yes," I continued, "but if we work night and day for the next two days we would in effect have another five days, we can sleep on the job when we need to and work nonstop until finish." Accepting that we had no alternative we arrived the following morning, the plan being that Bob and the other two guys would continue to remove the old floor, and I would clean and lay the hardboard underlay ready to receive the new flooring. I loosely fitted the hardboard panels to the area that I had cleared, and then went to the van to collect the air compressor and staple guns and set about stapling the panels to the old floor. Pleased that we were making some progress, I started to staple the panels into position. Almost immediately, the staple gun jammed. Undeterred, I cleared the jammed gun and continued, the same thing happened again and again. Confused as to why this should happen, I cleared the gun once more and fired a staple into an uncovered patch of the old floor, the same thing happened, the staple would not penetrate the original old maple wood planking which was used for the surface of the stage when it was first constructed. Kneeling on the floor, I sat back to rest on my legs and gave a long sigh when I realised what we would have to do. I called Bob over and explained what the problem was and what I thought we should do. Bob continued as before, and I went to a hardware shop at the end of the street, I explained to the shop manager what had happened and purchased his stock of half inch (12mm) countersunk wood screws, and requested that he organise a special delivery of a much larger quantity ready for collection that afternoon.

I returned and started work knowing we really had a serious problem on our hands; every hardboard panel would now have to be screwed to the old floor with a screw spacing of six inches (15 centimetres). I attacked the task with a vengeance, slow at first then working up to a rhythm and progress, albeit slow progress. We continued working all that day and through the night apart from rest periods, Bob and the two guys continued uplifting the old flooring with me following behind screw fixing the hardboard underlay. By the morning of the third day, the uplifting of the old floor and laying the hardboard had been completed and by midday we were ready to start laying the new Armourfloor sheet flooring. The Theatre Manager, with a concerned look on his face, appeared to inspect our progress, his visits becoming more frequent as the work progressed, anxious as to whether we would finish on time. His visit during the afternoon produced a sigh of relief when he saw we were laying the new flooring, "Do you think you will finish?" he said, directing his question at Bob and myself. "We are totally drained and in need of sleep," Bob said, "so we propose to leave the site later and return early in the morning, it will be a long hard day but we should finish on time."

We arrived at the site before seven that morning; we had until six o'clock that evening to finish. Working as two pairs and having food and drink as we worked, we were able to maximise our effort, but it was touch and go if we would finish on time. There was still an hour and a half before the performance was to start at six thirty, before that time we had to lay the two largest and most difficult sheets of flooring. All four of us went at it like madmen, working against the clock, there was a lot of activity on and around the stage, bantering between the technicians and stagehands as to whether we would make it or not. It didn't help when some of the Tiller Girls, with long legs and feathers, stood around us watching what we were doing, laughing and giggling amongst themselves. We were fitting the last sheet of flooring when the sound of instruments being tuned came from the orchestra pit in front of the stage, and buzzing chatter coming from in front of the curtain as the public flowed down the aisles looking for their allocated seats. Just before six o'clock we fitted the last piece, everyone around us cheered and clapped softy then they went about their business now that the crisis was over. Bob, myself and the two guys allowed ourselves a few moments to ease the tension and concern that had built up over the past few days, then removed surplus materials, tools and equipment which was loaded in the van. The Theatre Manager, relieved of the worried look, walked towards Bob and I, saying, "You had me worried, but you managed it." As we spoke, he looked at the new floor, and at the same time nodded with approval, then in mid-sentence froze with a look of horror on his face. Unable to speak due to the shock, he pointed to where the revolving stage used to be. Bob and I looked in the direction he was pointing, but saw nothing so turned to look at the Theatre Manager who screamed out, "THE REVOLVING STAGE," then walked away holding his head.

Everybody in the area was alerted to the situation and converged to the centre looking at where the revolving stage should be. "I've laid the bloody flooring over it," I said to Bob. Devastated because of what had happened, we knew we only had twenty minutes to put it right or we would be in serious trouble. I isolated myself from the milling people on the stage to think of a solution; seconds later I asked one of the stagehands if it would be possible to see underneath the revolving stage. Moments later, I was back on the stage explaining to Bob and the other guys what I proposed.

The joint between the edge of the main stage and the edge of the revolving stage was capped by a steel trim, with a space between, just wide enough to pass a hand saw blade between. Convinced it might work, I told Bob and the guys what I was proposing. The plan was I would go to the basement to get under the stage then drill a series of holes up between the two steel trims, the thickness and width of a hand saw blade. Then from on top of the stage, Bob would pass the hand saw blade down the slot between the trims and start sawing, he would saw in one direction and one of the guys would saw in the other direction, I would remain underneath the stage to make sure we didn't saw through the light cables! My heart was pounding and my head felt like it was about to explode as I watched the saw blades following the circle. The orchestra, now in tune, was playing music from the show and above I could hear the entertainers walking across to get into position ready for when the curtain goes up. I watched the saw blades going up and down willing them to go faster, as they worked their way around the circle. It seemed to be taking ages but in truth we finished sawing and by the time I got back on stage, covered head to foot in saw dust, it had taken fifteen minutes. Relieved that I was able to save the day, and a hell of a lot of cost and embarrassment, I moved to one side of the stage to shake myself free of the coating of sawdust, then realised we should make sure that the revolving stage worked O.K. I quickly spoke to the Stage Foreman, who ordered the revolving stage cleared, as he ran to the switch and turned it on, it revolved then stopped, there was a shot term panic while we passed the saw once more through the offending section. The stage revolved and stopped a few times, until it continued to revolve as before.

Everybody was smiling once more as we were ushered from the stage and the entertainers positioned themselves ready for the start of the show. A few moments later the orchestra that had been playing soft background music suddenly came alive, the audience went silent as the lights dimmed and the curtain started to rise then erupted with excitement. Feeling really knackered but relieved we made it, we loaded the van, cleaned ourselves up a bit and then went back inside to watch the show from the side of the stage. The Theatre Manager, who had not hung himself after all, saw us watching the show then moved off in a different direction, a short while later he reappeared and walked towards us, I thought to throw us out, but he didn't. He came quietly towards us, and in a whispered voice said, "I want to thank you for working so hard to finish the job," and handed each of us four complementary tickets, which was a nice gesture. Working at the

London Palladium and the heart stopping problems we encountered always brings a smile to my face whenever I recall those days. It was also on that occasion that I learnt to never make a decision based on an assumption, had I insisted on a closer inspection when we carried out the survey in the first place, we would have known what we were letting ourselves in for.

July 1962, 22 years old, I learned fast and soon showed signs of developing a head for business and eagerness to drive forward. Vi had already given birth to our daughter, Carole, and our son, Lee, made his entrance later that year. We formed our own flooring company and called it R & L Carvall Ltd, Flooring Contractors. Over the next few years we worked hard expanding our business year after year, employing more people as we expanded. Vi worked with us as our bookkeeper and kept control of our finances, it was mostly all work and no play during those days.

1967. Bob and I were no longer on our knees laying floors. We ran the business as equal partners dealing with all the bigger jobs ourselves, by that time our younger brother, Danny, joined the company as well as us employing site surveyors and full time floor layers. We occupied offices with limited storage at West Green Road, Tottenham, North London; the flooring company eventually grew to become one of the largest flooring companies in the U.K. employing twenty floor layers. When we received enquiries for flooring work there was, on occasion, ceramic tiling work that we didn't tender for. Seeing a way of expanding our business, we started to submit our estimates to our clients to include flooring and ceramic wall tiling. It wasn't long before ceramic wall and floor tiling expanded to become a substantial part of our overall business, and required an operating title more in keeping with the ceramic wall and floor tiling business that was developing, thus Val-Fix Ltd, our second company was formed. We moved in and out of various properties to accommodate our expansion and as the company grew, we needed to buy and store more and more materials to feed to our contracts. In those days there was no such thing as a wholesale supplier of flooring materials, everything you needed had to be purchased direct from the manufacturer, who usually had a delivery service to our area, one day a week. An impossible situation to be in if you have ten or so contracts to complete each week, something needed to be done to eliminate the supply problem. Over the following weeks the issue about getting supplies delivered more frequently occupied my mind, I tried to come up with some way of not relying on a once a week delivery and become independent of the materials manufacturers. I was working late one Thursday evening and went to the store to check on some materials for a job that was starting the next day; we had everything we needed on that occasion, I then looked at a line of jobs still awaiting the arrival of materials before they could be delivered to their respective sites. The only way to overcome the problem, I thought to myself, was to carry the level of stock necessary to cover most eventualities, but the cost would make it unaffordable.

Still looking at the stock but not seeing anything, my mind was spinning like a roulette wheel, my eyes focused once more as I realised that most of our competitors have the same problem with materials availability as we do, what if I buy materials in bulk and sell it to them, why don't we set up a company in London that supplies flooring materials to the trade at manufacturer prices, on a next day delivery basis? I didn't get much support for the idea from Bob when I outlined what I was proposing; instead I was given a number of reasons why it wouldn't work, all of which I answered to the contrary, but eventually he went along with it. First I had to explain to the people around me who needed to know what I was proposing, secondly run my idea past our bank manager and talk him into increasing our overdraft (the sod wouldn't do it without our house as collateral) then convince the individual manufacturers to supply me with materials on credit at a 20% discount. It was an uphill struggle, what I was proposing had never been done before, so they were very cautious, they understood my thinking when I told them that they would save money if they deliver one full load of materials to me instead of four or five small loads. The manufacturers came around to my way of thinking in the end, although, in some instances I only managed a discount of 15%, but it was a start. It was not long before I had a range of preparation materials, tiles and sheet flooring and a range of accessories, all available to the trade on a next day delivery basis. My next task was to convince our competitors to become our customers. That wasn't going to be easy, but I had an ace up my sleeve!

Before I started to talk to other flooring companies about buying their materials from a wholesaler instead of direct from the manufacturer, I first had to form a new independent company, neutral to all the flooring companies who hopefully would become our customers, I called the new company Flooring Supplies (Tottenham) Ltd, but it was known throughout the trade as Flooring Supplies. Anticipating that I might be put to the test when talking to other companies, I got myself organised beforehand. I acquired a storage area local to our offices, received the initial consignment of stock from the manufacturers, purchased a van and had Flooring Supplies painted along both sides, so as to look presentable when we delivered the goods. I talked a retired floor layer friend of mine, with plenty of knowledge, into answering the phone, armed with a temporary brochure; I was ready to lock horns with our potential customers. I selected medium sized companies to call on first, mainly because I had been in contact with some of them in the past and they would listen to what I had to say, my salesman pitch was roughly the same every time I made a call, explaining that for the first time, contractors can pick up the phone and order from our stock range of products, everything they need, at the same price as before, and it would be delivered the next day. They would usually follow by saying, "Why should we buy from a competitor?" I would reply, "Flooring Supplies is not a competitor, it is an independent company that can help you increase your business," (this is where I produce my ace) "and also," I would continue, "if a customer walked into your office and wanted you to complete a contract over the weekend or start the job the next day, you wouldn't be able to do it, but now you can, if you can't wait for a next day delivery, you can collect from our store the same day." My sales pitch worked, some companies saw the advantage and placed orders pretty well straight away, others quickly followed, the bigger companies were reluctant at first to switch but we eventually did business with almost all the companies in and around London on an ongoing basis. Over the next few years Flooring Supplies Ltd expanded, opening thirteen branches nationally, it employed one hundred and twenty people and had an annual turnover by the end of 1976 of around four and half million. I look back over that time in my life, being a sort of pioneer if you like, thinking through an idea, and turning it into reality. Being a new idea, there was no one before you to copy from, you are on your own. To say it was easy would be untrue, there were plenty of people watching and waiting for me to make a mess of things so they could say I told you so, fortunately, that didn't happen.

1977. We were known as the Carvall Group Ltd who, in turn, owned R&L Carvall Ltd, Val-Fix Ltd and Flooring Supplies (Tottenham) Ltd. We occupied a 40,000 sq. foot (3717 metres) office and warehouse premises which was also our head office. I was the chairman of the group and a 48% shareholder, Bob and Danny had 52% shareholding between them. I could have insisted that on the basis that I had been responsible for bringing us this far I should therefore have a majority shareholding. I thought along the lines that we were a family business and in it together, irrespective who was the driving force. I instead proposed that my brothers, Bob and Dan, have 52% between them, and in so doing guaranteeing that, if at any time I come up with an idea, and I can't convince them it is worth pursuing, I can be out voted. This arrangement, I thought, would involve my brothers more, and bring in an element of caution in my thinking and decision making in the future. Unfortunately, my quest to involve my brothers more was the worst decision of my life, and led to me being voted off the board as chairman and dismissed from the company I had built. This devastating incident happened a little further along the road, so till then I will continue with the story.

You may recall that I said earlier, it wouldn't be possible for me to include everything that happened to me or what I did as I worked my way through the University of Life. However, what I am about to tell you is another incident, and one of many, that deserves a mention because, like everything else, it actually happened. I was responsible for putting into motion a chain of events that changed the British ceramic floor and wall tile industry into what it is today. To start at the beginning, I need to take you back to 1973, if my memory serves me right, we were doing pretty well for ourselves, I was dividing my time between the companies, Flooring Supplies was expanding like crazy and the contracting side of the business had a full order book. Flooring Supplies branches throughout the country had developed into fully stocked depots and for a year or so we had a monopoly of the market. Unfortunately, it wasn't long after that our first competitor appeared and soon after that, small companies copying our idea were popping up all over the place. Conscious that I had to keep ahead of the competition, I started to look at adding complementary products to our stock range. The carpet industry at that time still worked the old way and there was opportunity to include commercial carpeting without much reorganisation, but I didn't know enough about the carpet industry and people who may not be so easy to convince. The other possibility was ceramic tiles, I felt more comfortable with it, I wasn't an expert by any means, but through Val-Fix Ltd, I acquired some knowledge over the years so I was more confident, but never ruled out carpets altogether.

Having decided to have a closer look at the British ceramic tile industry, I started by compiling a list of manufacturers and was surprised that basically there were only four manufacturers, and one importer of German ceramics. I collected samples and spoke to some of the manufacturers but received a negative response, from what I could make out manufacturing methods and the finished product was twenty years out of date, tile finishes were limited to short ranges of plain colours and old designs. I soon decided that moving into ceramic tile distribution in its present form wasn't for Flooring Supplies. I knew I had to do something to keep ahead of the competition by expanding the product range and, for a time, I did this by becoming a national distributer for two additional flooring brands, but my gut feeling at that time told me I needed to find something fresh, something new. Every flooring company throughout the country knew who Flooring Supplies Ltd was but I felt that I had to do something to keep the name at the front, so to speak. I pondered the problem for a while, eventually deciding what was needed was London's, and the country's as a whole, first Contract Flooring Exhibition. It hadn't been done before so I was a bit apprehensive as I set about putting it together. I looked at various venues but they were either too expensive or too large, eventually deciding that the main warehouse at our Tottenham head office would suit the purpose nicely. I discussed my proposal with Bob and Dan; they thought I had gone mad as I explained what I was proposing to do, but when I got to the part when I said, "I will take all the stock out of the warehouse and store it outside in the open for a day and a night," they said I was definitely mad. I contacted our suppliers who readily agreed to take part. The date was set for Britain's first Contract Flooring Exhibition on 25th September 1969; I prayed that on the day it wouldn't rain. Neil, the Warehouse Manager, wasn't too happy when I told him what I was going to do and that I needed his help if I was to achieve what I had planned and the event being a success. Neil recovered from a near seizure, the colour restored to his usually rosy cheeks, and breathing back to normal, I continued, "You have been asking me for an opportunity to re-organise and maximise the warehouse space, well now you will have the opportunity, and you can order the additional shelving you need to achieve it."

In the days leading up to the first Contract Flooring Exhibition, I was running around like a headless chicken making sure everything was going to plan, and it was going to happen. I personally visited as many of our customers as I could, I phoned or sent invitations to the remainder and our representatives were kept busy following up the invitations to make sure they were coming. The response was overwhelming, not because I was that popular, it was probably because of the free bar and buffet! The day finally arrived, it was hard work but we would be ready to open the doors to visitors at 5pm. Twenty exhibitor booths, each stocked with the latest materials and equipment, were positioned around the perimeter and through the centre. An official programme containing exhibition information was available at the entrance, flags, banners and posters all with a strong bias promotionally towards Flooring Supplies Ltd were displayed everywhere. The two free bars and buffet were open for business and awaiting custom, background music was playing, we were ready, all we needed was for the people to turn up. At 5pm only about ten of the expected number had arrived, I can still remember walking around the exhibition area at that time, talking to exhibitors, the piercing eyes watching me, some hoping that

I had got it wrong. The hour between 5 and 6pm that evening was the longest hour of my life, as the hour closed, I started to wonder if in fact I had got it wrong. Feeling a bit uncomfortable, I made my way to the main entrance to get some fresh air and to think about what I would do if it all turns out one hell of a mess. I stepped outside into the street and the expected quiet resonating from factories that had closed for the day. Attracted by the noise of car doors closing, I looked in that direction to see a large number of people walking towards me, some I knew, giving me a wave. With tearful eyes, I returned the wave and at the same time thought, just maybe, I had got it right after all.

From that point on people kept coming, based on the number of programmes handed out, there were around 450 visitors packed into our small exhibition area, I spent the evening reconnecting with old friends, talking to new customers and making sure everything was running smoothly. Apart from someone complaining that the beer was warm, and another who had too much warm beer and had to be ejected, it all worked out fine. It was one o'clock next morning, I was the last one to leave, the doors were made secure, I sat for a few moments reflecting on the evening's events now that it was behind me, I met a lot of old friends, people I first met when starting as an apprentice floor layer, most were still on their knees laying floors, but I had managed to elevate myself to where I was at that time, I wondered what they really thought. My thoughts drifted to Bob and Dan, they didn't give me any help to put the exhibition together, and it was particularly noticeable that they hardly spoke to me during the evening; it would have been a compliment if they had patted me on the back and said to me, well done, for a change. I was back at the office at six the following morning, allowing myself one day to help get everything relocated into the warehouse and back to normal trading the following day. From then on the relationship between Bob, Dan and me wasn't quite the same; we went about our allotted duties within the company as normal but without any of the usual banter or joking like brothers do. The situation didn't deteriorate further so I had no cause to enquire if there was a problem I needed to deal with, apart from that everything carried on normally and we prospered.

It was late 1973, the Contract Flooring Exhibition was a memory and as chairman, I got back into the routine of dealing with finance and general group matters, as well as visiting some of the larger contracts to check on progress and have a chat to the guys on site. It was on one such occasion I visited our site just off Slone Street, London. I liked these site visits, it kept me in touch with the people I worked with, I usually arrived early to meet the guys, have a look around the site then buy them, and myself, breakfast at the local café. On the way to the café on this particular day we walked past an exclusive Spanish store called Casa Pupo, if my memory serves me right, a real up-market store, as we walked past, I glanced at the display and noticed what looked like a 9 inch (225 mm x 225 mm) glazed tile with a teapot on top. We walked on to the café and within thirty minutes we were on our way back, I was keen to have another look at the tile. Through the window I studied the tile, it was a bit knobbly (you could see it was handmade) and had a white glaze surface, painted over with yellow and black to a fleur-de-lis design. Frozen to the spot, I just stared at the tile, my mind trying to make sense of what I was looking at, the two tilers who were with me looked at the tile but didn't see what I saw. Without saying another word, I walked into the store and asked at the reception if I could speak to the owner, I wanted to ask some questions about the teapot stand! After some strange looks, paper shuffling and phone calls, a rather short, slim, well-dressed man appeared and introduced himself as Señor Cassias, the owner of the store. I explained who I was and why I was interested in the teapot stand, I also asked him if he could supply the tiles in larger quantities, "Why?" he asked, "Because

I think I can sell them," I replied. A week later I had another meeting with Señor Cassias who confirmed that he could supply a larger quantity, but it would take some time because they are individually hand painted. I had already made up my mind as to what I was going to say to Señor Cassias if he said he could supply larger quantities. Hearing the news, I looked him straight in the eye and said, "I have a proposal to put to you," he didn't flinch, I said, "I will order from you and pay for enough tiles to complete a large bathroom. When the tiles arrive I want you to let me use the main shop window and I will build a complete bathroom and tile it throughout with your tiles. If what I believe will happen actually happens, that is, people from the area will see the display in your shop window and may want to buy hand painted tiles for themselves, one of our site surveyors will measure the quantity required for installation and submit the customer a supply and install price, if successful, we place an order for the tiles direct with you." He stood motionless thinking though what I had just said, after a few moments he looked at me and with his right hand pointed at the display area, "You want me to give you my window to sell tiles?" "Yes," I said. Then I went on to explain, "At the moment you cannot buy hand painted tiles in Britain suitable for tiling a bathroom, we could be the first, and your window display will be in the top ten magazines and the talk of London." A bit optimistic, but it got a response. Señor Cassias looked at me, then turned to the young lady at reception and said, "Please get Mr Carvall a coffee," then turned back to me to say, "Make yourself comfortable, I have to go to my office." Señor Cassias returned fifteen minutes later accompanied by another man, who I understood to be his partner; they spoke in Spanish to one another for a minute or two then Señor Cassias said to me, "How long will you want the window?" "One week to complete the bathroom, and four weeks to see what happens, after that you decide." He gave a long sigh that seemed to go on forever, and then said, "How many tiles will you need?" Bob already knew what I was doing so I was in high spirit (not the liquid sort) and eager to tell him what I'd managed to achieve.

The mind splitting potential of what I was playing with wound me up like a taut spring. I had found the new product range I had been looking for; all I had to do now was get it to the marketplace, easier said than done. By the time I reached the office, I had the bones of a plan worked out in my mind. I made straight for Bob's office to tell him the good news, outlining what had happened at my meeting with Señor Cassias and the financial potential if we could market the tiles through our branches, ending by saying, "If we do it right we will be ahead of the competition by two years." Bob listened to what I had to say, but at the same time rolled his tongue around his mouth, something he did automatically when he wasn't altogether interested in something I was telling him, neither did he ask any questions nor show any enthusiasm. I was disappointed at the lack of interest but was determined not to let this opportunity slip through my fingers. The thought of being the first commercial importer and distributer of hand painted tiles really fired me up, the financial potential of what I had stumbled on had taken hold of me and nothing or nobody was going to stop me.

My deal with Señor Cassias was the first step, turning teapot stands into bathroom tiles, my agreement remained firm and I would honour the arrangement to the letter. However, there was nothing in our agreement that said I couldn't travel to Spain to talk to tile manufacturers and organise my own supplies. While we were waiting for the tiles to arrive for Casa Pupo's display window, and so as to not waste any time, I asked Vi to join me on a short business and pleasure trip to Spain to visit and make contact with tile manufacturers, with the view to setting up a supply line and stock quantities sufficient to feed our thirteen branches, also the trip to Spain would be a bit of a novelty for the both of us. Most of the so called factories we called at turned out to be small corrugated tin buildings in the middle of nowhere with no hope of producing what I needed. Eventually though, we tracked down two companies who showed interest and were keen to do business with me. From the standard stock colours and designs from both factories I was able to select a range that we would offer for sale in the U.K. Having been assured that the quantities we required and delivery time would be met, I collected the samples they provided, and satisfied that a deal had been put together, we finished the last few days of our holiday. After a week in the office to catch up on what had been happening, I made an appointment with the manager of our bank, National Westminster Bank, Gray's-Inn Road, London, to find out what we had to do to set up letters of credit to cover each consignment of tiles.

I produced the colourful tile samples I brought back from Spain to show Bob and Dan and our contract managers who expressed interest. I said that the first consignment would arrive in six weeks, before then, we would need to design and produce tile sample boards for our representatives to present the tiles to our ceramic tile customers. We would also need a tile show area at the office main entrance for our walk in trade customers, and a price list and brochure. There wasn't much time and it was hard work bringing everything together, our presentation needed to reflect the unique quality of the expensive tiles we were offering, so to help the sales team we were able to produce, from the hand samples I brought back from Spain, a glitzy brochure and price list indicating a trade discount structure. Everybody involved with the new product range attended short training sessions to ensure that they had a thorough knowledge of the product and to give our customers confidence. Everything was ready and the staff enthusiastically waited for our first consignment to arrive.

I guess at this stage I should mention that everything didn't exactly go like clockwork, I had my share of problems, at various stages I made mistakes in one way or another and sometimes things didn't turn out as planned. One serious problem I had remained undetected and reared its ugly head when we were building the bathroom in the display window at the Casa Pupo. The window had been sealed from the public's prying eyes inside and outside the store, the guys doing the work had completed erecting the false walls to simulate a bathroom, comprising of a back wall and two end panels, the remaining side was open to allow the public to eventually see into the three sided bathroom. I was on site the day the tiles arrived, and soon after, we were offering up the tiles to achieve the best pattern effect before fixing into position. The tilers were about to start work when one of them said to me, "Where are the round edge tiles?" You could have heard a pin drop, it went that quiet, I stopped breathing for a moment or two while my mind darted in all directions to source a solution. My breathing kicked in as I thought to myself, —— —g hell (not the Queen's English I know, but I couldn't help myself on that occasion). The problem that caused so much concern was that I didn't order a quantity of tiles with a radius on one edge to facilitate finishing on corners and edges. I felt worse when I realised that four tiles made a complete pattern, so we would need four tiles each with a radius on a different edge, I thought to myself, I'm in the shit up to my neck this time. I just sat there looking at the tiles then at the mock-up bathroom, not knowing which way to turn; the guys went to the café around the corner for a cup of tea, leaving me alone to think about my problems. With the burden of responsibility weighing heavily on my shoulders, I started to consider the possibility that I might have to tell Señor Cassias that I had cocked up, made a mess of things and would need time to sort it out. Still sitting, I looked around the store for inspiration, and at the same time turned over the tile I had in my hand, I noticed that the biscuit (the tile base) was softer than British tiles and a bit sandy, I then for some reason looked once more at a heavily patterned wallpaper forming a backdrop of another display. Remaining focused on the wallpaper for a moment, unable to make a connection between the two, I suddenly realised I was looking at the answer - disregard the old way, that is, using special tiles with radius edges, we would fit the tiles like they hang wallpaper, when you come to a vertical edge, you simply cut the tile and sand the biscuit at forty-five degrees to form a ninety degree angle. A good tiler would have no problem working this way and, as it happened, I had two of the best tilers working on the window display. When the guys returned, I told them about my solution to the problem and they immediately went about proving whether it could be done that way or not. I watched them work, they quickly produced and tested samples for approval; agreeing that we had found the answer, the guys started tiling the bathroom.

Señor Cassias was unaware of the near catastrophe a few hours earlier when he looked in to check the progress, by that time the tilers had covered a large wall area and tested the new method of tiling around corners, it was looking good. Señor Cassias told me that the following week he had arranged to unveil the tiled bathroom at an open evening and press reception including special guests and celebrities; I assured him the display would be ready. We finished the tiling work two days later, the guys had done a wonderful job, and it looked spectacular, Señor Cassias was overwhelmed with the end result and was running around like a dog with two tails. After we cleaned the display it was handed over to the store design department to add the furnishings, bits and pieces and the detail that goes into window displays, when everyone had finished, it really did look something special.

The reception was a grand affair, I had to hand it to Señor Cassias, he knew how to put a reception together to attract the right people, the centre of attraction and what everybody was talking about was the tiled bathroom, because it was something new, the press made a big thing of it, making the front cover or centre pages of the top magazines. It had all worked out O.K. in the end. Sales of tiles through the store continued for a year or so but eventually the store decided for one reason or another to stop selling tiles, but we did alright while it lasted.

A few weeks after the success of the Casa Pupo open evening, our first consignment arrived, we had a few issues to start with but we worked it out and in a short time, hand painted ceramic tiles, associated materials and accessories were being sold through our depots nationally, sales grew month after month to become a large part of Flooring Supplies Ltd's business. Eventually though, we decided that because the ceramic tile sales had grown so much we needed someone from the top to run it, after due consideration, Danny, our younger brother, was given the job. Focusing only on the ceramic sales, he was able to take it to another level, and to give credit where due, he was responsible for attending trade exhibitions and establishing in-house tile shops in all the major stores throughout London which generated business that required weekly shipments from an increasing number of Spanish and Italian tile manufacturers. Sadly, two years or so after we pioneered the idea of selling hand painted tiles in Britain, tile shops were popping up everywhere, growing to what it is today. Regardless of the competition, we remained the dominant supplier for many years. If at some time you pass a tile shop, big or small, you can say to yourself, I know who started that.

The years leading up to 1978 didn't produce anything new, my attention was focused mainly on holding the group together, we were very profitable but the depots were spread all over the country, and that started to worry me. My relationship between Bob and Dan had deteriorated, we didn't argue or anything like that, we generally agreed about company policy and decisions that had to be made, but that was it, we never spent time together just to chat. Just for the hell of it and to set myself another challenge, I decided to learn to fly a helicopter, I signed up for a course of training with Trent Helicopters based at Luton Airport, the course lasted almost a year because I had to study at night and do my flight training when I had spare time and at weekends, ending when I passed my flight test and oral examination, I received my Helicopter Private Pilot Licence towards the end of 1974. I felt quite pleased with myself at my achievement; the staff at the office had been following my progress and gave me encouragement when I looked a bit haggard as a result of the strain. My brothers never spoke to me about my flying, or asked me how I was progressing, nor indeed did they attend the small party organised by the staff to celebrate me receiving my Helicopter Pilot Licence.

The companies prospered over the following three years or so, my job as chairman of the group was to make sure that the companies within the group continued to remain profitable, as well as keeping an eye open for any opportunities that may come along. I looked at a few things but nothing really interested me to a point that I should look further. I spent some of my time checking the cost of maintaining the depots spread around the country, the staffing and stock cost in relation to long term sales performance, that sort of thing.

I began to think of various ways we may be able to expand the business, nothing specific, more as a result of a gut feeling that maybe we should be doing something different. In the meantime, we were being forced to close the Glasgow depot because we were finding it difficult, as an English company, to continue selling in Scotland, especially now that Scottish companies were opening up. Also the manager at the Dublin depot indicated that he wanted to take over the depot and we were expecting his offer any time. The same applied to the Norwich depot, which just about kept its head above water, and the suggestion from the manager for him to buy the stock from us and run the depot himself was an opportunity not to be missed. I didn't want to delay the letting go of Glasgow, Dublin, and Norwich, so I told Brother Bob what I wanted to do and the reason why, he just said, "It's up to you what you do." I looked at him, and then said, "It's not up to me, it's up to us," "I said, you do what you want to," he repeated. I was concerned about the response I received, but went about dealing with the closures as described. Over the following weeks I completed an individual cost analysis for each of the remaining depots, to confirm the cost to keep them open. The individual depot cost varied but they were all operating profitably so there was no reason to panic, but in a year or so it may be a different story. I told Bob about my concern, and the long term viability of the depots, and that I was looking at various options available to us. The day to day business of my office, dealing with finance matters and meetings with suppliers occupied most of my time, so the investigative work I was doing into the future of Flooring Supplies Ltd was taking longer than I had hoped. Nevertheless, the information I had compiled so far started alarm bells ringing, realising that there was now some urgency, I gathered the remaining information I needed and was able to put a plan of action together. What I was looking at was a bitter pill to swallow, and what's more I didn't think my brothers could handle it.

I had committed the result of my investigations to paper a week previously, I had not shown it to anyone else, fearing that perhaps I had got it wrong. Thumbing through my papers one more time, I convinced myself that I hadn't got it wrong and what I was proposing was the right course of action, but how do I convince brothers Bob and Danny to sell off profitable depots? The long term viability of Flooring Supplies Ltd in its present form is questionable, to secure its future we would need to sell or close all the remaining depots other than the main depot and head office at Tottenham, and the depot at Coulsdon, South London.

My proposal for the future was that we re-organise the 40,000 square foot (3717 metres) office and warehouse building at Tottenham to accommodate smaller administrative offices and the remainder of the building be used as a warehouse and distribution centre of flooring materials for the whole of the south of England. Included in this proposal would be a cash and collect facility (as I called it in those days). The idea was that customers who collected their own materials would get a collection discount, I didn't know it then, but what I was proposing was a form of cash and carry, which came along later. The bitter part of the pill was why sell profitable depots? Profitable then but in a year or two I didn't think so, much easier to sell depots now that are profitable and maybe fetch a premium price, than wait and have to close them and walk away with your tail between your legs. The whole process of change would take a year to complete, and would include some heart breaking decisions. At a meeting dedicated to this issue, Bob and Dan listened to what I had to say, there was no discussion or questions put to me about the information I had accumulated or its authenticity. I concluded by saying, "You can delay what I am proposing but you can't put it off. If we do it might drag us down."

The meeting with Bob and Dan a few days previously didn't produce a response so I didn't know whether to include it on the agenda for the board meeting the following morning. Bob and Dan were out of the office that day, so we were unable to have our usual brief meeting in preparation for the board meeting. The following morning, I arrived early to complete the details of a report relating to general matters that I was to present at the meeting at 10 o'clock. There was a strange atmosphere in the office that morning, at one point I thought I caught a glimpse of one of the auditors from the firm we used and someone I hadn't seen before talking to Danny, people were acting a bit odd. Bob and Dan were already in the boardroom when I entered,

I immediately noticed that they didn't have the usual paperwork in front of them and they avoided eye contact when I looked at them, the non-shareholding Directors, long term employees who had been appointed Directors along the way, entered and sat down. Seeing that everybody was present, I called the meeting to order and was about to start my summary when Dan stood up and looked at me then said, "Before the meeting deals with any business, I want to propose a vote of no confidence in the chairman," then brother Bob stood and looked at me saying he seconded the vote of no confidence, and to consider myself no longer chairman or a member of the board and asked me to leave the room. Bob then indicated to everyone that the meeting would be rescheduled. Stunned by what I had just heard, I just sat there, I looked at everyone around the table, and they were shocked and clearly didn't know it was going to happen. I was left alone in the boardroom to slowly collect my papers and, for the first time in my life, not knowing what to do. I returned to my office and poured myself a cup of coffee, leaving it untouched, I made my way to Bob's office, the people he was talking to quickly vacated the room as I walked in. I looked at him and said, as I tried to put a lighter tone to the conversation, "I take it you will be taking on the job as chairman, so what job will I be doing?" He looked at me with such hatred in his eyes, it shocked me, he then said, "There is no job," then walked out of the office leaving me standing alone. I told Vi and my secretary what had happened, then Vi and I left the building and drove ourselves home.

At home, I finally accepted that I was no longer part of the organisation I had spent my life building, and being responsible for, and the mechanism I had put in place to protect it against wrong decision making, had been used by my brothers to remove me. I also knew that the hatred towards me that surfaced was so bitter that working with them again would not be possible, and there would be no turning back. The following morning I went to the office to collect my bits and pieces, also to have a word with Bob to see if I could make some sense out of what had happened. When I arrived Bob wasn't there so I went to my office to collect my things, as I did I passed Danny's office and he was sitting at his desk, so I entered. I went to speak to him but noticed he had made out a cheque payable to himself for a large amount of money, and it was on the desk in front of him. I asked, "Why have you written out that cheque to yourself?" he looked sheepish and didn't reply. I grabbed the cheque and went to find brother Bob, who had just arrived. "Can I have word?" I said, pointing towards his office, I closed the door and thrust the cheque in front of him, "Did you authorise this payment?" I said, "It's none of your business," he replied. I paused for a moment, and then said, "That's where you are wrong, you managed to remove me from the company, but I am still a majority shareholder and payments such as this need the approval of all three shareholders, and I am not approving this payment."

Feeling a bit like my old self once more, I thought for a moment then I looked into Bob's eyes and the hate they contained, and said, "Is this what it is all about, Danny needs money, and you have a jealous hatred of me because of what I have achieved?" There was no response to my question, so I continued, "You needn't worry yourself, I want to be as far away from you two as I can possibly be." I handed Bob a proposal I had drawn up on a sheet of paper indicating the price I would accept for my shares, part in cash, the rest in assets, valuing it at about half price as an incentive to do a deal. Within a few days the transfer of the shares was completed severing any further contact or connection. From that point on I never again visited the company or had any contact with my brothers whatsoever. Over the weeks that followed, I had plenty of time to reflect on what had happened and what the future held. For twenty years I had blinkered myself from everything other than building the business, during that time I didn't pay as much attention as I should have to my lovely wife Vi, my daughter Carole, and son Lee. I saw Vi every day, she worked with me at the office, Vi was always there but it was as though at times I didn't see her, and Carole and Lee were at home when I was there but I didn't see them grow up. I never forgave myself for the way I treated them by putting the business before my family. Now that I only had the family to worry about, I tried to be more of a husband and dad. Unfortunately, it didn't quite work out like that; previously, between 7am and 7pm, Monday to Friday I was never there, so Vi and the kids did what they wanted and had their own routine, to suddenly find another person around the house messed everything up, resulting in a shouting match for the slightest reason, but it was short lived and we soon got used to living together. It was the end of 1978, we had one of our now regular family meetings, on that occasion we discussed the proposal to sell our house at Broxbourne, Hertfordshire and move to the Bournemouth area, Hampshire. There was resistance from Carole, being the oldest, because she would lose contact with her friends but in the end we agreed to make the move. The next day, I drove alone to Bournemouth to have a look around, calling at estate agents in the town to check out the house prices and whether there were any vacant commercial premises available in the area. The morning produced a selection of houses to view locally and a commercial premise situated at a place called Milford-on-Sea, the Sea part of Milford-on-Sea was like a magnet to me, the information about the houses ended up on the back seat of the car and I drove straight to Milford-on-Sea. The location was perfect, a small village with its own harbour at Keyhaven a stone's throw along the road, and the Solent water that raced between the Isle of Wight and Hurst Castle in full view and a short distance from the commercial premises at Laundry Lane I had come to see. I couldn't believe what I had stumbled on; I knew this would be our new home. The following weekend, I drove Vi, Carole and Lee to Milford-on-Sea, I managed to convince everyone that this was our new home and went about finding a house to live in. The village estate agent soon produced a house that put a smile on everyone's faces and we moved in six weeks after. As part of my share sale agreement, I acquired the group's interest in a small marine cooker and heater manufacturer called Taylor's Paraffin. Situated on the east coast, it was a bit run down but it had a good reputation within the marine industry and so I thought that I could do something with it. I moved the company, together with the two remaining employees, to the premises at Milford then set about revitalising the business. During the years leading up to 1982, I was able to get Taylor's Paraffin back into the marketplace, so to speak, we were doing O.K. but the product range was out of date and in need of restyling.

I didn't have the time to go through the process of designing, manufacturing and getting type approval of a new range and coincidentally, I visited a motorhome exhibition and looked over an American built motorhome. Inside, and set neatly in the kitchen area was a modern four burner stove produced by the Suburban Manufacturing Company, Dayton, Tennessee, U.S.A. I corresponded with the company and they seemed to be interested in supplying me with cookers, so the next step was to pay them a visit to see if I could put something together. We arranged for someone to look after Carole and Lee for a few days then Vi and I flew to New York, then took an internal flight to Chattanooga, stayed overnight at the famous Chattanooga station (now a hotel), you know the song, Chattanooga Choo Choo, track 29. The next morning, I drove the two hour journey to Dayton and the Suburban factory. It was a huge place, but like a lot of big manufacturing facilities throughout the U.S.A. was winding down and soon to close as a result of the recession that had ravaged the country for the past two years, and soon to devastate the rest of the world. But luckily they had a hell of a lot of stock they wanted to place at a price that brought a smile to my face. We had a look at what they had and how they made it, and decided to buy all they had.

When Vi and I returned to the U.K. I brought with me one complete cooker and a four burner hob as excess baggage so that I could work on them to see what we had to do to convert them to British standard, automatic lighting and flame failure, etc. The conversion procedure was set up and ready, including British instructions for use by the time the first consignment arrived. It wasn't long after that I was visiting my existing and new customers, to show them the new range of cookers, and the steady flow of orders that followed. I was turning the small business into something bigger. The arrangement with Suburban Manufacturing worked out fine and later I added their range of Gas RV heaters (recreational vehicle heaters) to our range and another string to my bow, so to speak. The stock of cookers at Suburban Manufacturing would run out by the end of the year so I had to make a decision as to what I would do before that happened. The recession that devastated America's economy did the same throughout Europe, and in particular the U.K., turning into the world recession of 1982. Thousands of British companies were wiped out, Taylor's Paraffin included. The marine and leisure industries just died, nobody could sell anything, luckily for me my stock was low at the time and I tried real hard to keep going, but it was hopeless. I eventually sold the company to a marine equipment manufacturer for a modest sum and looked for something else to do. I always managed to provide for my family and was willing to look at anything I could turn into a business. The recession dragged on and the recovery still seemed a long way off. I still occupied the business premises and as luck would have it, some friends of mine who ran a board and panel business from North London called R.P. Panel Ltd asked me if I would run a branch for them based at our premises. I considered their proposal, bearing in mind that the rent for the premises would be paid and I would be paid a wage, so I decided to give it a go. We concluded a deal but I insisted that I work on a commission only basis. Within a year I was outselling the stock they could supply, leading to the owners deciding to withdraw from our arrangement. I offered to buy the stock, and from then on Vi and I were owners of a board and panel business. A year or so later, I acquired an interest in a sawmill in the New Forest, which we ended up owning. The board and panel business and the sawmill ran side by side, the panel business remained profitable but for some reason I couldn't find out why the sawmill wasn't making a profit, all my costings indicated that we should have been, but we didn't, it was baffling but I was determined to get to the bottom of it. The situation relating to the profitability of the sawmill continued. I was dividing my time between the board and panel business based at Milford, and the sawmill based in the New Forest, overall we were making a profit and business was improving, so I let the situation continue on that basis for a while.

By that time, I had let my Helicopter Licence lapse and became a member of Bournemouth Flying Club so as to keep flying, and managed to work my way through the flight training and the oral exam to acquire my Fixed Wing Private Pilot Licence. Vi and I spent some of our leisure time at the club and got to know a lot of people and made many friends. Over the time we were members, the cost of flying had risen to a point it was becoming unaffordable for pilots with a limited budget, so there was a quest by some of the members to find cheaper ways of flying. Mike, a friend and fellow pilot, and I decided to look into the possibility of building and owning our own aircraft, we spent the evenings and weekends looking at the sales data of various home built aircraft, although cheaper to run, they were generally expensive to buy. Undeterred, we looked at the possibility of buying a built or part built plane. Weeks later, we found what we were looking for and at a price we could afford. A few days later, Mike and I were the proud owners of a part completed F.R.E.D. (short for Flying Runabout Experimental Design), a High Wing Monoplane. The previous owner, for one reason or another, couldn't finish it but he had completed a lot of the work and what he had done looked pretty good. The aircraft was on its wheels and manoeuvrable, the engine was installed, propeller fixed in position and running but it was almost another year before Fred was ready to fly, during that time Fred was parked in Mike's front garden and the neighbours weren't too happy when we occasionally fired Fred up, so we moved it to Bournemouth airport to deal with the final touches and adjustments ready for Fred's first flight.

At this stage of my story I should mention that as well as being fairly lucky in business, I have been lucky enough to still be alive, throughout my life there has been many instances when I should have departed this world, but somehow I have managed to hang

A younger Les sitting in FRED engine running

in there. On the occasion I am about to describe to you, I think you will find what happened unnerving, was it luck, or fate, or was there a hand on my shoulder that day? I haven't spoken much about the incident and this is the first time I have written about it. I also have a tendency to elaborate a bit when describing some parts of the story, perhaps it's the way I come to terms with a brush with the almighty. What I am about to tell you is a true account of what happened. It was during 1984, Fred had occupied a small space in one of the aircraft hangers at the airport, it had been ready for its first flight for three months or so but to be truthful neither of us had the balls to fly it. Just so you know, when you build an aircraft you have to have the work that you have done at each stage of construction examined and signed off by a certified aircraft engineer. This procedure continues until the aircraft is completed to a point when it is ready for a flight test, and hopefully after signed off as fit to fly. Well we did all that and our paperwork was in order, but the problem was we hadn't been able to secure the services of a test pilot to carry out the flight test, perhaps they knew something we didn't know? So Fred sat there at the back of the hanger looking sorry for himself and Mike and I were getting more frustrated, turning up at weekends to sit in Fred with the engine running but going nowhere. On this particular day, I went to the office at Milford as usual, dealt with the pile of paperwork on my desk then got the orders for delivery the next day ready for when the driver returned and we loaded his lorry.

I finished what needed to be done and went upstairs to my office to make myself a cup of tea then for some reason, and I don't know why, I picked up the phone and dialled Mike's number, he answered and I calmly said, "Hi Mike, I am going to fly Fred today, see you at the hanger at two this afternoon." I arrived at the hanger a little before two o'clock, parked the car then made my way to the air traffic control tower to ask the guys if I could taxi Fred up and down on the runway if not in use, and if it all worked out, I might try a circuit. They were as excited as I was to see Fred fly, most people working around the airport knew about Fred and, like us, wanted to see the little plane in the air. When I returned to the hanger Mike had already moved Fred from the back of the hanger and parked it close to the short stretch of taxiway leading onto the unused runway. I noticed that during the few moments I was alone, my lunch had started to turn liquid and my backside was sending a message to my brain telling me that I shouldn't be doing this. Overriding the urge to say I didn't feel very well and abort the test flight, I continued to carry out my pre-flight check, and made sure I had enough fuel for a circuit of the airfield, as normal, the tank was full. All eyes were on me as I slid into the cockpit seat like an experienced test pilot, my artificial smile reflecting confidence was directed at the people who had gathered, but under my breath, I was cursing myself for not using the toilet before I put on my flying suit and boarded Fred, adding to my workload by having to fly with clenched cheeks. The chatter died as I spoke into the handheld radio to ask the tower for permission to use the runway, permission granted, I turned on the fuel, switched on both magnetos, looked around the aircraft then called out clear prop and a moment later, Mike swung the propeller and the converted VW car engine fired into life. I glanced at the instruments and saw that they were working, I had a quick look around, and then increased the engine revs and I rolled forward. Fred was what we call a tail dragger, two wheels at the front and a small wheel at the back, I immediately noticed that it was light on the tail, meaning that when you increase the revs the tail had a tendency to lift slightly, no problem, as long as I knew it happens. I taxied along the runway, turning this way and that way, to get a feel of the rudder and response of the controls. At the end of the runway I turned Fred so that I was facing down the runway and almost into wind, the direction for take-off, if I got that far. With the brakes on, I increased the engine revs to maximum to carry out a mag check, while the engine is running at maximum revs you first switch off one magneto, the engine revs drop but it keeps running, then you switch the mag back on and the revs recover, the procedure is the same for the other mag. When carrying out the mag check procedure, and if the engine stops while you are doing it, you don't go flying. Fred's mags checked out O.K. and everything seemed to be working. I took a deep breath and called the tower for permission to carry out an aborted take-off, clearance was given. I quickly glanced at Mike and the now larger group of people, then pushed the throttle forward as far as it would go, released the brakes, and we were off. Slow at first followed by the tail lifting and the speed increasing to 45 knots, at that point Fred felt as though it was about to become airborne, so I eased the throttle back and Fred slowed quickly allowing me to turn some distance before the end of the runway. I taxied back along the runway to my starting point intending to repeat the same procedure, but this time I intended to reach a higher speed before I abort the take-off. I completed my checks then called the tower for permission to carry out a second aborted take-off, permission was once again granted; I pushed the throttle forward and confidently headed down the runway, I was watching the speed indicator in between glances along the runway to make sure that I was going straight, eager to reach 55 knots before aborting, watching and willing the speed to increase, I noticed that the rumble sound of Fred rolling down the runway had ceased.

I looked sideways then down, my eyes sprung out of their sockets, like they were on springs and my backside resembled and sounded like a bottle of champagne that had just popped its cork, I was ten feet (three metres) in the air flying along the remainder of the runway and too late to abort. I was trying to remember what to do when the radio came to life and a calming voice of the controller said, "We weren't expecting that, but don't worry we are watching you, continue to do a right hand circuit and land." I tried to acknowledge his instruction but my tongue wouldn't work, by the time I reached the end of the runway I was five hundred feet off the ground, flying straight but somehow Fred was pointing slightly to the right. I decided to correct the situation by applying left rudder to straighten before turning right as instructed, I applied left rudder, but more than intended causing Fred to bank left and we headed away from the airport. I called the tower and told them that the rudder is sensitive, I over-corrected so could I continue along the cast to the Needles then return to Bournemouth? The assuring voice replied, "Continue at your discretion and contact approach," which I did. Cleared to continue, I flew Fred along the coast at an altitude of one thousand five hundred feet in an easterly direction, my air speed was 60 knots and I had a tail wind of 15 knots. Therefore, my speed over the ground was about 75 knots, and not long before I would reach the Needles Lighthouse and make my turn to fly back to Bournemouth. I completed my turn and was heading back to the airfield, the flight so far seemed fine, the controls were light and easy to operate, and Fred flew well enough considering the limiting power of the little engine. Getting back to the airfield was to take longer because the tail wind had now become a head wind, so our 60 knot airspeed was now reduced to 45 knots over the ground, and it would be about thirty five minutes before we reach the runway. This is where it gets a bit unsettling, if the flight to the runway had taken fifty minutes I wouldn't be telling this story! I was still flying at one thousand five hundred feet and had the airfield in sight; I contacted approach and then the tower who instructed me to continue at my discretion and to land on the runway not in use as before. Still at the same altitude, I lined Fred up with the runway then froze. I said to myself, I managed to get up here, but how the bloody hell do I get down? I was getting close to the runway so I needed to make a decision, I looked at the throttle then gingerly pulled it towards me and the engine slowed, at the same time I pushed the stick forward so that Fred adopted a slight nose down attitude and descended slowly. When I thought I was low enough at that stage for my angle of approach, I increased the power and levelled out, I repeated the process a few times, each time reducing sufficient height so that I crossed the runway threshold and made a perfect landing a short way further along. Relieved to be back on the ground, I taxied towards Mike and the people who had been waiting for my return, but became alarmed when the mass of people started to move toward me, concerned that there might be an accident, I swung Fred around, quickly carried out a mag check and switched off the engine and fuel then eased myself out of the cockpit. Mike was jumping up and down like a small boy who had got locked in a toy shop overnight. "It's my turn now; it's my turn now," he repeated. Mike settled himself down into the cockpit seat and I explained what to expect when applying the controls, we checked to make sure there was enough fuel then Mike contacted the tower for permission to carry out an aborted take-off followed by a circuit, at the same time carrying out his mag check then he rolled forward. Mike completed the taxi and aborted take-off then returned to the threshold end of the runway to line up for take-off and a circuit. The whole procedure from the time I landed and Mike lined up ready for take-off was about fifteen minutes.

All eyes were on Mike sitting in Fred at the beginning of the runway; engine idling, presumably waiting for the tower to give him clearance to take-off. A moment later, Mike waved then pushed the throttle forward to maximum revs. The noise and chatter from the people behind me suddenly stopped, we were all looking at Mike open mouthed at seeing the propeller detach itself from the front of the engine, and go spinning across the runway. The engine now with no load on it from the propeller screamed as it over revved and stopped. Mike remained sitting in Fred, his face grey with fright, the people behind me started to talk to each other and someone patted me on the shoulder and whispered, "You were lucky." I walked to where Fred, with Mike still sitting in it, was waiting, I asked him if he was alright, then said, "How lucky can we be?" Together, we pushed Fred back to the hanger without another word being spoken. No one could shed any light as to why the propeller came off; it was fitted correctly by the previous owner and signed off by an engineer in the normal way. We repaired Fred but didn't have the stomach to fly it again so we sold it. I have often wondered if Fred was something more than wood, steel and canvas and had a mind of its own. Think about it, the propeller remained attached to the engine long enough for me to land safely and live, the propeller continued to remain attached long enough for Mike to complete the aborted take-off and taxi back to the threshold and it remained so while the engine was idling waiting for permission to take-off. It only detached itself when Mike was cleared for take-off and Fred at full revs started to roll forward to fly a circuit. We were lucky that day.

It was some time before I told Vi what had happened that day at the airport, and a lot longer before I was able to push the incident to the back of my mind and once more focus on the business. I was determined to find out why the sawmill wasn't showing a profit, I measured a number of logs to establish the usable timber yield before they went through the mill, and I measured and priced the sawn timber that the logs produced. So providing I sold enough timber we would make a profit, at the end of the month I costed out all the sales invoices for the month, the cost of the timber, production cost and overhead, also the estimated stock value, the result was the mill made a profit. Knowing that the mill was making a profit I looked elsewhere for an answer. There were five people working at the sawmill, the Foreman, the Sawyer, (the man who worked the machine that cut the logs) and three brothers who turned their hand to anything that needed to be done in or around the mill. Still puzzled as to why we were showing a profit but didn't have enough money at the end of the month to pay the bills, I spoke to the Sawyer, who was different from the other guys, a clean cut family man with a wife and kids to support. Anyway, I put my dilemma to him to see if somehow I was measuring the logs incorrectly, we chatted for a while, then looking around to make sure we weren't observed, he said come to the mill at seven in the morning, then went back to work. Realising he had taken a risk, and so as not to compromise him, I stayed by the machine to watch him work and to make notes. The Foreman joined me by the machine to see what I was doing, to throw him off the scent so to speak, I said, "I am measuring the timber we get from that log." The following morning it was a little before seven, I parked the car and walked along a track that entered the mill from the forest, almost immediately I could hear the high pitched buzz of the saw working and the dull hum of the dust extraction system. As I approached the mill, I left the track using the bushes around its perimeter for cover. At that time in the morning the quietness of the forest exaggerates the sound of the working mill, producing a few more decibels higher than normal. Hidden in the bushes so close, the sound of the working mill was deafening and my heart was pounding like a bass drum within my chest as I eased my head up to have a look.

I slowly raised my head to see what was going on and hopefully find the reason for the lack of profitability, what I wasn't prepared for was the sight of a well organised production team running the sawmill. Remaining concealed in the bushes, I worked my way around the mill to make sure I had a clear understanding of what was going on. The Foreman was running the show, the three brothers were doing the fetching and carrying, selecting only the best logs, they would process it to produce cut-to-size timber to order then load it onto a waiting lorry, when the load was complete they piled fire logs on top to conceal the timber. It was about seven thirty, I had seen all that I wanted, then I back-tracked along the lane to the car, paused for moment to question whether I should drive into the mill guns blazing or go and fetch the police, I opened the door of the car and started to drive away saying to myself, sod the police they can wait, I want to catch those b*stards red-handed. There was a risk in what I was going to do but I was so incensed at what they had been doing, I wanted to look in the Foreman's eyes when I told him I had been watching him for the last half hour. I arrived at the gates of the sawmill, parking the car so as to block the entrance, I got out and locked the car then went to my office, placed my case on the desk then walked outside, the Foreman said, "Good morning," as he walked past. I ignored him and went to the three brothers and told them to switch off their machines and go outside and wait, I indicated to the Foreman, who was tossing more fire logs on the lorry for final concealment of the cut timber underneath, to join me in the centre of the mill. Once together, I looked into the Foreman's eyes and said, "What are you doing?" He replied, "We needed to start early this morning Boss because we have a lot of work to do." I took a pace closer, still looking into his eyes, and said, "Let me tell you what I have been doing, for the last half hour I have been watching you work the mill and load the timber you produced on that lorry," pointing in its direction, "then watching you cover the timber over with fire logs. I guess you have been doing it for a long time even though you knew I have been struggling to find the wages at times," I then went on to say, "You b*stards can do one of two things. You can wait for the police (I made that up on the spur of the moment) or give me the keys to the mill, unload my timber off that lorry and then go, the choice is yours." They spoke a moment between themselves, the Foreman handed me the keys, and then they set about unloading the lorry. I let them leave, thankful that I had found the reason why the mill wasn't making a profit, I phoned the police later that morning and told a detective what had happened, he arrived at the mill thirty minutes later so I could confirm what I had told him over the phone and to have a walk around the mill. We returned to my office to tidy up the details, he also asked me if I wanted to bring charges, I said, "What's the point? It will cost a lot of money and time and they will walk away free in the end. Its best left that people will know what they did and why they got the sack." As the detective got up to go he turned to me and said, "What you did was dangerous, they could have hit you over the head and buried you somewhere in the forest and we would have never found you." "A possibility, but unlikely," I replied, "I wanted to catch them b*stards red-handed." I employed replacement labour, reorganised various parts of the mill and we were soon operating efficiently and at a profit. At the end of 1985 I managed to sell the lease of the building we occupied at Milford-on-Sea to a yacht building company, the overhead crane was ideal for them and suited me because I had been thinking of moving the board and panel business to the sawmill. To complete the move I had to first erect a suitable building, with the money from the sale of the lease at Milford and a loan from the bank we were able to move the board and panel business to the sawmill eight weeks later.

Between the years 1986 to 1990, the sawmill and the board and panel business kept their heads above water but nothing exceptional happened other than we were getting a lot more machining work, that is, when a company placed an order for standard size boards they sometimes asked if we could cut it to size, drill it or shape it as required, I called it a machining service charge and it was lucrative, so I promoted the service to our customers as well as offering it to our competitors, it seemed there was a need for this service, it expanded to become a sizable part of our business. Towards the end of 1998 my friendly bank manager turned out to be not so friendly and asked me to reduce my overdraft which was running at eighty thousand pounds at the time, I wrote back to him to say that I didn't have any cash available at the moment, delaying tactics really. Unfortunately it was only the beginning of a lengthy correspondence that ended with a meeting at the manager's office and a proposal from me as to how I would reduce the overdraft. Before I go any further I suggest you never trust a bank manager. From the very beginning of my working life I have had a love hate attitude when dealing with bank managers, they want to screw me and I try to screw them. In the early days when running the Carvall Group Ltd, my overdraft peaked at about two hundred and fifty thousand, and as long as your overdraft level fluctuates, you are a valued customer with clout. With that level of overdraft you will probably be one of his largest accounts so he will want to keep you happy. You can talk to him as equals, negotiate a better rate of interest, and usually get your own way when you want to extend the overdraft on occasion. But at some point he will mention, probably over lunch, that head office has asked if you would consider reducing the overdraft. At that point, the game of out-foxing the fox begins. There are companies who, in my view, shouldn't be in business and probably deserve to be in the clutches of the bank, but I have known of good established companies who for one reason or another have found themselves in financial difficulties and turned to the bank for help but eventually are refused and have to close with the loss of jobs, I felt sorry for those people. Over the years I have paid one bank or another a fortune in interest charges and get personal satisfaction when I get a chance to screw one of them, to pay them back, if you like, for the many times they wouldn't help me. I am not a nasty vindictive person, a long memory I might have for the many times I got screwed and had to grin and bear it, but now it was payback time. My branch was one of a national bank that had recently been acquired by the faceless ones from the far side of the world so the branches were under pressure to call in the loans, of which one was ours. I read the correspondence between the bank manager and myself once more to refresh my memory ready for my meeting the next morning; throughout the correspondence they were asking if I could pay back or reduce the overdraft, not telling me. I somehow got the feeling there might be a deal on the table. I arrived for our meeting and dealt with the pleasantries, I then got a lecture about my overdraft, yes it was lower than it was a year ago and it fluctuates (you have heard this bit before). "But head office has asked if you can make a substantial reduction." We looked at each other for a moment or two, the game of out-foxing the fox was about to begin. I explained that business had been slow, customers were not paying their bills on time, and raw material prices were rising. "It's a difficult time to reduce my overdraft," I said, "Yes I realise that," the manager replied, "but will you agree to a reduction each month?" "Yes," I said, "but ten pound a month won't help much will it?" I could see the manager grinding his teeth together in frustration.

We verbally parried and thrust at each other, scoring and losing points until eventually he said, "My hands are tied, I have been asked to arrive at a settlement with you to clear your overdraft," I knew this was coming so I drew it out a little longer just to make it look good, "When you say settlement what do you mean?" The manager shifted in his chair, swallowed then said, "Can you raise any money at all?" I rubbed my chin for a moment to give the impression I was thinking, and at the same time lowered my head to conceal a grin that was threatening to become a laugh. I recovered my hard done by posture then looked him in the eye and said, "It may be possible to raise thirty thousand pounds," I sort of half ducked expecting him to explode, but instead he said, "When can you pay it?" Suspicious it could be a trap, I quickly said, "I don't have the money, I will have to borrow it from friends and family." "Put your offer to me in writing," he said, as he stood to signal the meeting had ended. I was about to leave, but before I did, I said, "This payment, if I can raise it, and you accept, will it clear my overdraft?" "Yes it would," he replied, I shook his hand and left. I thought about the meeting at the bank that day and couldn't resist trying to screw them for a bit more, so I wrote back to the manager telling him that I overestimated the amount I could raise, and am now only able to raise twenty four thousand. Expecting to have to compromise, I received a reply accepting my offer and asking when I could pay. With great satisfaction, I cleared my overdraft two weeks later. It was a gratifying feeling to win for a change.

July 3rd 1990, somehow I reached the age of fifty; our children were now adults and building their own lives and were living close by. I had already made my mind up that there was no future for me with the sawmill and decided to sell it, contrastingly, the board and panel business, particularly the machining side of the business, was doing O.K. and I had a good feeling about it. By the end of 1992, I sold the sawmill and moved the board and panel business to Gore Road industrial estate, New Milton, half way between Southampton and Bournemouth, occupying a small industrial unit and employing three people plus myself. Machining other people's materials meant that we didn't need any stock of our own, we got paid for the work we did. It was great, I drove the truck to collect and deliver back the finished work to our customer; also it was an excuse to make sure that they were satisfied with the work we were doing, and sometimes collect another job at the same time. I never missed an opportunity to sniff out a new customer or expand the business, I really felt good at that time. By 1994 the board and panel business had expanded, we moved into manufacturing standard sized white melamine shelving which I sold to fitted furniture companies and shops, we still employed the same number of people at that time, even though we were doing more work, we just got better at doing it. It was one day during the summer, I can't remember the exact date, anyway, I was in the workshop at the time when a man, who I hadn't seen before, walked in and asked for the office, "Can I help you?" I said as he passed me a piece of paper with a list of sizes hand written on it. As I looked at the list he said, "The Manager of the builders' merchants on the corner said you may be able to supply white melamine panels cut and edged to these sizes." I said, "We can do that, I will work out a price and you can collect the following morning," our price was accepted and payment made, the customer, with a relieved look on his face, then turned to leave, I asked, "By the way, what do you want the panels for?" "Cubicles" he said, "toilet cubicles." Becoming curious I said, "Why didn't you buy them from the merchant at the end of the road?" "You must be joking," he replied, "the manager at the merchant told me that basically, there are three manufacturers, if I send one of them an enquiry and if I am lucky, I will receive it in three to four weeks. When it arrives it's likely to be damaged, it's a waste of time trying to sell toilet cubicles." My natural instinct to spot an opportunity was in racing mode, I needed to find out more about toilet cubicles, who makes them, and why the manufacturers have such a bad reputation. I kept my new found interest to myself for the time being, carrying out my investigative enquiries in between my normal daily work load. Within three weeks I had a pretty good idea as to what constitutes a range of cubicles, the panel sizes required, hardware and general items. I also found out why the manufacturers had such a bad reputation, sure enough there were basically three main manufacturers at that time, who supplied builders' merchants, who in turn supplied building contractors and other trade customers throughout the U.K. The reason for the bad reputation arose because all three manufacturers produced other products as their main business and so cubicles was just a side line with no marketing impetus. There were also three or four small specialist cubical companies that had their own niche in the market. The product ticked all the boxes, a national marketplace, a builders' merchant network covering the whole of the country, and our little factory already geared up to produce panel products. If I do it right we could have a basic range available to the trade within three months, and with luck we might catch the competition asleep on the job, boy was I getting excited. I acquired brochures from the competition and spent as much time as I could allow sneaking in and out of gents' toilets like some pervert with a tape measure, pad and pencil, measuring various cubical configurations. I was glad to get that over with, I wasn't very happy with some of the looks I was getting. I had accumulated all that I needed to get the show on the road, initially deciding that our customers could have any colour they like, as long as it was white. I then set about producing prototypes for testing purposes and photography for a double sided A4 brochure, so far so good.

I had already decided what the name of the new company should be, it didn't spring to mind so to speak, Cubical Systems Ltd came to me while driving one day, I knew it was the right name, the minute it rolled of the end of my tongue. I was eager to avoid mistakes of the past and so put this enterprise together using my skill and business experience amassed over the past thirty years. First I needed to decide whether to deal direct with the end user and bypass the builders' merchant, or deal exclusively through builders' merchants. Experience over the years has taught me that the most important part of business is getting paid, you earn a bit more when you deal direct, but you always attract bad debts. Dealing through blue chip companies like builders' merchants, you earn a little less but you always get paid. I told Vi what was going through my mind, she has always been the Financial Director so dealing exclusively through builders' merchants received a nod of approval and our preferred option was adopted. The next thing was to come up with a merchant sales package showing the merchant a generous profit, remove any hassle from the transaction, and create trust and confidence between us as the manufacturer and the salesman working for the merchant, not easily done. I needed to get this right so I took all the time it required to think through all the options until I arrived at a proposal that would deal with the inherent problems, but building up trust with the salesman took some time to achieve. What I was proposing was that the salesman does nothing other than source the enquiry and sends his customer the estimate; this is how it worked. The merchant salesman at the trade counter tells his customers, "By the way, we now supply toilet cubicles," and eventually his customer will come back and say, "I would like a price for toilet cubicles."

At that point the customer will either hand the salesman a drawing indicating what is required, or ask if someone could carry out a site survey, if the latter be the case we would represent the merchant on site, either way the information is passed to us, we then formulate an estimate which is based on the information from the drawing or the site visit. All estimates include a 20% merchant discount, this way the merchant simply copies our estimate and hands it to his customer within two or three days, rather than weeks. If our estimate is accepted we would manufacture and deliver it direct to the customer on behalf of the merchant, avoiding damage from double handling, and at the same time show the customer how to install it, if there were any problems we would sort it out with the customer direct, avoiding merchant involvement. I committed the transaction procedure to paper together with all other aspects of what I was proposing to do, ready for when I break the news of what I had been doing during the past weeks to those around me. I closed the factory one Friday afternoon and told everyone about toilet cubicles and what part everyone would play. I upgraded one of the lads in the workshop to manage the machining business and a few weeks later I was ready to give it a go. Armed with black and white brochures and technical information, I set myself a target of ten calls a day, dividing up the south of England into areas, I planned to sell cubicles every other day and deal with our other business in between.

It was slow at first due to the reluctance of the merchant salesman to let me come in contact with their customer, but we eventually got over their reluctance, it was six months or more before the occasional order turned into a steady flow of enquiries and orders. Our little factory was going flat out, the idea that you can have any colour you like as long as it is white soon became white, grey or magnolia, two more people joined the production team and Simon, our son-in-law, joined the company as Sales Manager to concentrate on sales, to be honest, one of my better decisions, if Simon heard me say that, I will never hear the end of it, it allowed me to focus on increasing production to meet the demand we were creating. The building merchant's salesmen realised that selling toilet cubicles was easy, because we did all the work, and it helped them reach their monthly sales target. I was confident at the beginning that what I was going to do had potential, but I didn't expect to reach the level of business we did in such a short time. Our 2,000 square foot premises became 5,000 square foot (464 metre), the seven people became twelve, and the first of a number of representatives joined the company. Our cash flow got a shot in the arm in the form of a loan from Vi's aunt so everything was going along nicely.

1997, towards the end of the year the merchants we were dealing with became unsettled, the competition had finally woken up to what was happening, realising they were no longer receiving any orders, they complained to the merchants, and referred to their exclusive supply agreement which apparently states that the merchant can only buy cubicles from one of the big three manufacturers. The business slowed for a week or two but the guys behind the counter, seeing that their monthly target would be hard to achieve without Cubical Systems, disregarded head office instruction to only buy from the big three, and continued to place their orders with us. It was too late anyway for the big three, we had our foot in the door and they couldn't close it.

2000, Cubical Systems Ltd was another player on the field, within two years or so of starting the business we had become a force to be reckoned with, our market share increased year after year. Our one man design department, me to be precise, kept pace with the ever increasing demand by introducing new ideas, styles and designs and expanding our manufacturing facility to include laminated vanity units and wall panelling. The production facility and offices had increased to 20,000 square feet (1858 metres) and was laid out to include departments for hardware, panel production, laminating and wrapping and dispatch. We had become a family business by that time and the staff that joined us at the beginning were still with us, although elevated to positions of responsibility within the company, the total number of people employed was about twenty five. Cubical Systems had certainly worried the competition, they became very active in trying to claim back their lost business by offering discounts and special deals, but we just kept to our plan, delivered on time and gave a good service. Looking to the future, I could see the demand growing for a low priced, in the box, one size fits all cubical design. It was a low priced range that was occupying more and more production time that would normally be allocated to higher priced ranges. There were two options open to me, get a bigger factory or get someone else to make it for us. I talked to a company in Belgium to make and box it for us, I called it Trade Pack, and within six months we were selling off the shelf to customers who wanted it immediately and didn't want to pay too much. I also corresponded with a hardware company located in Aligarh, India, they came to see me to show me what they could do, I then went to India to visit their factory and have a look for myself. When I got to the factory, it was like something out of the 1920s. The Indian family who owned the company became, and still are, very close lovable friends, during my first visit I spent a lot of time with Rohit, the owner of the company, advising him what he should do to bring his company into the twenty first century, and what's more, what he needed to do if he wanted to export to customers around the world. Rohit and Anu, his lovely wife, were quick learners, each time I re-visited their factory I saw that they had put into place the changes or improvements I had suggested the previous time. By the time of my last visit, Rohit had got the hang of it and didn't need me to tell him what to do any more, even to this day Rohit sends me details of his progress, to give credit where it's due, they have done pretty well for themselves.

Cubicle Systems just kept growing, it was a happy place to work, everyone was smartly turned out in company dress yet we maintained an informal atmosphere, we were successful because we worked as a team, from the top down, I knew everyone personally. I had plans for the future and at 67 years old I still felt that I could drive the company forward, but the opportunity to do so eluded me.

Part two

Conception, Preparation and Departure

At 68 and head of a successful family business, I got to wonder what I would do with myself if I didn't have the business to occupy my time. The older I got the more I thought about it. I didn't know it at the time but that scenario was soon to resolve itself. Looking back over the previous seventeen years or so, I had started with an idea, no money to speak of, but I had a gut feeling I could make it work. Over the following years Cubicle Systems Ltd, our company, became a well-run, profitable family business, creating work for seventy-four people and with a turnover of around five million. We did a good job, our market share increased every year and we were aiming to be the best, but not necessarily the biggest, washroom manufacturer in the country. There had been tentative enquiries to find out if I would be prepared to talk about selling, but to be truthful, I wasn't interested, although I knew someday I would have to let go. The day I was dreading arrived. One of our largest customers decided that they wanted to buy our company. It was indicated that if they didn't buy our company they would buy a competitor, and we would lose their business. The threat didn't worry me, but it was a way of putting pressure on us to sell, so we had to look at all the options. At a family meeting to discuss the issue, the general consensus was that it was a good offer and time for me to step down. The rest of the family had had enough anyway, so it was agreed we should accept the offer. Reluctantly, I went along with it. To be truthful it wasn't the right time to be negotiating the sale of the business, the family was in turmoil and distraught from watching our son, Lee, dying from cancer. Lee left us for another place, on the 4th of June 2008. It shouldn't be like this, parents are supposed to go before the children. When Lee died, we never realised we could experience such pain, my wife Vi has coped better than I have. There isn't a day that passes I don't think of him. Just after we buried Lee, I realised that the new owners of our business hadn't contacted me to show them how we ran our business so successfully. I guess they didn't need my help, so I was out of a job. The last time that happened to me was 52 years previously, I was sixteen at the time and sitting in a dole office, I made a pact with myself then, never to come back to a place like that ever again. Anyway, I tried to come to terms with my predicament, over the next two years I did what retired people do, but there's only so much painting, gardening, and pushing a trolley around the supermarket you can do. To give me something to do, I would call in at my old company on occasion just to keep in touch with my friends, but the management didn't really want me turning up to remind the guys of the good old days. I was getting seriously 'p—-ed' off and turning into a nasty person, I didn't like it at all.

It was September 2010, Vi and I were in Greece on holiday with our friends, Marion and Denis Bayles, I was bored of sitting around, but soon came to life when someone mentioned that it would be a good idea to drive to the monastery town of Meteora, up in the mountains, about a four hour drive. I suppose visiting Monasteries is what old folks do. I'm not over religious, but thought it an opportunity to make my peace with the almighty, you never know, we could be having a one to one conversation at any time. The following day, we were off. I can tell you if you ever need to get some experience driving on bad roads, have a drive across the Greek Mountains, you will get the experience but it won't do the car any good. We arrived during late afternoon, booked ourselves into a small but cosy hotel in the centre of town; we freshened up, fed and thoroughly watered ourselves then decided to turn in early.

The next morning, awake at daybreak and first down for breakfast, we planned our route for the day, and were keen to get going. If you have strong religious tendencies, I guess that Meteora is a place for you. Visiting the Monasteries, their location, solitude and opulence is breathtaking. Sitting quietly taking it all in, you get the feeling that you are as close as you can get to those who have left before us and only a handshake away from the man himself, we all shed tears that day. As the sun began its journey towards the horizon, so was our will to live, we were totally knackered, and desperately needing to get back to the hotel before we fell asleep standing up with our eyes open. The sanctuary of the hotel and a few drinks helped to revive us enough to decide what we did that evening and the following day. I didn't take much notice of the discussion, but the outcome was that we would give touring the clubs and bars till three in the morning a miss!! We chose to have an early night instead and then in the morning have a leisurely drive back to Lefkas, our base in Greece. Not wishing to travel the way we had come, I suggested that we take the mountain road as far as the new motorway, recently completed, follow it for about 40 kilometres, then pick up the old road again. All agreed, breakfast and paying completed, we were on our way again. The bone-shaking, car rattling journey along the Greek mountain road reminded me to make a mental note never to drive that road again. We eventually reached the summit of the mountain and drove through a curtain of mist into brilliant sunshine, what a view. Far below in the distance we could see the new motorway. Pleased at leaving the mountain road behind, we arrived at a slip road that led on to the motorway but saw that it was closed. A police car was blocking the access, causing a line of cars to form. We had been waiting about fifteen minutes then I decided to see what was causing the delay. I spoke to a police officer who informed me that the road was closed momentarily to allow rally cars to pass, this immediately aroused my interest. I returned to the car and told everybody what was happening and then found myself a high vantage point to await the passing of the rally. It wasn't long before I could see a long line of cars in the distance with headlights on, heading our way, I don't know why but I started to get excited. As the line drew closer, I could see that they were classic cars of all descriptions, saloons of varying iconic names, sports cars, even London taxis. As they passed by, each car had displayed on the door, Peking to Paris Rally. By this time I was in a world of my own, just sitting there taking it all in, I had found what I was looking for, I wanted to become a rally driver.

The rally passed by, I was still sitting there thinking about what I had just seen, oblivious to the noise of car horns and people shouting coming from a long queue backed up behind my car that was blocking the entrance to the motorway. Getting down from my vantage point proved more difficult than climbing up, aggravating the situation. I was then on the receiving end of a Greek version of road rage, and the threat to wrench the doors of my car if I didn't get moving. Clear of the hassle I had caused, we were on the motorway and driving in the general direction we wanted to go. The conversation as I drove was normal, including our encounter with the Peking to Paris Rally. I was listening to the conversation in the car, but my mind was thinking about what I needed to do to become a rally driver, and at the same time, was deciding to keep the idea of taking up rally driving to myself for the time being. Over the following weeks, it started to take shape in my head, rally clubs, maps and routes, the car I would need, what the cost would be. There was nothing stopping me having a go. It was at this point in time that I mentioned what I was planning to my lovely wife, she understood, saying it would keep me busy, and out from under her feet. Apart from giving me what I thought was a nod of approval and mentioning the bit about boys and their toys, and all that, I proceeded to get myself organised.

Deciding what car to buy was just another problem to solve, the list of options was endless, and also the price varied so much. The cost at the top end was frighteningly expensive and would deter budding rally drivers with limited funds. Thinking about it, I decided that I didn't want an ex-rally car, I wanted to prepare my own car from scratch, the idea being if it goes wrong I should be able to fix it myself. Rightly or wrongly, I decided to buy a 1973 Reliant Scimitar, no on-board computers or gizmos, a good solid car that I could prepare myself. Finding what I wanted wasn't difficult, I made my purchase then put the car in my garage ready to be worked on. Everything was working out so far, but I needed to give thought as to how I could bring it all together. It was one of those cold, wet winter nights during December 2010 that I decided to have one more look at the maps. Opening out on the table a map of the world to have a closer look at the rally routes that I had marked out previously, I don't know why, I suddenly found myself looking at the bigger picture. I was curious to see if it would be possible to drive all the way around the world. Fascinated by this problem, I set aside what I should have been doing to focus on the problem of driving around the world. I didn't know it then, but I was hooked and spent the next three years proving that I could do it. It wasn't long before the idea of rally driving went out of the window to clear the way for me to focus on the challenge I had set myself. As time went by, I could think of nothing else, weighing up the options, deciding whether or not I was too old or indeed had the determination and ability to take on a task that would be demanding for someone half my age. As the days passed I became more determined. I knew that there would be problems and difficulties but was convinced that there was no obstacle that I couldn't overcome, providing I could get myself properly organised so that I didn't fall at the first hurdle. I made my decision to drive around the world, now I wanted to move forward, I looked long and hard at what I was proposing to do, I had no previous experience I could call on other than that I acquired from the University of Life over the past 71 years, this was all new to me. To get things moving I listed the issues that needed attention, Funding, route, departure date, vehicle, equipment, preparation, all would be looked at individually, but hopefully would come together as one later. At this stage, I hadn't spoken to anybody about what I was planning, not even my wife, although I think she knew I was up to no good! Vi didn't ask any questions, so I didn't volunteer any information, and left it at that, my first mistake! We managed to organise a short break and visited our house on Lefkas Island, Greece, to catch the last of the sun before the winter set in. When we were there last time, I remember meeting and remained on nodding terms with Keith Rimmer, a retired professional photographer. When recalling our brief meeting, I remembered that when we were chatting I felt comfortable and listened with interest when he spoke about his photographic experiences and knowledge about websites. I met Keith again at Porto, a bar in the Marina. We acknowledged each other and a little later I re-introduced myself asking if I could have a word with him. I had to make it quick, Vi was watching, her ears were revolving like two miniature long-range listening devices, trying to pick up what I was saying. I explained briefly what I was planning and asked if we could meet so that I could outline everything in more detail. We met the following day, Keith and his wife Penny lived on their boat which was birthed at the Marina. We met and spent some time going over every aspect of what I was proposing to do. The outcome of our meeting was that Keith became as enthusiastic as I was, offering to set up our website and become my technical adviser, working with me throughout the duration of the project and after. Above all Keith and Penny became and remained my very close friends.

January 2011, everything was coming together nicely, but I couldn't make a decision as to the vehicle I would use. Looking at the options available, all were expensive, heavy if you got bogged down, high fuel consumption, and difficult to fix if they break down, and I couldn't see any point in dragging all that steel around the world. Some days later the problem resolved itself. I was sitting in a small room that I called my office looking out of the window, thinking to myself that I will have to make a decision about what car I will use. My train of thought led nowhere, so I collected up the bits of kit I had purchased the day before to take to the garage to add to all the other equipment I had assembled. On my way back to the house, thinking about nothing in particular, I walked past Vi's car and was about to enter the house, then stopped, turned and looked once more at Vi's car. I was frozen to the spot, my mind asking and answering some of the questions I had posed for myself, as to what I needed from a car I would use. Vi had purchased a Suzuki Jimny three years previously, she loved it, totally reliable, probably the cheapest 4x4 available, good fuel economy, lightweight. Within minutes most of the boxes had been mentally ticked. I was all over the car like a prospective buyer. I couldn't believe it, all the time I spent looking at various off-roaders, I was in fact every day walking past the one car that would suit me, but I didn't realise it. To make sure I had the right car, I contacted various people who knew about these things, explaining what I was proposing, and also asking whether they thought the car was suitable. The replies I received were a glowing testimonial as to the ability of the little Suzuki Jimny to do the job. I felt confident enough to arrange a meeting with Simon Whitely, General Manager of Newmans Suzuki, Southampton, to explain what I was proposing. Simon promised to contact Suzuki G.B. at Milton Keynes to see what they had to say about it. A few days later I contacted Simon who informed me that he had received a reply from Suzuki, confirming what I already knew. They said that with some preparation and the Jimny's reputation it would handle what I was proposing.

It was becoming obvious that I was up to something, Vi hadn't said anything, or questioned me, but after 54 years of being together, I knew she didn't miss much! Maybe it was time to talk to her, but I had a feeling this wasn't going to be easy. We had been together for a long time, we had our ups and downs, but always felt we should be together, Vi had never objected when I told her I wanted to do 'this' or 'that' or come up with some crazy idea, she normally let me get on with it. So I had no reason to think it would be any different when I told her what I had been doing during the past two months. I waited for what I thought was the right time to broach the subject. I was working in the garage and could see that Vi was in the kitchen preparing lunch, she looked at me and smiled. I returned the gesture with a wave, thinking now's the time. Taking a few deep breaths, I stepped into the kitchen and sat down, "I'm not doing rally driving now," I said, Vi stopped what she was doing, giving me all her attention, "What are you doing then?" she asked. I cleared my dry throat and managed to say, "I'm going to drive around the world." Vi just stared at me, I could see she was thinking, then said "How long will it take?" "Six months," I replied. "What am I going to do while you are away?" "No, no," I said, trying the jolly approach, "you don't understand, we will drive around together." At that point I thought I saw smoke coming out of Vi's ears, my lovely placid poodle of a wife turned into a rottweiler, growling at me. I have never seen her so angry, Vi told me where I could poke my project, and in no uncertain terms, there was no way she was roughing it around the world in a Jimny. To which I snapped back without thinking, "OK, I will go without you, but either way, I'm going whether you like it or not."

I wished I hadn't said that, Vi was devastated. I never intended for this to happen and hated myself for creating a situation that upset her so much, but the damage was done. She wasn't too happy and I was a bit shaken myself. I sat there for a few minutes in silence trying to think of something to say. I then plucked up courage and in an attempt to break the ice, I went to speak to Vi but saw she had tears in her eyes and was clearly upset. "What do you want me to say?" she asked, "Well," I said, jokingly, "do I take it that you don't want to drive around the world?" The smoke came out of her ears once more so I took refuge in the garage to think about what had happened and where, if need be, was the warmest place to sleep. I have never seen Vi so upset, I felt bad that it had caused a rift between us. In next to no time the whole family and some of our friends knew about my planned journey, followed by visits to the house to see and pacify Vi, also to give me a look that said everything. Vi and I didn't speak much and moved about the house in silence, avoiding unnecessary eye contact, it was to be like this for the next three months, I tried to break the ice again but she would have none of it. I am not a callous person, I misjudged Vi's reaction, it's the last thing I wanted to do, upset her and the family, but when it was mentioned that I was retired or too old to drive around the world, it just made me more determined to do it, to prove them wrong. I wasn't the person to be seen with for a while, I was the one who was going off and leaving his wife at home on her own. It was noticeable how some of my family and friends, particularly the wives, didn't spend much time talking to me. There wasn't any aggression or rudeness, it was just like there was a wall between us and I was on the wrong side. On occasion someone would break ranks and tell me what they thought of me, I was saddened by this but it was something that I had to get used to, as it may have got messy later.

Pushing to one side my personal problems, I made sure that the jobs around the house were attended to in the normal way, fetching and carrying, the trolley pushing around the supermarket were all dealt with without comment. I was eager not to aggravate the situation. Any time I had to myself, was spent in my office compiling lists of one sort or another, or just a place to sit and think about what had happened over the past weeks. A day or so later, I decided I needed some air, to get away from everything for a while. Being a member of our local yacht club I thought that I would pay the club a visit, find a quiet corner, settle down with a coffee, make some notes and think about what I need to do next. Instead, I ended up making my second mistake! I had been at the club for a short while thinking various options through, when I was approached by my good friend and close neighbour, Alan Butler. We exchanged pleasantries and brought ourselves up to date as to what had been happening recently, avoiding what I was working on at the moment. It wasn't long however, before Alan enquired about the notes I was writing, not wishing to be rude, or avoid the question I reluctantly said, "I'm planning to drive around the world." I spent the next hour outlining the details, and answering a multitude of questions that Alan put to me. He wasn't just curious. Every Wednesday evening, I and a few other old guys, including Alan would meet at the club and argue about putting the world to rights. We called ourselves 'The Grumpy Old Men's Club.' We would sit there moaning about everything until late in the evening, getting well-oiled in the process, until being collected and taken home. This particular night, I arrived a little later than usual, Alan was already there and met me as I walked in, then steered me to a quiet table, asking if he could have a word with me. "About the journey around the world," he said, "I would like to come with you, but for only part of the way and share the driving."

We spent the rest of the evening talking about the journey and the implication if Alan joined me. When it was time to go, I said that I would give his proposal consideration and talk to him again at the weekend. The dilemma I had to consider was that, from the beginning, I had decided that I would drive my vehicle all the way around the world as part of a personal challenge I had set for myself. There was no question of me sharing the driving. Suddenly the simplicity of what I was doing became complicated, it wasn't that I thought Alan and I were not compatible, bearing in mind that we would be confined together for long periods, as we travel. Alan would be a good companion, it's just that, at some stage of the journey I would have a driving companion, but when he left to go back to the U.K. I would be on my own. What if Vi decided to come. It seemed that I was creating a problem for myself that I could do without. The following Saturday, Vi and I had been invited to a barbecue organised by friends, who were staying at the time near Southampton, but they also divided the remainder of their time between Greece and South Africa. While at the barbecue I met Glyn Maher, who I had also met previously in Greece. After reacquainting ourselves, and as part of the general conversation, I mentioned my proposal to drive around the world. Glyn, retired and on his own, asked all the right questions, concluding that he would be interested to take part. The following week I spoke to Charles Scott, another acquaintance, who also expressed interest. There were four of us now, I didn't know where this was leading me, I needed time to think about what was happening, how would it work out if Vi decided to join me after all, but I guess this was wishful thinking.

The recent interest shown resulted in me having to re-think my original plan, the thought of me to simply drive a Suzuki Jimny by myself around the world was about to change. My simple one vehicle journey looked like becoming a much larger, more complicated and seriously demanding project, divided into four stages, involving two vehicles, one I would drive myself all the way around as previously planned, a second vehicle would be driven by eight drivers, two drivers each stage, sharing the driving. At the same time, creating for me a logistical nightmare, and an unanswered question, how would it be funded? My head was spinning trying to get to grips with the task I had set myself.

Aggravating the situation, was the thought that after a lifetime in business, answerable only to myself, I could arrive at a situation whereby, every time I want to do something, or make a decision I would first have to get the approval of a committee of one sort or another. I made a mental note, I couldn't live with that, it wasn't going to happen. Every day that passed, more interest was generated, news of what I was doing circulated quickly and soon became general knowledge, ideas and suggestions were coming from all directions, I urgently needed to get control of the situation. I phoned the guys to arrange a meeting for a few days' time, to agree a project plan and get everybody pointing in the same direction. I decided to use the days before the meeting to do nothing else but focus on producing the plan. Vi could see I had the bit between my teeth, leaving me to work everything out, but helping in her own way, by keeping me properly fed and watered. I sat in my little office for hours trying to work out how I could bring everything together as one plan, properly managed and funded. I accepted that it would be a much larger project involving a lot more people, two vehicles and necessary equipment, route and itinerary, registering as a charity, also organising the filming of the journey. The situation was not what I wanted at all, I felt sick, looking at the endless list of things to be done, I wanted to throw everything into the air and say, "Sod it," I was seriously thinking about stopping it, pulling the plug, the list of what I had to do was just too much.

I was looking at the computer but seeing nothing, my mind had drifted away, I was mentally closing down. I sat for a while, pleased that I had decided not to continue, but to be truthful I was kidding myself, I'm not a quitter. I had another look at everything, at the same time saying to myself, "When you were running the company and had a project to put together, what would you do?" Immediately, it became clear, I didn't know much about charities and fund raising, I would need help with that, but the rest I would run as a business, I would produce a Project Management Plan, budget controls and accountability, the principles are the same. The first thing was to appoint myself Project Director, so that I could make decisions and drive the project forward, next, but not urgent, would be to make an application and register ourselves as a fund raising charity which would also be the organising and managing authority for the project. Our charity needed a name, as all the guys taking part were in their seventies, the name I proposed was 'Heaven Can Wait I'm Busy'. Four of the guys, including myself, would be trustees of the new charity and would be responsible for organising the journey around the world, as an event, in 2013. The event also needed a name. Thinking about the age of the guys once more, it would probably be the last chance the guys would have to do something spectacular before we leave this place, I thought that we should call it 'The Ultimate Challenge'. To accommodate those already committed and those needed to make up the number of drivers required, The Ultimate Challenge would be divided into four stages and would need two Suzuki Jimnys. One I would drive alone, unaided the whole distance around the world. My determination to do this from the beginning remained the same regardless of the changes. The second vehicle would be driven by those wishing to experience driving for one stage of the journey; the vehicle would be driven by two people on a shared basis, at each stage. From this point on, I suggested that those taking part in The Ultimate Challenge, be referred to as 'road crew'.

The road crew would comprise myself and possibly a cameraman accommodated in vehicle one. Vehicle two would make available eight places for road crew wishing to take part in one of the four stages. The road crew, including myself, would each make a financial contribution to cover all costs and expenses, related to participation. As I tried to calculate what the likely cost would be to drive around the world, I also realised that before we could do anything, we would need a sizable amount of cash available at the beginning to enable us to purchase and prepare the vehicles, to cover essential costs to give confidence to sponsors by being properly organised and adequately funded. At a guess, I estimated we would need initially around £50k to get the show on the road, plus the road crew estimated contribution of £6k from each of those taking part. It seemed a lot of money, but at this stage I could only guess what the total cost would be. Preparing the management plan, draft costings and as many details that I could think of would be a priority but pretty straight forward when compared to the logistical and financial nightmare that lay ahead. I produced the draft management plan, keeping it simple and in a presentable form ready for the meeting with the guys. I was happy with what I had put together. However, I had no idea where the money we needed to get the show on the road was coming from, and I was sure I wouldn't be able to persuade the guys to pay their contribution up front, so I had some serious thinking to do. Vi was still a bit frosty with me, but made sure I was fed properly, she also brought me tea and biscuits regularly while I was putting everything together.

On occasion, Vi would show a little interest in what I was doing, it was on one such occasion, showing more than her usual interest, I decided to raise the question of the £50k, the worst that could happen is that I would end up sleeping in the garage for a while. The opportunity presented itself, I was exaggerating my huffing and puffing routine, Vi said "What are you after?" pausing for a moment I said, "Can we make available the money we need?" At the same time I still wondered if the camp bed was in the garage. Vi looked at me, her eyes were rolling like a fruit machine. For safety sake, I took a step backwards to be closer to the door and the safety of the garage. Silence, when it comes, can be blissful, and defers further discussion, the trouble was I didn't know what Vi was thinking. Silence continued, I quietly moved about the house, trying not to be noticed or make any noise. When passing the lobby I would look, just in case my bags had been packed and placed there for me, together with a note, indicating that my short stay in the garage had become permanent. The meeting with the guys took place as planned, but before we discussed the management plan, I wanted to explain to everybody, to make sure that everyone understood why I wanted to drive around the world in the first place. My original idea was for me to drive a vehicle on my own all the way around the world. To plan and put into place a route and itinerary that would include meeting famous people, visit places of interest, taking part in activities and events if the opportunity presents itself, must remain as I originally planned. On the basis that the route and itinerary would be acceptable to everyone it would be possible to include suggestions or proposals put forward by the road crew, indicating specific places to visit, introducing some flexibility. The proposal to change from one man, one car, to a ten man, two car project, would create a number of problems, but provided it didn't affect or compromise my original idea, I felt sure we could bring the project together. I presented the management plan, also detailing the reasoning for me to be in a position to make decisions, and be able to drive the project forward as Project Director, without first seeking approval. I argued that too much time would be lost trying to get everybody together for non-scheduled meetings. The proposal was that we would meet every two weeks to discuss and agree what needed to be done and as Project Director, I would then get on with it. The management plan was approved in principle but I had no answer as far as where the funding was coming from, other than to say, I was working on it. Those confirmed as taking part as road crew so far including myself, were Alan Butler, Charles Scott and Glyn Maher. We also appointed ourselves as trustees, myself as Chairman, thus our charity, 'Heaven Can Wait I'm Busy' came into being. My appointment as Project Director of The Ultimate Challenge was also confirmed. Having a free hand, I was able to concentrate on bringing the project together; I didn't worry too much at the time about the road crew, although we still needed to find five more crew to fill the eight places available. There had already been a number of people who had expressed interest, asking me to contact them later, so I was confident that I would make up the numbers. Raising the money and getting the show on the road was my main concern, spending many hours trying to make contact with P.R. people at the major companies in the area, to see if I could talk them into becoming a sponsor or whether they would support us, in some way. I was really up against it; I couldn't have picked a worse time to speak to people about sponsorship, or support. The country was in the middle of an unprecedented world recession, charity funding cut, and the media awash with high profile events looking for funding, it was going to be difficult, but it was early days yet. I'm from the old school and a great believer in the old saying 'as one door closes another opens.'

2011, I spent the weeks to April beavering away, detailing and dividing up the project into sections with clear objectives. The more I studied the project, the more I saw how big, expensive, and out of control it could become if I didn't maintain a firm grip on the situation. Contrary to my original thinking, there couldn't be much flexibility once the planned route and itinerary had been agreed. We could end up with a situation where one of the guys taking part in one of the stages may want to amend the route and itinerary to include places he wants to visit. On the other hand, the person sitting next to him may want to do something totally different. Heaven knows what sort of mess we would get into trying to accommodate everybody. The idea of flexibility needed to be severely limited, the route chosen and start date firmly established as soon as possible so that everyone taking part would have something to work to. Having a look at my now very tatty map of the world, and the original route I had previously highlighted, indicating the countries we would travel through, I realised that I required a lot more information before the route could be finalised. I needed to locate a map supplier, who stocked detailed road maps printed in English of Poland, particularly Belarus, Russia, Ukraine, Kazakhstan, Mongolia, and Japan, also current maps of Europe, Canada, and the U.S.A. It wasn't that easy, but after many phone calls and emails it was suggested to me that I got in touch with Stanfords, who could supply what I wanted. A few days later, I visited their London office to collect the pre-ordered maps I required. I explained what I was proposing to do and why I needed the maps, the staff were very helpful and became a source of information and help to me throughout the time the project was coming together.

I spent the next two weeks studying the maps to confirm the route and weather conditions we could expect as we travel. The start date was critical, starting too early could mean encountering snow as we travel through northern Europe, Ukraine and Russia. Leaving it too late could also mean driving through the early winter snow in Canada, Alaska and the northern states of the U.S.A. We needed a date to focus on, a decision had to be made, if we departed the U.K. Sunday 28th April, the snow in Europe would have mainly cleared, leaving us only to worry about snow in some parts of Russia. I spent many hours working out how long it would take to drive around the world including sea time to ship the vehicles across the Sea of Japan, also the Pacific and the Atlantic Ocean. At this stage of the planning, the best I could do was a calculated guess. It would take between five and six months, arriving back in the U.K. around September, or October. I knew that there was a lot more work to be done before the route was finalised, but at least we knew the start date and where we were going. The next thing to think about was the route itinerary.

I already had a starting point, in the form of a list of people that I would like to meet, also historic and other interesting places I would like to visit. High on my list of people to meet was Mikhail Gorbachev, ex-President of Russia, and Lech Walesa, ex-President of Poland. You might think to yourself, why would someone who grew up at Hackney, East London have an interest in meeting such distinguished people? There are two reasons, the first, they were both born to poor families, and against all the odds grew up to become President and stood rock solid for what they believed in. The second reason was, people would give me a funny look when I mentioned that I would like to meet such distinguished people someday, just to shake their hand and have a chat. It would be an achievement for me to meet them, you know, it's like something personal. The weeks passed quickly, it was like spinning plates. I had so many things on the go at the same time, emails to this or that company, phone calls, chasing up information, meetings, running backward and forwards keeping everything spinning.

Every day I was working on something to do with the project, I needed to slow down, maybe rest a bit at weekends, make an effort to spend some time with my long suffering wife. I made myself slow down, spending more time with Vi was important and helped to ease the pressure, everything became more manageable, I even got some free time at the weekend, just what I needed. Through the summer, various parts of the project I had been working on were coming together nicely, there were regular meetings with the guys, and everybody seemed to be happy with the way things were going. At each meeting I made sure that everyone was kept informed of my progress and handed out copies of relevant documentation. At one such meeting, I emphasised that we would be travelling without any backup or support team, in the event that we got into trouble or had a problem we could only rely on ourselves to sort it out. Bearing this in mind, members of the road crew would have to take part in a training programme so as to be able to deal with emergency roadside and general first aid, vehicle recovery and repair, to learn of road survival, familiarisation of vehicles and equipment, application for visas, and inoculations against diseases, the list was endless, but needed to be dealt with as soon as possible. The summer was the usual mix of days of rain and sunshine; I guess I should be thankful that I am still here to 'moan' about the weather! At summer's end and in spite of many meetings with potential sponsors, I had not been able to secure sponsorship and the cash we needed to get the show on the road. During one of my sessions where I would sit quietly sifting through the paperwork to see if I had missed anything, it occurred to me that out of all the countries that we would be travelling through only the U.K., Canada, and the U.S.A. were English speaking. Europe we could deal with, but Belarus, Ukraine, Kazakhstan, Mongolia, and particularly Russia and Japan we may need some help. I contacted Keith to ask how he was getting on with the website, also to have a general chat about how I was progressing. I mentioned my concern about travelling through Belarus, Ukraine, Kazakhstan, Mongolia, Russia and Japan and that we might have a language problem and suggested it would be helpful if we could find somebody who speaks Russian to travel with us for that part of the journey. We discussed various possibilities and options available to us, but to start with, Keith agreed to have a look on the internet to see if there was anyone in Russia that I could contact. Within a few hours, Keith phoned me to say he had found someone, and had forwarded the info. It didn't take me long to study the information Keith had sent and agree that he could be just the person I was looking for. Mikhail Rybochkin operates a small business, escorting small groups of people on road tours to central and remote parts of Russia. The following day, I sent an email with an attachment to Mikhail explaining who I was, and what I was planning, and whether he or someone else would be available to join us at Brest, Belarus, travelling east through Russia, via Moscow to Kazakhstan, Mongolia, then on through eastern Russia to Magadan, our destination. A week or so later, I received an enthusiastic reply in English, saying he was pleased that I contacted him, subject to more information and agreeing terms, he would be pleased to join us, the words 'agreeing terms' rang up another cost on my mental cash register, aggravating the already existing funding problems. The roller coaster ride, the twists and turns, progressing two paces forward then one back became more regular, fortunately I have a remedy when it happens, when I feel a bit low, I put on hold all the things on my mind I know I have to do and concentrate on something I know I want to do, like talking to Simon Whitley, General Manager, of Newmans Suzuki, Southampton about helping with the two Suzuki Jimnys we would need.

I was awake early and dealt with the jobs I had to do, leaving enough time to make myself presentable and on the road to meet Simon at Newmans Suzuki at around twelve o'clock. I had previously phoned Simon and he remembered me from our discussion some time ago. I told him that I had made a lot of progress since our last conversation and was now at a stage where I wanted to talk about the two vehicles we needed and if Suzuki could help in some way. Simon was very supportive and encouraging so I was looking forward to our meeting; I only hoped he wouldn't mention anything about the funding. On arrival Simon was waiting for me, and he listened to what I had to say. I must have been speaking for fifteen minutes, trying to cover as much about the project as I could. It must have sounded like the spiel coming from a door-to-door brush salesman, not letting the customer getting a word in! Simon sat through my presentation without saying a word, or was it not being able to? I finished what I had to say, we sat looking at each other for a second or two in silence, Simon then said, "I think you should talk to Guy Foster, the Managing Director; he will be interested and may be able to help. But unfortunately he is not available today." Relieved that there was some interest, I produced a copy of the Project Management Plan and handed it to Simon, for him to look at and then pass it on to Guy Foster the M.D. to avoid over-staying my welcome, I thanked Simon for his help and stood up to go, he said, "Give me a ring, I will see if Guy has some free time and arrange a meeting." Then as an afterthought, he handed me a card and casually mentioned that I should contact, Mr Alun Parry, Head of Press and P.R. at Suzuki G.B. who may be able to help. Driving home through the forest, I felt pleased with myself that something positive came out of the meeting, plus I had a contact at Suzuki head office to follow up. I emailed Alun Parry at Suzuki, introducing myself and what I was proposing to do, and saying that I would like to send by post a general overview as to what the project is all about, including a copy of the Project Management Plan. I emphasised that we were proposing to use two Suzuki Jimnys to drive around the world and was there anything Suzuki could do to help? Some days later I received a courteous reply apologising for the delay in getting back to me and saying he would be interested to receive the information. He then continued that he had commitments and would contact me on his return to the office. As promised, Alun contacted me to ask if we could meet, and suggested as time was limited, we meet at Fleet Services on the M3 motorway. We met a few days later, he already had a good idea about the project from the information I had sent him, so I guess the meeting was all about Alun having a look at me, and to make sure I wasn't some sort of crank. I must have convinced him, because he said he was interested and would talk to his people at Suzuki, then organise a meeting to be held at Newmans the Suzuki dealership at Southampton.

My batteries recharged from the encouraging meeting with Alun, I set about dealing with the project matters I had previously put on hold, the problems caused by the lack of funding occurred more frequently to become a constant worry. I had mentioned to Vi some time ago about whether we could make the funding available, I didn't get the reaction I was hoping for, so didn't pursue it any further. At the beginning of November I was at home in my office, shuffling the paperwork for the hundredth time. Vi popped her head around the office door and asked how everything was going, knowing I was struggling with the funding. I said, "There are a number of companies that will help with equipment, but I can't find anyone willing to sponsor us for the fifty thousand, we need to get the show on the road." "Do you have to have the whole amount at once?" Vi asked, "No not really," I replied, "why are you asking?" "Well," Vi said, "if you can't find anybody to help fund the project we will have to fund it ourselves."

There are times when a husband and wife close ranks and work together when a situation such as this occurs. We are by no means rich by today's standard but let's say we are comfortable, the down side to all this is that my now reinstated, lovely wife is in charge of our modest fortune, it's not like the old days. I just can't put my hand in the cash box and grab a handful any more; I have to go through a long process of softening Vi up plus looking sorry for myself and sulking a bit, before she will come to the rescue! I knew she would come around in the end, but I must confess, she had me worried that time. I should be thankful to Vi for supporting me and the project, after all we were saying bye-bye to a large chunk of our daughter Carole's inheritance. But then if she hadn't agreed to help me I would have been seriously in the poo up to my neck and the project wouldn't have turned out as it did. Free of the funding burden, I was able to discuss the project with potential sponsors head held high, and without the need to avoid the question. If asked about funding, I would say that we had funding, but avoid where it had come from, other than if there was some benefit or gain. Of course, the guys at the next meeting, plus others who needed to know were informed that the funding problem was behind us. It gave everybody confidence and a tremendous lift. It all moved pretty rapidly from then on, everything was coming together, without too much hassle. The weeks of indecision, not being able to agree, finalise or put a lid on various parts of the project I had been working on had come to an end. I had several meetings at Newmans Suzuki, on occasion, Glyn Maher or one of our team would accompany me. Guy Foster, M.D. and Simon Whitley, General Manager were very supportive, and made me welcome on each occasion. We discussed all aspects of the project, but in particular the availability and cost of the two new Suzuki Jimnys we were going to need, also servicing, training and supply of spare parts and so on.

Alun Parry had been kept informed in the meantime of our progress. It was during a recent phone conversation that I notified him that we now had the initial funding we needed and looked forward to our meeting at Newmans the following week. I had already informed the guys about the funding so there was a jolly atmosphere when I attended our next meeting. I handed out the minutes from the last meeting and outlined my progress to date. I said that I had a meeting with Suzuki next week, Alun Parry would be there and I hoped to agree a competitive price for two Jimnys and would let everyone know the outcome at the next meeting.

I was driving through the New Forest on my way to the meeting at Newmans, hoping that I might be offered some sort of discount if we order two Jimnys, and maybe some help with the spare parts. I made a point of being professional and organised and always kept everybody up to date and informed as to our progress. I was apprehensive when I sat down at the meeting. I outlined our progress in as much detail as possible, then finished by saying that we were now in a position to purchase the two Jimnys. Alun and Guy had sat in silence listening to what I had to say, pausing for a moment or two to refer to his notes, Alun then said, "I have been talking to the senior management at Suzuki G.B. about your project, they are very interested and I have kept them informed as to your progress and they have authorised me, on behalf of Suzuki G.B. to help you any way we can." Alun asked who was providing the funding, I had to explain that in spite of my best efforts I had not been able to secure funding from a would be sponsor, so to get the show on the road, and to make sure the journey happens, my wife and I had agreed to donate fifty thousand pounds to the project.

I then added that it was a way of letting everyone know that I was totally committed to the project and intended to see that the crew, a bunch of old guys in their seventies, drive around the world, and arrive back, the crew unharmed and the vehicles undamaged.

Alun was pleased to hear what I had to say, then said to me, "Your confidence and determination to see it through is very reassuring, we would like to help as much as possible, and this is the deal. I have been authorised to offer you one new Suzuki Jimny as a gift to the charity, and a spares package for each vehicle, worldwide service and support through the Suzuki dealer network as you travel. Also Suzuki will pay the cost of the graphics to both vehicles plus promotional exposure." I had hoped that Suzuki would help in some way but I was totally unprepared for the generosity and help offered. I will never forget the smile on Alun Parry's face, looking at him I wondered if I had heard correctly, I maintained my composure as best I could, it took a while for it to sink in. My head was spinning as we discussed the details of the offer, Alun continued, "The vehicle, when required, will be supplied by Newmans," I said to Guy that I would contact the trustees to notify them of the offer from Suzuki G.B. and would place an order for the second vehicle within a few days so that both vehicles could be supplied at the same time. Still dazed, I asked Guy if the crew could take part in a short mechanical and service training programme in the event we damage a vehicle and need to carry out emergency repairs. Agreeing to help, Guy also said that he would work with us to set up the spare parts package for each vehicle, and any general preparation support we needed. The business concluded for the day, I thanked everyone for their kind support, saying that I would be in touch after I'd had a chance to talk to the guys then left, elated that all my hard work had paid off. Boy what a day.

March 2012, I had been corresponding with Mikhail Rybochkin, my Russian contact, the outcome being he would join our merry band as interpreter, and we would meet somewhere near the Belarus border. I told Mikhail that I wanted to meet Mikhail Gorbachev and could he put me in touch with his office, which he did. I emailed the contact address Mikhail had given me two or three times but didn't receive any reply, frustrated at not receiving a reply and concerned that I needed to meet Mikhail Rybochkin in person, I talked Vi into accompanying me on a trip to Moscow in two weeks' time, the idea being that I could call at Mikhail Gorbachev's office and arrange a time to meet him, and at the same time meet Mikhail Rybochkin. Two days before we flew to Moscow, Mikhail Rybochkin emailed me to say his father had died and wouldn't be able to make it. Having paid our money, Vi and I decided to go anyway. It was our first trip to Russia, we were pleasantly surprised in some ways but the old cold war feeling was still evident, believe it or not a plain clothed KGB agent sat in the lounge of our hotel all day checking on the movements of the guests, a bit spooky. We spent our time being tourists, and there's plenty to see if you're that way inclined. The morning of the second day, I asked the hall porter if he could find out where Mikhail Gorbachev's office was located, I spoke to him the next day and he said he hadn't been able to find it, but he would ask the taxi drivers while I waited. He came back a few minutes later and told me that Gorbachev's office and house where he lived when in Moscow was in a secure enclosure and nobody was allowed in without an appointment. Oh well, I guess you can't say I didn't try, the annoying thing was that shortly after, I found out Mikhail Gorbachev was in Berlin at the time, it just wasn't to be. And just to add insult to injury Mikhail Rybochkin emailed me to say he wouldn't be joining us as interpreter after all.

April 2012, relieved of the burden of funding and acquiring the vehicles, which I immediately registered in my name as LC02SUZ and LC03SUZ for administration reasons, I was able to focus on bringing everything together. The long list of issues I needed to attend to that had been on hold because of the lack of funding were no longer on the back burner, they became a list of priorities that I had to urgently work through. During the previous year I visited the London office of Save the Children, to explain what I was proposing to do and that maybe we could raise some money for the charity at the same time. My proposal was met with enthusiasm by the Save the Children management and details were finalised in time to be included as part of the vehicle graphics. I had a little over 12 months to get everything in place and be at the starting gate as planned, so had a free hand to get on with the job, no baggage of officialdom to worry about, apart from keeping the guys informed and asking for their help if I needed it. My first job was to design the graphics to be applied to the vehicles, I drew what I thought would be eye-catching and at the same time display a message for the public letting them know who we were and what we were doing. Armed with my sketches, I drove 02 to visit a company who did the graphics for my company vehicles when I was in business, to ask if they could help. I knew the boss and arrived at the time arranged, I assumed that I would receive a warm welcome and eventually a competitive price. What a miserable sod he turned out to be, he must have got out of the bed the wrong side that morning, because he turned out to be the most unhelpful and uncooperative person I had come across for a long time. Fortunately, I have dealt with people like him in the past, how they survive in business is anyone's guess. Anyway, I told him what I thought of him, scooped up my sketches and left. As I drove home I thought about what happened to try and make sense of it, I knew the person in question fairly well he seemed a bit up himself at times, so to speak, but not a bad bloke, he tried to make amends with me a few times, after the incident but he got a p——-off look, instead! Undeterred, I thumbed through the local trade directory the following day and saw that there was a graphics company local to me. I phoned New Forest Signs and got through to Trevor Stickland, the owner, I explained to Trevor who I was and what I wanted to talk to him about and agreed to meet the following day. I arrived at the address Trevor had given to me, his office was also his house located in a row of houses in a residential street. I parked outside his house behind the company van then followed the arrow and sign saying office at the rear. Confronted by a large garage that had been converted into an office and print shop, I banged on the door and hoped for the best. Moments later, bolts on the inside slid to one side, the door opened and Trevor appeared grinning like a Cheshire cat and introduced himself, then went on to say, "I have been thinking about what you told me and I would like to help." We talked for some time on that occasion and worked together over the following week or so. Using my draft sketches as a starting point, Trevor designed and produced a most spectacular design that met all my requirements and, if approved by Suzuki G.B. and our guys, would be applied to 02 and 03. There was never any doubt, the design was approved and Trevor Stickland and New Forest Signs took charge of our graphics and, later-on, sponsors' graphics transforming our two plain pearl white Suzuki Jimnys into two stunning to look at vehicles.

Glyn, Les, Vi, and helpers took the 'Road Show' to the New Forest Show as part of the publicity for the project

Next on my list of priorities was to decide what modifications we needed to apply to the vehicles. I made numerous phone calls, met and spoke to a number of people who know about these things and I listened with interest to what they had to say, however, the advice as to what I would need or not need to do, the modifications I might or might not need to apply to the vehicles and kit required was conflicting and confusing, to say the least.

May 2012, by the end of the month the vehicle specification started to worry me, I had pretty well decided what I was going to do, but before committing myself, I contacted a specialist vehicle preparation company to find out what it would cost to have the vehicles prepared for us. I soon realised the cost was prohibitive and finalised my decision to take on and manage the preparation myself. Keep it simple was uppermost on my mind as I drew up the specification, working from the bottom up. We would need steel rims and all-terrain tyres, up-rated shock absorbers and springs, to increase ground clearance by a further 2" (50mm), braided stainless steel brake lines, and manually operated free running hubs fitted to the front wheels, required so that we can disengage the front wheels from the four wheel drive system when running on paved roads for long distances and it should reduce tyre wear and fuel consumption. Apart from the short list of mods the vehicles would be standard, facilitating maintainability and servicing as we travel. Confident that the mods to the standard vehicles was all that we needed, I put it at the back of my mind for the time being as the work needn't be completed until later in the year. Trevor completed the graphics so I was able to adopt 02 as my car for use when on official business, meeting potential sponsors and press and P.R. opportunities, also it is the car I would personally drive around the world.

June 2012, I met with Alan, Charles and Glyn frequently to keep them informed as to my progress and the priority list I was working on. I had a number of things on the go as we entered the month; one being a fund raising road show that I had been working on, the idea was that throughout the summer months we would use 02 and 03 together with display boards prepared for us by Trevor of New Forest Signs describing who we are, what we are doing, and why we are doing it, Glyn, who gratefully volunteered to help, and myself would attend as many summer shows, fairs and events in the south as we could to promote the project, sell promotional T shirts and caps and for £5 you could have your name printed and displayed on one of the vehicles, there was also a guess the mileage competition. The road show was a strain and tiring, but it helped to create public awareness and raised a bit of money as well, which was helpful. Towards the end of the summer I was receiving emails and phone calls from one organisation or another asking if we would attend their show as a guest exhibitor, which we did do on occasion. Everything seemed to be coming together nicely, but not everything worked out as I had hoped. Generally I was able to work at my list of priorities and drive the project forward. One particular issue, of the many I had to solve, was how much fuel we would use and its likely cost, for each vehicle. I pondered over this problem for hours, racking my brains trying to arrive at some sort of answer that didn't rely on guessing too much, assumptions or what Suzuki say about how many miles we would get from a litre of 95 octane fuel. To arrive at and use a calculation that would tell me how many litres of fuel I was likely to use, I needed to first prove to myself that the information I produce is as accurate as possible. I studied the manufacturer's information relating to standard maximum Jimny payload and expected fuel consumption, but because we would be operating outside the manufacturer's limitations I decided to start with a clean sheet of paper, so to speak.

Using 02 as a test vehicle, I removed the rear seat assembly, and in so doing created a reasonable space that I could do something with, I then drove 02 with an almost empty fuel tank to a local sand and gravel company to use their weighbridge. Having established the nett weight of 02 at 2447 pounds (1110 kilos) excluding fuel, all I needed to do was to weigh the kit and equipment each vehicle would be carrying, add the weight of a tank full of fuel, plus 40 litres of fuel in cans, driver, and passenger if applicable, and I would arrive at a gross weight. The exercise seemed simple enough but in truth it was a nightmare, having to decide at an early stage what the list of kit and equipment each vehicle would include. It was a little over two weeks by the time I arrived at an all up weight of 3251 pounds (1475 kilos). Knowing the loaded weight of 02, I could now set about finding out how many miles a loaded Jimny would travel for each litre of fuel used. To do this I loaded 02 with 840 pounds (381 kilos) of engineering bricks to achieve the all up vehicle weight required, I then drove it around for a day or two, just to get some idea what the loaded vehicle feels like to drive. I hadn't seen Keith and Penny for some time, so a meeting to deal with matters relating to the website was long overdue. Glyn, by this stage, had become closely involved with the preparation and jumped at the chance to join me when I mentioned that I was going to drive to Suffolk to meet Keith and at the same time use the 350 mile round trip to identify the best cruising speed and the amount of fuel we use. I was looking forward to visiting Keith and his wife Penny, the day I chose for the journey was dry and sunny, I set off very early, excited at the prospect of getting out of the office, so to speak, a sort of day away from the usual things I had been doing recently. I collected Glyn on the way then drove through the New Forest to connect with the M27, then along the M3 to the M25 clockwise to the A12 towards Ipswich. 02 settled down nicely, cruising at a steady 55 mph, a shade under 3000 rpm. I briefly played with different cruising speeds, but 55 mph seemed about right. I made a note of 02's mileage at the start with a full tank of fuel, so after an enjoyable meeting with Keith we headed back the way we had come, refuelling and making note of the mileage, before joining the M25 anti-clockwise. Glyn drove from there on leaving me free to calculate how much fuel we used. 02 averaged 8 miles to a litre, or 36 miles to a U.K. gallon. For the purpose of converting litres to imperial U.K. gallons, I used the calculation of 4.5 litres being equivalent to 1 U.K. gallon or as near as damn it. I checked the fuel consumption on a number of occasions over the following months and the result was the same. I now knew what our fuel consumption was likely to be when driving on paved road surfaces at 55 mph throughout Europe, Canada and the U.S.A. However, I expected the fuel consumption to increase dramatically and miles to a litre of fuel reduce to an average of 5.5 miles to a litre (about 25 miles to a U.K. gallon) when driving through Ukraine, Kazakhstan, Russia, and in particular Mongolia. Perhaps a bit pessimistic but better to be on the safe side. The distance we would travel on land to drive around the world is about 19,000 miles. I worked out the distance we would travel on paved road surfaces, travelling through Europe, Canada and the U.S.A. to be about 11,000 miles. Based on 8 miles to a litre we would consume 1375 litres (or 305 gallons) of fuel for each vehicle. The distance we would travel to cross Ukraine, Kazakhstan, Russia and Mongolia is about 8000 miles. Based on 5.5 miles to a litre we would consume 1454 litres (or 323 gallons) of fuel. The expected total number of litres of fuel each vehicle would consume to drive around the world would be in the region of 2829 litres (or 628 gallons).

I now knew how much fuel we were likely to consume, what I needed to know next was how much I would pay for it, not easy at a time when the world is experiencing financial meltdown. About the time I was working on these calculations, I was paying £1.30 a litre at the local garage and the price was set to rise further. The U.K. price per litre was about the same as throughout the rest of Europe. Ukraine, Kazakhstan, Russia, Mongolia, Canada and the U.S.A. we would pay less, but by how much I would have to guess, bearing in mind the current financial climate. My best effort at calculating what the price should be produced an average figure per litre of £1.20, probably higher than it was likely to be, but better that I budget on the high side, to make sure we didn't run out of money to buy fuel. I wasn't looking forward to the outcome of my calculations, but, if we actually required the estimated 2829 litres of fuel for each vehicle at an average of £1.20 per litre the cost would be £3394 for each vehicle. "Bloody hell", I murmured to myself as I pencilled a note to remind me to allow £8000 in the budget for vehicle fuel and running repairs.

July and August, I was running around like a headless chicken, beavering away at my list, attending shows and above all keeping Vi and the family happy. Every week we seemed to be at one show or another, and when I wasn't doing that I was meeting with sponsors or equipment suppliers, trying to get something for nothing, it wasn't a good time to do that, but those who did help in one way or another had their company name or logo displayed on one of the vehicles. I was at the New Forest Show the previous month, the owner of Red 5 Off-Road Adventure Company introduced himself. He seemed to know what he was talking about and got my full attention when he mentioned that I should fit stone guards to protect the exposed engine sumps, and other vulnerable parts, he then went on to say that he knew somebody at Cooper Tyres who might be interested to supply our tyres. I thanked him for his help and thought no more about it. The next day I got a phone call from our contact at Red 5, saying that he had spoken to Mr Shane Ryde, his contact at Cooper Tires and they were interested and would I give Shane a ring? I got in contact with Shane and explained what we were doing and where we were going, he listened to what I had to say. I wasn't used to a sponsor having a positive attitude to a promotional opportunity, and unprepared for Shane's response. "Let me know what the wheel rim size is, I would recommend our all terrain tyres, and I will send you 6 tyres for each vehicle, supplied with the compliments of the company, they will be sent direct from the factory in America and will be with you in about six weeks." I thanked Shane for his help and generosity, insisting he send me a sample of the Cooper Tyres logo to be displayed on the vehicles; it's really nice when something comes together. For some reason my conversation with Red 5 remained on my mind, particularly the part about fitting stone guards to protect the engine sumps. On one of those rare occasions when I was able to sit still and think for a while, I was sitting in my garage looking at 02 as my mind wandered back to my conversation with Red 5, I felt uneasy, I was looking at something but not seeing it, if you know what I mean. I walked to the front of 02 standing motionless for a while just looking at the bodywork, still not finding what I was looking for, I rolled out a length of carpet I use when shimmying under cars, then on my back but with only my head and shoulders actually under 02 I could see why we needed stone guards. One good thump from a sizable rock would cause unrepairable damage and put the vehicle out of the game so to speak. Having seen what needed to be done and about to push myself out from under 02, I looked up and saw the unprotected radiator, headlight assemblies, and other vital parts hidden behind thin body panels.

The standard assembly arrangement is fine for the average owner and general use but for what we were doing we needed to protect the vehicles' vulnerable parts. So pleased I had found what I had been looking for, I raised my head higher than need be and connected heavily with an unforgiving object causing me to see stars and wince with pain. I lay under the front of 02 for a minute or two waiting for my vision to return and the throbbing pain and a rapidly rising bump on my head to become manageable. I eventually dragged myself out from under 02 and sat back in my chair holding my head and thinking to myself, who do I know in the sheet metal business?

September was a busy time; I spent the whole of the month picking away at my priorities list in between meetings with the guys and attending one meeting or another to arrange training sessions for myself and the rest of the crew relating to roadside first aid, action to be taken in the event of an accident, emergency repair and maintenance of the vehicles, advanced driving assessment, tent erecting and equipment familiarisation, visa requirements and documentation, validity of personal health insurance, inoculations and en route health management. The list was endless but I had to arrange the sessions and in some cases together with an expert able to lecture us on specific subjects. The bump on my head had long since receded but the need to beef up the bodywork and protect the vehicles' vitals remained at the forefront of my mind. I made a list of what I thought needed to be done and remembered that I worked with a small company when I was in business that was located close by to my factory,

I made a mental note to pay Robert, the owner, a visit when I had a chance. A few days later, I paid a visit to Precise Sheet Metal and to meet the owner, Robert Rickman. On arrival, I was told by the occupant of the building that Precise Sheet Metal had relocated to the airfield industrial estate at Christchurch, about five miles away. Undeterred, I drove to the new location and met Robert, we hadn't seen each other for some time but within minutes I had a cup of tea in my hand and was talking to Robert about what I was doing and what I wanted. I pointed at 02, at the same time explaining that I wanted a price for him to fabricate and fit a replacement steel front bumper and bulbar with a mesh panel welded in place to protect the radiator and head lamp assemblies, also I would need a stone guard to protect the engine sump and steering gear. At the rear of the car I wanted to fit a steel bumper with a steel gate that would support a spare wheel that weighs 24 pounds. Both bumpers would be fitted direct to the chassis to allow free movement of the vehicle body. The last Item was to fabricate an aluminium tray fitted to the roof to carry a second spare wheel, extra fuel and sundry bulk items. I said to Robert, "I have two vehicles, so I will need two of everything." Then went on to say, "I know it's not your normal line of work but if you can help me I would appreciate it and hopefully at a price that is acceptable to you and what I can live with." The following week I again visited Robert, dreading what the price would be. While Robert was making the tea I asked him if he had managed to sort a price out for me, he didn't answer but went on to say, "Do you remember the day you first came to see me to ask if I could do some work for you?" "Vaguely," I said, "why?" "Well, you didn't know at the time but I was about to go out of business because I didn't have any work, you saved my business and my livelihood and I have never forgotten it." "I remember now," I said, "I did hear you were in trouble and a lot of our work was going to another company whose director was too friendly with our buyer, I thought I would upset their little arrangement by transferring some of the work to you, I argued that it would be better placed with you being closer to our factory."

"When you owned your business I received a lot of work from you, and you always paid me on time. It's now my turn to say thank you for what you did for me, and my turn to do something for you. I will make the parts you need free of charge and together we will fit them to the vehicles at my workshop." I was overwhelmed by Robert's kind gesture, I said, "I didn't expect you to do the work for nothing, let me pay something towards the cost," Robert was insistent and would not hear about a contribution from me, "I want to do it for you, and that's an end to the matter, let's work out how much material we will need." What was that old saying we have in business? Help people when you are on the way up, you never know, you may need their help if you are on the way down! Robert was as good as his word, the body modifications were completed during the following weeks. The technical parts I had ordered would arrive within a few days and should coincide with the arrival of the Cooper tyres, allowing me sufficient time to complete 02 and 03 to journey specification before the end of the year.

October, November, and December, everything seemed to be coming together and I was able to sign off items on my list as completed. By the end of December, Glyn and I collected 02 and 03 from Tes garage of Lymington, off road specialists, who came to my rescue offering to fit the various technical upgrade parts I had accumulated for a very modest sum, and avoiding many hours on my back underneath the vehicles. All that remained for me to do was to design, fabricate and install a false floor and draw system for each vehicle to maximise the load space and they would be ready. Realising early enough that by the end of the year I was likely to be knackered, Vi, in her wisdom, booked a two week holiday over Christmas and the New Year period at the Canary

Islands, to spend some time together and for me to recharge my batteries. I concealed as much paperwork, maps and notes that I had made about one thing or another, into my case and covered them up with my clothes so that Vi didn't see them, there were some long standing issues I wasn't happy with that needed a second look. The route and itinerary was put together in a draft form a year before, based on the information I had at that time, since then there had been some changes to the route that needed to be included. With only four months before departure I wanted to have a closer look, to make sure the changes were included and that I had got it right. Some time ago I found out that the proposed plan to ship the two Jimmys from Magadan located at the north eastern corner of Russia, to Anchorage, Alaska, U.S.A. wasn't possible because the Bering Strait is frozen over for most of the year, and there is no reliable shipping service available. Vladivostok, located further south and facing the Sea of Japan, was my second choice and ideally located for entering Japan.

Our stay over Christmas at the Canary Islands was blissful, I didn't realise how tired and worn out I really was, I just slept for the best part of two days. I must have needed it because on the third morning I awoke fully energised and was soon ploughing through the work I had brought with me. Vi and I, together with hundreds of other people, walked along the seafront in the afternoon ending the stroll at the local harbour to give the boats in the marina a cursory glance before we walked back the way we had come. One day when we ended our stroll at the marina we were confronted by a number of jumbo sized trailers loaded with ocean going rowing boats that were destined to take part in the crossing to the Caribbean.

The owner of the company who produced the high-tech rowing boats was there; I introduced myself and told him that at the end of April we would start our journey around the world. Making sure that Vi wasn't looking, I took the opportunity to have a brief chat with him about what I would have to do to receive all the relevant information relating to me rowing across from the Canary Islands to the Caribbean, January 2014. I needn't have bothered, because while I was talking to the man, Vi had realised what I was up to and crept up behind me and whispered in my ear, "Don't even think about it!" Feeling a bit subdued at having been caught in the act, I spent the rest of our holiday paying penance, recharging my batteries and enjoying myself, in between jumping to attention every time my name was called, followed by 'yes dear', or 'no dear' to whatever question was fired at me. The holiday came to an end too quickly, we had just got into the holiday routine when it was time to return to the U.K. and the journey around the world.

January 2013, by the end of the month we completed the modifications to both 02 and 03 and fitted the special parts including my pièce de résistance, the raised plywood false floor and draw system for each vehicle. Vi was watching me through the kitchen window as I was working on the false floors, she brought me my cup of tea and biscuits as usual, then nodding towards the open backs of the vehicles, Vi said, "It's a funny thing, you can make fitted furniture for the cars in next to no time, but I have been waiting two months for you to hang a picture in the lounge." I mumbled something unprintable, scooped up a handful of tools and made my way to the lounge to hang the picture, and in so doing avoid any tension building between Vi and myself. When I returned from our short holiday I made a point of having a closer look at the itinerary, bearing in mind that Mikhail Rybochkin had decided not to join us after all, and as it wasn't possible to meet Mikhail Gorbachev, there was no longer any reason for us to visit Belarus or Moscow. The countries that we would now visit were France, Belgium, Germany, Poland, Slovakia, Hungary, Ukraine, Russia, Kazakhstan, Mongolia, Japan Alaska, Canada, and U.S.A. I was also concerned that I hadn't allowed enough time in the event that we encounter delays en route; the more I thought about it the more I was convinced that we should leave on Sunday 31st March, a month earlier and not 30th April as previously proposed. I put my proposals to the guys at the next meeting and explained my reasons for leaving a month earlier. Everyone was in agreement so our revised route, itinerary and departure date of Sunday 31st March was adopted and written into our program, and everyone who needed to know of our decision was notified. 02 and 03 were ready apart from being kitted out, they really did look smart and impressive, all I needed to do now was concentrate on crew training and bring everybody together so that we work as a team. At that time the committed crew comprised of myself, Alan Butler, Glyn Maher and Roger Winkworth, Charles Scott was unable to take part due to health reasons, but remained a part of the team as financial secretary. For everything to work as originally proposed we would need eight crew members to drive 03 around the world in four stages with two crew members sharing the driving at each stage. 02 would be driven by me on my own, unaided around the world, the film cameraman would occupy 02's passenger seat. Over the previous months I had spoken to a number of people who indicated their interest and it was time to talk to them again. I contacted those I had spoken to previously, and on each occasion I was given one reason or another why they couldn't take part. I told the guys of my predicament and saw the first signs of concern on their faces. I changed my original plan so as to accommodate the additional people who had shown interest, and in so doing created yet another problem for myself.

The sort of people who would take on a journey around the world aren't exactly waiting on street corners for me to approach them, I decided to place a carefully worded advertisement in the local paper and within a day of its publication I received a call from Graham Higgins. Being local, we met at my house and immediately warmed to each other, I explained to Graham my predicament and the reason for the advertisement and it wasn't long before Graham was as excited as I was and said he would think about it and would call me the next day. True to his word, Graham phoned me to say he would like to join our merry band and could we meet that morning to deal with the details, during our meeting I mentioned that we needed another four crew members if we were going to make it work.

I was grateful that Graham had agreed to join us, even more so when he phoned me a few days later to ask if we still need crew, and if so he has a friend who is interested and would like to meet me, the following day I met Mike Bailey for the first time. Mike, Graham, and I chatted for some time, I was particularly interested when Mike mentioned he had rally driving experience in his early days, as we chatted I felt compatible with Mike but it wasn't the same as when I first met Graham. By the end of the meeting, Mike was as enthusiastic as the rest of us and signed up a day or two later. Confident that I would find the three remaining crew members needed, I turned my thoughts to the crew training program we had in place, and the remaining kit I still had to track down. I was ever mindful that we would be on our own once we start our journey; we had no backup team to look after us if we got into trouble, so we would have to deal with any problems if and when they happen ourselves. During the following weeks the crew attended training sessions at Newmans Suzuki, Southampton, covering vehicle servicing and maintenance, roadside collision repairs and vehicle recovery. One afternoon we all assembled at Alan Butler's house to meet the St John Ambulance nurse for a crash course in first aid just in case we needed to apply emergency treatment at the roadside. Endless hours were spent familiarising ourselves with the vehicles and equipment, satellite phone and tracking systems, tent erecting and use of the galley equipment should the need arise. If the training sessions didn't accelerate the aging process, sorting out our visas and organising our vaccinations surely did.

February was the start of a period that pushed me to the limit; Roland Spencer joined the crew then left shortly after as a result of the financial commitment required. Then came the devastating news that Alan Butler could no longer take part due to serious health issues that needed immediate attention. Six weeks before departure I found myself in a position where I had crew for stage three and four but no crew for stages one and two, the situation wasn't looking good at all. If I couldn't find crew I would somehow have to start the journey, complete stage one and two and deliver 03 to Graham and Mike on 9th May at Novosibirsk, Russia, ready for the start of stage three, the journey across Russia. I didn't panic as a result of my predicament; it was just another problem I had to solve and I decided to see what happens during the next few days. I continued to do my once a week early morning five minute slot on the Julian Clegg radio show, broadcast on B.B.C. Radio Solent, Julian became a big fan of our project and agreed to flag us off when we leave, as well as continuing our weekly broadcast by satellite phone as we travelled around the world. Fortunately, I was being looked after by Maureen Wycherly, a close friend of Vi and I, Maureen was the Project P.R. Manager, she kept me pointing in the right direction and made sure that I was in the right place at the right time to link up with Julian Clegg as well as many other P.R. engagements.

It was about that time I first contacted the Novotel Southampton, I made an appointment to see Glen Findley, Hotel Manager, and Claire Smith, Events Manager. I explained who I was and what I was doing; I asked if it would be possible to organise a reception at the start of our journey around the world from the hotel. I then went on to indicate that there would be a large number of guests, local T.V. and radio, and that Julian Clegg would read a dedication before flagging us off at midday. Glen and Claire listened to what I had to say, Claire asked a few questions, they had a short discussion between themselves, then Glen said, "How many guests do you think will be here?" "About one hundred and fifty," I replied. Glen paused for a moment as though thinking then said, "The hotel will provide refreshments free of charge as well allowing the two vehicles to be parked close to the reception, and for you to display promotional flags and banners for best effect." The generosity shown by Glen and Claire and the Novotel was heart warming, especially when things seemed to be going wrong. Just before my meeting with Glen and Claire finished, I asked Claire if there was a preferential rate if I only use Novotel hotels as we travel through Europe. I produced a copy of our itinerary indicating that we would be stopping overnight at the cities on that list; Claire turned the pages from the list I had given her, and then said that she would look into it and get back to me. A few days later I was passing through Southampton and decided to call at the Novotel to see if Claire had any news for me. Within a few minutes, Claire collected me at reception and we made our way to the hospitality area. Claire opened a file she had with her then said, "I have emailed the Novotel hotels in most of the cities indicated on the itinerary notifying them that you are special guests and to help if they can, and the date you are expected to arrive. What the individual hotel will do will vary, but they will look after you." I thanked Claire for all her hard work, finishing by saying that Maureen would be in touch with her soon to tidy up the loose ends relating to the P.R. and the start date. I was grateful for what Glen and Claire were doing for us and felt confident that the departure reception would be professionally organised.

As we got closer to departure day the crew meetings became more frequent and concern was continuously being raised about the lack of crew for stage one and two. I assured everyone that nobody was more concerned about the situation than me, and I was doing everything I could to find a solution. To be truthful I privately accepted that there was a strong possibility that we wouldn't find the crew we need and that I should have a plan B in place, just in case. I remembered when I was exchanging emails with my very good friend Iwona, a lovely Polish lady; she was my contact in Poland and helped to arrange for me to meet Lech Walesa. I recalled she mentioned in one of her emails that her partner, Mariusz, ran an off road adventure company, I knew it was a long shot but I emailed Iwona explaining the situation and asked whether Mariusz had any free time available between 14th April to 10th May to drive 03 from Budapest in Hungary to Novosibirsk in Russia. The next day I received a reply saying he was available from 18th but he didn't have a visa for Russia. I was relieved that I had a plan B, that is, I would drive 02 and Mariusz would drive 03 from Budapest to Novosibirsk to arrive on or before 9th May ready for Graham and Mike and myself to drive 02 and 03 on stage three as scheduled. The remainder of plan B was still to be finalised, I needed to find a driver willing to drive 03 from Southampton, England on March 31st to Budapest in Hungary and arrive there around 14th April. Plan B was taking shape so I decided to focus on some of the other issues that were causing concern.

It was the end of February, I was in Southampton collecting some of the last few items still required, and as it was close by, I called at Roger Winkworth's office to discuss various issues outstanding, and had a cup of coffee, then made my way home. When I arrived home I gave Vi her usual cuddle then went to my office and fired up my laptop, by the time I got myself a cup of tea I was ready to see what had arrived in my inbox.

I noticed there was an email from Roger, but dealt with everything else before I looked to see what Roger wanted. I read his short note and remained looking at the screen dumfounded. The part my eyes remained focused on was, 'I will no longer be able to take part due to unforeseen financial commitment elsewhere' and so on. The news was sickening, I was with Roger that morning and he never mentioned a thing, I tried to phone Roger but got nowhere. The following day the guys and I met for our regular meeting and I told them about Roger's email and indicated that it would be easier to find someone to join us for stage four and I would start work on it straight away. We dealt with matters outstanding then I mentioned that Alan, although no longer taking part, Graham and Mike had all paid their contribution, Glyn who was at the meeting and Roger who wasn't, we now knew why, still hadn't paid. I asked Glyn if there was a reason why he hadn't paid, he said there wasn't and he would pay it at the next meeting. After the meeting Alan came to me and said, "Look, I know you have a lot going on at the moment, so I don't want you to worry about paying me back my contribution, it is my fault that I am too ill to go and you made it clear that the contribution, once paid, was not refundable, look on it as a gift to the project, I will try and claim it from my insurance." I was humbled by what Alan had just said to me, bearing in mind I knew how much he wanted to take part and how seriously ill he was. Three weeks to go, Roger Winkworth emailed me to say his financial situation had changed and he could now come, and would pay his contribution at the next meeting. 02 and 03 were as ready as they would ever be, all the paperwork was in place, the problem concerning worldwide vehicle insurance was resolved, both vehicles were covered by U.K. insurance while driving in Europe, when we enter Ukraine and other countries en route I would have to buy insurance at the border. I needn't have worried myself, obtaining car insurance, like many other issues I unnecessarily worried about, turned out to be easy to deal with and hassle free.

Thursday 21st March, I remember it very clearly, I was sitting in my office early evening checking to make sure I had not overlooked anything when the phone rang and a moment later Vi opened the door to say Roland was on the phone. We talked briefly then Roland said, "Are you still looking for crew for stage one?" "Yes," I said, hoping that Roland had changed his mind about joining us. Roland continued, "It's probably not what you want to hear but I will put it to you anyway. My friend Keith Twyford and I have been talking, we know the problem you are having trying to find crew for stage one and two, and if it is of any help Keith and I will drive 03 from Southampton on the 31st to Budapest, Hungary, and we will pay all our own expenses. I wish we could have joined you officially but it wasn't to be, is our suggestion of any help?" I wanted to say yes immediately but I needed time to think it through, "Can I ring you back in ten minutes?" I continued to remain seated, facing the wall in front of me, my head in my hands, it was like a crushing weight had been lifted off my shoulders, and I now had a workable plan B. I thought through Roland and Keith's proposal to make sure there were no hidden problems, then phoned Roland back and said, "On the face of it your proposal would be acceptable but I will have to run it past the guys at our meeting the following day for their approval," I thanked Roland and said I would call him back tomorrow afternoon.

Two weeks before departure, the guys assembled at my house as usual for the meeting, Glyn and Roger arrived and sat down, when Roger emailed me to ask if he could re-join, I didn't make it difficult for him I simply said it would be O.K. and left it at that. The meeting discussed one or two urgent matters then I read through a long list of headings relating to every part of the project, explaining what it was and how I had dealt with it. I handed everyone a revised copy of the route and itinerary to study. I also handed out a copy of the programme and timetable relating to the run up and departure from the Novotel, and I answered satisfactorily all the questions directed at me. I drew the meeting's attention to the current situation relating to stages one and two; I admitted that I had not been successful as far as locating paying crew, but so as to ensure that we start as planned I proposed to refer to 03 and stages one and two as delivery stages. I then went on to notify everybody that I received an offer the day before from Roland Spencer who everyone already knew, and Keith Twyford, a friend known to Alan and myself, to drive 03 between them from Southampton on 31st March to Budapest, arriving 14th April, they would pay all their own expenses. I also said, "Mariusz, a Polish man and experienced driver, is available to drive 03 from Budapest on or about 18th April and arrive at Novosibirsk Russia on or before 9th May, ready for Graham and Mike to take over and drive stage three as originally planned. Wherever possible, 02, driven only by myself, and 03 will follow the planned route and itinerary and take part in the planned organised events, as though driven by paying crew. Any additional costs or expenses relating to these changes will be covered by me." Various questions were raised and put forward, but in the end I said, "Our options are clear, if the crew taking part in stages three and four are unable to help out with stages one and two, we either have to use a delivery crew to get 03 to Novosibirsk, or we have to stop now." As I had hoped my proposal was accepted as our best option, and I was relieved that I had managed to overcome yet another challenging problem. The remaining item on the agenda was to review the project finances; I outlined the project's financial situation. I went on to say, "The amount remaining in the project account, plus the £6000 contribution from each of Alan, Graham, Mike, Glyn and Roger, will not be enough to completely fund the journey." I continued, "From what I have calculated we will run out of funds before we reach our shippers at Newark on the east coast of the U.S.A." I suggested that I keep a close eye on our cost as we travel and deal with any shortfall if or when it happens. I asked Glyn and Roger if they were going to pay their contribution, all eyes were on them when they produced their cheques and laid them on the table. Relieved that they had finally paid, I thanked them as I picked up their cheques and glanced at them to make sure there were no errors, as I did I noticed that both cheques were made out for £5000 and not £6000, the agreed amount. With the cheques in my hand I turned to Glyn and Roger and said, "This is the wrong amount," Roger said, "That's all I have got," Glyn said, "Same for me." I just looked at them as I tried to work out what to say next. I knew what I wanted to say, but it would have meant me finding a replacement crew for stage four. I said, "You have known for a long time what your contribution was to be, why have you left it to this late stage to spring this on me?" I think it was Graham who interjected by saying, "Look, Alan, Mike, and myself have paid the correct amount, if that's all they want to pay it's alright with us," "With respect," I replied, "it's not alright with me." I looked back at Roger and Glyn and said, "You will be driving 03 through Canada and the U.S.A. for 24 days at no extra cost other than the £6000 contribution you committed to, a modest amount for a journey of a lifetime."

I looked at Glyn and Roger, and said, "Because of our financial situation and short notice, I have no alternative but to accept the amount you want to pay, and at the same time refund £1000 each to Alan, Graham and Mike so they pay the same as you, and in effect you are responsible for wiping out £5000 of the project funds, something we can ill afford." The meeting drew to a close and I showed everyone out then returned to my office to think through what had happened. My conclusion was that what had just happened was probably the first of a number of instances or disagreements I would have to deal with before I arrive back in the U.K. I was a fool to not consider the possibility that the crew might want to do something that I didn't or go somewhere that wasn't included in the itinerary; I cursed myself for not taking the likely situation seriously. My best course of action was to try to avoid it happening in the first place. One thing I was sure of, I was in the process of turning an idea into reality, my determination to drive the project forward had brought us this far and would continue to do so until we arrive back to the U.K. safely, no amount of problems I was likely to experience as I travel would prevent me from driving around the world. I decided to put what happened the previous Friday behind me and focus on what had to be done before we depart in fourteen days' time. I had a meeting with Roland and Keith to formalise my previous discussion with Roland and confirmed the arrangements for them to join us for stage one. We spent some time going over the route and itinerary and it was clear that they were taking the delivery of 03 to Budapest seriously, and when not talking about the project, Roland and Keith always seemed to be laughing about one thing or another, just what I needed. The same day, I emailed Mariusz to let him know officially that I would like him to join us and to confirm the financial arrangement we had already discussed. Relieved that stage one and two was back on track, I turned my attention to the cameraman. A few weeks previously a friend put me in touch with a cameraman who I then contacted, he said he was interested and would contact me again nearer to departure date. Because he hadn't contacted me as promised I was a little concerned when I gave him a call, after a number of unanswered calls to contact him, I decided to look elsewhere for a cameraman. I spoke to Maureen Wycherly, our P.R. Manager, who suggested that she put an ad on our website, a day or so later she phoned me to say she had been contacted by a cameraman who said he was interested and would I give him a call. That evening I rang the number Maureen had given me and Gary answered, he sounded pleasant enough, I introduced myself and asked if he was working at the moment, he said he wasn't, I then went on to say who I was and what we were doing, and that we were looking for a cameraman to join us and film the journey from departure day, Sunday 31st March departing from Southampton to Budapest, Hungary, a fourteen day journey. Interviewing cameramen was not an everyday occurrence for me so my questions were mainly related to whether he would be able to join us at the Novotel Southampton about midday Saturday 30th. He said he would be there, but he was short of funds and could I book and pay for his rail ticket to Southampton? I should have picked up on the reason why he couldn't buy his own ticket but it didn't register, I said to Gary, "Although I am the head of the project my filming experience is limited so if you don't mind I would like you to talk with David Ellery of Viewpoint Productions, who will be putting the film together, and Keith Rimmer, Manager of our website and a professional photographer." I explained to David and Keith that I would like them to interview Gary to see if he could do what we want.

The following day David and Keith came back to me to say Gary answered the questions and as far as they could see he could do the job. I phoned Gary to say he had got the job and confirmed the financial arrangement we briefly discussed the last time we spoke, I then thanked him and said, "I look forward to meeting you on the 30th." Gary was the last link in the endless chain of things I'd had to do over the past two years or so, I had checked and rechecked everything and I guess we were as ready as we would ever be. Sitting at my desk in my sanctuary of an office, I looked around me, the map of the world and list of one thing or another pinned to the walls. My self-adhesive coloured squares with scribbled notes to remind me to deal with this or that hung by the corner along the edge of the shelf above my desk awaiting removal and consignment to the waste bin. I looked around my office, as though it was for the last time, stood and walked out the door, turning the light off as I did, I couldn't help reflecting, was it the end of the beginning, or beginning of the end.

Part three
No turning back

I first started thinking about driving around the world during December 2010, the successes and failures, disappointments and achievement, the personal highs and lows and unbelievable problems that I had experienced along the way would test any man and his family to the limit. The two years and four months bringing the project together was behind me now but I sometimes wonder how I managed to achieve what I did. It may have been a different story if I didn't have the support of Vi and the team. I was in my 71st year when I started bringing everything together and in my 73rd year when we set off on our journey. During that time I still had the energy and the knack to get things done. Bringing everything together during the last year was bad enough but the few weeks running up to departure day was an absolute nightmare, pushing me to the limit as to whether at that late stage I abort or not, however, I hung in there. Saturday, the last day before departure, my family either called at the house or made contact in one way or another to see how Vi was bearing up and how I felt. I had a stock answer "I'm O.K. it will be alright once we get started." In truth, I was worried sick. I spent the day between keeping the family happy and for the umpteenth time checking the vehicles and equipment, going over the documentation, passports, visas and all the other paperwork I had amassed that I needed, there was always that nagging feeling that I had overlooked something but tomorrow at 12 o'clock what we haven't got we go without!

Saturday evening, the family got together locally to celebrate my leaving in the morning, or was it the last supper! It was a jolly affair, questions were asked about what would I do if this or that happens. I would answer as best I could but in reality we had no support team tagging along to look after us. If we got into trouble we would have to sort it out ourselves. I said my goodbyes to those who couldn't make the send-off reception then Vi and I made our way home for an early night. Vi was very attentive, making small talk, I could see it in her eyes she was concerned that something might happen to me, for the first time in our lives we would be apart for a long time. I didn't sleep at all that night; I tried not to disturb Vi, I laid there trying to find some mental rest to slow my brain down for a few hours so that I would be fresh for the morning, but it never happened. I lay awake mentally going over everything, cross checking this and that, how would Gary, the cameraman work out? I didn't really know him. The vehicles were overloaded, would they be alright? The send-off reception at the Novotel, would everyone be there? The press, radio, all the guests? Would it rain? Everything seemed to be going round and round in my head over and over again. My ability to hold everything together was shattered when I visited my doctor and he confirmed to me the result of the tests that I'd had two weeks before and his recommendation. Considering my predicament, I asked my doctor if we could keep it to ourselves. I watched the first signs of dawn inching above the horizon and finding its way into our bedroom. I slid out of bed trying not to disturb Vi, but when I looked at her she was looking at me with a twinkle in her eye, being the gentleman I am I got back into bed. A short while later I got out again with a smile on my face and was feeling pleased with myself. I looked out of the window at the two Jimnys, I saw them as two metal horses waiting for their riders to arrive. I was impressed by the way they had turned out, they looked the part. I thought for a moment, wondering if they would perform as well as they looked. I showered, shaved and dressed myself to look like Indiana Jones' dad, ate a hearty breakfast, gave Vi some extra cuddles, leathered the early morning dew off the vehicles, we were ready to go.

Roland arrived a little earlier than planned to collect 03, after leaving he would collect Keith, stop at his home to say goodbye to some friends then drive on to Southampton. It was soon time for me to leave, the house was deadly quiet, Vi was there with Maureen, our Press and P.R. Manager and friend who had flown down from Leeds to take charge at the reception and to be on hand together with my daughter Carole in the event that Vi had difficulty coping. I could see that they were waiting for me to leave so that they could make their own way independently. The last few minutes, I dithered around doing nothing in particular, I reminded Vi that the cruise ships were at the docks and there was likely to be traffic jams. Feeling a bit apprehensive I said, "It's time for me to go." They both watched as I climbed into 02 commenting, "Don't get lost on the way to Southampton." I looked into Vi's eyes as I turned out of the drive, we both knew it would be difficult being apart for such a long time but she promised she would be strong when the time came. As I left for the thirty minute or so drive to Southampton I felt a little bit sick with the constant worry about the many things that could go wrong, the effect of the late crew changes and financial disagreement, a cameraman joining us at Southampton who I had only met the day before. These issues and many others were constantly on my mind. Entering the main road from where we lived, I noticed that there was some frost still lingering and the roads were wet. The little Suzuki Jimny felt comfortable to drive, the reassuring purr from the little engine that was about to take on a man size job and the Cooper tyres that gave a sort of sure footed feeling on the road felt good. The problems ahead of me were still on my mind as I approached the first bend in the road, I lifted my foot off the gas and laid it over the top of the brake just in case as this bend regularly claims a victim. As I approached the bend I heard a muffled bang followed by bits of cars flying through the air in all directions. It looked as though there might have been a patch of ice because there were two cars imbedded into each other. The drivers looked O.K., more people arrived to help out and everything was under control so I discreetly slipped away to continue my journey. Alone, I sat thinking to myself as I drove to Southampton about the accident that I had just witnessed and all the other issues that had occupied my mind recently, to hell with it, I thought, what will be will be. I then stopped thinking about all the issues spinning around in my head, I wiped my mind clean so to speak, got rid of the rubbish so as to focus only on what lay ahead of me. Relieved that I no longer carried the mental burden of the past and what might happen, I ran through what was organised for the departure reception knowing I could rely on the Novotel Southampton's Glen Findley, the Hotel Manager, and Claire Smith, Events Manager, very professional people who were organising the facilities. The press, local radio and T.V., photographers, guests, flags and banners, it should all happen. I arrived later than intended, relieved to see Roland and Keith were already working with others to get the flags and banners in place. I positioned the vehicles for display and best effect, the press, radio, T.V. and photographers were all there as promised. Dignitaries, family and friends of the crew and guests were all milling about. When everything was in place, I and the rest of the crew made ourselves available to the media for interviews and photography. I was overwhelmed and relieved with the turnout, I took the opportunity to thank personally Alun Parry, Press and P.R., Suzuki G.B. and Guy Foster, M.D. of Newmans Suzuki, Southampton for having confidence in me and their support over the past year or so and continuing support as we travel. I also thanked as many of our sponsors I could find. Then I gave my lovely wife Vi a final hug and Maureen an extra squeeze as she reminded me not to get lost. A final goodbye to Keith Rimmer, his camera clicking away in all directions, I didn't give Keith a squeeze, he might have got carried away, so I shook his hand.

I tried to get to everyone who had helped us in one way or another. When a reporter asked me how I felt now that we were finally on our way, I said, "I am very uneasy at being parted from my wife for such a long time, it's been a long and difficult road to get us here today, so now I guess I just want to get going." Our very good friend Julian Clegg, presenter at Radio Solent was there to flag us off, I asked everybody to make ready for us to leave in five minutes, I hung on to Vi as long as I could, tears in her eyes, I gave her another last cuddle and a long lasting smacker of a kiss and said goodbye to her and our daughter Carole and the rest of the family, friends and well-wishers. We lined up the two vehicles for the final photos, Julian Clegg said a prayer and a few words, we then got in our vehicles and we were flagged off. Everybody was waving us off as we rolled forward, I and Gary, the cameraman, in 02, Roland Spencer and Keith Twyford in 03. I gave Vi a final look and a slight nod as we passed. We were on our way around the world. I knew my way around Southampton but I wasn't about to risk making a fool of myself as we left, like taking a wrong turn and ending up doing a tour of the city via the one way system before we found our way out, I would be reminded of it for the rest of my life. To be on the safe side, a few days earlier I did a dry run and fortunately found that one of the roads I was to have taken was closed! Just as well, when we were flagged off we were followed through the city by an escort from a Suzuki Owners' Club, horns sounding, flags flying from the front of their vehicles, could you imagine it, the whole lot of us, driving down a blocked street, then having to back up, just the thought of it is enough to wake me up screaming at night. Relieved to be clear of Southampton, and proud of the way the send-off turned out, it was time for our escort to leave us, waving and flashing their lights and giving us a long blast of their horns as they turned off to make their way home. We were on our own at last.

We finally made it, we were on our way cruising along the M3 at a steady 55 mph, on occasion, cars overtaking sounded their horns, flashed their lights, and gave us the thumbs up as they passed, it was a nice feeling. We kept in touch with each other with our communicators loaned to us for the journey, chatting about the send-off and general bantering. At last, I started to settle down relaxing a bit, the twisted knot in my gut brought on by my concern about the reception coming together as planned and leaving on time had gone. The journey to the Channel Tunnel gave me an opportunity to have a chat to Gary Scott, our cameraman for stage one, he joined us at very short notice. My initial contact by phone was the week before and we only met in person the day before we left. So there was no opportunity to eye each other up or get to know each other beforehand, not an ideal situation bearing in mind the time we would be together in 02. After a short tea and pee stop and to make sure that the vehicles and kit were O.K. and satisfied that all the bits secured on top were still with us, we continued to the tunnel, arriving in time for our booking on the 2.50pm train. We occupied ourselves during the 35 minute journey, running through our itinerary, in particular our schedule for the following day. It had taken me a long time to put the itinerary together, communicating mainly by email; as I recall, the only phone conversation I had was with a German lady at the Nurburgring, the old racing circuit South of Koln, Germany. After a few attempts to contact the Nurburgring reception itself and not an agent I finally got through to a lady who spoke excellent English with a strong German accent," HOW CAN I HELP YOU?" she bellowed down the phone. I swallowed hard, then explained who we were and what we were doing, then asked if it would be possible to drive our cars around the circuit during the afternoon of April 1st, "ONE MOMENT," she replied conversing in German with a colleague, then switching back to English "YOU CAN COME."

I was excited at the prospect of actually driving around the Nurburgring, I must admit I had my fingers crossed hoping it was going to happen. Before we would arrive at the Nurburgring I had planned to visit the European Parliament during the morning to give them a tongue lashing about a number of things, in particular why, when the whole world was in recession having to make drastic cuts and savings, and in some cases people starving, the retirement home for failed politicians, the European Parliament who supposedly run Europe, were giving themselves pay rises, and drinking 100 Euro bottles of wine with their lunch, all at our expense. I really get fired up every time I think about it.

Having rested from the short train journey through the tunnel we were released into Europe, part of the largest land mass of the world that would take a challenging 60 days to transit by the time we reach Vladivostok, our destination for our ferry connection to Japan. The sun shone, our mini convoy flowed with the weekend traffic arriving at the Novotel Bruxelles a little after 7.30pm, knackered but still upright. Claire Smith, Events Manager at the Novotel, Southampton had been so helpful, Claire had a copy of our itinerary and forward booked accommodation for us at special low rates. Wherever we stayed at a Novotel we were given the V.I.P. treatment and looked after, in return we would organise a photo shoot with the manager and staff centred around the two Jimnys.

Monday 1st April, day 2, I was so pleased that Roland and Keith had joined me for the first stage of the journey, two of the nicest people to be with, we pretty well laughed about everything, just what I needed. Rested, fed and thoroughly watered the night before and a hearty breakfast the following morning, I was ready to lock horns with the faceless ones at the European Parliament. I acquired a local map and traced the route to our destination; the traffic was noticeably quiet for a Monday, it wasn't until we arrived at the parliament building that we found out that Monday

Brussels to Nurburg

1st of April was a holiday. We parked outside the parliament building and stood there in amazement; looking around, it appeared that the parliament was one of a number of buildings that came under the title of the European Parliament. How do they keep track of the thousands of paper shufflers? Sleeping off their lunch in the afternoon, the answer is they probably don't. For me it was a bit depressing to see the opulence of the place also knowing that it is funded by the hard working tax payer, heaven help us. As there were not many people around us we were able to organise Gary to get the camera and equipment set up to film Roland, Keith and myself having a discussion in front of the parliament building, also interviewing each of us about what lay ahead. I had planned to visit the other European Parliament at Strasbourg on our way to the Nurburgring but quite frankly I would probably end up being dragged away by the police if I went there. I mentioned to the guys, "I don't think I can take much more of this, how about bypassing Strasbourg?" They didn't need much persuading at my proposal. In the meantime, Gary had finished filming and was packing the kit into 02 as we spread our map on the bonnet to identify the route that would take us direct to the Nurburgring. Navigating our way out of Brussels, we soon settled down to the three hour drive, we were excited at the thought of driving around the Nurburgring but to be truthful I hadn't a clue as to what would happen when we got there. I tried to explain to the lady who I previously spoke to at the Nurburgring that we were driving 4x4 vehicles not race cars, but all I could get in reply was, "YOU CAN COME."

We were in a jolly mood as we travelled towards our destination; there had been some bantering between Roland,

Keith and myself over the intercom and during our stop for fuel and coffee. We had about 45 minutes before arriving at the Nurburgring by 2.30pm. I had noticed that Gary hadn't said much since the last fuel stop; he kept looking at the camera equipment stowed behind his seat, turning it over as though looking for something and was clearly agitated. We had another quiet spell and I was getting concerned now that maybe I was missing something. Driving a bit further there was still no comment from Gary; I asked him if there was a problem, pausing for a moment he then said, "You have left the camera bag at the parliament building at Brussels." Hearing what he had just said I looked at him, "What do you mean I have left it? You are the cameraman, it's your responsibility to look after the camera equipment, what have we actually lost?" I asked. "The camera bag," he replied, distant alarm bells started ringing. This was the first of many issues relating to filming I had to deal with as we travelled, some quite serious which I had to overcome by the time we arrived at Budapest, Hungary. Driving in silence, I thought

Arriving at Nurburgring

through the situation and concluded that when it comes down to it we only lost the bag, I could buy a replacement. To ease the situation I turned to Gary and said, "It's a two hour drive back to Brussels, the bag probably won't be there anyway, so our best option is to continue as planned, I will buy a replacement." To soften the situation I said, "Don't worry about it, we can't put right what has happened, but in future the security and safety of the camera equipment is paramount and your responsibility. Also please make sure that everything you need for filming is ready for immediate use at all times and if you have any problems at all please tell me." To clear the atmosphere further I chatted to Gary, who by this time was wound up tighter than an over-wound clock spring. I asked if he had any ideas for filming once we got to the Nurburgring, I also mentioned that if we were able to get on the track we would only have one opportunity to film so we needed to be organised. Watching Gary working briefly, I had enough confidence to let him deal with the filming. I spoke to the guys in 03 through the handheld radio, explaining that the Nurburgring was just ahead and that I would follow the signs and hope it leads to the ticket office. I guess at this point I should mention I tend to see the funny side of a situation or incident so please bear with me if I get carried away on occasion and elaborate a bit when describing what happened.

We eventually arrived at the circuit and found our way to the main office building, parked the cars and stretched our legs for a moment. Gary was already at work with the camera, I asked the guys to wait while I went into the building to enquire as to where the ticket office was located. Concerned that they might send me away when they saw the cars, I casually walked along the path to the entrance doors at the ground floor of a totally glassed multi-story building. I swaggered up to the doors as though I had just stepped out of a Ferrari, yanked at the door expecting it to be closed and it opened slightly but felt like one of those doors that secured the bullion at Fort Knox, I could imagine people watching me from the inside struggling with the door as I tried to open it. I pulled as hard as I could at the door, smiling and giving the impression for those watching that I was super human but to be truthful I had a vein the size of a garden hosepipe protruding from my neck and my arm muscles were about to give in. The door was open far enough for me to squeeze through to the inside, I then let it go, the bang that followed as the door relocated the frame was deafening.

Having negotiated the outer door, I was immediately confronted by another set of half glazed double doors leading to a cathedral sized, marble clad, public area. Situated in the centre was the longest curved counter I have ever seen, sitting in the middle 'alone' was a solitary lady with an unimpressed look on her face. Sandwiched between the two sets of doors I could see that apart from the lady behind the counter and me, the place was empty and as quiet as a tax office waiting room. Knowing what to expect when I tried to open the inner door, I took a few deep breaths, hyped up my muscles, grabbed the handle with both hands and gave the door all I had. Unprepared for the lack of resistance, it came towards me like the speed of light, ready to smack me in the face, if it wasn't for the toe of my right shoe protruding a few millimetres in front of my nose. Surprised at what had happened I let the door go, the toe of my shoe now acting as a spring then sent the door at speed in the opposite direction, the almighty bang that followed when the door relocated into its frame reverberated throughout the building and frightened the hell out of the lady behind the counter, causing her to become airborne momentarily. Still sandwiched between the doors, I composed myself, opened the inner door once more and stepped inside, my right crumpled shoe now squeaking and my big toe throbbing, I made my way to the counter. The lady I now will refer to as Greta, who sounded very much like the person

I first contacted said "CAN I HELP YOU?" speaking in English with a strong German accent, "Yes," I said, I explained who I was and what we were doing, also that I had been in contact with her office some weeks ago and I was told that if we arrived on the 1st of April it would be an open day and we would be allowed to drive our vehicles around the track. "THAT IS CORRECT, TODAY IS OPEN DAY," she boomed back, relieved that I had got it right, I asked, "Where do I pay?" "YOU PAY NOW." Hesitant with the next question I said, "We don't exactly have race cars," "NO PROBLEM IT IS OPEN DAY." "There is one more question," I said, looking to see her reaction, "we have a film cameraman with us to film as we go around is that O.K.?" "FILMING IS FORBODEN WINK, WINK," she said. I looked at her for a second or two did she wink at me or did Greta have a twitch in her left eye?!! I tried that one again, I said, "Are you saying that taking pictures is not allowed?" "FILMING IS FORBODEN, WINK, WINK," she did it again only this time screwing the left side of her face up to look like Popeye to make sure that I got the message, I couldn't believe it. I paid 26 Euros for a ticket for each car and was told to hand them to the attendant at the track entrance. I thanked Greta for her help, giving her a couple of winks then made for the door. I emerged smiling, holding the tickets for the guys to see as both doors closed behind me sounding like a twelve gauge shotgun at a clay shoot.

Arriving at the circuit entrance, the attendant indicated to us to wait at the gate that leads on to the track, just sitting there taking in the unbelievable atmosphere, excited that we finally made it, our adrenalin pumping through our veins as we watched fast cars of all descriptions flying past in front of our eyes at break neck speed. I really couldn't believe I was actually going to drive the Nurburgring. We had been parked for a few minutes, waiting and watching the fast boys speeding past racing each other, the wind vortex created rocking our little cars as they sped down the

Out on the track at the Nurburgring

track. As we waited, I assumed that at some point the fast cars would come off the circuit and the slow cars including us would have their turn. Startled by the attendant banging the car to get my attention to lower the window he asked for my ticket and then indicated for me to go through the gate just as an assortment of BMWs, Porsches, Ferraris, and Aston Martins flashed past. I thought that there had been a mistake letting us on the track to mix it with the fast boys.

I looked at the attendant, as we turned onto the track he was shouting "GO, GO, GO". I looked in my mirror to make sure that Roland and Keith in 03 were behind me then floored the accelerator to get to the first corner before they did, then eased off the power having reminded myself of the decision we made earlier about not doing anything that might end up damaging the vehicles. Glancing at the rear mirror once more to see how the guys were getting on behind me, I saw 03 about to be swallowed whole by a pack of the fast boys who had been travelling down the straight at about 140 mph (225 km) to suddenly find us travelling at 65 mph (105 km) occupying the fast line into the first of many bends. The blue haze and the smell of rubber from aggressive braking was enough to create a mini eclipse as more cars piled up behind us, unable to overtake. I focused on the rapidly approaching corner, undecided as to the fastest way to get around the bend so as to free up the traffic behind knowing that 02 was 264lb (about 120kg) overweight, most of that was on top so trying to side drift around the bend didn't seem likely, I thought that my option was to straighten out the bend as best I could and see what happens. The sure footed Cooper tyres designed to perform on unsurfaced roads didn't take kindly to sliding sideways, my attempt to create a drift ended up more like a two wheel wobble as I went around. The two BMWs tailgating me through the bend suddenly dropped back when they saw 02 at an alarming angle and Gary leaning out of the window hanging on for dear life with one hand and the camera in the other filming our progress. Exiting the bend having frightened the life out of Gary, I then tried to compose myself and re-think my strategy

Unsurprisingly, the heavily loaded 4x4s failed to pass anything on the Nurburgring!

ready for the next bend. The loud roar as the cars, that we had bottled up, broke free and passed, was deafening, I couldn't see their faces but it must be a local custom, a one finger wave.

I was getting the hang of it as we drove further around the circuit; the experience was breath-taking. The crowds of spectators were waving to us as we passed, we waved back as though we had just won a race and we were on the lap of honour. 03, fed up with being the car behind, did a sneaky manoeuvre and passed us. Gary managed to capture this manoeuvre on camera, he also kept the camera rolling most of the time, securing a lot of footage for when the time came to put the film together. Driving the Nurburgring was a box I always wanted to tick, I never imagined I would ever get the opportunity to actually do it but I did and savoured every moment of the experience. I thought of the famous drivers who had raced here in the past, the glory, the tragedy, the many tales the circuit could tell. For some reason I tried to imagine the chaos we must have caused when the fast boys found us driving on their circuit. I could see the funny side of it, imagining an elderly couple returning from visiting the supermarket taking a wrong turn and somehow finding themselves driving around the Nurburgring and mixing it with the fast boys. The very thought of the situation made me laugh, it started as a chuckle, then developed into a long laughing bout, tears streaming from my eyes as my warped sense of humour took charge. Sadly, up ahead there were flashing lights and signs indicating that our time on the circuit had come to an end, an attendant directed us to a slip road and reality. The twenty-one kilometre Nurburgring doesn't discriminate about age, if you can walk and drive, if you are an old petrol head or whether you are wasting away waiting for the end but would like to go out with a bang, book yourself a ticket for an open day at the Nurburgring. Ask the wife if you can borrow her car, blow caution to the wind, if you make it around the circuit the wife's car will probably have to go home on a low loader but you will feel great. Excited at having driven the Nurburgring, the adrenalin still surging through our bodies, the verbal exchanges between the two cars reflected our achievement.

After driving a few miles we refuelled the cars, checked our route to Cochin, our overnight stop, and reflected once more about the Nurburgring. Continuing our eastward journey we arrived at Cochin late afternoon, a picturesque town situated on the banks of the Moselle River, a drive along the river's edge led us to a small inviting hotel overlooking the water. It had been a wonderful day.

Tuesday 2nd April, day 3, I needed to be out of bed early and get myself ready to receive a phone call at 8.30am from Julian Clegg, presenter of Julian's People UK BBC Radio Solent for a short live interview, a sort of progress report for the listeners. This was to be a once weekly interview as we travelled around the world. After being fed and watered the plan was to make for Bingen, situated on the banks of the Rhine, on the way we stopped for lunch at Trier, reported to be the oldest town in Germany. We spent an hour or so visiting the old town and at the same time looking for a replacement for the camera bag we left behind at Brussels. Departing Trier later than planned, Roland and Keith asked if they could make their own way to Bingen, I agreed but knew the rule was that we should always remain in contact to offer support if need be in the event that one of us has an accident. Uneasy about being out of contact, we made our way independently. I had been driving for about an hour along roads under construction, temporary road signs, and diversions, when the TomTom decided to stop working, resulting in me getting well and truly lost. After a bit of head scratching, I decided to head for the nearest village to seek assistance. My German was a mixture of French, Greek and Italian so that didn't help and got me nowhere. In the centre of a village I stopped for a moment to decide what to do, at the same time a door of the house opposite opened, a black man, the biggest I have ever seen, came out and walked towards me, I got out of 02 and walked to meet him, as we met, he said in English with an American accent, "Hi buddy, you look lost," I explained that I was trying to get to Bingen on the Rhine and somehow took a wrong turn. "The roads around here are mostly closed today," he said, "I'm not surprised you are lost." He was very helpful and gave me directions that eventually got us back on the road to Bingen, arriving there two hours later than Roland and Keith. I phoned them to find out where they were. When we met they wouldn't accept any excuses, adding that if I got lost every time I was on my own heaven knows where I would end up! Needless to say I was on the receiving end of their banter for the rest of the evening.

Wednesday 3rd April, day 4, although the weather forecast for the day was sunny, it was bitterly cold as we checked the vehicles. We were in no hurry to get going, our appointment at Bensheim was a two and half hour drive, we didn't have to be there until 1 o'clock so there was no rush. I took the opportunity to walk some way along the water's edge, stopping to look across to the other side, I found myself thinking about the soldiers, our guys, paddling across the Rhine in rubber boats towards the end of WW2, wondering if they would make it to the other side, very brave people. Continuing to walk I turned my attention to thinking about the itinerary over the next few days, that day we were to visit the Suzuki European Headquarters at Bensheim at lunch time to receive a cheque from the team at Suzuki on behalf of Save the Children, at 3 o'clock we had to say goodbye and make our way to Leipzig, a 4 hour journey and our stopover that evening. The following morning, it was essential that we departed Leipzig as early as possible if we intended to reach our destination. We had a 670 mile, 12 hour journey to Gdansk, Poland to meet

Receiving the cheque on behalf of Save The Children at Suzuki Europe at Bensheim

the retired president Mr Lech Walesa, on the 5th. Thinking about the meeting with Lech Walesa, I wondered if I had managed to get it organised properly, if I didn't when we got there it would be one hell of a mess!

The guys were waiting for me when I returned from my walk; we soon checked out and were on the road once more to Brensheim. We arrived at the Suzuki European Headquarters on time as requested and were met by the marketing team who would explain to us over lunch what they had planned. The lunch break was short, there was a photo shoot with us and the marketing team, the two Jimnys acting as a backdrop, the visit concluded with the European Marketing Manager presenting a donation to us on behalf of Suzuki for the Save the Children charity. Being treated like celebrities, giving interviews to the press was something we had to get used to. It was time to move on once more, we thanked everybody, said our goodbyes and were heading to Leipzig as planned. The Novotel in the centre of the city was a welcome sight after almost a 5 hour drive. It had taken longer than anticipated, arriving at 8pm. The staff at the reception were expecting our arrival and were very helpful. Fed, watered and the cars refuelled ready to go early in the morning, we decided to call it a night and get as much rest as we could in preparation for the journey the following day.

Thursday 4th April, day 5, we met for breakfast just before seven, stuffing as much food as we could get inside ourselves, it was going to be a very long day, I had my hands full keeping 03 in constant view, also monitoring the route we took. Gary helped on occasion but I couldn't rely on him as filming was his main priority. Gdansk, Poland was entered into the TomTom and everything was working fine for an hour or so. Travelling along a modern multi-lane highway, 03 was in view behind but the traffic volume had increased, making it difficult to change lanes. Ahead of us was what we used to call a spaghetti junction, you know the sort of thing, roads going off in all directions. I followed the sign to Gdansk and at the same time checked to make sure the guys were still behind me, there was no sign of them. I looked around and saw that they were slightly ahead and three lanes to my right. Calling Roland to tell him he was in the wrong lane, replying he said they were heading for Gdansk via the new toll road. Unable to switch lanes and look at our map at the same time I continued along the multi-lane road, following the signs to Gdansk, hoping that I would connect with the new road at some point. I had driven fifteen miles looking for an opportunity to turn and backtrack to follow 03's route but nothing presented itself, forcing me to drive further along and finally to continue all the way on the old road. The multi-lane new section of road ended to become a single lane and mayhem. The cars and their occupants, backed up at the end of the three lanes, turned into Kamikaze drivers as they tried to get to the roughly patched, pothole riddled, single lane road that would eventually take us to Gdansk. The heavens

Gdansk to Auschwitz

opened and it rained continuously for the rest of the day, creating miserable driving conditions as the line of traffic crawled along unable to avoid the potholes. Aggravating the orderly single lane each way of slow moving traffic, the Kamikaze death and glory drivers, forcing an opening between the contra flowing single lanes, were driving along the centre of the road, zig-zagging their way through. When they met another nutter coming in the opposite direction they played chicken for a bit, if they bottled out, they just turned right forcing some poor devil off the road to create a space. It happened to me on one occasion, I saw this huge 4x4 growling and clawing its way up the centre, determined not to let it through, I moved slightly to the left; undeterred, he kept coming and was alarmingly close. I saw that the driver was an old man, he had trouble breathing and his glasses were steamed up, so pretty safe to give him some verbal abuse, he saw that I lowered the window and was looking at me, I leant over shouting in my best English East London grammar, "Pi—off," or words to that effect! He gave me a blank look and eased past.

Needless to say the old boy didn't understand a word I said, just as well, un-noticed sitting behind the driver was a one man rugby team sporting a pair of matching cauliflower ears and a broken nose, you know the type of person that would rip the doors off 02 just for a laugh, I looked ahead, closed the window and slid down in my seat. The remainder of the journey to Gdansk was sole destroying; it seemed to go on forever. We eventually arrived at 8pm, totally drained. Roland and Keith were in the watering hole awaiting our arrival. In front of me at the reception was a tall and very fit guy talking to the receptionist, I listened with interest to his Polish accent, when he had finished he remained at the counter. I introduced myself to the receptionist, booked Gary and myself in and turned to go to the room when the big guy introduced himself. In perfect English with an exaggerated London accent, "Hi I'm Kevin," he said "what are you guys doing here?" At that point Roland and Keith joined us, and were introduced, I explained who we were, what we were doing and why we were doing it, then I asked why he was in Poland. "I live here," he said, "I'm a fireman, my partner is Polish and we have four children." It wasn't that simple though, as we spoke over a beer it came out that Kevin, the fireman, was a celebrity in Poland, he regularly appears on T.V. and radio and attracts the press. A few years back, Kevin, then working as a fireman in the U.K., met a Polish girl who had lured him to Poland, and never went back, she must be one hell of a girl! He learnt to speak Polish, transferred to the Polish fire service, showed them how it's done in the U.K. and never looked back. I mentioned to Kevin that we had an appointment the following morning with Lech Walesa, the retired President, he gave me directions as to where his office was located, expressing his surprise that Lech Walesa had agreed to a meeting. We spent some time talking to Kev, but we needed to have a discussion between ourselves to prepare for our meeting in the morning, we thanked Kevin, wished him well, and said our goodbyes, a nice guy.

Friday 5ᵗʰ April, day 6, our appointment was scheduled for 11 o'clock. Lech Walesa's office was located in the old town close to the dock area. Leaving the hotel early to make sure we arrived at his office at 10.30am as instructed, as we drove, I recalled conversations I had a year or so ago, people's reaction when I said that I was trying to arrange a meeting with Lech Walesa, retired

President of Poland, they didn't take me seriously so heaven knows what was said behind my back but I persevered, we would know soon enough if they were right. Lech Walesa didn't speak English so through a Polish friend, I arranged for Magda, a young Polish lady, to act as our interpreter and to meet us outside a building in the centre of the old town called The Green Gate. We parked the vehicles a short distance from the office, everyone was a bit subdued, and my stomach was in a knot, anxious that I had got it right. Gary was going to film the interview so he took his time to make sure that he had everything he needed, the equipment distributed between us, we made our way to the building and the office which was situated on the top floor. It was deadly quiet as I knocked and entered the reception room which was unattended, waiting for a few minutes for something to happen, I felt a cold sweat working its way up my back, I started to think that maybe I had got it wrong. A young lady entered the room and introduced herself in perfect English as secretary to Mr President, indicating that we be seated then continued, saying that Joanna, the President's Personal Assistant, would be with us in a moment.

Relieved that it was going to happen, I reflected on my limited correspondence I'd had with Joanna, how professional and helpful she was at that time, wondering what she looked like. An old man dreaming again. While we were waiting, I checked with Roland and Keith to make sure they had a note of the questions they were going to ask Mr President, we were overwhelmed at the thought of meeting Lech Walesa, the man in the next room. One of two large double doors of an adjoining room soon opened slowly, a petite, well-dressed regal looking elderly lady entered the room. Being seated while we were waiting, we stood respectfully as she walked towards us. In impeccable English she said, "Good morning, my name is Joanna," looking at the paperwork held in her hand, she asked, "Who is Leslie?" I stepped forward and introduced myself, looking a bit confused Joanna said for some

Iwona and Mariusz, friends of Les who helped arrange the meeting with Lech Walesa

reason she assumed Leslie was a lady. I replied, "It can be if spelt Lesley." I introduced Roland and Keith and then indicated towards and introduced Gary, also Magda, who acted as our interpreter. I asked if there was a specific procedure when talking to the President, Joanna replied saying that we would be sitting around a table with Lech Walesa at the head, "When asking a question, refer to Mr Lech Walesa as Mr President." Joanna explained that there was a film crew just finishing, "Please be seated, Mr President will meet you in a moment." We all looked at one another, the tension eased but we were overwhelmed that at long last we were going to meet the man himself.

The double doors opened, the film crew emerged carrying their equipment with Joanna snapping at their heels like a sheep dog. Closing the outer door on the departing film crew, Joanna turned to us and said, "Mr President will see you now, please follow me." Joanna paused long enough for us to compose ourselves, we then followed her through the double doors. The room was quite large, bright and traditionally furnished, to the right, close to a window benefiting from the natural light, was an ornate antique oblong table and matching chairs, Mr President, Lech Walesa stood in the centre of the room waiting to greet us as we entered. Seeing him in the flesh for the first time, he looked slightly taller and a little thinner than I imagined him to be, he didn't smile as Joanna introduced me and I at last shook his hand. Standing in the same room as him was a privilege for me. Joanna introduced Roland and Keith then Gary and Magda. Lech Walesa then indicated to us to sit down. Joanna looked at me as though she was waiting for me to say something. I responded by saying, "Joanna, perhaps I should start by telling Mr President who we are and what we are doing." Turning to Magda to make sure that she was ready and then looking back at Lech Walesa and speaking at a pace that Magda could handle, I said, "Mr President, I first want to thank you for your time and it has long been a personal ambition to meet you." I then proceeded to outline briefly what we were doing. He became very interested and jolly when he realised that it was not a run of the mill interview; asking a number of questions, he became excited when I said that those taking part were in their seventies. When I had finished he had a pretty good idea what our project was all about, the meeting became more relaxed and less formal. "Mr President," I said, "Roland, Keith and myself have questions we would like to ask, if we may?" I said, "I have a question that I had hoped one day to ask you. I would like to take you back to 1970, the days of unrest at Gdansk, the time when you stood in the line with other Solidarity shipyard workers facing the tanks, it was a standoff for a while, what was going through your mind at that time and what made you decide to take one step forward?"

Lech Walesa thought for a moment as though rethinking what happened that day then smiled saying, "Someone had to step forward otherwise we would have been there all day," and he laughed. I'm sure there was more to it than that but satisfied, I didn't pursue it further. Roland and Keith put their questions to Lech Walesa, his replies reflecting the casual atmosphere that had become quite jovial. Noting that we had reached the end of our allotted time, choosing the right moment I said, "Mr President, it seems that our time with you has passed so quickly, on behalf of myself, Roland and Keith, I would like to thank you for the opportunity to meet you and to show our appreciation can I ask if you would like to join us? We have a spare seat." Lech Walesa laughed at the thought of joining us, he said that he was too busy with his charity work also that he was only sixty eight, too young to join us, Lech Walesa then spoke to Joanna who related to me that Mr President said there was no urgency for us to leave, so we continued a little longer chatting and Gary carried on filming. I asked Joanna, "Is it possible to take pictures shaking hands with Mr President, and as a group?" She agreed to my request and at the same time signalled to a man who had been standing at the back of the room to come forward and collect our cameras and take pictures on our behalf. I thanked Lech Walesa and Joanna for their kind hospitality and just before leaving he produced signed copies of a small book covering his life story that he presented to each of us. There was a light-hearted atmosphere as they escorted us to the outer door. I thanked Lech Walesa, Joanna, and the staff once more for the kindness shown to us during our visit.

We emerged from the ground floor of the building overwhelmed at the meeting. I will never forget the feeling when I shook Lech Walesa's hand, a real nice man. It was bitterly cold, the last of the winter snow piled up everywhere making it difficult at times to remain upright, to avoid the risk of falling over we decided the safest place for us would be sitting down in a bar that offered food. Over a beer and lunch, we chatted about our meeting with Lech Walesa. I admitted that I had concerns that it might not have happened but was relieved that it did. It was a pity that I couldn't get it together to meet Mikhail Gorbachev. I tried real hard, but it wasn't to be. You may be thinking why did I want to meet Lech Walesa and Mikhail Gorbachev? Well, they both achieved greatness, Lech Walesa came from a poor and humble background, becoming a shipyard electrician and through his effort and circumstance became a figurehead of Solidarity then went on to become the President of Poland. Mikhail Gorbachev started life born to a poor farming family and through sheer hard work, guts and determination, rose to become the most powerful man in Russia and responsible for ending the days of the iron curtain, two great people. The remainder of the day we spent sightseeing around the old town and visiting the war memorial. During the last war the Nazis really treated the Polish people badly. It saddened me when I read what happened but somehow they survived. I liked Poland and the Polish people, if I can remain upright and breathing long enough, I would like to go back some time.

Saturday 6th April, day 7, exhilarated by what we had achieved the day before, we checked and refuelled the vehicles then pointed ourselves south for the 190 mile drive to Poznan where I had arranged a face to face meeting with my very good friends, Iwona and Mariusz, I wanted to thank them personally for their help when I was trying to organise the meeting with Lech Walesa. We entered the old city of Poznan early that evening and arrived at our destination. 03, which was being driven by Keith at the time was cut up so badly by another car, how they avoided a collision heaven knows, Keith's quick reaction avoided a possible a disaster, I have to say the screeching of tyres and the unrepeatable language made me focus a bit more on my driving. We found our way to a high rise Russian style apartment block, their apartment was situated half way up. There was no lift, so we were fighting for air by the time we got there. It was a pleasure to meet at last, to thank Iwona, for her help and to talk to Mariusz in detail about his agreement in joining me for stage two of the journey, Hungary to Novosibirsk, Russia. Prior to departure date, I had difficulty organising crew for stage two, at one point I thought that I and another person, who I had yet to find, would drive the vehicles from Budapest, Hungary to Novosibirsk in Russia and be there ready for when Graham and Mike arrive by air on the 9th of May for the start of stage three of the journey. Mariusz had time available and offered to help which resolved the situation, he is a nice guy; he spoke a little Russian and had a lot of experience from running his own adventure company, and knew the route we were taking, so he would be helpful, particularly at border crossings. Pleasantries and business concluded we left the small but comfortable apartment to relocate to a traditional Polish basement restaurant, after a few local beers and a meal, my memory gets a bit vague, I don't remember much until I awoke in the morning, looked into the mirror and saw an old man looking back at me, must have been strong beer!

Sunday 7th April, day 8, we had another meeting with Mariusz just to review what was agreed the night before and say our goodbyes then faced south once more for the 300 mile or so drive to Katowice. After driving for three hours through forest and farmland, on roads with serious potholes, we finally emerged onto a highway that would take us direct to Katowice. I was feeling pleased with myself that morning, Roland led the way out of the city avoiding the roads that were closed for a marathon, we ended up getting well and truly lost, we got it sorted out eventually and were on our way again but I made a note to remember this incident ready for when Roland rubs it in when I occasionally get us lost. The road to Katowice seemed O.K. but we soon experienced a sort of osculating or rolling effect caused by the wheels of the high volume of heavy goods traffic. The two lanes in either direction had deep ruts made by the tyres of the heavy lorries. The deep ruts were wider than the wheel spacing of the

Jimnys, causing us to drive with one wheel in the rut, requiring a lot of concentration to keep it there. Just when you think you have it under control, the little Jimny, as if it has a mind of its own, jumps across to the other rut just to see if you are awake, surprised at what has happened, you overreact with the steering, creating a rolling effect as you roll from one rut to the other while you make up your mind which one to stay in. About 7 hours after we started, we sort of rolled into Katowice. As I was not sharing the driving, I felt totally knackered by the time we located our friendly Novotel and booked ourselves in. Roland and Keith decided to walk into the city centre to have a look around, I decided to rest up a bit, as well as catch up on my paperwork; we would meet in the hotel bar later.

The short rest brought me back to life and about ready for a beer, Roland, Keith and Gary, who had finished filming for the day, were already seated in the lounge chatting to someone who had joined them. I arrived and was introduced to Max Mendel, a young doctor, who went on to say that he was one of a group of young doctors who owned Suzukis, and other makes of off-roaders, they formed a club in Poland called the Mud Doctors and have been following our journey and itinerary via our website and local radio. Max saw that our itinerary indicated we would be staying at the Novotel Katowice so he decided to pay us a visit. It was a pleasure to meet and talk to Max, we spent a pleasant hour or so chatting about what we were doing and why we were doing it, also as we would be returning to the hotel the following afternoon after visiting Auschwitz, we agreed to a photo session that evening with some of the club members who would very much like to meet us and have a look at our vehicles. Max was a happy man when he left, having tracked us down and arranged the meeting for the following evening, he couldn't wait to tell the guys back at the club.

Monday 8th April, day 9, feeling the benefit of an early night, I finished the remainder of my paperwork, I had a shower, consumed a large breakfast and was ready to go by 8.30am; it was a beautiful, cold but sunny morning, mounds of snow resisting the onset of spring. Roland and Keith were already cleaning 03, mumbling something about, "Can't get up in the morning," when I joined them to clean 02. We agreed with the manager for him to take some pictures so the Jimnys needed a bit of a clean to remove the muddy splashes received after days connecting with water filled potholes. To show our appreciation to the Novotels that we stopped at as we travelled through Europe in return for the special rate we were charged and the V.I.P. treatment we received, we made ourselves available for a group picture, whenever time permitted, to include us and the Jimnys, the manager and staff. I liked these mini photo shoots, us old guys being surrounded by pretty young girls, it's a tough job but someone's got to do it!! We were on the road again by 11am, making our way to Auschwitz to pay our respects. The drive wasn't

The entrance to the infamous Second World War Prison Camp at Auschwitz

long and it was quiet, there was none of the usual bantering over the radio, I guess we were a bit apprehensive as to what we would find when we got there. I didn't realise at the time that what I have always referred to as Auschwitz, was in fact three separate camps, Auschwitz 1 and Auschwitz 2 - Birkenau, are close together and located at the town of Oswiecim. Auschwitz 3 is located at Monowitz, six kilometres further away.

As we arrived at the visitor centre there were police everywhere, we were told that we could not go any closer as Auschwitz was closed for a V.I.P. Jewish Memorial Day. There were restricted group tours we could have joined but we really wanted to do our own thing, we saw what we could, it was enough to get some idea of the scale of what went on there. Depressed at what we had seen and disappointed at not having access to the camp itself, we sought comfort in a cup of coffee and discussed what to do with ourselves for the rest of the day. One or two places to visit were mentioned, I kept quiet, I knew what was coming. A while ago, I had mentioned that Zabrze coal mine at the town of Gliwice is open to the public, knowing that it would clash with our visit to Auschwitz and we wouldn't have time to do both, I thought no more of it. The truth is, I'm not too keen on going underground, that's for rabbits and badgers. The thought of going down a mine in a steel cage and having to rely on the man at the top to bring me up again isn't my idea of fun.

I didn't let the guys know that I was a bit scared at the thought of going down the mine; I was hoping that something would happen so that I wouldn't have to go. Unfortunately, what I hoped for didn't happen. I was reminded that I had mentioned the mine at Gliwice, Keith and Roland thought it would be a great idea to go down a mine, I felt sick at the thought of it. For the sake of keeping the guys happy, we headed for Gliwice and the mine arriving a little after 2.00pm. It was a big enough place spread over many acres, a tall structure with a huge wheel on top driving cables that disappeared into a smaller building at its base, attached to this was what looked like a small office with people in it. Keith, Roland and, reluctantly, I entered the office to ask what the procedure was for us to go down the mine, we didn't speak much Polish and they spoke the same amount of English but they understood what we wanted. A spokesman for the group pointed at a clock and said, "Finish today." Adopting my disappointed expression I said, "What a shame I was really looking forward to it." Relieved but still looking disappointed the guys and I started to walk back to the vehicles, as we did a well-dressed man came out of the other smaller building, some sort of manager, and headed straight for us indicating that we should wait, he wanted to speak to us, I was getting that bad feeling again. Keith and Roland, with theatrical tears of disappointment in their eyes, pointed at the vehicles, explaining that we had driven a long way so we could visit the mine but the people in the office said that it was closed. Just my luck, the man, his first name translated into English was Brian, happened to be the manager in charge of organising tours down the mine, I was getting sicker by the minute, I let Roland and Keith talk to Brian while I thought of various excuses I could use for not going down, Roland turned to me and said, "Guess what? He's going to take us on a private tour of the mine," ooh SH-T.

Not wishing to go on record that I was too scared, I followed as they made their way to a building close to the entrance to the lift, a place where you got kitted out ready to go down. We were logged in as six for the descent, four of us including Gary, who had been keeping the camera rolling ever since we arrived at the mine and no doubt captured at some point the look of fear on my face, Brian and the lift operator made up the number. We were issued with hard hats, you know the sort of hat, one size fits all, I adjusted my hat to fit as best I could but it was still too big, if it wasn't for my ears I wouldn't have been able to see at all. Brian said, "Ready, we go," and headed out of the door with Keith and Roland close behind and me following at the rear. I was dreading the whole thing, my stomach contracted, I was sweating, my mouth was dry, my tongue wouldn't work, I couldn't speak properly and to top it all, I thought that I detected a slight movement at my rear end! I could hear the guys calling; I smelt the damp, musty air coming up the shaft as I came to my senses. Standing in front and looking at the yellow painted cage, suspended by what looked like a piece of thick string, everyone was already inside the cage, the lift operator waiting to slide the gate across as soon as I stepped in. I tried to swallow but nothing happened; forcing myself, I stepped forward into the cage, as I did I looked down through the wide gap between the threshold and the cage, the hole going down looked like it went on forever. I never got the chance to make a run for it, the lift operator pulled me into the cage, slid the door closed and operated the descent lever and a bell rang all in one slick movement. Before I knew what happened, we were dropping like a stone, hanging on for grim death, my hat lifted from my head releasing my hair to follow me down, my eyelids and nostrils acted like air scoops, my cheeks were flapping like a flag in a storm and my top lip had rolled up to expose my teeth and it appeared that I was grinning on the way down.

Descending the three hundred metres at around twelve metres a second, I was inwardly screaming, fighting my own battle to control my fear; I glanced at Keith, Roland and Gary, their individual grey faces concealing their inner thoughts. Nobody could speak, the noise was ear splitting, the descent was frightening, the dull light shining from Brian's hat lamp cast shadows that added to the tension the deeper we went. We continued to descend, still clinging on for dear life, unprepared when the cage slowed so violently I gave out a muffle yelp, followed by a reminder from my rear end that it was under pressure and about to run amuck! The remainder of the descent to the coalface was much slower, allowing us to recover from the ordeal, also for me to avoid having to ask Brian if he could loan me a pair of pants. The coalface was pitch black, Brian asked us to wait while he tried to find the light switch, we stood there clinging to each other like four boys frightened of the bogyman, the light flickered on then went off again, some distance away we could hear Brian cursing in Polish then thankfully the light came on. Brian came into view at the end of the tunnel muttering to himself as he walked towards us, he reminded me of the Mad Hatter, you know the rabbit with the top hat in Alice in Wonderland. Brian explained that we must stay together because it is dangerous, there are regular cave-ins, the power fails and the lift can be out of order sometimes for days! It was at that point that I realised we were the victims of a well-rehearsed routine to scare the living daylights out of unsuspecting visitors like me.

Confident that I had seen through the ruse, I got control of myself allowing the tension from being three hundred metres underground to ease. With heads and knees bent to achieve a crouched position, we followed Brian along the five foot (one and a half metre) high tunnel towards the coalface, Keith being over six foot (1.82 metres) struggled to get low enough, resulting in his head making contact with the roof as we shuffled along. When we arrived at the actual coalface I was horrified when I saw the conditions in which the miners had to work and above their heads thousands of tons of coal, rock and earth, supported only by wooden sticks. Brian said that sometimes the wooden shores make a sound like ice cracking before they collapse and cause a cave-in, as though on cue, there was a loud crack, Brian shouted, "Cave-in," then ran along the tunnel; scared stiff, the rest of us ran like hell following Brian, who was laughing his head off as we emerged from the dark into a brightly lit two hundred seat, modern, banqueting facility. The fifty yard dash had left us pale faced and short of breath but relieved that it was a joke and not the real thing. Brian was still laughing when I came up from behind to strangle him, but had second thoughts when I realised that I might need to borrow that pair of trousers after all. The tour lasted about an hour, we saw pretty well everything and experienced what it would be like working down a mine. The ride to the surface was less dramatic, relieved to be breathing fresh air once more, we thanked Brian for looking after us, but I couldn't resist asking him how he managed to get the timber shore holding up the roof to make the cracking sound when it did, he looked at me with a twinkle in his eye and said, "I didn't make it happen!" We just looked at one another. Roland, Keith, Gary and myself really had a great time, it was a real privilege to meet Brian and for him to personally escort us on a V.I.P. tour of the facility, I laid it on a bit when describing my fear of going down holes in the ground, I wasn't happy about doing it, that's for sure, but I'm glad I did, an experience I will never forget.

Reluctantly, we said goodbye to Brian, the mine and the town of Gliwice, then headed back to the Novotel at Katowice for a beer and a shower ready for our meeting and photo session with Max and the Mud Doctors. Max arrived together with another seven or so knobbly and dented Suzuki off-roaders and crew, a great bunch of guys, we spent a long time talking to them, they took turns to have their picture taken sitting in the Jimnys and asked a lot of technical questions about the vehicles and our journey around the world. It was a pleasure to meet the young Mud Doctors and so refreshing to come across such enthusiasm and support for what we were doing. After an hour I indicated to Max that I had one or two things to attend to, I thanked everyone for coming and meeting with us and we said our goodbyes, they left only after they had lined up to drive off, doing a circuit of the car park, horns sounding, engines revving and waving as they left. Tired, we had forgotten that we were in our seventies, it had been a long day, we were knackered and ready for bed.

Tuesday 9th April, day 10, I was up early, expecting a phone call from Julian Clegg at Radio Solent for my once weekly live slot to let the people at home know that we were still breathing. During our short stay at the Novotel Katowice the hospitality afforded to us by George the General Manager and his staff was exemplary, they couldn't do enough for us. The night before we left, George phoned the Mercure Novotel Bratislava, to tell them we were coming and to take good care of us. I was a bit sad when we said goodbye to George and the staff, nice people but time to move on. Our drive to Bratislava, Slovakia, was about 225 miles, having time to spare we decided to revisit Auschwitz once more, last time we were disappointed, but hoped this time we would have better luck. Arriving mid-morning, we were shocked, it was mayhem, and there were hordes of people everywhere, plus bus loads trying to park and hundreds queuing at the ticket office. Disheartened at seeing the chaos, we were also disappointed that we wouldn't have the opportunity to pay our respects to the people who suffered at these camps. I was, however, heartened when surveying the crowds of people, I noticed that the majority seemed to be children of all ages, girls and boys, excited, noisy and jolly as they waited in long lines to collect their tickets, I wondered how jolly they would be when they emerge after the tour, it's tough on the kids, but they need to know what went on in that place if they are going to prevent it happening in the future.

It took a while to get clear of the build-up of traffic around Auschwitz and to exit the town of Oswiecim on our way to Bratislava, once more disappointed at not being able to do a tour of Auschwitz, perhaps another time, the sun was shining and we were heading south once more, crossing into the Czech Republic at the town of Cieszyn, then after another twenty miles or so we crossed the border into Slovakia then on to Bratislava. The route took us along secondary narrow roads, mainly through forests and open country, the road surface resembled an endless slab of Swiss cheese, they hadn't got around to repairing the roads after the winter snow, there were potholes everywhere, causing the traffic to move slower. As a result, our arrival at Bratislava was later than anticipated. We located and checked into the Mercure Novotel at the city of Bratislava at 5.30pm, Gary travelled with me in 02 when not filming, as well as sharing a hotel room during overnight stops, this arrangement was fine with me as it gave me an opportunity each evening to keep an eye on the camera equipment and make sure that the batteries, and everything else that needed charging, would be charged.

Over the last few days it was noticeable that when not filming, Gary kept himself to himself, he didn't say much to me, Roland or Keith, his face seemed to have taken on a vacant, blank, wide eyed look. I asked Gary a number of times if he was alright, he would say yes but nothing more, I was beginning to wonder if an exchange of words we'd had was the cause of the problem. Reflecting on what had happened on that occasion, I don't exactly remember what I said and I didn't make a note of it at the time either, because I didn't think I needed to. At a guess it was the day after our drive around the Nurburgring, Gary filmed the drive around the ring from the passenger seat of 02, and I think he did O.K., but he still seemed upset, possibly as a result of the conversation I had with him about him leaving the camera bag behind at Brussels. There hadn't been much conversation between us as I drove; I tried to think of topics that might interest him so as to get us talking, sometimes it worked other times it didn't, perhaps it's me, maybe I had got it wrong but it seemed to me that what interested him wouldn't necessarily interest me. Gary, I guess, was about fifty but the topics that interested him, and he would talk about, didn't relate to his age. We spoke about the graphics on the cars and the crew's T shirt design, then, for the want of something to talk about I remembered seeing some block head in Southampton, wearing a black T shirt with serious anti-

German slogans on the front and something even more obscene on the back. The man must have had a blank space where his brain should have been, however, I mentioned to Gary that I had seen the T shirt and I felt that people shouldn't be allowed in public displaying obscenities on T shirts, not only is it in bad taste and offensive to people, children as young as four can read. I waited for Gary to say something, to continue the dialogue but nothing was forthcoming, we sat in silence as I continued to drive, eventually Gary turned to me and said, "I can wear a T shirt with whatever I want on it," "Yes you can," I replied, "all I am saying is that there should be some self-imposed guidelines that T shirt printers should work to, to prevent the bad prints getting on the streets." I guess I must have pressed the red button, he became verbally over-heated about T shirts, becoming slightly unhinged and saying other things unrelated that were leading in a direction I didn't want to go. I politely had to say, "Look Gary, can I stop you there? I don't want to go down that route," he stopped speaking, gave me a strange look, and never said another word until we arrived at Bratislava. We were at the hotel reception; dealing with formalities I asked Gary if we had all the equipment but he didn't answer. Keith and Roland decided, as there was time, they would walk in to the city and have a look around, "O.K." I said, "we will see you in the bar later," then Gary and l went to our room. Gary still hadn't said much and his facial expression I thought had worsened, we entered the room, Gary put the bags down and got into bed fully clothed, boots and all. I didn't know what to make of the situation, I sorted the equipment out and put the batteries on charge, updated my diary and showered ready to meet the guys. I sat on my bed for a while looking at Gary, I had a bad feeling as I thought about what I would do if Gary was to quit and wanted to go home. I cursed myself for allowing the situation to develop then reflected on the day we first met. Gary joined us at the last minute and I first met him face to face the day before departure day, as we chatted he answered all my questions particularly the one where I said something like, "Everything seems O.K. but is there anything else I should know?" "Not that I can think of," he said.

David, the MD at Viewpoint Productions, who would be producing the film, also Keith Rimmer, a friend and top class professional photographer who also happens to be the project website manager, they are both experts in their own field and, at my request, interviewed Gary over the phone and confirmed to me that he could do the job. Under the circumstances there wasn't much more I could have done. Whatever the outcome, I was stuck with the situation so I would take it one day at a time. Recalling once again my first meeting with Gary, I remembered our discussion about the equipment, he knew his way around our camera and kit that went with it, so I guess it helped to convince me he was the man for the job and didn't enquire further, on reflection the question I should have asked was, "Can you tell me what work you have done over the last two years?" I had sat on the edge of my bed long enough thinking and it was getting dark, I made my mind up that when an opportunity presented itself I would try to get Gary to open up so that we could get talking and maybe ask some questions. Gary was sound asleep, he must eat I thought so I woke him to say I'm going to dinner, he opened his eyes, "You must eat," I repeated, as far as I can recall, he rolled over and went back to sleep. Earlier, Keith and Roland, during their stroll around the town had come across a traditional Slovakian restaurant that they planned to revisit later for our evening meal. I met the guys at the hotel bar, I mentioned that Gary seemed a bit odd and to be truthful, I can't remember whether Gary joined us or not for a meal that evening. Anyway, it was time to eat, Roland, clutching a piece of paper with the name and address of the restaurant, organised a taxi, showed the address to the driver, we piled in and away we went. The taxi had been flowing with the traffic for about five minutes when Roland said, "I think we are going the wrong way," he turned to the driver and said, "This is not the way," the driver didn't respond and kept driving, becoming alarmed, we told the driver to stop the car, once again he didn't respond but turned to say that the restaurant we wanted to go to was no good and he was taking us to a better one. Roland was hopping mad when the taxi finally stopped and the driver said this is good, Roland would have none of it and demanded that the taxi driver take us to where we originally wanted to go, we finally arrived, Roland gave the driver what he thought the fare should have been in the first place then we walked away, the driver shouting something like, "Tight arse English man".

Wednesday 10th April, day 11, awake in my bed in the hotel and relieved that I had got back O.K. after the fracas with the taxi driver, Gary wasn't in his bed. I remembered that I had a discussion the night before with Keith and Roland and decided that as we were ahead of schedule and that Bratislava train station was just around the corner, we would travel by train to Vienna and do some sightseeing. When I went down, Roland, Keith and Gary were tucking into a healthy breakfast that individually would feed a family of four. Relaxed at the thought of having a day of R&R we made our way to the station and the hour train journey to Vienna. It was my first visit to Vienna, I was immediately impressed by the lack of modern unsightly glass office blocks, the city seemed to glow with old world charm, old buildings, statues, churches, St Stephen's Cathedral, opera and music at every corner. We had our lunch at an open air restaurant, the sun was shining, faint music in the background. After our meal and a beer to wash it down, we reviewed our programme and itinerary for the next few days. Gary had got his act together that day; he seemed to be a different person from the day before and was blending in with the rest of us as part of the team. Our visit to Vienna was well worth the effort, but by the end of the day we were all so tired, we decided to spend the rest of the evening at the hotel resting ready for an early start in the morning to Budapest, Hungary.

Thursday 11th April, day 12, the journey from Bratislava, Slovakia to Budapest, Hungary we estimated would be about a four hour journey. There was no urgency to get to our destination so we ambled along, dodging potholes and taking in the scenery, it was a bright sunny day and an opportunity to have a talk to Gary. I had driven for about an hour, during that time I had tried to start a conversation, about nothing in particular, you know just to get us talking, but he didn't respond, he sat in the passenger seat looking out of the window with a blank look on his face. We arrived at the Hungarian un-manned border crossing knowing that I needed to purchase a transit ticket, vignette or some sort of toll charge if you like for each of the vehicles. There was no facility to pay at the crossing, bewildered as to what to do I entered a building set back from the road and found out that tickets are available at a roadside café two hundred metres back the way we had come. I purchased two tickets at a cost of 10 Euros each, valid for four weeks. After a coffee and sandwich we were on our way again. Gary still sat in silence, at this point I'd had enough, I turned to face him and said, "Are you going to sit there all day and say nothing?" Pausing for a moment or two he then turned to me and said, "You told me that you didn't want to talk to me," I thought for a moment, what the hell is he talking about? Then realised he was referring to our discussion about the T shirts. I replied, "What I said was that I didn't want to continue the discussion because it's not something I wanted to talk about," "I can say what I want to," he replied, "I know you can," I continued, "but some of what you were saying was sick and disgusting. I have heard it all before, I'm sorry, I don't need it at my time of life, look," I said, "we have to talk so why don't you tell me about how you got into the film industry and what work you have done?" at that point Gary seemed to change once more, he became pleasant to listen to, the blank look on his face had gone. I listened intently to what Gary had to say, way back he had attended a college course that focused on filming and camera work, he worked for various companies over the years, as far as I understood for one reason or another the jobs didn't last, the time up to when he joined our little group he had been in and out of work through ill-health, he had tried his hand at forklift driving, training as a chef, eight months prior to joining us he hadn't worked at all. It was my turn to sit in silence; I thought to myself oh bloody hell! Coming to my senses, I said tactfully, "Gary, when we met for the first time, I said to you is there anything I should know about, you said no. You should have mentioned it, what was the reason you were off work for such a long time?" I asked, "I had problems with depression but I am O.K. now," I sighed with disbelief. Not knowing what else to say, I drove in silence for a while thinking about how to deal with the situation, also whether my decision to ask Gary to stay with me for stage two was now viable. As I drove, I considered the options available to me and concluded that I needed Gary to help if he would and now was as good a time as any to ask. "Gary," I said, "I have a problem, can you help? I have to drive both vehicles to Warszawa by Sunday 21st April ready to meet Mariusz, my Polish friend, he will drive 03, I will drive 02, we have to be at Novosibirsk in Russia to meet Graham and Mike on the 9th of May, our arrangement is still the same except you will fly home from Warszawa and not Budapest." To be fair to Gary it didn't take him long to say he would help. We arrived at the Novotel Danube around 4.00pm, the manager came out to meet us, he spoke excellent English, he had managed Novotels at Dublin and Portsmouth, he was an ardent Portsmouth football supporter, mention anything to him about football and he goes into his routine, "Pompee, Pompee, Pompee," a great guy. He had previously motivated his staff to expect our arrival so they were ready and waiting when we arrived, they really treated us as something special.

Stage one, a thirteen day, 2648 mile journey through Europe almost completed, we were able, over a beer, to reflect on what we had achieved, when you consider the itinerary was put together by me mainly during the long winter evenings at home in my little office, we didn't do too badly. I started the journey hoping that I had got it right, my concern as to the safety and wellbeing of those who travelled with me was always on my mind. Looking back, I needn't have worried so much, Roland and Keith turned out to be the best travelling companions I could have travelled with, they shared responsibility and were a laugh a minute. I developed a bit of a habit, of which they never missed an opportunity to remind me of, and that was, whenever I was being filmed or included in a photoshoot, I would find a mirror, comb my hair and take my glasses off, they thought it was hilarious, well I had to look my best for the camera! I already knew that Roland and Keith's wives Jill and Chris were arriving that afternoon, so when released from their commitment to stage one the following day, the guys and their wives would become tourists and stay at Budapest for a short holiday. What I didn't know and was pleasantly surprised to hear was that Vi, at short notice, had decided to join them and myself for a few days break before I started stage two of the journey.

Friday 12th April, day 13, refreshed, we met for breakfast early, we needed to be on the road to complete the seventy mile drive to the Suzuki European car manufacturing facility at Esztergom, Magyar, not far from Budapest. The arrangement was that we would be there at 10am to meet Victoria Ruska, P.R.

Manager of Suzuki Europe, who had organised a photoshoot that included shaking hands with the Managing Director and his team, they all took turns to sit in the cars to have their picture taken at the wheel, we were then taken on a tour of the factory. When the time came to leave, we were presented with an assortment of children's toys which we would present on behalf of Suzuki to the children at the orphanage I had arranged to visit when we arrive at Samara in Russia. Once again, we said our goodbyes and made our way back to Budapest and a few days' rest. Later that afternoon, the wives arrived, I spent the rest of the day catching up with family news and telling Vi how successful I thought stage one was. Although I had mentioned it before during our phone conversations over the past days, I raised my concern about what had happened between Gary and myself, he seemed to be alright at the moment, but his mood swings worried me. That evening, we were to meet for a meal at the hotel. Gary had a room of his own and slept most of the afternoon, he knew what the arrangements were for the evening so when he didn't join us at the bar for a drink before we sat down, I called his room to find out where he was, as I was doing so he emerged from the lift looking terrible, he had that look again, a chalky-white blank look on his face, wide red-rimmed eyes, mouth open and tongue partly protruding. Clearly there was something not quite right and I had to deal with it urgently. I said to Gary about joining us, he said he wasn't up to it, I introduced him to the ladies, he was polite and chatted for a moment then offered his apologies for not joining us and left. We just sat there wondering what to make of it all. I broke the silence by saying, "He seems to be getting worse, he gets mood swings, one minute he's up together, the next minute he looks and acts like someone who is ill and needs help." If Gary was O.K. in the morning, I would talk to him and try to find out what the problem was before we went any further.

Saturday 13th April, day 14, we all met for breakfast, refreshed and relieved knowing that we were having a few days rest before the start of stage two. Roland and Jill and Keith and Chris were keen to explore Budapest, I wanted to have a chat with Gary so Vi and I did our own thing later. The guys left to do their walkabout and I asked Gary if we could have a chat and moved to a quiet part of the lounge, ordered coffee then I asked Gary if I could say what was on my mind first, Vi joined us and sat listening to what was being said. I spoke at length referring to the situation I was now in, the incidents that had occurred from the time when the camera bag was left behind at Brussels, the erratic behaviour, the fact that he didn't tell me that he hadn't worked for some time before he joined our venture, the mood swings, also I had to ask the questions rather than him volunteering the information, I wanted to know now what the problem was. I then went on to ask if he was ill or suffering from anything. Gary didn't respond straight away, his eyes glazed over, I felt bad having to ask these questions, Gary was clearly distressed, unable to respond, Vi broke the silence sympathetically asking Gary if he was taking any medication he said, "Yes." Vi continued, "What is the medication for?" Gary replied, "To control bouts of depression," for heaven's sake, or words to that effect, I said to myself, wanting to bang my head on the nearest wall. I had to get up and walk over to the window and the panoramic view of the Danube, I stood there but my eyes saw nothing. I returned to where Gary and Vi were sitting. "It appears," Vi said, "when Gary left Southampton he only had a small amount of medication so for the last week or so he has been stretching it out to make it last, the dosage being so low it has had no effect." "If that's what's causing the problem," I said, "let's go and buy some more pills." Gary, pleased that he was soon to get some medication, perked up a bit, the three of us were soon pacing it out along the Danube to cross at the first bridge to the old city shopping area and a chemist shop for the supply of the magic pills.

We located the chemist we had been directed to, who we thought would be able to help but were told that what we wanted was only available by prescription from a doctor, one step forward, one back. We tried two other chemists but the answer was the same, what do we do now? We made our way back to the hotel wondering what to do next when I had a thought, perhaps the hotel manager could help. It was about 4.00pm when we spoke to the hotel manager and explained the situation, "No problem," he said, "I will phone the hotel doctor to ask if he will come and examine Gary and provide a prescription." The doctor arrived within an hour, spending some time with Gary, then relieving me of 80 Euros and issuing a prescription for enough medication to last the next three weeks. Too knackered to do any more that day, we decided to collect the pills the next morning when we were to have a walk around the old town. We sat in the lounge chatting to await the return of the guys from their walkabout. They arrived back a short while after and joined us at the bar, eager to tell us where they had been and what they had seen. By that time, Gary had gone to his room, so when asked what sort of day we'd had, all I could say was, "Not much sightseeing but it looks like we are getting Gary back on track, with luck we will collect a supply of Gary's medication in the morning," saving the details of the day's events for another time. That evening I wanted to be on my own for a while, I needed time to think before we were going out for dinner later. I went to the hotel lounge early, got a beer and found a quiet corner with a stunning view of the Danube and part of the city by night. I just sat there mulling over in my mind what had happened over the past thirteen days, what we had achieved, the leisurely drive through Europe, the itinerary worked out O.K., the comradery and jolly good nature of my travelling companions and the unexpected meeting with Vi, and even sorting Gary out didn't seem a problem anymore, it seemed too easy, what concerned me more was the uncertainty of what lay ahead.

Sunday 14th & Monday 15th April, day 15-16, kitted out to look like tourists, we embarked on a walking tour of the city, calling at the chemist shop en route to collect Gary's pills and at the same time being relieved of another 40 Euros. I lost count of the number of bridges we crossed and re-crossed, the undercover market, the tea we drank at the pre-war ornate tea rooms with violin music in the background; they really have to be seen to be believed. On a sad note, Hungary and Budapest in particular was severely mauled during the last war.

The Hungarian people suffered badly, like most of Europe. Evidence of the conflict is all around you as you make your way through the city, I guess they leave it that way to remind people what happened. I am not a religious person but I wanted to visit and pay my respects at the Jewish memorial, and one or two other memorials dedicated to those who lost their lives at that time. I particularly wanted to visit the memorial site at the edge of the Danube River, located close to the Academy of Science. People, mostly Jews, were lined up along the river bank and shot by members of the arrow cross militia, their bodies were then dumped into the river, their crime being of a different religion. In the past when I have visited a country or place that at some time in its past had been the location of human suffering I would try and make the time to see and understand what happened and pay my respects to those who suffered. On one occasion after visiting a famous battle site, I told a friend about it he said, "I have been to that place but there's nothing there," I tried to explain that of course there's nothing there, the battle took place two thousand or more years ago, I went there to stand on the spot where it took place, to imagine what it was like facing an enemy, close hand to hand fighting, so close, you can smell their breath and sweat as he tries to end your life with a sword or axe, it terrifies me just to think of it. I have no doubt by now that you have realised history interests me, so I tend to get carried away on

Bronze casts of shoes are a memorial to Jewish people executed on the bank of the Danube

occasion. We did what tourists do during the two days, I made an extra effort to be close to Vi, not missing an opportunity to give her a cuddle whenever I could and a bit extra if I could get away with it, I knew our parting the following day would be painful and heart wrenching. If it all went according to plan we wouldn't see each other for the next four months and fourteen days, when you consider the longest time we have been apart since we first met fifty six years ago, is three weeks, this parting was to be a trial of strength for both of us. At the hotel, I had an opportunity to have another talk with Gary, he looked visually better, I asked how he felt, "Much better," he said, I also asked if he was still O.K. to drive with me to Warszawa, "Yes," he said. I thought for a moment, then said to Gary, "What are you doing after you arrive home? I mean do you have any work lined up?" "No," he said, I thought for another moment then I said, "If you are going home to sit in an armchair and watch television not earning any money, why not stay with me as cameraman for stage two which finishes at Novosibirsk on Thursday 9th May, then fly home from there?" Gary thought about it for a minute or two then said "If it's alright with my wife, I will stay," he went to his room to phone his wife, returning a short while after to confirm that everything was O.K. for him to stay. The next problem was to arrange, at very short notice, Gary's visas for Ukraine, Kazakhstan and Russia. I phoned my visas agent Tayfun Dirik at Scott's Travel Management, London and explained the situation, also what I required and that it had to be sent to me to arrive at our address at Warszawa no later than Monday 22nd, we discussed the problem at length and the options available to us, the outcome from our discussion was that Gary's passport was with him in Poland and there was not enough time to send it to London so Gary would be provided with a new passport including visas. The general information required for the new passport including passport photos and visas was provided by email, everything was in place and was handled on a high priority basis, it wasn't cheap but the service was excellent, I knew the new passport containing the visas would arrive as promised.

Tuesday 16th April, day 17, the previous evening was a sort of a farewell get together, a jolly affair but behind the happy go lucky show I put on for Vi's benefit, I was deeply worried that she would be on her own for such a long time. The day had come for Gary and I to leave; I awoke early, made tea for both of us and opened the window to a blue sky and a bright sun that reflected from the water of the Danube into our room. Vi and I laid awake talking about things in general, Vi cried when she said, "What will I do if you don't come back?"

It started to get to me at that point, I had to take a deep breath and hold back my emotions before I could say, "Don't be silly, of course I'm coming back," my mind drifting for a moment, reflecting on the thousands of miles and all the countries ahead of me. I pulled myself together then said to Vi "There's no turning back now, we both have to be strong when the time comes."

By the time Vi was ready for breakfast, I had packed my personal things and equipment I kept in the room for safety, carried it with me and placed it into 02 before going into breakfast. We all arrived together and tucked into our breakfasts. Gary, Roland, Keith and I ate more than we should have, I guess most men are on the seafood diet, you know the one, see food and eat it. So far that morning there had been no comment about me getting lost or 'don't forget to comb my hair and to remove my glasses when I pose for the camera', as though on cue Roland was laughing his head off saying. "Try not to get lost and don't forget the comb and glasses," "Bast—d," I said, and then added, "seriously though I'm going to miss you guys."

It was getting near 12 o'clock, the time I had planned to leave, 02 and 03 had been checked and refuelled days ago so a walk around was all that was needed, I made sure that our destination Nyiregyhaza, a 147 mile journey, was entered into both TomToms and pencilled in on the road maps as back up, we tested for the umpteenth time the Motorolo handheld radios to make sure that they were working, everything checked out so we were ready to leave. The hotel manager and most of his staff, also a number of guests from the hotel, Roland, Keith, their wives, and of course my dear, lovely, long-suffering Vi were waving and cheering, I waved back, turned to Vi to give her a smacker of a kiss, she had tears running down her cheeks, I gave her one last squeeze and another long kiss, turned, got into 02 and drove away. As I left, I glanced at the rear view mirror to make sure that Gary was close behind me and saw Vi being comforted by Jill and Chris, I felt sick seeing Vi so unhappy and suffering, I knew she would be looked after for the remainder of her stay at Budapest and the journey home, but how would she feel when opening the door and stepping into an empty house.

Apart from family and friends visiting occasionally she would be on her own for a long time, but I was in it up to my neck now and determined to see it through to the end. I spoke to Gary as we made our way through the city heading in the direction of Nyiregyhaza, our first overnight stop. Gary seemed cheerful and talkative, I had previously reminded him to stay as close to me as safety would allow as we drove through the city, if for some reason we were separated, I was to stop and keep him in visual contact, if we lost sight of one another and out of contact by radio we were to park the vehicles and walk back to where we lost contact, and try to make contact by mobile phone. I needn't have concerned myself, Gary was there whenever I looked to check. We arrived at our destination late afternoon, found suitable accommodation and settled down for the evening. Over a meal, I ran through our schedule for the next few days, having already roughly outlined what I was proposing the day before but I now had an opportunity to clarify the details. I continued by saying, "The following morning, Wednesday 17th, we will travel two hundred and sixty two miles to the Corona hotel, our overnight stop at Tyskie, a small town close to Auschwitz and Birkenau."

Thursday 18th April, day 19, I was awake early, ready to receive the scheduled once weekly phone call from Julian Clegg B.B.C. Radio Solent, the folks at home like to follow our progress. I said to Gary, "Before we leave for Warszawa, we will visit Auschwitz once again, if it's not too busy this time, we will join an organised tour, take pictures and film as much as we need, then during the afternoon continue to the Holiday Inn close to the airport at Warszawa. We will remain at Warszawa awaiting your passport, due to arrive on Monday 22nd, Mariusz, my Polish friend who will be joining us for stage two, plans to arrive at 2 o'clock Tuesday 23rd, if it happens as I have indicated, we will be on our way sometime after 2 o'clock Tuesday to Chelm, then cross the border into Ukraine the following morning." I followed that by saying, "Did you understand all that?" He said, "Yes, most of it," "O.K."

I replied, "if you are not sure about anything, please ask me."

Surprisingly, what I had planned to do over those next few days we actually achieved, the radio interview with Julian Clegg was O.K., there weren't as many people queuing at Auschwitz, so third time lucky, we tagged onto an English speaking group of people with a tour guide so we saw and heard for ourselves what went on at that terrible place. I couldn't help shedding a tear when I saw what systematic pain and suffering had been inflicted on those poor people. Gary managed to film what he wanted, avoiding some sensitive areas. Feeling a bit subdued at the end of the tour, we continued our journey to Warszawa and the Holiday Inn at the airport. We were able to spend a day or so sightseeing in and around Warszawa, Gary's new passport arrived as promised and Mariusz stepped off of a bus that had stopped opposite the Holiday Inn at two o'clock on Tuesday 23rd, exactly at the time he said he would be there. To say I was pleased that it had all come together as I had hoped would be an understatement. After welcoming Mariusz, I then said we were already to go, but being a professional, he insisted that he have a look around and check things for himself, after the inspection we discussed the route we were to take, the distance, and time of arrival. At about 2.30pm that afternoon, we fired up the little Jimnys and started phase two of our journey, a one hundred and forty mile, pothole riddled, four hour drive to Chelm, our overnight stop and border crossing into the Ukraine. Up to a few weeks before departure date, I had no crew, the people who had earlier indicated that they would like to take part notified me at short notice that for one reason or another they were no longer available for stage two, so I was desperate and prepared to do whatever it would take to get the two vehicles from Budapest to Novosibirsk, Russia before Thursday 9th May ready for the arrival of Graham Higgins and Mike Bailey who were to join me for stage three. At the last minute and with gratified relief I got an email from Mariusz who

Les waits for Mariusz in Warszawa and for Stage 2 to begin.

I had been corresponding with to say he had been able to reschedule and was now available to join us, boy was I relieved, not only is he a nice guy, he speaks a little Russian and has a lot of experience, very helpful at border crossings. Later that day, we arrived at Chelm and were soon directed to clean and moderately priced accommodation, over a beer we discussed our plan for the next day, Mariusz said he had crossed at this border crossing previously then went on to say, "The actual crossing is only a short distance from the town but before we get there we will encounter long queues of trucks and cars and large numbers of people milling about," continuing, he said, "we will ignore the queues and drive directly to the gates of the crossing, when we get there I will talk to the guards, hopefully it will take an hour to cross, but we could be there all day." Wondering what awaited us in the morning, we ate our last meal in Poland and went to bed early.

Wednesday 24th April, day 25, we finished our breakfast and were on the road once more by 7.30am, the border crossing didn't

Les, Guy and Alun meeting at Newmans Suzuki showroom, Southampton discussing and approving Les' proposals.

Alun Parry, Head of Press and PR Automotive Division Suzuki GB, to the right of Les, and Guy Foster Managing Director, Newmans Suzuki Southampton handing over the vehicles to Les.

O2 and O3 high up at Tes Garage, Lymington, the mechanics fitting the kit Les had purchased previously, larger wheel rims and tyres, high lift shock absorbers and springs, and armoured brake fluid pipes.

Les and Robert Rickman, Managing Director of Precise Sheet Metal Engineering, Christchurch, Les and Robert fitting steel bumpers, front bull bar, rear steel bumper and spare wheel gate, aluminium top tray and engine sump guard.

Graham, Glyn and Les, a tea break during checking and final loading of the equipment into O2 and O3.

Les and Graham at Newmans Southampton receiving instruction from the workshop manager relating to daily and weekly vehicle checks and what inspections we need to make in the event of an accident.

Roger Winkworth, Glyn Maher, Mike Bailey, Alan Butler, Keith Twyford, Roland Spencer, Les and Gary Scott, our cameraman, having their picture taken before the start.

The press, TV and radio were there to see us off.

Les giving wife Vi and daughter Carole a last hug before leaving.

Julian Clegg, BBC South presenter flagging the guys off on their journey around the world.

Inside the cathedral at Trier, reputed to be the oldest town in Germany.

w Gdańsku

↓

BIURO
LECHA
WAŁĘSY

*Les, Roland and Keith at the
entrance to Lech Walesa's office.*

Inside Auschwitz, flowers at the wall of remembrance.

A group picture taken at Lech Walesa's office after our meeting and receiving a signed copy of his book. Lech Walesa flanked by Les, Keith and Roland, Gary and our interpreter behind.

The guys at rest during a brief visit to Vienna, on our way to Budapest.

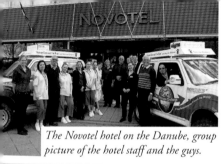

The Novotel hotel on the Danube, group picture of the hotel staff and the guys.

Overlooking the Danube, Budapest.

Volgograd, previously known as Stalingrad, a church erected on the site of the bloodiest battle of WW2.

The memorial site known as hill 102, an 83 metre high statue of a young woman wielding a sword representing mother Russia.

A sad occasion, a visit to a local children's orphanage supported by Suzuki Sumara, all the toys in the world is no substitute for a Mum and Dad. We all shed a tear that day.

open until 9 o'clock but we wanted to get as close to the gates as we could ready for when they opened. We soon encountered the end of the queue that seemed to go on forever as we made our way to the crossing, engines running, smoke and exhaust gases blowing the dust from the unsurfaced dirt road creating a purple coloured haze that instinctively made you reach for a handkerchief to cover your nose and mouth. The air cleared as we approached the gates, we weren't to be first but we would be included in the first batch when the gates opened. We sat in the cars while the time passed, our two sparkling, brightly coloured blue and white Jimnys surrounded by smoking overloaded lorries and old clapped out cars would have made a great picture, but the stern faced border guards on the other side of the gates were watching us closely for any excuse to confiscate our cameras. At 9 o'clock, one gate opened, Mariusz walked to the front and spoke to one of the guards who then marched to an office, returning moments later with someone more senior, orders were given and the two gates in front of us opened. There was some shouting at the drivers of the cars in front to let us through, feeling a bit big headed, thinking we would be getting the V.I.P. treatment, we were ushered through the gates that made a loud metal to metal bang as they closed together once we had passed through. We had entered the Polish side of the crossing and were directed to park at a waiting area, leave the vehicles and take our documents to the customs office, once inside we passed through immigration, customs and police who checked the vehicles' insurance and our driver's licences. All the hours I had worked during the preparation prior to start date, to make sure that all our paperwork was in order had paid off, you needed to have available the original of each document relating to each vehicle including vehicle registration paper and purchase invoice showing V.A.T. paid, plus driver's licence and passport, plus six colour copies of each. Our car insurance cover ended at the Polish border; I had

The next stage of the journey: to Ukraine

planned to purchase insurance once we crossed the border. I was first to complete the paperwork then was requested by a smiling English speaking guard to wait outside by the vehicles. I went outside to wait, surprised at being the only vehicles in what I would call no-man's land, the short stretch of road between Poland at one end and Ukraine at the other. While I waited for the guys to join me, I looked along the road to the Ukraine border, a group of pan faced guards sporting oversized, round-rimed hats, some rims bigger than others, waiting for their turn to give us a going over, it was an uneasy feeling waiting to cross into a country not long freed from communism, I couldn't help recalling one of the old spy films, I imagined Michael Caine supported by K.G.B. heavies being dragged towards me out of the mist and rain, as part of some exchange deal. Mariusz and Gary joined me a few minutes later then we drove the hundred metres or so to the Ukraine side of the crossing, the procedure was repeated but a problem occurred at customs over the ownership of the vehicles, both vehicles were registered in my name; as I understand it, foreigners were not allowed to own more than one vehicle, so I had to sign a declaration stating that I entered Ukraine with two vehicles and when we cross the border at Luhansk into Russia, it would be stamped by the Ukraine customs to say that I left the country with two vehicles. It was about an hour before we were released on to the Ukrainian roads, I barely had time to get into top gear when we passed a rundown wooden shed on our left, Mariusz called me over the radio to say that the shack we passed was the car insurance office, we stopped and decided that now was as good

Crossing the border from Poland into Ukraine

a time as any, we turned and made our way back to the rundown but brightly decorated shed and parked.

It was hard to believe that this ten by six foot rundown garden shed was an insurance office, I peered through the lace-curtained, recycled glassed window, slotted into a hole cut out with a chain saw, roughly positioned in the centre of the side facing the road, two pleasant looking round-faced smiling ladies traditionally dressed, head scarf tied under the chin, full length flower pattern apron, black thick stockings and boots, beckoned us to enter. Realising that space was limited, Mariusz and I entered what looked like a miniature bordello, not that I know what a bordello is (that's for the benefit of my wife!). Mariusz spoke to the lady sitting behind a desk, followed by a few minutes of form filling, then the ladies, still smiling, relieved me of a 90 dollar fee for each vehicle for insurance for a four week period. Mariusz must have mentioned where we were going and what we were doing, because once we had completed the business side of things, the ladies produced their cameras, off came the scarfs and aprons, a recoating of makeup and hair check, a quick dusting of their boots then they strutted outside like two fading supermodels, well not quite. We went along with the model charade for a few minutes, making them feel good, taking pictures of them sitting in the cars, and other pictures they wanted, it only took a few minutes of our time but it meant a lot to those two ladies that we spent it with them. Legally insured and on our way again, it was a little after ten thirty and another sunny day, the plan was to push hard to reach Kyiv, the capital, by about 8 o'clock that night, a 324 mile, 10 hour journey, it would be a long day.

Once clear of the border town and driving east along the M07 motorway, things seemed to settle down, it felt like we had entered a sort of period of calm, the traffic was light, cruising long distances before an intersection change allowed us to maintain our 55 mph cruising speed to our destination. Both Jimnys were running sweet, confidence in my decision to use the Suzuki Jimny was becoming stronger the further we travelled, content to sit in 02 hour after hour, the rhythmical sound of the little engine working quietly in the background allowing me to think clearly about anything that came into my head. I hadn't thought about it up until now, but sitting comfortably in my ample-spaced well-cushioned seat, I found myself thinking about the amount of time I would spend in 02 driving on my own. I reminded myself of the decision I made at the very beginning that I would drive a Suzuki Jimny myself around the world, no shared driving; nobody else would get their hands on the steering wheel of my car. Although I realised that the passenger seat would be occupied at times by a cameraman or another passenger, no one would ever get their bum on the driving seat of 02. Prior to departure day, one or two of the guys did indicate that they should also drive 02, mostly I didn't take any notice but if I had to reply to the suggestion I would be quite firm with whoever it was and say, "Not a chance, don't even ask," whoever it was usually got the message. Concentrating once more on my driving, checking that 03 was behind me, then using the radio to contact Mariusz, I asked if everything was O.K. "Yes," he said, then continued, "when are we stopping?" "In about an hour, we can rest, eat and refuel at the same time," I replied. I thought for a moment, feeling a bit uneasy about dumping Gary on to him when we left Warszawa, he said he didn't mind but I still didn't feel right not telling him about Gary's depression problem, I made a mental note to mention it at the next opportunity. We made a turn onto a secondary road and soon came across a serious road accident, two lorries collided with one another, the lorry cabs were smashed beyond recognition, as the traffic crawled past the unforgettable scene, the police and ambulance people were in the process of extracting what was left of the drivers.

It was a sombre reminder of what can happen, I didn't have anyone with me in the cab that I could talk to about what we had just seen, falling asleep while driving became a serious problem for me both mentally and physically as the distance we drove increased. I guess it's the penalty I paid for not sharing the driving. I estimated at the time that it would take forty three days, including rest time, to cover the distance from Warszawa to Vladivostok, Russia, arriving Tuesday 28th May, day 59, during that time I would be sitting alone in the cab of 02, driving distances of anything up to 450 miles and 10 hours driving time in a day. During my working life I often drove five or six hundred miles including visiting ten customers all in a day, but I was younger then, I also had twice as much energy. Thinking about it as I drove that day, I told myself that come what may I could not stop if I was tired, to do so would mean that 03 would also have to stop, any time lost may result in not arriving at our destination as planned, time lost one day would have to be made up the next day, if not the problem gets complicated. Somehow I would have to stay awake.

As we motored on through the Ukrainian countryside we couldn't help to notice that the terrain to the north was pretty flat, no hills, just gentle rises and shallow dips, to the south west was the Carpathian Mountains rising to around fifteen hundred metres, but generally Ukraine is a flat country with lush green vegetation and large forests. On either side of the road were farms, the buildings gaily decorated forming a colourful picture with the wheat fields as a backdrop, the picturesque villages with golden domed churches that were never out of view, the occasional glimpse of women in traditional dress and men riding on horse-drawn carts created interest as we passed. We needed to refuel so we stopped at a modern European looking motorway service area, the sort of thing you would see anywhere throughout Europe. Come to think of it, the motorways, road signs and bridges all looked European, Ukraine being a relatively poor country and at that time wasn't part of the European Union, how could they finance the construction of all these new motorways, another question I would like to ask the faceless ones at Brussels given half a chance. Fed and fuelled, we were on the road again, Mariusz and Gary seemed O.K., Gary filming whenever an opportunity presented itself, Mariusz elected to drive 03 all the time, the afternoon was uneventful apart from the noticeable increase in heavy goods traffic the closer we got to Kyiv. It was early evening, an hour or so before we were to arrive at Kyiv. Just sixty miles to the north was Chernobyl, the site of the world's worst nuclear accident on April 26th 1986. No. 4 reactor got out of control and exploded, the aftermath spewing out over the countryside caused the death of thousands of men, women and children, those first to die were the people who pushed caution and self-preservation to one side; the workers at the site, firemen, soldiers, also local people who didn't understand what had happened or the seriousness of the situation all died. Twenty-eight years after the incident people, particularly children, are still suffering. My heart goes out to those who have suffered so much. They are being looked after properly now, but that's no compensation for what has happened to them or the effect it will have on them for the rest of their lives. The reason I know a little bit about what happened at Chernobyl, apart from what was published in the papers and on the news at the time, was because I knew from the research I did in relation to planning the route that we would pass close to Chernobyl. I then contacted a company who, believe it or not, organised tours in and around the plant, also you could get close to no. 4 reactor if you wanted to risk it. Apart from the tour being very expensive you had to wear a rubber suit and carry a geiger-counter, at that point I decided what little hair I still had, I would like to keep, a visit to Saint Sophia Cathedral at Kyiv sounded like a better idea.

We arrived at Kyiv early that evening, pretty tired after the ten hour drive, we soon found a small, clean and comfortable hotel at a price that made me smile. By the time we had showered and got ourselves a meal and a beer it was 10 o'clock and too late to walk to the Dnipro River and back as we had planned, so we decide to call it a day, get a good night's rest and an early start the following morning.

Thursday 25th April, day 26, fed and refreshed from a good night's sleep, we were on the road once more, mixing with the early morning traffic through Kyiv city centre, across the bridge over the Dnipro River to re-join the M03 motorway that would take us all the way to Kharkiv, a 300 mile, 7 hour journey. We'd carried out a thorough check of the vehicles and refuelled at a garage opposite our hotel that morning, the roads looked good and the traffic light, we were hoping to achieve a higher average speed than previously, stopping briefly for fuel, and lunch later in the day, then arriving at Kharkiv at around 4 o'clock in the afternoon, allowing us an opportunity to walk around the town during the evening. For some reason, there seemed to be police everywhere, driving our identical gaily coloured Jimnys fairly close together along the motorway attracted their attention, we passed a parked police Lada prompting the two man crew into action, I waited a few minutes for the smoking Lada, making a noise like a chesty cough, to come alongside, the Lada's driver and commander who occupied the passenger seat both sporting tight-lipped, wrinkled faces, looked surprised when I waved at them. The police Lada stayed with us for a moment or two giving us the once over, the Lada, feeling the strain from the dash to catch us fell back immersed in its own exhaust smoke. We attracted the police continuously throughout the day, generally it was only interest but at the lunch stop they wanted to see inside the vehicles and to know where we were going, I said that we were driving around the world, pointing to the side of my Jimny, they didn't understand a word I said but they let us go. The remainder of our journey to Kharkiv was uneventful, arriving at the time predicted. My first impression as we entered Kharkiv was the Russian communist look of the buildings, run down and dirty in places, predominately drab looking, low-cost square blockhouse style buildings, a place that maybe is 30 years behind the rest of the world, I hoped to get a closer look later. Mariusz took the initiative, asking a taxi driver, in Russian, for directions to a hotel, we tried to understand his directions but lost it half way through, I asked Mariusz to say we would follow him, just as well, after fifteen minutes we ended up in the middle of the city, we would never had found it ourselves. I thanked and paid the taxi driver, looking up at the marble entrance and polished brass grab rails leading up the steps to the revolving doors, I stepped forward thinking this isn't going to be cheap. But as it turned out it wasn't expensive either, plus it had secure parking, we were in the centre of the city, saving us walking miles later, and maybe we'd get some decent food for a change. Walking about the city later, I noticed, although free from Russia, this part of the Ukraine has a large population of Russian speaking people, there seemed to be plenty of monuments and dedication plaques wherever you went, and from what I could see mostly dedicated to Russians. As with most cities, the city centres seem to benefit from modern buildings, parks, open space and amenities and in general look smart and tidy, whereas the suburbs are left at the bottom of the pecking order. The people are pleasant enough and those I spoke to asking for help or assistance went out of their way to help me. Sadly time had run out once more, well not quite, time enough for one last beer at the hotel before bed.

Friday 26th April, day 27, driving across the city of Kharkiv to re-join the M03 motorway and travel in a south easterly direction, passing through Sloviansk, Kramatorsk, Stakhanov and then on to Luhansk and the Ukraine Russian border crossing was the day's objective, a 274 mile, 9 hour journey. Over breakfast, prior to leaving, I had a word with Mariusz, asking if he was happy about the way things were going, and was he still O.K. about Gary travelling in 03 with him, I said, "He doesn't talk too much," "I know," he said, "he sleeps most of the time," "He shouldn't be doing that," I replied, at the same time thinking to myself, that's why he hadn't been very active with the camera during the last day or so. Mariusz said to me that when we arrive at the border he would do all the talking, we were to stay close together and have the papers ready to show if needed. I had a chat to Gary over a second cup of coffee asking if he was happy to continue driving with Mariusz he said that it was O.K. with him, he looked a bit paler, but cheerful enough. We finished our breakfast and were collecting the gear together to put into the vehicles; I turned to Gary and said, "I am happy with the filming generally but I wonder if maybe we have missed one or two opportunities over the past day or so," I went on to say, "I know we have been doing a lot of motorway driving, limiting what you can film, but I still think we missed some opportunities. What I would like to suggest is that if I see a filming opportunity at any time, particularly when we are driving, I will call you on the radio to draw your attention to it and we can decide jointly whether to film it or not." Gary seemed to accept the arrangement; Mariusz looked at me with a smile on his face as we walked towards the vehicles.

Zigzagging our way across the city of Kharkiv to re-join the M03 motorway took longer than anticipated due to the early morning traffic and a diversion that sent us in every direction other than the way we wanted to go. Eventually we joined the motorway; our intended route was in an easterly direction arriving at Luhansk at about four o'clock. Merging in with the flow of the traffic, I relaxed and thought about our arrival at the border and whether we would encounter any problems, I reminded myself to stay close to Mariusz, watch, listen and learn from what is said and done, because after the 9th of May, Mariusz and Gary would be on their way home, I would have to deal with border crossings and day to day language problems myself. My attention focused on the slowing traffic in front, after only 9 miles the four lane each way motorway had ended, the four lane orderly traffic moments before had turned hostile and aggressive towards each other as they jostled to join the continuing old but now two lane road. We eventually made it onto the two lanes hemmed in by two continuous lines of traffic that first accelerated then slowed. As we moved forward slowly I wondered what the delay was, the vehicles at the front seemed to hesitate before going forward, unable to see what the problem was, I waited my turn. We continued moving forward slowly, I could hear bangs and scraping noises also the smell of burning rubber coming from somewhere in front of me. I crawled forward slowly, then the car in front stopped, then cautiously eased forward once more, the front wheels of the car disappeared followed by a sound of metal to concrete coming together then a sickening scraping metal sound as he maintained the forward momentum, the car's front wheels spinning and creating blue smoke and the smell of burning rubber as the front of the car clawed itself out of what looked more like a trench. I rolled forward, seeing for the first time what was once a very wide and deep crack that the traffic had worn into a nasty looking trench stretching across both traffic lanes. I looked at the hole in the road, flinching as a car to my left locked horns with the concrete that showed no mercy.

Touching the button to select four wheel drive, then waiting for the reassuring click as it engaged, choosing second gear on this occasion, I then eased 02 forward, the partially braked wheels and Cooper man size tyres absorbing the shock as 02 at a nose down angle made contact with the bottom of the trench. With just enough engine revs to keep momentum, plus a little help from the Jimny's short wheel base chassis, 02 popped out the other side like cork from a bottle of champagne, no metal to concrete contact and the Cooper tyres undamaged. At the wheel of 03, Mariusz dealt with the situation in his own way but the outcome was the same. Shouting, "That's how it's done boys," and waving at the envious looking drivers, we accelerated along the road. Although the whole episode lasted no more than 10 minutes it seemed much longer, the remainder of the drive to Luhansk dragged on forever, hold ups of one sort or another, dodging suspension-busting pot holes the size of vacated missile bunkers, and the losing a battle to digest a plateful of something greasy I had for lunch which was creating a rumble in my tummy that may turn lethal later.

It was late in the day when we arrived at Luhansk, a short drive to the town of Donetsk and the actual border crossing that hopefully would let us loose on Russian soil. We arrived at the border crossing at 4.45pm and joined the short queue waiting to cross, it wasn't long before we were called forward by a smartly dressed Ukrainian man in plain clothes and speaking good English, who asked us to bring our paperwork and follow him. We were asked a few questions as our passports were stamped and returned, he glanced at the paperwork, I explained that I was the owner of both vehicles but that didn't seem to interest him, he said thank you and wished us a safe journey. Surprised at being processed so quickly, we stood by the cars for a moment, wondering if it would be the same at the Russian side of the border. The iron gates at the Russian end of no-man's-land were opened by two armed border guards, who directed us to park in front of a small office; four more unarmed guards sprang into action as we rolled to a stop. Dealing with one vehicle at a time, the man in charge indicated to his men to give me and 02 the onceover; after a few minutes poking around inside the cab the boss man, pointing at the back door, said, "Open," unlocking the tailgate then carefully opening the door enough to look in, to make sure that none of the tightly packed contents was about to fall out. Opening the door slowly with one hand and holding the kit in position with the other, I stood there arms and legs spread apart holding everything in place while the boss man decided what to do. He poked around a bit, opened a bag containing my dirty washing then decided not to pursue it further and turned his attention to 03 and the guys. The vehicle checks completed, we were taken to customs and police, who wanted to know who we were, what we were doing, and where we were going, our passports, in particular the visas they contained, attracted special interest. Mariusz explained that we were driving around the world and that most of the people doing the driving were over seventy, at that point the atmosphere changed, the stern faces were replaced with beaming smiles and hand shaking. Still smiling, our paperwork was handed back to us and we were told we could go. The gates closed behind us once more, we were relieved as we entered Russia for the first time, and only the second border crossing out of a total of 9 excluding Europe we would cross as we travel around the world. As before, I purchased car insurance but this time it was valid for two months and covered both vehicles for the whole of Russia, Kazakhstan and Mongolia, and until our arrival at Vladivostok at the beginning of June. As before, a similar looking shed, but different smiling ladies who very politely relieved me of another 90 dollars for each vehicle.

It was evening, with the border crossing and acquiring car insurance once more behind us, we made our way through the streets of the small town of Luganx, the first town we came to, looking for suitable accommodation for the night but found nothing. We eventually arrived at the centre of the town, expecting to see a hotel but again nothing. I decided to ask someone, nearest to me was a sort of small club, I went inside, the only person there was a stunningly pretty young girl behind the bar, I said, "I am sorry I only speak English, can you direct me to a hotel?" she responded immediately in impeccable English by saying that the hotel in Luganx is closed, but there was one at Kamensk-Shakhtinsky, the next town. Surprised, I asked, "Are you Russian?" "Yes," she said, I continued, "Where did you learn to speak English so well?" "At school," she replied, "I also speak German and French." I thought for a moment then went on to say, "You speak four languages, you should be working in Europe as an interpreter not wasting your life in this place as a barmaid," "I know," she said, "I have tried, there is no work so I can't save enough money to go to Europe," I was feeling very sorry for the girl, "Look," I said, "I wish I could stay longer but I have to go, I know it is not easy for you but don't give up hope," I turned and walked away thinking I didn't even ask her what her name was. We eventually booked ourselves into a small hotel and restaurant just outside the town of Kamensk-Shakhtinsky, fifty miles further on, we had been on the go all day and we were shattered, by the time we had eaten, it was almost 10 o'clock when we got back to our rooms. Gary was asleep by the time I made sure that the camera equipment was safe and the batteries were on charge, I sat up in bed writing notes in my diary, at that point I must have fallen asleep because I awoke at 6.30 the next morning, still sitting upright and with my opened diary on my lap.

Saturday 27th April, day 28, I remember waking early sitting up in bed thinking about the events the day before, I glanced at my diary and noticed that we had driven 4323 miles so far. We had pretty well driven the length of Europe, the guys uninjured and cars undamaged, but Russia, Kazakhstan, and Mongolia would be a whole new ball game.

I had time that morning to tidy up my paperwork and give myself a long overdue shave and check the vehicles before breakfast, as I went to leave the room, I woke Gary to tell him what the time was and that I would meet him for breakfast in 20 minutes. Mariusz's room was two doors along the corridor, as I went to knock on the door, it opened and Mariusz stepped out ready to go, we made our way to 02 and 03 parked in the hotel secure compound, stowed our gear and completed the checks on the vehicles, knowing that the Jimny's reassuring reliability makes this task a formality. At breakfast we briefly discussed the plan for the day, mentioning that we were in Russia now and that we should take extra care. At a little after 8 o'clock we were on our way once more, driving to Volgograd, a 222 mile, 7 hour journey. The old highway to Volgograd was an open surfaced two lanes each way road with potholes and cracks accounting for about 30% of the road surface, requiring maximum concentration while driving if we wanted to arrive at our destination undamaged. It was difficult enough maintaining our 55 mph cruising speed and dodging cracks and potholes when the traffic is light, but when the volume of traffic increases you become locked in the traffic flow, unable to see what is ahead of you until it is too late. It was constantly on my mind that we might seriously damage the overloaded vehicles in some way and not be able to complete the journey, but looking back over our achievement, I needn't have concerned myself. The journey to Volgograd dragged on a bit, the repetitive scenery of farmland, colourful villages and golden domed churches were interesting enough but beyond that there was not much variation. After a while my interest waned and I drifted into my thinking mode. For some reason I recalled that over dinner one evening at home, it was mentioned that there wasn't much time for sightseeing, I must admit, at the time I struggled to give a satisfactory answer then thinking back to when I first started to put the plan together, I remembered, Alan Butler, a real nice guy, the first person to ask if he could join me, he wanted to visit various places, but in the end I had to say it wouldn't be possible. I explained to Alan at the time and gave the same reply when the question arose later, "The Ultimate Challenge is not a sightseeing tour, neither is it a jolly for the boys, it's all about proving that guys in their 70s can plan, organise and drive two Suzuki Jimnys around the world and arrive back, the crew unharmed and vehicles undamaged." Not paying attention, I hit a deep crack in the road, causing me and the kit in the back to become momentarily airborne, the thump that followed as I relocated my seat caused, for the first time, a slight pain in my groin, reminding me that all wasn't well in that department, also it must have unsettled me as there now was some urgency to have a pee! It was time for fuel and food so I called Mariusz to confirm that we would stop for lunch at the next opportunity. I thought about the slight pain in my groin and the meeting I had with my doctor a few weeks before departure, he wanted me to have more tests to confirm his diagnosis relating to my medical condition, I know it was foolish, but I decided the tests would have to wait until I got back, and so I kept the unwelcome news to myself. I didn't even tell my lovely wife Vi, she had enough on her mind without me adding to it. Only two people knew my predicament at that time, my doctor, who left the decision up to me, and myself. I was too involved to pull out and I felt O.K. apart from wanting to pee more often than usual, I had no reason until now to think about it. Unfortunately, my problem regularly reared its ugly head as my journey and the story unfolds. We did everything we needed to do at the service area and were soon on our way again. The road surface improved during the afternoon, allowing us to catch up on the lost time in the morning, we arrived at the city of Volgograd that afternoon at 4.30pm and located and booked into a small, moderately priced guest house overlooking the Volga River.

Volgograd, or better known as Stalingrad to the older generation, was the location of the fiercest and bloodiest battle of WW2, lasting 199 days, ending February 1943 and claiming around 1.5 million lives. The Russian forces, under Marshal Zhukov, fought and defeated Field Marshal von Paulus and the German army, marking a turning point of the war that Germany never recovered from. After the war, Stalingrad was rebuilt and renamed Volgograd, mainly as a tribute to those who died or took part, but also because Stalin was losing favour at that time. That evening, we had time to walk to the city centre to have a look around, the following morning being a Sunday, we had allowed ourselves a few hours to visit the vast memorial site overlooking the Volga River.

Sunday 28ᵗʰ April, day 29, the weather was perfect, it was a beautiful, cloudless sunny day, we arrived at the memorial site and just stood there for a moment, mesmerised by the stunning panoramic view of the wide Volga River and the city silhouetted in the background by the early morning sunrise. The location and weather were perfect for filming, Gary and I carried the filming equipment to Hill 102, the spot where some of the fiercest fighting took place, known today as Mamayev Kurgan or (Mamay Mound). To commemorate the site, an 83 metre high statue of a young woman, representing Mother Russia, wielding a sword has been erected. Gary set the camera up ready to film me talking in general about Volgograd, with the memorial site and the statue of Mother Russia in the background. This was where I took my glasses off and combed what's left of my hair. Gary and I had been filming for a little over an hour when he said to me that he could not film any more, he had used all the batteries, I replied, "That can't be right, the camera batteries should last four hours." Concerned at the situation, I made a mental note to put the batteries on charge myself that evening, I was annoyed that we couldn't film anymore, the conditions were perfect. We loaded the filming equipment back into the vehicles then completed the tour of the site a bit disappointed. It was 11.30am before we were travelling east once more, to Saratov, a 232 mile, 6 hour journey, luckily the roads were mostly clear of traffic allowing us to maintain our cruising speed. Later that afternoon we stopped at a roadside pump to refuel, as usual Mariusz went to the cash window and said, in broken Russian, "We want to fill two cars with petrol and pay for them both with one credit card," expecting them to hold on to the card while we filled the tanks, but this time it was different. The procedure was the same, only this time the lady at the window said to Mariusz we could only fill each car with 25 litres, Mariusz tried to find out why but got nowhere. It meant that we had to stop for fuel more often to keep the tanks topped up; payment was by card if I could convince them it was valid, other times I would pay cash, we carried 40 litres of fuel in cans on each vehicle just in case but from then on we topped up as often as we could to be on the safe side.

At 6.30pm we drifted into Saratov, a rundown sort of place, some of the buildings looked tired, in need of repair and a coat of paint, dust and dirt everywhere, the old style buses bouncing over potholes full of stagnant water that splashed passers-by. We stopped at the first hotel we came across, it looked O.K., the rooms were basic and the sheets were clean, the rest, well nothing a glass or two of beer and something to eat wouldn't overcome. We were too tired to go walking; we parked the vehicles in a secure compound at the rear of the hotel and settled down for the night. We finished our meal, remaining at the table to discuss the route to Samara the following morning. I remembered the problem we'd had with the camera batteries, I asked Gary if we could go to our room to check the camera equipment to find out why the batteries do not hold the charge.

Gary didn't say anything as we went to our room; I collected all the camera equipment together including the backup miniature GoPro camera. I asked Gary to identify each piece of kit so that I would know what its function was, so far so good. I then asked if he could show me the batteries and chargers, these were paired together so that I could see which charger was used to charge specific batteries. It all looked O.K., I couldn't see any problem. At that point Mariusz entered our room, I told him what the problem was, he picked up one of the camera batteries then looked at the charger, then turning to look at me he said that it was the wrong charger for that battery, explaining that it did not have enough power to charge a battery that size. I looked at Gary, his face drained of colour, I was expecting an explanation but nothing was forthcoming, "Why are we not using the correct charger?" I said firmly, "It was in the bag that was left at Brussels," he replied, I looked at him wanting to say something but all that came out was, "Ho-o-sh—t, you have known about this all this time and you never thought to tell me, why?" I asked, I don't remember what his reply was because I was formulating my next question, "Was there anything else in the bag?" Looking sorry for himself, using his fingers to count a list of items that he knew was in the bag, I just looked at him dumfounded. I lay on my bed looking up to the ceiling for most of the night, wondering how it would affect the filming and considering the options available. It was highly unlikely that the replacement kit would be available at Samara, the next big city, so my best option was to contact David Ellery, Viewpoint Productions, who would be producing the film and who supplied the filming equipment, email a list of the items to be reordered and have them delivered to Graham Higgins, or Mike Bailey, they would bring the items with them when they fly to Novosibirsk on 9th May to join me for stage 3, problem solved. I had a word with Gary the next morning to put him at ease, he was clearly upset about the whole business, also to explain what I was proposing.

Monday 29th April, day 30, I remember this day very well, we departed Saratov about 8am, the route that day was in a north-easterly direction to Samara, a 257 mile, 8 hour journey. While at the hotel the night before, I had a conversation with a Russian man who spoke some English, he told me that the road to Samara was very bad and there were a lot of accidents, some good news would be nice for a change! The plan was to arrive at Samara that day to be on hand ready for a Suzuki press conference at 12 o'clock the following day. The Russian guy I spoke to at the hotel wasn't joking; the road to Samara was the worst so far. Easing ourselves onto the main road and into the continuous flow of traffic to become a part of a nose-to-tail two lane block of vehicles travelling in the same direction, I told myself to relax, there was nothing I could do, just go with the flow, as they say. Mariusz was a few cars behind me, just visible in my mirror so I settled down; lately I had let my driving get a bit sloppy, taking unnecessary chances when overtaking, it's not really like me, I didn't realise it at the time, I was driving like a Russian. Sitting comfortably, I became complacent about what was going on around me thinking of everything other than my driving, suddenly there was a screech of tyres then a bang, then another two bangs in succession, cars were hitting each other, the car in front braked aggressively, shocked by what was unfolding in front of me, I instinctively turned the wheel to the right missing the car in front by the thickness of a cigarette paper and ending up bumping over some rough ground before stopping and switching off the engine. I sat there for a moment looking at the mayhem going on behind me, thinking I was lucky that time, let it be a warning I said to myself. If only I would take notice of what I tell myself!

Restarting the engine, I continued along the rough ground to get ahead of the accident, Mariusz being some way behind avoided the carnage and was following. We got ourselves back onto the road, the traffic was less, but the road condition remained the same, regardless of the conditions we were able maintain a reasonable speed for the rest of the morning. It was nearly midday, I spoke to Mariusz, suggesting that we refuel and get something to eat at the service area 30 minutes further along the road. It was not what I expected as we rolled to a stop; it was

'Mr Fix-it 1' - at work?

a scruffy, ageing three pump garage, a small workshop one side and café the other. We got out of the cars and stretched ourselves, Gary pointed to the rear left shock absorber on 02 saying that it was hanging down, Mariusz and I shimmied under 02 to get a better look, sure enough, the left hand rear shock absorber bottom bracket bolt had sheared, "Not surprised," I said, "with the extra weight I'm carrying, it looks like the potholes have claimed another victim." I had to make a decision whether we carry on to Samara to get it fixed there, or ask at the garage workshop to see if they could weld it. Luckily the workshop was open, Mariusz explained to the young lad in charge what the problem was and asked if he could weld it, he gave us the Russian version of, "No problem," saying it would take an hour, laughing he pointed to the café. I went to walk towards the café then turned to ask the lad, indicating with my dirty hands where can I wash, laughing once again he pointed to the café. Mariusz, Gary and I sauntered over to the café, it was a bit of a dump but the coffee and pies were welcome. There were a few people sitting at a table, I indicated with my hands, where can I wash, they started laughing, the younger one of the group couldn't contain himself, exposing a mouth full of black teeth as he pointed to a door at the far end of the café. Turning the grime-encrusted door knob, I entered a passage with three or four doors leading off either side and a partially opened door at the far end. The whole place was painted fire engine red and smelt a bit sweaty; there was no indication as to which door was the wash room so I walked to the end of the corridor and pushed the door open a little further and looked in, expecting to find a washroom, the room was small and red, there was an iron framed bed and mattress that had been hammered to death, sitting on the bed was a round faced lady clad in bra and knickers, strong enough to pull a customer's head off if he tried to pay by credit card. At that point I realised I was in a brothel, not wishing to overstay my welcome I held out my hands to indicate I wanted the washroom, but she must have thought that I wanted to grab something. Startled, the lady gasped and stood up ready to come at me throwing punches, seeing my hands were dirty and realising I wasn't a customer she gave me a cheeky wink and pointed to a door along the corridor. I cleaned myself up then passed more scantily clad ladies on the way out. Back in the café, everyone was laughing, I said to Mariusz and Gary, "That's one hell of a washroom." The lad at the workshop welded the shock absorber back into position, I must admit the job looked a bit amateurish but fingers crossed, we headed for Samara arriving around 5pm that evening. I have mentioned a few times about the cracks and potholes in the roads, but I have to say the city of Samara is something else, the roads are in such bad condition you can't drive in a straight line although there are two lanes each way. To go forward you join a single line of traffic that resembles a snake as it twists and turns across two lanes avoiding unbelievable suspension busting huge potholes. We checked into a small hotel in the centre of the city, I then contacted Ksenia Grebenkina, Suzuki P.R. Team Manager, who had flown in for the occasion and had been awaiting our arrival so as to let us know what the arrangements were for the press conference at 12 o'clock the following day.

Tuesday 30th April, day 31, the press conference wasn't until 12 o'clock so there was no rush to have an early breakfast; after we had eaten, we checked and cleaned the vehicles then made ourselves presentable for the benefit of the cameras. A courtesy car arrived, the driver asked if we would follow him to the venue, on arrival we were manoeuvred into position so that the Suzuki showroom formed a backdrop, the P.R. team attended to the final touches ready for the press and photographers to take pictures and ask questions, the session lasted an hour. After lunch we visited a local orphanage to hand over the presents given to us by the Suzuki management at the production facility at Magyar, Hungary. I had been thinking on and off for some time about the visit to the orphanage, I sometimes get emotional when confronted with this sort of thing, but went along anyway, I was glad I made the effort. We were met at the entrance by some of the children, they seemed happy enough and from what I saw didn't want for anything materially, the presents we had brought for them were of interest but they already had lots of toys, I could see it in their little faces that what they really wanted more than anything was the love of a mum and dad, I hoped the world will be kind to them as they grow up, reluctantly and with glassed eyes and feeling really sad, I said goodbye. Outside in the cool air we all took a moment to compose ourselves, I thanked the Suzuki team on behalf of Mariusz, Gary, and myself for their kind hospitality then turned east once more, heading for Sukhodoi and our overnight stop. On our way to Sukhodoi and in the middle of nowhere, the welded shock absorber bracket broke once more, I had no alternative but to continue driving, taking care to dodge

'Mr Fix-it 2' – a job well done!

the potholes as best we could. Eventually we came across a small workshop just off the main road, an old building but with modern equipment inside, the young lad (every man is a young lad at my age) came out, once again Mariusz explained what the problem was, pointing to the shock absorber, Mr Fix It 2, we shall call him, took one look then dived under 02 for a closer examination. Gary was active with the camera, showing a touch of professionalism as we went about the business of getting 02 back on the road. Mr Fix It 2 emerged from under 02, what Mariusz roughly translated to me wasn't exactly complimentary about the work Mr Fix It 1 did, on reflection what he actually said isn't printable, it was a pleasure to watch a professional at work, the preparation and welding itself was as good as it gets. Thankful that he had got me out of the mire! I went to pay, he asked for the equivalent of £8 in real money, as I went to give him a bit extra for a job well done, he stood back insisting he didn't want any more and wouldn't take it, I felt privileged to have met Mr Fix It 2. Confident that I had seen the last of the problem, we continued to Sukhodoi.

Wednesday 1st May, day 32, the journey to Zlatoust wasn't long but the road was reportedly bad and winds its way through the southern end of the Ural Mountains, if all went well, by the end of the day we should be close enough to the Russian Kazakhstan border, ready for an early start in the morning. Before going to sleep the previous night I had taken two paracetamol to ease the slight pain in my groin. I didn't feel too good when I woke up that morning, the slight pain was still there so I took another two paracetamol hoping I would feel better later, it also didn't help when I saw what our hostelry was offering for breakfast, settling for a bowl of cereal and coffee, I started the day lacking my usual energy. As we loaded the vehicles, I noticed that Gary looked a bit vacant, his face was a grey colour, and he didn't look quite right, I knew what the problem was anyway so did nothing about it.

02 was like a sort of comfort zone, once inside and doors closed I was isolated from the outside, not feeling quite myself, I was happy enough to settle down into my cushioned seat and just drive, watching the world go by, the pain in my groin had eased but I still didn't feel right. It was another bright, sunny, cloudless day the high altitude mountain air was clean and fresh, lakes and rivers sparkled from the sun's reflection as we drove past, the scenery was breathtaking. By the look of things, we were travelling through a Ural Mountain summer holiday area, small cabins, lodges and shops remained boarded up awaiting the summer season and visitors. Content to let Mariusz lead the way, I just followed. After stopping for fuel, food and a short rest, we were on our way to Zlatoust, a further two hour drive. Although feeling tired and a bit lethargic, I insisted that I take my turn at leading the way, the highway was single lane each way, with no hard shoulder at the side of the road and the traffic was light. I didn't feel like putting too much effort into overtaking manoeuvres, so I was content to follow the truck ahead of me, driving close behind and being sucked along at 55 mph. Fatigued and tired from driving long hours day after day with no proper sleep, I just sat there thinking what I had to do the following day, how my wife was coping at home on her own and anything else that came into my head. Realising that I had been behind the lorry long enough, I decided to overtake. Normally it's not a problem, first talk to the car nicely to get it excited, change down to 4th or 3rd gear, then wind up the little 1328cc engine by hitting the floor with the accelerator and away you go. I checked my rear mirror; there was one car behind but a long way back. I let the lorry move forward so I could have a look to see if I could overtake. I moved out to the oncoming traffic lane, the road ahead was clear apart from a white van coming towards me but there was plenty of time to overtake. Already travelling at 55 mph, I was short of additional power. I was already heavy on the accelerator, my

overloaded, low-powered little Jimny struggled to respond, I changed down to 4th and wound her up. I was slowly moving forward, the white van ahead was closer now but I still had time. The car behind had followed me to overtake, I looked ahead, the shock when I realised that there were two lorries not one, driving nose to tail, I still could make it. I coaxed my little car along the side of the first lorry at about 60 mph, my mouth had dried and beads of sweat formed on my forehead. "Make a decision," a voice resonated in my head. At this point, I was level with the driver of the first lorry, he could see the accident about to happen and looked down at me, our eyes met momentarily but I was still overtaking. "Make a decision, look for a way out," I said to myself as I glanced at the rear view mirror and seeing, to my horror, that the car behind was now on my rear bumper. At the same time, I noticed that my forward momentum was slowing and engine rpm was dropping, why, why, why? Desperately, I scanned the panel trying to find what was wrong, I changed down to 3rd gear, the little engine was screaming, I then realised it was not the engine, I was going up an incline, I won't make it. I looked ahead to see where the white van was, the shock that followed was a heart stopper, it wasn't a slow moving van, it was a fast moving white Toyota truck, lights flashing and horn screaming, coming straight at me. The alarm bell ringing in my head was deafening, there was nothing I could do, the Toyota kept coming, braking wheels and smoking tyres as it skidded towards me, no hard shoulder at the road edge to offer either of us sanctuary, the outcome was unavoidable. In desperation I stamped on 02's brakes as hard as I could, a futile gesture, before impact. The driver of the first lorry, watching the incident unfold, reacted spontaneously by applying his brakes to create a gap between his lorry cab and the back of the lorry in front, the Toyota was almost on me when I yanked the wheel to the right, not knowing if I would make it or not, as the Toyota flashed past, lights flashing and horn sounding.

Shaken, I passed between the two lorries, emerging out of the other side and managing to stop on a piece of flat ground marginally wider than 02, I felt terrible but I was able to take a few deep breaths and think about what happened. I have taken unnecessary risks a few times in my life and dodged death, but this time it really did scare the crap out of me; I got it seriously wrong this time. Driving off the road at the first opportunity, I waited for Mariusz and Gary to arrive. A few minutes later 03 rolled to a stop beside me, Mariusz lowered the window to ask if I was alright, "I'm O.K." I said, "that was close," he just smiled, shaking his head as we both continued the journey to Zlatoust, arriving early evening. We found a cheap and clean guest house close to the border, I asked Mariusz if he would share a room that night with Gary, I didn't tell him Gary's snoring was loud and sounded like a gorilla's mating call. It had been an eventful day; I needed to get a good night's sleep.

Thursday 2nd May, day 33, arriving early at the Russian Kazakhstan border crossing, I was refreshed and feeling much better after a good night's sleep and a decent breakfast. It was over an hour before the stern faced Russian border guards had finished with us and we made our way across to the Kazakhstan side. The formalities took another thirty minutes to complete, apart from answering a few questions relating to our paperwork, the process was straight forward and the officials were polite and helpful. I hadn't met anybody from Kazakhstan before, so the border crossing was my first encounter, from what I could see they are generally small people with round

Russia to Kazakhstan

smiley faces, the uniformed guards looked a bit comical, they wore huge angled wide brimmed hats, the higher up the pecking order you are the bigger the brim of your hat is. Our plan for the day was to get as far as Qostanay before nightfall, a 256 mile, 12 hour journey. That particular day I was expecting my once weekly call by satellite phone from Julian Clegg of B.B.C. Radio Solent U.K. time 8am, Kazakhstan time 11.30am, the further we travelled east the greater the time difference, very confusing at food times. Just before the call was due we stopped at the side of the road for a short break, a few minutes later the call came through and I was talking live to Steve, Julian's stand-in for that week. It only lasted a few minutes but I was able to give everyone an update. The weather remained kind to us for the rest of the day but it was pretty hard going maintaining our 55 mph cruising speed on roads that seemed to deteriorate the further east we went. I must admit I was pleasantly surprised at the stunning scenery, whether it was mountains, plains, rivers or lakes, it was spectacular. The 1250 mile journey across Kazakhstan would take about 5 days by the time we arrive at Rubtsovsk, the border town, where we would cross back into Russia to arrive at the city of Novosibirsk by 8th May. The little Jimnys seemed to be standing up to the daily punishment and fuel consumption was averaging about 34mpg (7.5 miles per litre) not bad for the little overloaded 4x4s. The remainder of the journey to Qostanay was uneventful, but I couldn't help noticing that the police seemed to be everywhere, stopping vehicles to check their papers and at the same time giving us an inquisitive glance as we passed. The journey seemed longer as we approached Qostanay, it was dark by the time we settled into a small guest house with food available. I had my rest from Gary's snoring so he and I were once again sharing a room, earlier in the day I had an opportunity to ask Mariusz if Gary had been filming, "Not really, he sleeps all day," was his I reply, I was concerned to hear this, I had been keeping an eye on Gary over the past few days to make sure that he captured on film our activities and anything else that would be of interest.

Up until the day before, he seemed to be keeping busy then nothing since. Before going to eat that evening I stayed in our room waiting for Gary to get ready, he didn't look too good, he had that grey blank expression on his face and his eyes were red and glazed, I asked if he was all right, "I want to go home," was his reply. Unprepared I said, "What do you mean, you want to go home we are in the middle of bloody nowhere?" Then thinking for a moment I said, "The nearest place you could get a flight to the U.K. is Novosibirsk, Russia, we will be there in 5 days anyway, it would be better if you stayed with us until then. Gary seemed to be falling apart, he kept repeating to himself as he packed his bag, "I want to go home, I want to go home." In a soft voice I said to him, "Stop what you are doing for a moment, sit down on the bed," I then said, "Gary you are not well, we need to stay together until I can get you on a plane, are you taking your medication?" "Yes but I'm running out," he replied, "How much medication do you have left?" he showed me, enough for about 3 days, "O.K.," I said, "why don't you have some food then take a pill and have an early night, see how you feel in the morning and you can make a decision then?" Gary picked at his food, the food was alright but I guess he didn't have an appetite, he stood up and went to our room without saying a word, Mariusz and I just looked at one other as he walked away. That night it was like trying to sleep next to someone using a chain saw, it seemed like hours before I finally fell asleep, then automatically opening my eyes again at 6.45am, it seemed that I had only been asleep for ten minutes.

Friday 3rd May, day 34, I dragged myself out of bed thinking how quiet it was as I applied some urgency to reach the bathroom before it was too late, standing there checking to see if I needed to drink more water, I looked down and became mesmerised, I could see what was happening but could hear nothing, my first thought was that I had gone deaf! Then turning to look in the mirror I once more saw an old man with red puffy eyes and toilet paper coming out of his ears looking at me, not a pretty sight. Looking a bit more presentable and thankful that I could hear once more, I awoke Gary, hoping for the best, he stopped snoring and opened his eyes, "How do you feel, can you manage some breakfast?" I said. Gary got up saying that he was feeling better. I related to our discussion we had the night before emphasising that the quickest way home is to stay with us, he didn't exactly say he understood the situation but I assumed he did. It was about 8am by the time we refuelled and checked the vehicles and were on our way to the capital city, Astana, a 420 mile, 10 hour journey if we had no problems that is. The day was uneventful, apart from some rain mid-morning, the first for two weeks, and a strong wind that blew all day. The traffic was light, but even so, cars passing in either direction would press their horn and wave at us, also when we stopped for food and fuel people gathered around us and the Jimnys to have their picture taken, I got the impression that they knew we were coming, maybe there was something in the press. Gary was still with us but he wasn't firing on all cylinders, he slept most of the time and only filmed when I asked him to, the mood swings reappeared, making it difficult when I wanted to speak to him, Gary had a serious problem that needed urgent attention, me arguing with him wouldn't help so I was happy to go along with the situation.

Approaching Astana from the west, it seems as though you drive across some sort of line, leaving the old Kazakhstan on one side and entering the new Kazakhstan on the other side. Astana, the capital since 1997, has grown into a modern style clean city, from the outskirts to the city centre the straight wide roads pass new modern buildings designed to be pleasing to the eye, surrounded by statues, monuments, parks and gardens.

Stopping at the car park and stretching ourselves, we were facing what I could best describe as a gold plated hotel, all three of us just stood there taking it all in, the whole of the outside of the building was covered in gold panels. Surprisingly though it wasn't expensive, so I booked a room for each of us and arranged that we meet for dinner at 7 o'clock. Mariusz and I met for dinner at the hotel restaurant as arranged, feeling out of place having been shown to a table in a huge room that doubled as a banqueting hall for five hundred people or more, I guess they expected to be busy, every table was laid with high quality china and cutlery, I swallowed slowly when I realised the surroundings and culinary opulence would be reflected in the price. We sat at the table sipping a beer for 30 minutes waiting for Gary to arrive, I said to Mariusz that I had better go to his room, he had probably fallen asleep, I made my way to Gary's room and knocked on the door but got no response. Thinking he may be asleep, I knocked once more but harder, still no response, perhaps he was wandering about somewhere, I turned to go, as I did I heard a sound coming from inside the room, I banged on the door a third time. This time the door opened, Gary, looking deranged, fully clothed and bag over his shoulder walked past me saying, "I'm going home you can't stop me, I want to go home," "Gary," I said, pausing to decide which wall to bang my head on, "if I could get you on a plane home tonight I would, I'm sick to death of accommodating your problems, you lied to me from the beginning, you have messed up the camera equipment, I had to sort out your medication at Budapest, and of late I have had to put up with your Jekyll and Hyde mental state, quite frankly, I have had it up to here with you," pointing to my forehead, "now you pull yourself together, I'm not standing for any more of your nonsense." I said, "Its 8 o'clock, you're not going anywhere, take your gear back to your room and be at the restaurant in 5 minutes, you have f—ked up our evening, so I had better go and square things with Mariusz." I relayed what had happened to Mariusz, he wasn't surprised, by then we had lost our appetite, I finished the remainder of my beer thinking about what would happen in the morning. Gary joined Mariusz and me at the table, he didn't say much, I asked him what he would like to eat, "I'm not particularly hungry," he replied, I looked at Mariusz and suggested that we find a café that the locals use, Gary then said he would like a burger if he could get one, I paid for the beers then we went outside. The hotel porter was carrying someone's bags to a waiting taxi, when he had finished I asked him if there was a café nearby that serves good food, he smiled and gave me directions to a family owned establishment just a few minutes away, the food was good and the atmosphere was great. It had been another long and tiring day so after our meal we all had an early night and agreed to meet at 7am for breakfast and be on the road before 8 o'clock.

Saturday 4th May, day 35, we met for breakfast as arranged, even Gary was on time, looking better than the night before, we discussed our route for the day and agreed that we would refuel at the first opportunity. Sounding like a general addressing his men, before going over the top I said, "I would also like to mention that I have been told that the Kazakhstan police are notorious for stopping foreign motorists for speeding and threatening the driver if the fine isn't paid in dollars on the spot, so be very careful, especially at crossroads at the top of hills, the police apparently conceal themselves on the far side of the hill, as you approach the top all you can see is the brim of a policeman's hat and a handheld speed camera searching for the unwary." I took this advice seriously so to be prepared and to be on the safe side, I put $75 in my right breast pocket and $50 in my left breast pocket just in case the guys got stopped.

It was another beautiful day, the road was pretty rough but we managed to miss the potholes. We applied caution as we approached each crossroads, particularly at the top of hills, slowing to about 30 mph there were signs indicating the speed limit of 75, 50, and 30 kph all within a 100 metres. The 308 mile journey to Pavlodar, I estimated, would take 8 hours, arriving about 5 o'clock that evening. Mariusz and Gary led in 03 and I followed a short distance behind in 02. We had been driving for about an hour and a half when we came across two police Ladas at the side of the road and four policeman stopping cars at random. Mariusz, in 03, tried not to make eye contact with a policeman waving what looked like an oversized red lollipop, indicating to him to stop, Mariusz ignoring the shouts and whistles, continued to drive past but a second policeman stepped in front of 03, waving his lollipop and forcing 03 to stop. I saw what happened from a distance then came upon the scene moments later as I cruised past unnoticed, laughing to myself as I stopped at a safe distance to see what happens. After a few minutes the police lost interest and let 03 go, it came to a stop alongside me, I wound the window down still laughing, "I told you to be careful," I said jokingly to Mariusz and Gary, "I had better lead, you two guys look too suspicious!" 03 was stopped twice that day but didn't get fined. A few kilometres further on we stopped at a sort of roadside café, it didn't look too good from the outside but the pies and a cup of tea were O.K. There was a garage close by so we took the opportunity to refuel but once again if I paid with my credit card, I was only allowed 25 litres for each vehicle. It was about that time I started to seriously consider how I would deal with the day to day language problems when we arrive at Novosibirsk and Mariusz returns to Poland, up until now Mariusz had used his limited Russian when we wanted fuel, food, accommodation, border crossings, and a number of other times when a few words of Russian has come in handy, something else to keep me awake at night. Bearing in mind the daily issues that I had to deal with, I thought that I had managed everything pretty well so far; it all seemed to be working out fine, boy was I about to get my comeuppance that afternoon! Fuelled and fed, we were on our way to Pavlodar, thirty minutes into the journey I was thinking about what lay ahead, and whether Graham and Mike would arrive at Novosibirsk on the 9th of May as planned, and a number of other issues I needed to think about. I was driving along at 55 mph, not really concentrating on what I was doing then suddenly I realised that I was at the outskirts of a town, on an incline and coming up to a crossroad, late to react, I had passed the 75 and 50 kilometre signs then braked fairly hard to slow 02 to roll past the 30 km (20 mph) about right. Relieved, I looked ahead to see if there were any police in hiding, and there it was, the hat and speed camera getting taller as I drove closer, "Ooh sheeit," I said as the policeman waved his oversized red lollipop indicating that I should stop. I sat in the car getting my papers ready, I looked up as Mariusz and Gary drifted past in 03, laughing their heads off. The policeman wielding the lollipop pointed at me then at the Lada with two heavyweight policemen sitting in the back, as I walked to the Lada one of the back doors opened and as the overweight policeman extracted himself from the Lada, the car body lifted a hands width higher off the ground. Pointing at the open door and motioning with a jerk of his head that I should get in the back, I sat on the seat that he had just vacated, to my surprise the policeman that got out now wanted to get back in, I protested, looking at this huge backside being forced through the small door space, one cheek at a time, and blocking out the light as it homed in on the seat I was sitting on, desperate not to have this elephant sized sweaty bum drop in my lap, I leant forward just as he relocated his seat, causing the Lada to drop lower than before.

I was a little concerned as there was some shuffling going on behind me, yelping slightly as they grabbed hold of me, then was relieved as they pulled me back into the space they had made to become squashed between the two heavyweights, and held down in place by an arm across my shoulders. I sat clamped in the back trying not to breathe in the stale sweat-impregnated air while they decided what to do, eventually the speed camera was produced and played back showing that I was speeding, but before I could focus on the tiny screen it was switched off, from what I did see it wasn't 02 on the screen, "You speeding," they both said. I turned my head to protest but ended up looking at and smelling his sweaty armpit. Realising I was about to get screwed, I said, "How much is the fine?" and at the same time rubbed my thumb and forefinger together like an East London money lender, "23000 Kazakhstan Tenge," the one with the camera said. Not understanding, I indicated that they write it so I could see how much, the amount was scribbled on a piece of paper and put in front of my face, when I saw all those zeros I nearly passed out, but then recalled you get a lot of Tenge for the dollar, feeling a bit sick, I extracted my trapped arm and felt inside my jacket and produced my credit cards, I indicated that I could pay by card, smiling politely, if looks could kill, I would be dead now. Realising that they were not getting through to me, my back seat companions with threatening screwed up faces both said at the same time, "You have dollars." Startled into action I said, "I have no money," as I patted the pockets of my coat, working up to my top right hand pocket which I patted a few times, then with a surprised look I took out the papers I kept there and shuffled through them looking even more surprised when $75 appeared. I was quickly relieved of my dollars as they asked for more; I just gave him a blank look. They said a few words to each other, and then they both leaned over me and said, "You can go, you say nothing." Relieved to be out of the sweat-impregnated Lada and sitting in 02, I could see the guys in 03 waiting for me further along the road, as I rolled alongside, Mariusz and Gary just looked at me for a moment then they both burst out laughing, I could see the funny side of it and laughed also. With tears in our eyes I said, "That's what not to do, but still be careful." Unfortunately for me, the police had not finished with me I was still on their hook and about to be reeled in for a second time. An hour further along the road, I got stopped again, it followed the same procedure, only this time there was no play back of me speeding and they went straight to the point saying I was going too fast and I had to pay the fine with American dollars, I did my little bit of play acting and parted with my remaining $50 then was told I could go, once again the policeman put his finger to his lips and said to me, "You say nothing." I guess the whole thing was a set up from the start to the finish, when I got stopped the first time, I suspect they notified their friends ahead that we were coming and that the money was in my left breast pocket. On reflection, when Mariusz and Gary got stopped the first time, I'm not so sure that they didn't tell the police that the man with the money is driving 02! The guys in 03 were in hysterics when I passed them to take the lead; I knew they would be reminding me of that afternoon and rub it in at every opportunity. In spite of my encounters with the police, we made good time and arrived at Pavlodar late that evening, another 308 miles completed. It had been a real eventful day, but one I would not like to repeat, we were all tired from the long hours of driving, I took two paracetamol to help me sleep but I was awake on and off throughout the night thinking about what was ahead of me and how I would cope when Mariusz leaves.

Sunday 5th May, day 36, still feeling tired, I met Mariusz and Gary for breakfast, we then checked and fuelled the vehicles and were on the road by 8.30am driving east to Semey, a 216 mile, 7 hour journey, on roads that deteriorated further each day, causing 02 and 03 to get seriously knocked about. The stern talking to I had with Gary at Astana seemed to have brought him back to his senses, and to give him credit, he had made an effort since then and appeared to be back with us, as our cameraman. Picking our way around the cracks and potholes, I noticed for the first time the major road signs were in Kazakh and English, it didn't improve the road surface, but at least I knew where we were going. When the roads are so bad it makes it difficult to overtake, that morning I came up behind a slow moving lorry belching acrid blue smoke from its engine exhaust, also flicking stones from its back wheels, hitting 02's windscreen, I decided to overtake, one or two cars were ahead of my thinking and were already overtaking me and the lorry, as soon as they had passed I followed to overtake myself. I turned to the left to move out from behind the lorry to overtake, a simple manoeuvre as the traffic was light, as I was overtaking the lorry another vehicle followed close behind, no problem. Overtaking at about 40 mph, I looked ahead, the road was clear, my eyes then panned down to the road surface and focused on a water filled pothole I couldn't avoid, praying that it was not deep as I nosed dived, sending a mini surge of brown water up and over the bonnet and onto the windscreen, limiting my view and at the same time feeling a heavy metallic thump that travelled through the steering, jarring my arms and shoulders. The little Jimny bounced out of the pothole but the steering didn't feel right, also I had acquired a slight rattle and vibration that got worse as I slowed and turned off the road to investigate the damage. I had shimmied under the front of 02 to get a closer look when Mariusz and Gary in 03 stopped, I explained what happened, and that it looked like the torsion bar was damaged and the front right suspension arm had sheared a bolt, but was driveable. Reflecting on the situation, I suggested that we continue on to Semey at a slower pace and as the following day was Monday, I would get it looked at then, it was frustrating for the guys in 03 but there was not much I could do about it, if anything I needed to lighten the load 02 was carrying, that I couldn't do. After a while, we stopped for fuel and

217

refreshment at a roadside stop, I asked Mariusz if he would enquire if there was a workshop locally, a few minutes later he returned to say that there was a village further along the road, we would get a replacement bolt there. We found what looked like a workshop, the doors open and a car inside that was being worked on, as we waited for something to happen, a car turned off the road and stopped, Mariusz stepped forward as a man in his 50s introduced himself, asking Mariusz how he could help us, he listened to what Mariusz had to say. Then in his Sunday best clothes, this kind and very helpful man slid under the front of 02 to get a closer look at the problem, emerging to say that he could not do anything with the torsion bar but he thought he could find a bolt for the suspension arm. Bringing out from the back of the workshop into the daylight two rusty tins containing an assortment of nuts, bolts and washers, tipping the contents of both tins out on a patch of concrete close to 02, he then rummaged and selected a fist full of bolts then dived between the wheel arch and the wheel. This gentleman kept at it until he found the right bolt and fitted it to his satisfaction. I felt humbled and privileged to have met this Kazakhstani man, the only thing that mattered to him was that he could help, I asked Mariusz to find out how much I had to pay, in doing so he looked at me insulted, refusing payment, I shook his hand firmly and a little longer as Mariusz translated my sincere thanks for helping us.

As we drove away from his workshop, I couldn't help thinking what a real nice man he is, but if he thought I would go without paying something he was mistaken, it's not in my nature to take advantage or not pay my way, so we said goodbye but just before we left, our friend collected up the scattered bolts and took them inside the garage, as he had his back to us I placed $20 on his work bench. 02 patched up, we continued the journey to Semey, arriving early evening, it had been another long day but we made it in spite of the temporary repairs. We were directed to a small hostel on the east side of town, close to the road that would take us to Rubtsovsk, the Kazakhstan Russian border crossing and Barnaul the following morning. The three beds in one room accommodation was tidy enough but on this occasion food wasn't available, a ten minute walk produced a rundown café come restaurant, Mariusz doesn't read Russian so what passed as a menu wasn't any good to us, both Gary and I left it to Mariusz to order something for us. It arrived moments later and was placed in front of us, when I looked at what was on my plate my stomach jumped and contracted, it was some sort of fatty meat and potatoes plus an oversize helping of greasy liquid posing as gravy, but it smelt O.K. so I was willing to give it a try. Vi often says that I have a cast iron stomach and can eat anything that is put in front of me, well I struggled this time, chewing the meat was like trying to eat a pair of old trainers, not getting anywhere with the meat, I concentrated on the potatoes and fatty gravy, after a few mouthfuls I had to give it up as a bad job and ended the evening lying on my bed waiting for my stomach to make a decision, as to whether its contents were going down or coming up, unfortunately it came up.

Monday 6th May, day 37, Semey to Barnaul, a 272 mile, 9 hour journey, coffee and cereals were available at our accommodation so we were able to get an early start; our plan was to arrive at the border crossing by late afternoon, if there were no delays we would reach Barnaul about 7pm that evening. The weather continued to be kind to us that morning, driving 02 listening to the sweet sound of its engine busily working away under the bonnet, I couldn't help thinking that considering the bone shaking miles 02 and 03 have done so far, they seemed to be running nicely, then thinking to myself, Mongolia may be a different story. In a way, I seemed to feel comfortable in my little car, sort of secure sitting all alone in 02 just driving and thinking about anything that crossed my mind, I also thought more about what it would be like when we cross the border into Mongolia on 13th May. The previous winter, I got as much information as I could to be pre-warned as to what to expect when we arrive, what I found out about the driving conditions and no decent roads made depressing reading. I needed to cheer myself up and to help to pass the time, I thought I would teach myself to sing! It would be a nice surprise for Vi, I thought to myself, when the journey is over and I return home, bags in hand, seeing Vi, then bursting into song. Not being a sing along type of person, I haven't found it necessary to learn the words to songs, so I guess I'm what you call a 'la,la' person, anyway I made up my mind to have a go. The only song I knew some of the words to, was 'Oh, what a Beautiful Morning' la la la, etc from the show Oklahoma, there was only myself and my overnight bag on the passenger seat, who I talked to on occasion, so I could sing as loud as I liked, I cleared my throat and filled my lungs with air and launched my singing career, the pleasing to listen to sound I was expecting turned out to be something very different and not too pleasing to the ear. Thinking to myself that can't be right, I tried again only this time I expelled air as I belted out the words to the song, I produced the same noise as before, but this time with a slight cockney accent and a hissing sound as I expelled the air.

Disappointed, I sat in silence for a few minutes digesting the fact that my singing career had collapsed all around me and my talent should be restricted to bath times, to hell with it, I said to myself and sod-it, I didn't want to be a singer anyway. We stopped briefly for food and fuel late morning and expected to reach the border crossing at 3.30pm that afternoon, Mariusz and Gary were in good spirits and 03 was running nicely. I asked Gary if he would run through the filming so far, he responded professionally by going back over the last few days, outlining what he had filmed. Satisfied, I asked him if he would drive with me for the remainder of the journey in 02, filming 03 driving ahead of us. We needed more footage of 03 on the road, also it would give me an opportunity to have a chat with Gary. Mariusz, driving alone in 03, led the way for the benefit of filming, Gary and I followed in 02, I asked Gary if he was O.K., he replied saying that he was fine at the moment, I said that I was pleased that he had taken a lot of film, I also referred to our previous discussion when I spoke to him about using The Ultimate Challenge to head up his resume to get back into the film business full time, I said, "My offer still stands plus a letter of recommendation from me providing you get yourself sorted out." I also mentioned that the remainder of his fee plus expenses would be in his account by the 8th, "Your travelling expenses and ticket home I have ready for you, the problem is that you are scheduled to fly out on the 9th, but I want to ask you if you will leave on the 10th?" Gary didn't want to hear this and immediately adopted the vacant look I have seen many times over the past weeks. "I want to go home," he said, I replied, "You are but I need a favour, Graham and Mike will be arriving at Novosibirsk on the 9th, for stage 3, I would like you to film me greeting them when they arrive at the airport that evening, also checking the vehicles before we leave the following morning, could you do that for me?" I don't know why but Gary was really struggling with my request and said he would phone his wife. "I promised her that I will leave on the 9th," "Its only one more day, do your best for me," I said, Gary carried on filming but didn't say much during the afternoon. We arrived at the Rubtsovsk border crossing as predicted, the crossing itself was straight forward but once again the question of me owning both vehicles caused additional scrutiny, but eventually we were let through and were back on the Russian roads for the second time, arriving at Barnaul an hour later. We already had insurance cover but I needed to exchange some more of my rapidly depleting amount of dollars into roubles, this I was able to do at a money shop a short distance from the border, we then covered the remaining distance to Barnaul, arriving just before 7pm. We booked ourselves into a typical old style Russian hotel, the building was like a blockhouse, the type you see in any Russian city or town, the two rooms allocated to us were as bare and as basic as they come, the carpet was threadbare and the sheets and towels had seen better days, but then it didn't cost much and there was food available, any other uncertainties we overcame with the help of the local beer. It had been another long day.

Tuesday 7th May, day 38, I was sitting at the breakfast table waiting for Mariusz and Gary, reflecting on a another restless night, the same thoughts turning over and over again in my mind, Mariusz would be leaving soon, how would I cope with the language, he wouldn't be there if I have a problem, what would I do if the garage won't accept my card when I want fuel, I knew I had cash as a backup, but it wouldn't last forever, I still didn't know if Gary would stay until the 10th. All I had to do was hold everything together for one more day to reach Novosibirsk and complete stage 2. It was great fun sharing the journey with Roland and Keith, a laugh a minute, stage 2 was a different situation, my time with Mariusz and Gary, I will always remember and be grateful to them for helping me at short notice, enabling me to arrive at Novosibirsk on time.

I couldn't get Mongolia out of my mind, and what was waiting for me when I got there, the desert regularly challenges and catches off guard the most experienced people, so what chance would I have of getting our team of three and the two Jimnys driving east across 1100 miles of desert to UlaanBaatar, then turning north for another 200 miles to the border, the very thought of it worried the life out of me. Mariusz and Gary joined me for breakfast; Gary looked O.K. so I assumed that he had

Big Boy Lada

spoken to his wife and in due course would let me know if he was staying or not, I said cheerfully, "We will be eating our lunch today at Novosibirsk, a day ahead of schedule, and the completion of stage 2, the distance travelled will be 3291 miles and journey time 38 days by the time we reach Novosibirsk, well done to everybody." It was another fine sunny day, there was no rush that morning but we still had a 170 mile, 5 hour journey ahead of us. At 8.30am we were fuelled and on the road, driving in the direction of Novosibirsk, I noticed that 02 wasn't bouncing around as usual, then realised for the first time since crossing the border into the Ukraine that we were driving on a road that didn't have potholes so we were able to make good time. An hour or so into the journey, 03 was leading the way, we drove past a fairly modern service area, on our left. Positioned, one on either side of the main double door entrance into the building, was what I would describe as a big boy Lada, a modified Lada car body, mounted on an elevated chassis, powered by a huge V8 and running gear that would pull a tank. There was no indication from Gary in 03 to tell me we were stopping, so I called Gary using the intercom, Mariusz answered, saying, "Gary is asleep," "Did you see those big boy Ladas?" I said, "Let's turn around." We went back to the service area and managed to park the Jimnys close to the big boys to illustrate the size difference between the little Jimnys and the towering Lada big boys. Gary could see that I was cross with him, but we got the film I wanted so I was satisfied. We hadn't seen a pothole all morning; cruising along at a steady 55 mph, my right arm resting on the lowered window, breathing in the fresh crisp air, the humming sound of the Cooper tyres on smooth asphalt, blending with the reassuring purr of 02's little engine, was blissfully sweet. Not having to focus on the road surface so much, I had an opportunity to look at the countryside and scenery as we wound our way through lush green forested hills that looked fresh and energetic after the winter snow, the sparkling, cascading waterfalls racing from hilltops to freefall and join the rivers below, the panoramic view of nature would be a landscape artist's view of heaven. We would reach Novosibirsk in an hour, and in so doing, complete stage 2. Thinking to myself at the time, I know I get fired up when I am told I can't do something that I know I can do, but I never thought that in my lifetime I would actually be driving around the world someday, but here I am, it's Tuesday 7th May, day 38, a day early, I am roughly in the middle of Russia heading for the Southern Siberia city of Novosibirsk, I wasn't sure if I was a bloody idiot or a trailblazer for energetic, retired people, probably a bit of both! We entered Novosibirsk from the south and continued towards the city centre, as luck would have it, we passed the main Suzuki dealership on the way, I contacted Mariusz to say that I wanted to stop at the Suzuki dealership, the traffic was really heavy and we were on the opposite side of the four lane each way highway, going in the wrong direction, it took some time but eventually we arrived and stopped in front of the showroom. I pushed open the door to the showroom and stepped in, followed by Mariusz and Gary, looking like we had just walked off the set of a spaghetti western, a smartly dressed man walked towards us speaking Russian, I turned to Mariusz for help, he explained who we were, the man, who was the manager, replied that he had been informed by the Suzuki P.R. office at Moscow that we would be visiting Novosibirsk and to help in any way he can.

I explained through Mariusz that I would like them to service 02 and 03, also check and rectify the slight vibration coming from the running gear and steering, and rebalance the wheels if possible. It was almost 2 o'clock, we removed the camera equipment and our personal overnight kit from the vehicles, the Service Manager and a team of mechanics took charge, but not before I reminded him with the help of Mariusz's translation about the running gear and the vibration coming from the steering. The manager confirmed that the cars would be ready for collection by mid-morning the following day, also Suzuki had organised a press conference. Relieved that 02 and 03 would be ready to take on Mongolia, the least I could do in return was to be available for the press conference. We were taken to a hotel close to the city centre, it looked expensive, but it was only for three nights. We had lunch then spent the rest of the afternoon catching up on our sleep; Gary confirmed that he would stay the extra day, so all I needed to worry about was whether Graham and Mike would arrive as planned.

Wednesday 8th May, day 39, shaved and looking presentable, I called a taxi, we were requested to be at the showroom by 11 o'clock that day, on the way, I asked the driver to stop at a camping shop so that I could buy two single burner gas stoves and refill cartridges, we had a fully equipped galley in each vehicle but the single burner stove would be handy for making a hot drink and to avoid assembling the larger galley stove. Coming to

Management and engineers at Suzuki, Novosibirsk

a stop close to the showroom, I was pleasantly surprised to see 02 and 03 looking like new, positioned in front of the showroom, surrounded by coloured balloons and display boards. We were met by the manager who then spoke to Mariusz, explaining that what I had asked to be done had been completed and both vehicles road tested, he went on to say that as it was a press day, both cars had been vacuumed inside, washed and polished. Gary filmed Mariusz and me being interviewed by the press, they asked a lot of questions about the project, how far we had travelled, when it would finish, and so on, the session lasted about an hour. I said to Mariusz, "I had better find the manager and ask how much I have to pay," the manager appeared as if by magic, I asked Mariusz to ask about payment, he then spoke briefly to Mariusz, who in turn related it to me, saying that Suzuki has arranged to cover the cost, there would be no charge. Overwhelmed by Suzuki's generosity, I thanked everybody for the hospitality shown to us and for completing the work on the vehicles so quickly and then returned to the hotel. When we arrived back, I positioned

02 and 03 close to the main entrance for best effect and a possible discount of our bill at the end of our stay. The remainder of the afternoon and evening we spent sightseeing, to be truthful, and from what I saw, I didn't think Novosibirsk was a historical or cultural city, but fairly modern as Russian cities go, it was noticeably cleaner and the public services seemed properly organised. There was no shortage of bars or places to eat, if you are partial to a glass or two of Guinness you are well catered for, we passed a number of Irish bars on our walkabout, everything seemed expensive but I guess that's the price you pay if you live in a westernised city in the middle of Russia.

Thursday 9th May, day 40, I awoke at 4am, made myself a cup of tea, courtesy of the hotel, once more I had an unsettled night's sleep, once again thinking about a whole list of things that had been buzzing around inside my head for days, I stood by the window in my room watching the city coming to life but not actually seeing anything, as I mentally analysed the issues troubling me.

This was the day Mariusz flew back to Poland, so from now on, I would have to deal with everything he normally dealt with. Mariusz was always there to help at border crossings, getting fuel, food, also dealing with hotels and on occasion asking somebody if we were on the right road, English speaking Russians are few and far between where we were going, it really worried me. The following day, Gary was to leave us to go back to the U.K. so from then on, I

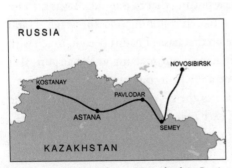

Across Kazakhstan and on to Novosibirsk in Russia

wouldn't have a cameraman until I arrive at Vancouver, Canada. Somehow I would have to deal with it myself. Apart from everything else giving me concern, there was another issue that I found myself thinking about the closer I got to Novosibirsk, this was the day I had planned to meet Graham Higgins and Mike Bailey at the airport at 5am, two people I hardly knew, Graham answered an advertisement I placed in the local paper saying what we were doing and that we had crew seats available. From the first time I met Graham I knew we would get on just fine, there wasn't much time before the start date so we didn't get much of a chance to really get to know each other, but I knew we would be O.K. together. Anyway, a short while after Graham joined us he contacted me to ask if I was still looking for crew, thinking for a moment I said, "I am," he went on to say that he knew someone who may be interested, "it's someone I know at the club," he said. I asked a few questions and agreed to a meeting. A day or two later, I met Mike Bailey for the first time, we chatted about the project and how he would fit in etc, I was particularly interested when he mentioned he had been involved with rally driving for British Leyland back in the 70s, he seemed a decent enough chap and I was grateful he wanted to join us and fill the remaining seat, but to be truthful I didn't feel the same when I met Mike for the first time as I did when I met Graham, we really didn't have time to get to know each other, putting that to one side, I was grateful to both Graham and Mike for joining me for stage 3 and arrangements were made on that basis. I hadn't been in touch with the guys since departure day so our meeting at the airport, if it was to happen, would be a credit to our organisation. Mariusz, Gary and I shared the taxi to the airport, when we arrived at the departure building, we exchanged an emotional farewell then, sadly, Gary and I made our way to arrivals, hoping to find the guys waiting for me but it wasn't to be, I had a look around, couldn't see them so I sat down opposite a pair of doors with an arrivals sign above and waited. Gary joined me after he had finished a cigarette, with the camera ready to roll the moment the guys appeared. While we sat waiting, I said to Gary, "We will wait for an hour, if nothing happens I will make some phone calls." I needn't have worried, 20 minutes later Graham and Mike appeared, looking like they hadn't slept for a week, I don't know who was surprised the most, them or me, I don't think either of us expected the other to be there.

The guys and I settled in the taxi that took us back to the hotel, it was a confidence boost for me now that we had met as planned, I asked if it was a good flight and how everything was at home. I also mentioned that I was pleased to see that their travelling bags were small, and about the weight agreed, as stowage space was limited. Gary sighed with relief when he heard Mike say that he had managed to bring the replacement parts for the filming kit that I ordered from David at Viewpoint Productions. I also mentioned that I had brought Mariusz to the airport that morning and he would be on his way to Poland during the day and Gary kindly agreed to stay for one more day so that he could film their arrival and the start of stage 3, leaving the hotel the following morning. After filming us leaving, Gary would be catching a flight to the U.K. We arrived back at the hotel; I registered Graham and Mike then suggested that they take their bags to their rooms and meet me for breakfast so that I could brief them as to what was happening during the next few days.

We met as arranged, I explained that after breakfast they should rest for a while, then early that afternoon we would meet so that I could brief them about the journey so far and our itinerary for the next few days, and familiarise themselves with the vehicle and equipment. Then added, "I would like to arrive at Kosh-Agach, close to the Russian Mongolian border by late Saturday, a two day, 540 mile journey, to achieve this we need to leave by 9am the following morning." The guys went to their rooms, Gary followed saying that as he was awake at 4am that morning, he also wanted to sleep for a while. Remaining at the table, I decided to make a note of some of the issues on my mind. I ordered a pot of coffee from a passing waiter, then took from my bag my note book and diary, I then thumbed through my papers and produced my map of Mongolia and spread it out on the table to study. I sat in silence, just staring at the map in front of me, then lent back on the chair and at the same time let out a huge sigh. Continuing to stare at the map, I turned the pages of my note book, glancing at previous entries before arriving at a clean page. I sat motionless for a moment focusing once more on the map and placed both elbows on the table, burying my face into my hands, blanking out the light and thinking about what lay ahead. If only I had said no to Alan when he asked if he could join me, I would only have myself to worry about and not the wellbeing of other people, vehicles, equipment and finance, dicing with death all the way across Europe, Russia and Kazakhstan so as to be at Novosibirsk by 9th May, and then the drive across Mongolia, a place that would terminate my breathing given half a chance. Startled back to reality when the waiter placed the coffee on the table, I looked up with red eyes and thanked him. I thought for a moment and then said to myself, there is no point thinking about what might have happened, I should think about what has actually happened and what I do from here on. O.K., I said to myself, stage 1 was a success, stage 2, although it was really a delivery trip, it was mission accomplished and a credit to Mariusz and Gary. Stage 3 may well be a different story but I have acquired some experience over the past weeks and I needed to express my confidence when talking to Graham and Mike, and eventually Glyn and Roger when I meet them at Vancouver, they should be under no illusion about what we are doing and how serious and dangerous it really is. At the planning stage of the itinerary and to help keep control of costs, it was always intended that once we had crossed the border into the Ukraine 40% of the overnight stops would be camping under the stars. I had given a lot of thought as to how far we would travel each day, the estimated distance we would travel depended on what country we were travelling through and the likely road surface, so there was a lot of guesswork when compiling the itinerary. The outcome of my observations as we drove stage 1 & 2 was that while I had got the driving time, in the main, right!!, I had omitted to include the time at the end of each day needed to find a campsite and erect the tents, the same applied in the morning for packing up before we got back on the road. It wasn't possible to adjust the itinerary, also to be fair to the guys, after a long day driving and arriving at the destination in the dark, to then have to erect tents would be too much to ask. After a bit of head scratching, I concluded that although both vehicles were kitted out for camping, it was not an option at that time. Overnight accommodation would continue as before although adding to our cost, it was essential that the guys get a good night's sleep. I reviewed the list of equipment and supplies that each vehicle was carrying; they also had been serviced and checked so were ready to tackle Mongolia. Later that day, Graham and Mike would have an opportunity to drive 03 locally so as to familiarise themselves ready for the following morning.

By the time I had transferred most of my thoughts onto paper, I felt a little better. The one entry I made in my book that I ringed around, and that really troubled me, was the prospect of having to deal with all those run of the mill things requiring a few words in Russian that Mariusz had previously dealt with. I was to be put to the test the following morning when we stopped for fuel, nobody would speak English, so if there was a problem with my card or I needed to explain that I wanted to pay for both vehicles with one card or if there's a limit to the amount of fuel I could have, I would have a problem. I had overstayed my welcome at the breakfast room, so decided to go to my room and call Vi to have a chat and tactfully mention to top up the project account to make sure that there was sufficient funds available for me to draw on.

I spent some time talking to Vi, reassuring her that I was O.K. and that I missed her very much, we laughed at a number of things mentioned, especially when I said, "I have to cut my own toenails and trim the hair growing out of my ears myself," I won't repeat what she said. Talking to Vi for a few minutes was something I looked forward to, we did the lovey dovey bit, then I said, "The next time I speak to you, it will be from Mongolia." It was late morning, I was feeling tired as a result of being awake since 4am, so I decided to snatch two hours' sleep before I met the guys. At around 2.30pm, I made my way to the lounge, Graham and Mike were already there, looking refreshed, it wasn't necessary that Gary be there, so I started by talking to them about the journey so far, then I outlined the itinerary and programme for stage 3. This included an early start the following morning, the two day drive to the Russia-Mongolia border, arriving Sunday, ready to cross on Monday 13th, and the 7 day, 1500 mile journey across Mongolia. I suggested to Graham and Mike that they take 03 for a drive so as to get a feeling for the car fully loaded, also to mix it with the traffic for a while to experience what it will be like when we leave the following morning. I then went on to say, "For safety reasons it is important that we remain in visual contact at all times, two vehicles travelling represent a lesser security risk if together, rather than driving a kilometre apart." I went on to remind them that the idea of using two vehicles was that if one vehicle had an accident or broke down, the other would be able to apply first aid, or tow the damaged vehicle if need be. I said, "In the event that we need to communicate with each other as we are driving, do so by using the Motorola handheld radio." The safety procedures had worked so far, so I asked that they would not deviate from these arrangements without first discussing it as a team.

Mike and Graham check out '03' before they set out on Stage 3 from Novosibirsk

The guys had taken 03 for a short drive, I sat in the hotel lounge waiting for the pot of tea I ordered when Gary appeared, I asked if he was O.K. he said, "I feel much better," I mentioned about him filming us leaving in the morning. I said, "I would like to leave by 10am so if you could film us checking the vehicles then driving off, we will then double back to collect the camera kit then be on our way." I handed Gary his flight ticket and explained the details relating to his flight home, I also gave him sufficient roubles, dollars, and U.K. pounds to cover his travelling expenses. I then said, "We won't have much time in the morning, so I would like to thank you now for helping me." The guys returned from their short drive and joined Gary and me in the lounge. We all stayed awhile, the discussion was mainly about what to expect when we cross the Mongolia border, I vaguely listened to what was being said but my mind was elsewhere. The following morning we would be setting off, I felt sick, I don't speak Russian, how could I communicate, it was driving me crazy, I could think of nothing else. Later that evening we had a meal then the guys decided to turn in early.

I went to my room and sat in silence for a long time, thinking about what would happen when I try to get fuel or food. It was nearly 12 o'clock when I got into bed, the same questions going round and round in my head. I lay in the dark thinking then suddenly I sat up and switched the light on at the same time saying to myself, "Leslie, it's so obvious you didn't see it". Elated that I had thought of a solution to my problem, I jumped out of bed, turned the pages of my writing pad and started writing, I wrote every question I was likely to ask, for example, please can you help? I don't speak Russian, I need fuel for two cars, can I pay by card for both cars or do I have to pay cash? I wrote every question I could think of, leaving a space below each one to accommodate a translation into Russian off what I had written. I compiled four pages by the time I had finished; all I had to do now was to sweet talk the English speaking lady at the reception to write in the gaps the Russian version of what I had written. Pleased with myself, I got into bed and had the best night's sleep for a long time.

Friday 10th May, day 41, I opened my eyes at 6.30am and lay motionless for a moment or two. I felt refreshed and energetic and at the same time realised that my head was no longer spinning. I then remembered my solution for dealing with my communication problem, I sprung out of bed (well I didn't exactly spring out of bed), showered, shaved and dressed in a clean set of clothes, I then looked in the mirror, irresistible, I thought to myself. Collecting my four pages, I made for the door then stopped and went back to the bathroom for a squirt of cologne, just for the benefit of the ladies at reception. Riding in the lift to the ground floor, I turned over the pages to make sure that I had written all that I needed, satisfied as the doors from the lift parted,

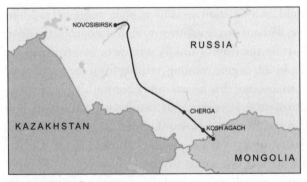

Russia to Mongolia

I made for the reception and the good looking lady who spoke English. Standing upwind so she would get a full strength sniff of my cologne, I politely asked if she could help me by translating into Russian what I had written in English. Unable to resist, she said that it would take a little time but if I returned in an hour it would be ready. I felt like a different person as I went back to my room, regaining my confidence that had been slipping lately, I was ready to lock horns with Mongolia. It was 9.45am by the time we finished breakfast and I had paid the hotel bill, then for the benefit of Gary filming, we simulated our departure, returning a few minutes later. I stowed the camera kit in the back of 02, once again thanking Gary and saying that I hope everything turns out O.K. for him. I then turned to Graham and Mike who were standing close to 03 saying, "Are you guys ready? Now remember, stay as close to me as you can so that you don't get lost or separated at traffic lights or in traffic, if we drive at 30 mph we should be alright, shall we go then?" As I turned towards 02 I heard Mike say in an argumentative tone, "It's your responsibility to make sure we don't get lost." I turned and just stared at him as I made up my mind what my reply would be, what I wanted to say wouldn't have been very complimentary, so instead, I said, "I can only drive one car at a time, stay close and you won't get lost."

Graham could see a situation developing, so he suggested to Mike that he drive, without saying another word, Mike opened the door of 03 and sat on the driver's seat. A minute or two had passed, I was sitting in 02, engine running, waiting for some movement from Mike to indicate that he was ready but nothing happened, becoming frustrated, I got out of 02 to ask what was wrong, but as I did, 03 rolled forward. Leaving the hotel car park, we entered the three lane highway via a slip road, I checked to see if Mike was behind, he was but some way back. I slowed to 20 mph expecting him to catch up but he didn't close the gap, seeing an emergency stopping area, I turned into it and stopped, hoping Mike had followed. As 03 arrived, I got out of 02 to ask Mike why he was driving at 20 mph. I don't think I got a reply, but I continued to say, "If we carry on like this, we will never get out of the city, please keep close and stay at 30 mph."

Mike didn't look happy and I can tell you I was as cross as hell at having to stop and once again ask Mike to drive a little faster. I got back into 02 and was about to drive off when a police Lada came to a stop across the front of me and two policemen got out and asked to see our papers. What a start to the day! I said to myself as I produced 02's papers and handed them to the policeman and at the same time pointed at the door of 02 indicating that we were driving around the world. The police shuffled through 02's papers, looked at the insurance then said a few words in Russian, handed back the papers then said something that I assumed meant you can go. Relieved that I didn't have to part with any money, we got ourselves back onto the highway, this time, 03 was doing a little better. Our journey out of the city was slow and we were separated at one point, I crossed a set of traffic lights but 03 didn't make it, I was able to wait further along the road and soon after we were back together. As I led the way out of the city I had plenty of time to think about what happened, I didn't think I said nor did anything that would cause Mike to react the way he did. If he was unhappy at the thought of driving through the city, he had plenty of opportunity to tell me. I have mentioned previously, I didn't have much time to get to know Mike before we left the U.K. so I had no idea he would react in the way he did. It worried me at the time, but then I thought that the best way to handle the situation would be to carry on as though it never happened and hope for the best. After we had been driving for 40 minutes I saw a transport service area to my right. I called Graham using the radio to say that we would stop for fuel and a coffee, 03 followed me to the fuel pumps, I stopped and got out of 02, clutching my four pages containing the translated questions, I asked the guys to watch the vehicles while I went to the cash window to arrange for the fuel. Folding the pages so as to isolate the question dealing with the purchase of fuel, I handed it to the lady on the other side of the window who gave me a strange look as she took and read the message, waiting for her reaction, she looked up smiling, saying something in Russian and pointing at a visa sign over the top of the cash window. I produced my card and handed it to her, she examined it for a moment then waving her hand, sent me back to the pumps to fill the cars, after filling both cars I collected my list of questions and put them into my pocket, out of sight for the time being, back at the pumps I said to guys in a blasé clever dick manner, you can fill up now. When the cars were fully fuelled, I walked back to the window rehearsing on the way the Russian for thank you, the transaction complete and my card safely back in my wallet, I said to the lady spa-si-ba (thank you) sounding like a native. With the city behind us, we were able to make better time on the roads, although cracked and uneven, they weren't too bad to drive on, I was leading and if I remember correctly, Graham was driving 03, I spoke to Mike on the handheld to say, "We need to increase our cruising speed to 55 mph as it's another 150 miles before we reach Biysk. I will drive at 55 mph just see if you can keep up." We didn't manage to achieve what I wanted, but the guys did O.K. bearing in mind it was their first day, we arrived at Biysk at around 6.30pm. We had been travelling for 8 hours by the time we found suitable accommodation, we were totally knackered. We rested for an hour then met for a beer at the small bar on the ground floor, we discussed the journey that day, no reference was made about the incident prior to starting that morning so I was happy to let sleeping dogs lie. I said to Graham and Mike, "You have had a day to get the hang of things and I am sure you understand the importance of keeping together." I then said, "The reason why we travel at 55 mph when we can is because of the long distances we sometimes have to travel, if we drive too slowly we will arrive at our destination in the dark, making it difficult to find accommodation. Also at 55 mph on a paved surface, the fuel economy is about 35 mpg. Travelling through Mongolia driving on mainly sand and flint tracks, we will be lucky if we manage 20 mpg." I went on to say that if they were unhappy about anything, to bring it to my attention so that we could discuss it. I thought that our chat over a beer brought us a little closer together; we walked some distance into the town to find a place to eat and have a look around. It was similar to many other towns I had passed through as I travelled east, yet it seemed to have a sort of friendly feel about it, the people were helpful and smiled when you tried to talk to them, giving the impression that they genuinely wanted to be helpful. On the way back to the hotel we spoke about the journey the following day, I said that I didn't have much information about the road conditions but from what I had read, the scenery in some parts is quite stunning.

Saturday 11th May, day 42, the bright early morning sun shone through the window of my room as I awoke from a deep, restful sleep, it was 6.30am. I had agreed to meet the guys for breakfast at 7am so I needed to get myself organised. I glanced out of the window at a cloudless sunny day, the roads were dry and there was hardly any wind, a perfect day for the drive to Kosh-Agach, a 328 mile, 9 hour journey. We met for breakfast, looking fresh and ready to take on the next stage of our journey; our accommodation wasn't expensive and therefore related to what was available for breakfast, I scanned the spread in front of me, trying to make my mind up as to whether it was breakfast or lunch. I have to say that I am a creature of habit when it comes to food, in the morning I tuck into cereals, figs or prunes and maybe toast, followed by a couple of cups of tea. If I feel reckless, I might have full English now and again when my wife is not around. What I was looking at on that occasion, was a bowl of hot boiled potatoes, cabbage and carrots, a jug of what looked like gravy, a basket of dry bread and several dishes of hot spices from mild to those that will set fire to your backside. Anyway, we managed to salvage something we could eat and eventually got ourselves on the road and heading south by 7.30am. An hour later we entered the Altai Republic, reputed to be a land of mountains, lakes and rivers, the roads were not very good but we were able to maintain a reasonable cruising speed. I was excited at the prospect of driving through unspoiled terrain and it wasn't long before the wide expanse of the Katun River appeared on my right, reflecting the morning sun and the lush green hills beyond. I drove with the window lowered, taking in deep breaths of cool, clean, crisp air that seemed to stimulate and energise my body, it was a great feeling. At Ust-Sema, the road veered to the right to Cherga then on to the Seminsky Pass, watched over by towering snow-capped mountains on either side of the road and musically sounding streams, converging and making their way south. Unable to pass by the breathtaking glimpse of nature, I stopped at a clearing followed by 03 and the guys, we got out of the cars and stood in silence, listening to nature going about its business. It was a moment in time that will never be forgotten. Surprisingly, the traffic was light and there were noticeably fewer heavy, overloaded lorries to contaminate the countryside. The towns we passed through pretty well all looked the same, over the years what started as a shack at the side of the track became a village at the side of the road, until finally it became a town with a major road running through it. Once through the towns though, you quickly enter the solitude of nature and the bliss of silence. Along the way and set back from the road we saw on occasion a colourfully decorated circular yurt (ger) which is a nomadic family house with a few animals close by. We managed to find a road side café, well it was an old shed really that looked like it was about to collapse when the next person slams the door, but the smell coming from the inside was inviting. I produced my magic notes and folded them so that the question I wanted was visible, it read 'Excuse me my Russian is limited can you help me please? We would like food and tea or coffee can you show me what you have? Thank you.' I handed it to a man behind the counter, he read what I had to say then handed it back to me, I quickly concealed it hoping the guys didn't see. I had no idea what we were eating but it tasted O.K. Feeling better after our meal, I suggested that we stop for fuel at the first opportunity to make sure that we could reach our destination. A few miles further along the road, there was a fairly modern service area and garage, the procedure to get fuel worked like clockwork, I was strutting about like a dog with two tails, but thought to myself, if I lose my four pages, I will be in the mire! It was time to let the guys know how I had been able to converse so well.

The remainder of our journey led us to the Chike-Taman pass, a spectacular valley watched over by menacing hills on both sides and Mount Baida away in the distance to the right. Also the spectacular view of snow capped Mount Aktru, 4044 metres high and Mount Maashey, 4177 metres. I felt humbled but also privileged, in a way, that life has allotted me an opportunity to travel along the road that winds its way through valley floors and over hills shadowed by mountains, isolated from the rest of the human race. For me, the experience was so overwhelming I have difficulty in describing it; perhaps I was living the dream. For almost 3 years I had worked to bring The Ultimate Challenge together, I used to think about visiting places like the ones that I have described, and wondered if I would ever be lucky enough to see it. There hadn't been much radio bantering that day, I guess Graham and Mike, like me, were overwhelmed by nature unfolding before our eyes. Driving alone day after day for up to 12 hours eventually started to have an effect on me. The loneliness throughout the day is interrupted only when we talk over the radio, and the short stops for fuel and food, the remainder of the time there is no one to talk to. I brought with me a collection of CDs to listen to but for some reason I never got around to it. I normally would just sit there, my eyes watching the road and occasionally glancing at the scenery as I thought about anything that came into my head. Before I continue I would like to touch on something personal, I mentioned earlier when describing what makes me tick, I stated then that in business I was never a hard person, more like firm when I had to be and compassionate and understanding when I needed to be. I have always been a bit emotional and shed a tear at the slightest excuse. Towards the end of 2007, my wife and I received a phone call from our son, Lee, telling us the life shattering news that he had terminal cancer, coming to terms with Lee's predicament was bad enough, but watching Lee go through the process of dying was unbearable, Vi and Carole, our daughter, and the rest of the family seemed to cope with the situation better than I could, and to this day I get very emotional when I think of our son, as I did that afternoon when Lee left for another place on 4th June 2008.

The journey continued to be spectacular and whilst I was looking at the scenery, I somehow thought of our son Lee, his time at school and as a teenager, also working with us in the family business. To say he was a rascal would be an understatement, I laughed to myself when I remembered the nickname I had for him, 'A Stroke a Minute Lee' is what I called him. It was a constant battle trying to catch him at the various schemes or fiddles he used to get up to. When we found out he was doing something he shouldn't, I would usually have a flaming row with him, on occasion I would give him the sack, only to reinstate him a few days later. We were always arguing about one thing or another, but we loved each other the way a father and son do, if only I could argue with him today.

Anyway that particular day, driving alone in 02, I found myself thinking about my son and how much I missed him. My eyes glassed for a moment then turned to tears, I couldn't help it, I drove for a while crying, until eventually I managed to compose myself and with red eyes, once again, focus on the road ahead. The remainder of our journey ran parallel with the Chuya River all the way to Kosh-Agach, our overnight stop. We arrived late afternoon; the town was situated at the eastern end of a huge valley, the Russian Mongolia border crossing was 60 miles further on. Kosh-Agach had the appearance of a shanty town with a few substantial buildings at its centre. I enquired about accommodation and was informed that there was only one place, a hostel across the street from where we were, we drove to the building and parked. We located the proprietor who informed us that he had a three bedded room available; the price was equivalent to about 30 dollars. The accommodation was a bit rough but warm and the sheets were clean, there was also a communal kitchen and washing facilities. I was able to talk to the hostel owner about crossing the border, he informed me that it was not open on Sunday, hearing the news, I asked if we could stay for two nights, and was there a restaurant, he said that two nights for the room was O.K., there was no restaurant in the town but he knew a club owner who may be able to help. To overcome situations such as this 02 and 03 both carried camping and galley equipment plus a comprehensive range of food, plus tea, coffee and pickings of one sort or another, so we were able to produce a meal for ourselves if we had to. As it turned out, we produced a meal for ourselves the first night and hoped to get a meal somewhere the following night.

Sunday 12th May, day 43, I woke early so as to be first in the shower in case the hot water was limited, feeling clean, shaved and dressed, I went outside to the vehicles to collect the breakfast plates and cutlery, then laid up a table in the kitchen, I was about ready when the guys entered the room. I rustled up ready for them a breakfast of dried fruit, figs and prunes, then cereals and coffee or tea. After breakfast, I suggested that we drive the 60 miles to the border to make sure we knew where it was and what to expect on Monday. It was a beautiful day, cold but sunny, and it wasn't long before we arrived at the border crossing and parked the cars. I had a pretty good idea how

the film camera worked so I ran some footage of the guys and the vehicles with the border crossing in the background. Graham and Mike were taking pictures as a man in plain clothes came out from a building in the centre of the compound and walked towards us, he said in broken English that the border was closed that day but would open Monday at 9am, he then went on to say that cameras were forbidden. We quickly took the hint and

Les preparing breakfast for the team

Tashanta Hostel – the overnight stop before crossing into Mongolia

got back into our cars and left. As we drove back to town, we deviated from the road to explore the surrounding area, stopping now and again and switching the engines off so as to look at the scenery in absolute silence. When we eventually got back to town, we topped up the fuel tanks and spent an hour checking the vehicles and equipment ready for the crossing into Mongolia the following morning. We managed to organise for ourselves what passed as a meal that evening, washed down with a local beer or two, it was a few minutes' walk to the hostel, the outside temperature had dropped considerably signalling an increase of our walking pace if we were to avoid being frozen to death before we got back inside.

Monday 13th May, day 44, we were ready to go by 7.45am and soon heading for the border, we wanted to be early. As we were passing the outskirts of the town, I glanced at the fuel gauge and noticed that I only had a little over half a tank of fuel, I was about to call 03, when Mike beat me to it to say that their tank was also only half full.

Mr Fix-it 2, a young man and a real professional the rewelding job he did for us needed no further attention.

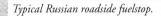

Typical Russian roadside fuelstop.

The owner of the one man business was so polite and helpful, it was a Sunday and he was in his clean clothes but that didn't deter him from helping us, such kindness.

Graham and Mike arriving at Novosibirsk as planned.

O3 following the track that crossed a river.

02 driving along a sand and grit road in Mongolia.

The guys stop for a short break at a village before continuing to drive through the desert.

Mongolian mounted herdsman.

Driving off the track to allow trucks coming in the opposite direction to pass.

A herd of yaks grazing.

A stretch of surfaced road as we approach a town.

Les and 02 descending from the bone shaking base of the soon to be completed road to re-join the old track.

Another short stretch of surfaced road ends to be replaced with a sand and flint track.

Passing a small village en route to Bayankongor, Mongolia.

Les pictured with two local lads wearing The Ultimate Challenge caps.

An invitation to see inside the immaculate and clean Mongolian ger.

Graham and Les each side of the petite Mongolian lady who made us so welcome.

At a roadside stop we saw a fully grown brown bear in a cage for people to look at.

A religious procession at Khabarovsk.

A lady in traditional costume out for a stroll on Sunday at Khabarovsk.

English speaking people at a stall at an open-air market.

We stopped to discuss the situation and concluded that both the vehicles must have had fuel siphoned out of the tanks overnight but were puzzled as to how it was done because the filler cap was locked and undamaged. We once again topped up our tanks and continued to the border. There were a few vehicles waiting when we arrived, it was after 9am but the gates remained closed, we sat around for a while, waiting for something to happen. At 9.30am two Russian border guards opened the gate and directed the cars in front of us to move to one side then beckoned us forward, indicating that we must park at the building in the centre of the compound, I collected the paperwork for both vehicles and entered the building, Graham and Mike followed behind. Inside, there were a lot of people milling around, I went to the nearest counter and spoke to the man we had seen the day before because I knew that he spoke English. I explained who we were, what we were doing and where we were going. I mentioned that both vehicles were registered in my name, he asked and I answered a number of questions, the passports were stamped and

Waiting at the Russia Mongolia border crossing

Filling our tanks and asking for directions at a Mongolian village

returned then we were told that we could go. Although I have driven across no man's land a number of times I still get that unsettling feeling that disappears quickly the moment the gates are opened on the other side. The crossing on this occasion was no exception, as we approached the Mongolian border control, the gate opened and we were given directions of where to go. The procedure was as before, but with additional passport scrutiny to make sure that our visas were valid. Once again, I had to explain why both vehicles were registered in my name, when I had satisfied them with my answer, we were handed back our passports and told we could go; the crossing on that occasion took about 40 minutes.

At last we had made it to Mongolia and as soon as they closed the gate behind us, we stopped for a moment to take it all in. I mentioned that I had driven almost 4000 miles and 44 days to get here, the question was, were we and the vehicles ready to take on what lay ahead of us. Looking down at the new smooth road surface, I said to the guys, "I think I have got it wrong about the roads, this is supposed to be a sand and flint track." It was 10.30am when we got back into the cars and continued to drive east through Mongolia, elated that we were driving along a new flat, wide road that was indicated on the map as under

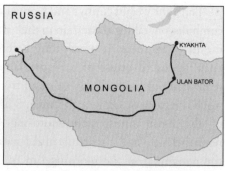

Across Mongolia

construction. I led the way, smiling to myself as I thought of all those months I had worried and concerned myself about the vehicles and ourselves being thrown around day after day as we navigated our way along the old sand and flint tracks they call roads. The handheld radios were alive with banter, rubbing it in, so to speak, about how I had got it wrong about the road surface, also that we would now make better time than predicted. Suddenly there was there was silence. We had been following the new road for a few kilometres, then it turned left at the base of a large hill and suddenly ended, it didn't go any further. Dumbfounded, I just let 02 roll to a stop inches short of the end of a laser straight cut dividing the new road, and the sand and flint track that snaked its way into the distance, I WAS LOOKING AT THE ROAD FROM HELL. Graham and Mike in 03 stopped by the side of me, we sat there in silence, I had got it right after all. Without another word, we coaxed 02 and 03 over the edge of the new road onto the sand track which was the width of a standard lorry, about 8 feet (2.4 metres), worn over a period of time so that the track surface was 12 inches (30 centimetres) lower than the surrounding tundra. Dropping over the edge onto a surprisingly hard surface, I felt reassured as the partially deflated Cooper tyres compensated for the unevenness caused by the exposed flint nodules.

The light weight Jimnys and Cooper tyres seemed the perfect combination, taking the terrain in their stride as though they were meant to be there, it wasn't long before confidence returned, enabling us to cruise at a comfortable 45 mph. I mentally reinstated our original plan to travel from the border and try to reach the town of Ulgit, a 237 mile, 8 hour journey across some of the most inhospitable motoring terrain in the world, nevertheless, I had a schedule and I meant to keep to it. Using the remainder of the morning sun to check the compass, we continued in a southerly direction, following the single track that had cut itself into the virgin tundra. Alone and isolated, we drove between sand mountains, across open plains until eventually we emerged from a gorge with sides so high sunlight never penetrated to the bottom, the single track that snaked ahead of us through a wide valley became lost as it merged to become one of many tracks that crossed each other.

Undecided as to which way to go, we noticed that a track led to a village far away to our left. There were no signs telling us which way to go so we headed for the village to ask for directions and if we were lucky, top up our tanks with fuel. Graham and Mike showed their map to a group of people who showed some interest, they looked at the map and pointed in the direction we should go. The single pump fuel facility only had available low octane fuel but needs must so we topped up the tanks and hoped for the best. 03 led as we continued our journey as directed but somehow we had taken a wrong turn that led us up the side of a fairly high hill; near the summit, the track, which was alarmingly close to the down side of the hill, was blocked.

To the right of the blockage were tyre tracks indicating that there was a way around the blocked road, I asked the guys in 03 to stay where they were to watch me in case I got into trouble. The hill was about 750 metres high, high enough to scare the living daylights out of me as I coaxed 02 down a 10 foot drop and followed the tyre tracks around the side of the hill that eventually led nowhere. I sat still, surveying the situation, 02 was at an alarming angle perched on the very edge of the hillside. Unable to open the driver's door to get out, if I did I would go over the edge, I decided to reverse back the way I had come, when I got back to where 03 and the guys had been waiting they were not there. Considering my predicament, I was facing the wrong way and I had a near vertical 10 foot climb to get 02 and myself back on track at the top, it wasn't going to be easy. I manoeuvred 02 as close to the rising hillside sufficiently to allow me to ease out of the driver side door then by hanging onto the roof tray, I was able to get to the back and away from the edge. Before attempting to drive myself out of the mess I was in I first needed to walk the muddy tyre ruts other cars had made. Feeling for and noting the hard ground I then had a close look at the near vertical 10 foot climb to see if I would get any traction on the way up, not an ideal situation, but with enough speed I thought I could do it. Walking back to 02, I thought to myself before I can do anything I first have to turn around and that wasn't going to be easy. I managed to get back into 02 after scraping as much mud as I could from my boots, there was nowhere to turn 02 around which meant that I would have to somehow reverse up the steep hillside. I drove forward once more to give me room, stopped then selected 4 wheel drive low range as my backside reminded me that what I was about to do was very dangerous. I looked in the mirror to see if the guys in 03 had returned but there was no sign.

I slowly reversed backwards and at the same time steered so that the left side of 02 worked itself out of the tyre ruts and up the hill, driving at an angle, the left wheels up high, the right side still in the ruts. I increased my speed and at the same time turned the steering wheel to the left, hoping that the 4 wheel drive would drag 02 around so that the back of the car was facing up hill. I was hoping it would work but was unprepared when the little

02 clawed itself around and would have climbed up the hill had I not put my foot on the brakes. Now pointing down the hill, my foot hard on the brakes, my body held in position by my seat belt but suspended clear of the seat and at a frightening angle made it difficult to maintain pressure on the brakes, ooh s—t, I said to myself as I was looking down the side of the very steep hill. The engine still running and managing to find 1st gear, I eased the pressure on the brake pedal, allowing 02 to roll downhill, as it did it nosedived into the mud and ruts. At the same time I turned the wheel to the right and increased the power slightly to complete the manoeuvre, we were facing the direction I wanted to go. I selected normal 4 wheel drive, took one last look at what I had to do, reminding myself that I had done it many times before on motorbikes years ago so it shouldn't be a problem now.

Still in 1st gear, I clenched my teeth, revved the engine and eased the clutch to get 02 rolling then quickly changed to 2nd and floored the pedal. The mud parted as I found grip and headed for the climb. Feeling confident, I kept the power on until I was sure I would make it then eased the power just before reaching the top allowing 02 to become airborne and bounce back onto the track. The whole incident lasted no more than 15-20 minutes although it seemed longer, I cleaned most of the mud that 02 had collected and was wiping my hands as Graham and Mike in 03 came along the track. I asked them where they had been, they replied saying they were looking for the road that will take us to Ulgij. Concerned that they went away and left me I looked at both of them and said in a stern voice to let them know I was annoyed, "I will remind you I said for safety and security reasons it is important that we remain in sight of one another at all times, you knew I was checking out that track around the hill and I asked you to wait, I had a serious problem back there and could have used some help." The incident passed without further reference, 03 led the way back towards the village and located the track we should have taken to take us to our destination, we were behind schedule so we needed to push ourselves if we wanted to arrive before dark. We followed the track, confidently dodging pockets of fluid sand that grab hold and almost stop the forward motion if you happen to drive into one. The track headed towards a seriously high hill, its presence visibly cut into the hillside forming a sand coloured line that zigzagged to the top. I wondered if somehow we were on the wrong track once more but high up there was a dust twirl making its way skyward, probably another vehicle so I guessed we were going the right way. The single track was as bad as it could be, behind us was the relatively flat tracks of the plains, in front of us was a track that was a boggy, rutted quagmire in places with rough cut-outs on the high side to facilitate passing converging vehicles and no second chance if the driver side wheels slip over the edge on the down side. We clawed our way up, it seemed to go on forever, I noticed that the higher we climbed the less power the engine was producing, until finally after using 1st gear for some time to keep going 02 would not climb any higher, the engine running rough panting like a horse that could go no further. I called 03 who were still climbing to tell them of my predicament, I mentioned that it was probably the high altitude and low octane fuel that was the cause and that they should keep going as long as they could, if they make the top wait for me there. I switched the engine off hoping it would start when needed.

I got out of 02 and walked around a bit to ease the slight pain in my groin caused, I hoped, by bouncing up and down for the last hour or so on a full bladder. Relieving myself and thinking about what I should do at the same time, I concluded that I would have to lighten the load on 02 but before I did there was one other option I thought I would try. Fortunately, I was parked close to a cut-out for passing and sufficient for me to turn 02 around so that I was facing down the hill, reverse gear being lower than first gear I was going to try driving backwards the remainder of the distance to the top. I sweet talked 02 into starting, selected rear wheel drive only, fed in enough power to do the job then eased the pressure off the clutch pedal. The back wheels spun initially cutting through the mud to find grip then 02 started to drag itself up the hill. Using the driver's side mirror only to guide me, I stayed close to the high side of the hill as we slowly clawed our way to the top. Graham and Mike were standing by 03 taking in the scenery surprised to see me emerging from the track facing the wrong way. We were high enough for the cold, low density air to affect our breathing but the view was stunning, from what we could see, going down the other side looked straight forward. We could see the track clearly from our vantage point at the top, twisting and turning as it descended to the valley floor then working its way in a southerly direction and disappearing into the distance. We still had a long way to go so after finishing something to eat and a cup of coffee produced out of the back of 02, we descended the hill and made our way along the valley floor that opened out to become a plain that stretched ahead of us as far as the eye could see. I was leading in 02 and 03 was some way back so as to avoid the dust and sand cloud created by 02. The track was bumpy and rutted in places but we managed to maintain a 40-45 mph, at that speed the dust churned up was horrendous. It was over an hour since we descended the hill to the valley floor, 03 and the guys had been behind eating my dust all that time, so I wasn't surprised when I looked in the driver side mirror to see 03 following a another track that worked its way more to the south. Thinking that they were going to turn to the left to re-join the main track in front of me to take their turn in the lead, I eased off the accelerator waiting for 03 to turn and take up their position ahead of me but they continued south increasing the distance between us. I called 03 on the handheld, Graham answered, I asked why had they left the main track Graham replied that the track they were taking re-joins the main track further on, I said, "It is dangerous to leave the main track and go off on your own," I continued talking but I got the feeling it was a one way conversation, there was no further contact. I watched as 03 made its way south, there was nothing I could do. If I left the main track to follow them there was no guarantee that we would find it again so I decided to follow the main track and keep an eye on them as long as I could. I continued along the track for another kilometre or so but I lost sight of 03 when the track took a turn behind a hill, when I came out the other side there was no sign of them. I stopped and scoured the horizon in the direction I thought they might be to see if there was any sign of a dust trail to pinpoint their position, there was nothing. I sat motionless, the silence of the desert broken only by the sound of 02's little engine reassuringly idling under the bonnet. Thinking about what I should do next, I turned off the engine and called 03 on the handheld but got no response, I continued calling for a few more minutes but still nothing happened. I gave a great sigh as I sat back in my seat thinking to myself that I had enough to think about without Graham and Mike adding to it, I did think at one point that maybe I should try to follow them then discarded the question saying to myself that it would only make matters worse.

Thinking what to do next I noticed that about half a kilometre ahead of me, the track I was on went up and over a small hill, I decided to drive the short distance to the top of the hill and try the handheld once more, the higher elevation would increase the transmitting distance, once in position I could see for miles all around me, it was desolate. I called 03 then waited, hoping for a response, but nothing, I called two or three more times, still nothing other than a slight click at the end of the last transmission motivating me to try once again, I called and waited, as I did Graham's voice came booming back loud and clear. Relieved that we were in contact with one another, I asked if he knew where they were, "I'm not sure," he said, "but if we drive east we should cross the track you are on," was his reply. I said, "Get up on high ground and watch in the direction where you think I am and I will try and create a dust trail and you look to see if you can see it." The stretch of track in front of me was pretty straight so leaving the high ground behind me, I coaxed 02 as fast as I could along the track causing dust to swirl high in the air, the call I was waiting for soon came. "I can see you," Graham said, "O.K." I replied, "I will reduce speed but keep the dust trail going so you can home in on it." There was enough dust in the air for the guys in 03 to pinpoint my position and not long after we made contact, 03 came into view from the right cutting its own trail through virgin tundra and stopping at a patch of sand used as a campsite by travellers in the past. I came to a stop close by, got out of the car and walked over and just looked at them for a moment then said, "What you did was stupid and irresponsible going off on your own, if you had rolled over or injured yourselves in some way I wouldn't have known what had happened or where to look for you, the same applies to me if I had an accident and you are not close by to help. We rely on each other for our safety and security," subdued they offered an apology, I then got back into 02 and we continued the journey.

You need to be a nomad to find your way around Mongolia, there are hardly any directional signs as you travel across the desert, our G.P.S. and TomTom in each vehicle stopped functioning when we entered Mongolia, the road maps were useful but the roads indicated on the maps as paved were mainly sand and flint so we had to navigate the old way. Fortunately, the sky was clear as we travelled and as luck would have it, we were generally driving in an easterly direction. Each morning, we would start our journey by facing the sun to make sure that we were on the right track and follow it. Providing the track didn't deviate too much we would eventually arrive at our destination,

I made it sound simple but it generally worked. To be fair to Graham and Mike, if we got lost they usually got it sorted out, their map work kept us pointing in the right direction all the way to Vladivostok. In spite of an already eventful day, we got lost again, the sand and tundra gave way to flint as we worked our way through a pass between mountains, on the other side there was a stream and tracks going off in all directions. We took the track we thought was the right one and followed it for quite a way then it ended in the middle of who knows where. We back tracked to a ger (a traditional Nomad dwelling) we had passed earlier nestling at the foot of a small hill, there were goats and chickens close by and an old motorbike at the side of the ger. We stopped and I knocked on the small door and stood back, the door opened and, surprisingly, a tall man ducked out of the door and smiled. Graham showed him the map, indicating with his finger that we wanted to go to Olgii (Ulgij), there was some head scratching then he realised what we were asking, he sprang into life pointing to the river and indicated that we must take the next turn after the river. I couldn't help looking around at the simple way the Nomads lived but then I thought, they don't have the westernised baggage we drag through life, who's got it right?!

We took pictures of him and his family then I went to 02 and retrieved a crash helmet that I was carrying in case we got thrown around in the cars at some point and needed head protection. I presented the helmet to the man who had trouble understanding it was a gift but we got there in the end, lovely people. We managed to find the track we were looking for and settled down to drive the remaining distance to our destination without further incident, arriving safely at about 6.30pm. The sun was still above the horizon when we drove along the main street and found a small hotel on the left close to the centre. We parked the vehicles in front of the hotel then went inside to organise our accommodation, the rooms were basic and clean enough and the good news was that we had secure parking. Since we started I had been concerned about the vehicles being broken into overnight so for a change I would get a good night's sleep knowing that the vehicles were secure. We unloaded our overnight kit and went to our rooms then returned to park 02 and 03 in the secure compound. Secure was questionable, the compound was a 6 feet wire fence with wooden gates, I forgot about my good night's sleep. After an hour's rest and a shower, we made our way to a local bistro recommended to us by the hotel owner but on the way I wanted to check on the vehicles. We went to the compound to make sure the gates were locked and saw that the gates were tied together with a length of light cord. We just looked at one another and laughed.

The smell of traditional cooking was overwhelming as we entered the bistro that was partly occupied by local people, always a good sign. The food on that occasion was a sort of mutton stew and tasted pretty good, bearing in mind we hadn't eaten much during the day. The sound of traditional music coming from a speaker on the counter created a welcoming atmosphere, the comings and goings of customers and those at tables didn't think it unnatural to be rubbing shoulders with three westerners; we sampled the local beer which didn't turn out too bad either. The bistro had that 'I want to stay' feeling so while we were getting properly oiled we chatted about the journey so far and what to expect the following day. I took the opportunity to clear the air and bring us closer together. "Look," I said, "I would like to talk to you as project director for a moment and then if you are agreeable I would like to put it all behind us. Today you were wrong in my view for what you did. On two occasions you divided the team by going off on your own, in doing so you put us all at risk. My objective is that we responsibly drive around the world and return home with the crew safe and the vehicles intact and undamaged. I will react if I see anything happening that is likely to reflect badly on the project as a whole or exposes the crew or vehicles to danger or damage. It doesn't mean you can't do anything on your own, it simply means we need to talk about and agree to what you want to do before you decide to do it. You also need to think and act responsibly while 03 is in your care, you have the use of 03 until we reach Vladivostok, thereafter it will be Glyn and Roger's responsibility but until then try and keep 03 clean inside and undamaged. One final thing I would like to mention, please accept my sincere apologies if you believe that I have said or done anything to offend you, we need to work together as a team so if there is any help and assistance you can contribute it will be appreciated." I then went on to say, "I have said what I wanted to say but unless there is something you wish to discuss further I would like to put today behind us."

Tuesday 14th May, day 45, the hotel didn't have much to offer us for breakfast so I awoke early, got myself ready and made my way to the 'security' enclosure. Firstly, to reassure myself that the vehicles had not been interfered with, also to collect our breakfast from the food stock carried in 02. The vehicles were O.K. and our cereals and coffee provided a good start to the day.

We didn't have far to go that day but from what I understood from the bistro owner the night before, the road was very bad, I noted what he said but beyond that I didn't take much more notice. Thinking for a moment, surely we have already experienced the worst Mongolia had to offer or have we? The journey to Khovd (Chowod) was about 145 miles; how long it would take us to get there I had no idea. Before departing Ulgij we found the local fuel pump and topped up our tanks with low octane petrol, at the same time hoping that the fuel wouldn't damage the engines. With helpful directions from the hotel owner, we located the road that would take us to our destination. The concrete of the town roads quickly turned to sand and flint but this time it wasn't the generally flat single track we travelled the day before. What we were looking at was a track three times wider than before, twisting and turning in a southerly direction, deeply rutted by overloaded lorries and trailers, the ruts snaking from one side then the other impeding our forward progress. Adding to the already dismal picture was that the track also oscillated like the rides at a fairground. The going was slow but the 4 wheel drive, Cooper tyres and the short wheelbase of the Jimnys seemed the right combination to keep us going in the right direction. After 2 hours of dragging ourselves out of ruts and over oscillations so close together and varying in height and depth that a long wheel based vehicle would have difficulty in transiting, the track surface condition eventually improved, there were less ruts but the oscillations remained.

Our progress was still slow, driving hour after hour, coaxing the cars up and down the never ending mini hills, the seat belt fighting with your body to hold you in position and the constant pain in your shoulders caused by your arms gripping the wheel and hanging on like grim death in an effort to stop sliding forward when you reach the bottom. We were all suffering and needed to stop frequently. The track surface continued to improve, the ruts petered out and the oscillations changed from hills to holes at varying intervals, created from pockets of fluid sand being pushed to the side of the track by the passing lorries. In an effort to catch up on the time lost that morning, we increased our speed to as much as the track conditions would allow. We eventually settled for a speed of around 35 mph, faster than before but not too fast if we had to stop quickly, the track had narrowed but was still bumpy, you couldn't just sit there half asleep, you had to watch for fluid sand patches and be ready to react if you had to. It was afternoon, the sun was high and behind us, causing the track colour to change to a lighter shade of brown, added to this, when travelling in an easterly direction and the sun is shining from behind (from the west), there are hardly any shadows to indicate that the road ahead of you is uneven and to apply caution. From the driver's seat all you see in front of you is a track that is all one colour and shows no sign or gives any warning that you are approaching a fluid sand hole. In front of you is a track, as far as you can see it's all the same colour giving the impression that it is flat and without any holes. What in fact happens is you drive at around 35 mph, not fast you may say, but fast enough if you are heading for trouble. You are looking at the track ahead of you but detect nothing, mainly because it's all the same colour, but now and again the track rises slightly, concealing a sharp drop in level on the far side and a sand hole. If unnoticed, even at our slow speed, you reach the edge quite fast and if you are not careful, you nose dive into soft sand and stop dead. Once is enough when it happens. Briefly, one other incident that happened and frightened the hell out of me was when I hit a patch of fluid sand at speed. We didn't have far to go to our destination, the track condition had got better so we were able to increase our speed.

The track ran parallel with what looked like a new road being built high above the desert floor, we tried to get up onto the base of the road but they made sure that people like us couldn't use it. Returning to the track and eager to get to our destination, I wound up 02 and headed along the track with the guys in 03 following some way behind. I was pleased with myself that I was bombing along at last at over 50mph as a result of the track regaining its hard flint and sand surface. Pleased that I was covering the ground once more, I got a bit complacent, not paying attention to the track, my mind wandered and I thought about the previous night and my discussion with the guys. I was happy they accepted what I had to say also it was noticeable that there was a much jollier atmosphere. I also reminded myself that I didn't exactly come out smelling of roses, I was also at fault and should have told the guys at the time that I accept some of the blame. Perhaps I had been over protective and needed to unwind, relax and enjoy what we were doing. Focusing on the track ahead once more, I noticed that a short section of the track had deep tyre ruts running through it. I didn't slow down because it was only a short stretch and the wheel ruts and 02 were going in the same direction. I entered the rutted section at a little under 50 mph, immediately dropping lower into the sand and was unprepared for the loss of directional control that followed. Avoiding the temptation to slam my foot onto the brake and aggravate the situation, I lightly applied the hand brake hoping it would slow me down and at the same time regain directional control. It didn't quite work out as I had hoped, I underestimated the amount of inertia driving 02 forward, so as I applied the hand brake, the back wheels locked solid causing the rear end to be dragged along by the free running front. 02 started to swing violently first to the right and then left increasing in ferocity at each turn causing it, with me inside, to lean over at an alarming angle until eventually leaping out of the sand and spinning around to the right and sliding sideways. The two left side wheels buried themselves into the sand as the last of the inertia pushed against the side of the top heavy 02 in a final effort to roll us over. I remember looking through the windscreen as the right side of 02 lifted into the air in what seemed like slow motion then hesitated as though deciding whether to roll all the way over or not. Fortunately for me, 02 rolled back and remained upright. The whole incident lasted no more than a few seconds but seemed a lot longer while it was happening. The dust was settling as 03 arrived to take the lead, I told them what had happened but didn't mention it again. Our overnight stop at Khovd (Chowd) was similar to the night before, the journey, although short in distance, really was hard going and took a lot out of us, we were shattered by the time we arrived at our destination. Mongolia was taking its toll.

Wednesday 15th May, day 46, the small guest house we stayed at surprised us by providing breakfast cereals, toast and coffee, not much but enough to keep us going till lunchtime. Over breakfast we chatted about the previous two days and hoped that the road that day would be much kinder to the vehicles. We agreed that the cars and ourselves had suffered a serious mauling and if it continued at the same ferocity we may not make it to the Russian border at Darkhan (Darchan), what lay ahead of us endorsed our concerns. The destination that day was Altai (Altay), a 226 mile, 9 hour journey. We fuelled and checked the vehicles and made sure that all the equipment was secure, the pump attendant confirmed that we were on the right track that headed in a south-easterly direction. Once again, the paved surface ended and was replaced by a sand and flint track as soon as we left the town, the condition of the track was better than expected and the experience we had gained since we first entered Mongolia enabled us to travel at 50 mph most of the time.

The track soon passed Khar-Us-Nuur, a large expanse of water, one of many scattered throughout Mongolia. We made better progress that day and the light hearted banter over the radio, 02 and 03 taking turns at leading and no incidents to cause concern all helped to make the journey enjoyable. According to my map the track all the way to Altai was the A0304 and the 80 mile section we were driving along was a narrow valley with tundra stretching to the base of high mountains set back on either side of the track. From time to time we would pass a mounted goat herdsman watching over a flock from the saddle of his horse and yaks grazing on the lush greenery close to water. On one occasion we passed a string of camels loaded with goods being led along a narrow path, the camels in Mongolia are dromedaries, slightly larger than normal and have two humps. We eventually arrived at Darvi (Darwi) at midday, about half way to our destination. There was no food available, only snacks from the village shop; we purchased what we wanted then moved on, stopping a short distance further on to make a hot drink and rustle up something to eat from the food stocks in the back of 02. Feeling refreshed after a hot meal and a short rest, we were eager to get going. The desert to our left was relatively flat tundra, as far as you could see to the right were mountains, 75 miles to the south east was the notorious Gobi desert and roughly 60 miles in a south westerly direction was the Mongolia-China border crossing at Bulgan Takashikyen. At that point I was feeling happy that we seemed to be working together as a team, we drove through the afternoon and never saw another person or vehicle until we arrived at a river crossing.

When we arrived at the river there was a group of young guys washing in the clear water, we were due for a short rest so took the opportunity to ask the guys about the condition of the track from there on. The guys looked like Arabs and they told us that they were delivering cars to Kazakhstan. We were told that the track to Altai was pretty good and the remainder of our journey would take about an hour and a half. We said our goodbyes then they drove off in the direction we had come from. It was time to cross the river, I walked to the edge of the water to see how deep it was and whether there were any boulders or obstructions in the middle. The river was about 80 feet (25 metres) wide and a little over 2 feet (60 centimetres) deep at its centre, it was low and had no fast flowing water in the middle so it looked O.K. to drive across. I said to Graham and Mike that I would go first and if they watch me they would be able to see how deep it was. I lined 02 up ready to cross making sure that both windows were closed then gave the thumbs up to the guys as I rolled forward, I took it real easy the four wheel drive slowly picking its way over the rocky river bottom to the other side. Once clear of the water, I parked 02 high up on the river bank, I got out then shouted to the guys in 03 to take it real slow then stood there watching confidently knowing nothing could go wrong. Mike was behind the wheel and immediately over revved the engine and followed by easing the pressure off the clutch pedal, allowing 03 to leap forward and hit the water like a Dambuster's bouncing bomb and the recommended slow speed was discarded and replaced with a quest to reach the other side as quickly as possible. The excessive speed through the water caused a mini tsunami to form that rolled up the front of the radiator over the bonnet and windscreen and entered the cab through the open windows soaking its occupants. I stood there open mouthed not wanting to accept what I had just witnessed as 03 emerged from the river shedding surplus water like a surfacing submarine. Not wishing to say something I would regret later I got back into 02 and continued towards our destination. I drove slowly to give Graham and Mike time to sort themselves out and catch up, there was no further contact or reference as to what happened that afternoon and we eventually arrived at Altai about 6pm.

Thursday 16th May, day 47, the previous evening passed jolly enough, Mike made no reference to what happened at the river so I decided not to mention it. We had another long day ahead of us, our routine of breakfast, vehicle checks and fuel completed we were on our way once more, our aim that day was to travel in an easterly direction to Bayankhongor (Bajanchongor), a 234 mile, 11 hour journey through some of the most inhospitable terrain Mongolia has to offer. Although we had to travel on sand and flint tracks there was a new road under construction (unfortunately none of it was finished when we were there) and it would run the length of Mongolia. On a number of occasions we tried to drive along the base of the unfinished road but the surface was left with a coarse corrugated finish that shook the hell out of the cars and its occupants, forcing us back to the track. Bouncing up and down hour after hour aggravated my bladder, necessitating more frequent pee stops, I couldn't help noticing that the guys in 03 and I must all be suffering from the same problem, when in the lead and I decided to stop for a pee, the guys also stopped for the same reason, when they were leading and decided to stop I would get a message that I also needed to stop. Not wishing to allow the distance we travel to be controlled by how long we can hold on to a full bladder we decided to stop about every 2 hours, heaven knows what the local herdsman thought when they passed, seeing the three of us abreast facing down wind drawing pictures in the sand, they must have thought it was an old English custom. It was very hard going all day, the track was firm but bumpy and uneven, sometimes we were able to maintain a reasonable speed, other times it had deteriorated forcing us to crawl along, picking our way around one obstruction after another, or leave the track altogether and drive across a section of desert to re-join the track a mile or so further on. It was particularly difficult for me having decided to drive 02 around the world on my own, I had to stay awake and keep going for long hours day after day regardless of the distance, it wasn't so bad for the guys in 03 as they shared the driving. That particular day was punishing, the morning was O.K. but as the day progressed I got tired from the constant jarring when 02 landed hard after a bump or swayed violently from side to side when crossing uneven ground. If it goes on long enough I eventually lose co-ordination, bracing myself to receive a shock after it already happened, eventually becoming lethargic and unable to get my timing right. At times, I just sat there and drove, hoping that it would end soon. We arrived at Bayankhongor close to 7 o'clock totally drained, luckily we found a guesthouse pretty quickly that had only one three bedded room available, it wasn't the Hilton but it was clean. We collected our kit and secured the vehicles then went to our room and dropped onto our beds exhausted. After an hour we were rested, showered and on our way to a local restaurant recommended to us, the food and beer was O.K. but we didn't prolong our stay because we were desperately in need of an early night.

Friday 17th May, day 48, I raided our food stock in the back of 02 and produced coffee and cereals that would keep us going during the morning but we would need something more substantial later. I purchased fruit and snacks from a local shop to eat while we were travelling and put to one side a meal from our stocks for lunch. That day we proposed to drive to Rushaant, a 219 mile, 7 hour journey over similar terrain as the day before, a depressing thought. We weren't exactly jumping for joy as we departed Bayankhongor, the vehicles were fuelled and up together and the sun was shining as we left the town. The people were nice enough but the town was a bit run down. The road out of the town was surfaced, following a sign printed in Mongolian and English that pointed in the direction of our destination, we soon left the town behind us.

Not allowing myself the luxury of the idea that the road would be surfaced from here on, I drove savouring the smooth surface, kidding myself and wondering, well perhaps the road is finished from here on. I needn't have bothered, a few miles further on, the paved surface ended and the track continued. Our progress was similar to the day before, hour after hour driving across the desert and tundra through fertile valleys and around hills and mountains, on occasion passing a nomad astride his horse watching as we passed. We emerged from the desert and entered Rushaant at 4pm, disappointed to find out that it was only a small village with no overnight accommodation. Graham, Mike and I discussed the situation and decided that there was no alternative but to continue to drive to Ulaanbaatar, the capital city, adding another 184 miles and 4 hours of driving to our journey. By the time we arrived at our destination I would have been driving for about 12 hours so I was looking forward to the planned rest the following day. 03 led the way so I didn't have much to worry about other than to follow them. It wasn't long before we were driving in the dark and eventually reached the outskirts of

Ulaanbaatar a little after 8pm, by that time the weather had changed to rain and reduced visibility. Entering a strange city at night is rarely easy but Ulaanbaatar was something else, pitch black, no street lighting, the two lanes each way road was gridlocked with horn sounding traffic in both directions. We managed to stay together as we worked our way towards the highly populated city centre arriving at 9pm. Still being carried along as part of the gridlocked traffic, I saw a modern looking hotel set back from the road, sounding my horn to get 03's attention we then extracted ourselves from the traffic and parked outside the hotel. I went inside to enquire about accommodation and returned moments later to ask the guys if they would like to inspect the rooms, they were expensive but as we had been battered about over the last few days, I thought that on this occasion the extra cost was justified. We managed to get a late meal at the hotel and were sound asleep soon after.

Saturday 18th May, day 49, confident that the worst was behind us, I looked forward to a rest day, we met for breakfast later than usual and spent some time discussing our progress so far and our route for the remainder of the journey to Vladivostok. During our conversation, I mentioned that the hotel was quite comfortable and a short distance to the centre. Mike said that he wanted to move to the Holiday Inn. I explained that we were only there for one more night so did we want to waste our time moving, but he was insistent. Reluctantly, I agreed and spent the next hour or so trying to find the Holiday Inn. We drove around the city and surrounding area unable to find the Holiday Inn, we did however pass the Ramada Hotel set in its own grounds in the middle of the city, it looked what it was, I didn't give it a second thought but Mike said he wanted to stay there. I replied that our budget wouldn't stretch to it but at this stage he was getting very insistent. I pondered as to what I should say, remembering when

I asked Mike, who is a professional photographer, if he would help out by becoming our film cameraman for this stage of the journey. Mike didn't hesitate to say he would do it and I was very grateful that he did, for that reason I should try to reciprocate if I could and at the same time diffuse the situation. I said to Mike, "Let's go to the Ramada reception and find out what the cost will be." The receptionist smiled at me as she said that she had a double and a single for one night for $450, I asked if she could help us with a discount because we are travelling around the world, smiling she said, "That's the price." Mike said that if we stay at the Ramada he would pay half the cost, it was still more than I had planned to pay but I agreed and we moved into the upmarket accommodation. The down side of this arrangement was that when I paid the bill I expected Mike to reimburse me as agreed but he never did.

What happened concerned me, it wasn't the money, it was just that Mike and I had an agreement and I kept my part, I'm a believer in the old saying, 'say what you do, do what you say'. We spent the rest of the day sightseeing, I have never seen so many people in one place at one time. It seemed that most of Mongolia's population was in Ulaanbaatar, nationalities from around the world, rich and not so rich, walking side by side. The tall western styled fully glazed buildings were erected on plots of land between traditional single story wood houses from the past. Over the centuries, the city grew and was known as Ikh Khuree (great camp) until 1924 when it was renamed Ulaanbaatar. The city vibrates with excitement as it embraces travellers arriving from faraway places who stop for rest and replenishment before moving on. The city of Ulaanbaatar is a Mecca and crossroads for travellers wishing to exchange information, to the west is Kazakhstan and Europe, to the south lies the Gobi desert and China, a few kilometres east is the suspected birth place and silver monument erected in the honour of Chinggis Khaan, to the north lies Russia.

We eventually arrived back at the Ramada after seeing as much as we could of that amazing city. For some reason, we needed the keys for 03. Mike, who had the keys last, searched his pockets two or three times but couldn't find them, in spite of our efforts they remained elusive. I issued Graham with the only spare key I had and left it at that.

Later that afternoon, I lay on my bed thinking about 03's keys when there was a knock on the door, Graham was standing there holding 03's keys, "Don't say anything," he said to me, then continued, "I was convinced that the keys were on Mike somewhere, I searched his jacket and found them in his pocket." Relieved, I thanked Graham and said that I would meet them for a beer later. Mike offered his apology for mislaying the keys, knowing that I was concerned about their loss. We chatted over a beer about Ulaanbaatar, its people and how vibrant it was, we all agreed that it would have been nice if we could stay longer. Mike complained about a pain in his knee, suggesting that he may have to see a doctor if it got any worse. We spent the rest of the evening feeding ourselves and seeing the city by night, unfortunately Mike's knee was getting worse so we headed back to the hotel, the receptionist confirmed that there was a doctor close by if required; reassured, Mike decided to try painkillers and a good night's sleep and review the situation in the morning.

Sunday 19th May, day 50, we met for breakfast early, Mike's knee was still painful and needed attention, Graham accompanied Mike to the doctor while I dealt with the formalities at the hotel and gave the vehicles a thorough check ready for our departure when they return. Mike and Graham arrived back an hour later, Mike said he felt better after the doctor massaged his knee, he also gave him strong painkillers to be taken if need be, Graham said he would be driving until Mike feels better. Before leaving, I adjusted the passenger seat in 03 to give Mike as much leg room as possible. We left the hotel at 10.30am, heading in a northerly direction to Darkhan (Darchan), a 165 mile, 6 hour journey and our overnight stop before the Mongolian Russian border crossing the following day. The road north was sort of paved, well the potholes represented a surface area greater than the paved surface area forcing us to zigzag our way along the road. The scenery had changed from sand and sparse greenery to open countryside that became greener the further north we travelled. We entered Darkhan at 4.30pm that afternoon, it was a small town built up on either side of the road that continued north, there was only one guest house situated in the centre of town and only one three bedded room available. It was a bit different to the Ramada but the price brought a smile to my face.

Monday 20ᵗʰ May, day 51, surprisingly, we managed to get a good night's sleep, waking refreshed and eager to get going, I put something together for breakfast and there was a jolly mood as we checked and fuelled the vehicles. Our plan and destination that day was to cross the Mongolian Russian border at Kyakhta at about midday then continue north to Ulan-Ude, hopefully arriving at our destination before dark, a 222 mile, 8 hour journey. We arrived at the border crossing at Kyakhta at 1pm, we were the only vehicles at the gate so I assumed we would be dealt with straight away. The gates were closed but there was a steady stream of border guards who came to inspect us and then returned to where they came from. We had been there for 45 minutes when a trusty old and battered Land Rover Defender rolled to a stop behind us and a young English couple got out and started chatting to us. It transpired that they had taken a similar route across Mongolia as ourselves and eventually got around to asking us how long it had taken us to cross. I replied, "7 days," they looked at us with an amazed 'you're kidding?' look, I said, "We crossed the border into Mongolia at Tashanta on the 13th." They thought for a moment then said, "It is normally a 10 day journey, how you guys did it in 7 days heaven knows, by the way how old are you guys?" Reluctant to talk about age unless there is some benefit, I hesitated as I side glanced Graham and Mike then said, "Most of us are in our 70s." "I don't believe it," said the young girl, screeching with excitement and at the same time saying, "I have got to take a picture of you guys." The young man asked me about the route we had taken, I explained and at the same time used my finger to trace the route we had taken on our map that was spread over the bonnet of 02. I said that the distance we had travelled from the time we entered Mongolia to where we were now was almost 1600 miles, 1200 miles of that was sand and flint track, the rest surfaced in places. After waiting an hour, four guards marched to where we were waiting, opened the gate and ushered us to a parking area. I made sure that I had the necessary documentation then, together with Graham and Mike, followed one of the guards to the customs office. The immigration and customs procedure took about 20 minutes and soon after, we were parked on the Russian side to repeat the process. The Russian customs officer questioned me for some time about why both vehicles were registered in my name, I tried to make myself understood but didn't get anywhere. The customs officer took my passport and Vehicle Registration papers and wandered off to another office, looking through the glazed office panels, I could see he was speaking to someone with a lot of medals and gold trimmings on his uniform, it was at that point I remembered the declaration I signed when I first crossed the border into Russia. It was in Russian but basically it stated that I took two vehicles into Russia and that I cannot leave unless I take the two vehicles with me when I go. I thumbed through all my paperwork and found what I wanted and held it up so that the people in the office could see. The officer I spoke to at the beginning collected the paper, also a copy of the letter from me authorising Graham and Mike to drive the vehicles, he returned a few minutes later with a smile on his face to say I could go.

Graham and Mike were waiting for me when I emerged from the office, I explained what the problem was and we were soon on our way. It had taken us about two hours from the time we arrived at the border to eventually being let loose on the other side. As we drove to Ulan-Ude, we passed a ger (a Mongolian style round house) set back from the road on our left, I called Mike who was acting as cameraman and asked if he thought it would be a good idea to stop and film us with the ger in the background. We left the road and drove to where the ger was situated, parked the cars close by then walked closer thinking that it was unoccupied, Graham and I prepared ourselves for filming while Mike got the camera set up.

As we were getting ourselves organised, the door of the ger opened and the smallest petite lady I have ever seen stepped out. Dressed traditionally, the charming, smiling lady beckoned us into her immaculately clean home indicating to us to sit down. Feeling at ease, I looked around and could not help but admire the way the inside of the ger was compartmented into sleeping, cooking and social areas and the inviting dry heat generated by a wood burning stove in the centre, topped with a steaming kettle. The lovely lady spoke no English but managed to communicate using hand and facial expressions, enthused with bubbling pride as she pointed out various features inside her home. Smiling continuously our little lady produced a tray containing three small glasses of what I assumed to be goats' milk and a plate of homemade biscuits; Graham and Mike were onto their second helping when I indicated to our little lady by rubbing my tummy that I was unable to accept her offering. Smiling, she nodded majestically, indicating that she understood, I hoped our little lady wasn't offended, I didn't want to risk it by aggravating my already volatile stomach and ending up with a dose of the Acapulco

Foxtrots! That would keep me close to a toilet for a few days. I reminded the guys that we had filming to finish and at the same time showed our cameras and asked for permission to take pictures, which was granted. I felt humbled by the hospitality shown to us by our lovely lady and as is the custom adopted by travellers, we left $5 on the table as we went outside. Mike was filming as Graham and I thanked our host for her hospitality, Mike also captured the ger and its surroundings at the same time. Saddened, we waved our farewell and made our way to the road and headed north to Ulan-Ude, arriving at 7pm, later than expected. The city looked more modern than most Russian cities we had passed through, perhaps it has benefited from being close to the prosperous and wealthy city of Ulaanbaatar. The hotels in the centre looked palatial and expensive but we eventually located one with a price I could live with. Over a meal, we discussed the route we would take the following day, I explained that we had to decide before we left Ulan-Ude whether we make a detour by turning west to visit the 387 mile (636 kilometre) long and 1637 metre deep freshwater Lake Baikal, adding a 250 mile round trip and an extra night to our journey or whether we turn east to Chita and thereafter continue in the direction we want to go, the choice was ours. The proposals for and against were discussed, resulting in the decision to proceed to Chita so as to make sure we arrive at Vladivostok on or around Tuesday 28th May, day 59.

Tuesday 21st May, day 52, although travelling in an easterly direction, we were further north and the likelihood of rain more frequent, behind us were the sand and flint tracks, ahead were paved roads. The distance to Chita was about 411 miles and took 12 hours of hard driving before arriving at our destination. It was dark as we made our way towards the centre, finding a hotel in the dark is never easy because of dodging the night time traffic and looking for a hotel at the same time. It must have shown because when we stopped at a set of traffic lights, a car stopped by the side of me, the driver, a young man, indicated to me to lower the window which I did. In broken English he asked if we had driven from England, I said, "Yes and we are going to Vladivostok." Seizing the opportunity, I asked if he could direct me to a hotel, he didn't understand my question so I simulated a sleeping posture to indicate that I wanted to sleep. He thought for a moment, then, realising what I meant, he said, "Follow me," and we arrived at a commercial hotel a few minutes later. We were asked to wait in the cars while he dashed inside then returned to us saying that the hotel was full and once again to follow him to another hotel which was able to accommodate us.

After we checked in we bought our Russian friends a beer and thanked them for their help, we then hastily placed our kit into our rooms then made our way to the hotel restaurant before it closed. The response and help we received that evening was typical, the Russian people generally went out of their way to help whenever we needed it. It had been a long and tiring day.

Wednesday 22nd May, day 53, another day, another long journey, fortunately, the hotel breakfast was pretty good so we ate as much as we could just in case there wasn't anything available along our route. By the time we finished checking and fuelling the cars and started the 370 mile, 11 hour journey to Mogocha it was 7.30am. Heading east, the road was surfaced but there were cracks and crater sized potholes everywhere, realising that we had to drive carefully if we were to avoid damaging the vehicles, we slowly picked our way along what looked like a lunar landscape. Our progress was slow and if it continued we would not reach our destination as planned. The single lane each way was as described but along the edge there was a strip of greenery slightly wider than 02. I contacted the guys in 03 to tell them that I was going to try and drive along the edge of the road and hopefully make a better time, I eased 02 over to the edge and increased speed, it was bumpy but I was able to travel at 45 mph. 03 followed my example, enabling us to cover the ground much faster, it seemed to work so we adopted the tactic whenever possible every time a bad section of road presented itself. Throughout the day the road followed a route that cut its way through mountains and descended to valley floors; we were cautiously crossing rivers by way of rickety old bridges and passing through deserted villages. We finally arrived at Mogocha around 7pm. The light was fading and from what we could see it was an old industrial town, seriously run down empty industrial buildings in an advanced stage of decay that had become a dumping ground for items that had outlived their usefulness. Poorly clothed pale skinned people stopped to look at us as we drove past then scurried off about their business. Heading for the town centre, we passed what looked like the police station, 03 stopped and Graham went inside to ask if there was a hotel in the town. He emerged after a while to tell Mike and myself that there was concern that we should not stay overnight but the station chief would come to talk to us. A few minutes later, the chief and five of his officers, one who could speak English, came to the front of the building where we were parked. There was a lengthy discussion between them as we stood and watched; eventually the young officer who spoke English stepped forward to explain the situation. "First," he said, "it is unsafe to leave your vehicles parked outside at night, they will be vandalised, what we recommend is that you remove your overnight things from the vehicles and park them overnight in our secure compound at the rear of the building. I will then take you in a patrol car to find accommodation for the night and in the morning I will collect you at 8 o'clock and bring you back to the police station to collect your vehicles." Amazed that they were going to so much trouble to help us, I asked our interpreter to thank the station chief and

Local police at Mogocha were very helpful

everybody for their kindness. We parked the vehicles and loaded our kit and camera equipment into the police car then set off to find somewhere to stay.

The first place was a derelict guest house that had been closed for some time; our driver, looking concerned, said, "I know one other place." We were then taken to an area of town dominated by small traditional wooden single story houses that surrounded a rail terminal that had become a storage facility for rusting steam engines, rail cars and equipment from a bygone age. The police car stopped outside the only two storey wood building in the vicinity. It looked like it was also some sort of club.

The policeman located the lady owner and after a short discussion confirmed that there was one room with three beds available for $30 a night. The dilapidated state of the building necessitated that we inspect the room beforehand but we knew we would have to take it or drive through the night. To say it was a grim sight as we walked up the stairs and along the corridor would be an understatement, the room, however, was a little tidier, centred at the far end was a huge iron radiator fed by 3 inch steel pipes running around the perimeter on both sides, reflecting enough heat to bake bread. We thanked our driver then returned to the room to have a closer look at what we had let ourselves in for. Sitting on our beds, getting slow roasted, we decided the room wasn't too bad as it was for only one night. Having got ourselves cleaned up and looking presentable, we went next door to the club to see if we could get something to eat; it transpired that the club was a meeting place in town for the youngsters. When we walked through the door everybody stopped talking and looked at us, in an effort to ease the stalemate I said, "Hi guys." The girl behind the bar asked if we were English, I said, "Yes," immediately the atmosphere changed, the chatting continued but was louder so as to make themselves heard, the group close to us engaged in conversation with Graham, Mike and myself to practise their English. As far as I could make out, the town, like so many throughout Russia, has been bypassed by change resulting in the demise of its localised industry, followed by unemployment and a steady decline of the town and the quality of life for its people. There is little work for the young, also the able bodied who are mainly unemployed are unable to accumulate enough money to move elsewhere to find work so are condemned to a life of vodka and state hand-outs. We spent the evening conversing mainly with younger people who had learnt English at school, answering their enquiring questions about us, also where we have come from and where we were going. In spite of the excitement, we managed to get a meal and washed it down with the local beer. It saddened me knowing that unless something drastic happens these lovely people have a bleak future.

Thursday 23rd May, day 54, I was up and washed before Graham and Mike, so that I could prepare our breakfast from what I collected from 02 before being locked in the compound. We were ready by 8am when the police car arrived to collect us as arranged. At the police station, we were taken to the compound to collect the vehicles, we loaded our kit then drove to the front of the building so that we could take pictures of the people who helped us and thank them for the help and kindness they had shown towards us, fantastic people. We made our way to the only fuel available in the town, located close to the old rail terminal, it consisted of a large square tank resting on old railway sleepers and a fuel pump that could only be switched on and off from inside a small office close by. We topped up our tanks with suspect low octane fuel hoping it would not damage the engines. At 9am, we were on our way east. Our planned destination that day was Magdagach, a 296 mile, 8 hour journey travelling along a road that was featured on our maps as a dotted line, usually meaning the road is under construction so we didn't know what to expect. Apparently, some time ago Russia's President, Vladimir Putin, decided that Russia needed a new super highway that would run from one end of Russia to the other and to make sure it all happens, he has taken responsibility for the project. I spoke to a lorry driver a few days before and he told me that work was underway but behind schedule so until it is finished we have to use the old road that is very bad. The driving conditions were as bad as the day before, demanding maximum concentration if we were to avoid breaking the vehicles. It wasn't long before we found out that the dotted line was a wide dirt track, accommodating nose to tail heavy traffic in both directions.

The thick dust generated by the traffic made it impossible to see beyond the back of the vehicle in front, limiting possible overtaking opportunities and causing traffic to back up behind. The situation improved as our route took us higher up mountainsides into cleaner air and improved visability; at the same time causing the over loaded lorries to use lower gears and slowly grind their way up, allowing us to overtake in relative safety.

It remained like that throughout the day, we stopped to refuel twice and at the same time washed the dust down with cups of coffee and food available from the garage café. The mountainous terrain seemed to go on forever and I was gratified that Graham and Mike took it all in their stride, enabling us to cover the ground as fast as we did. We seemed to be working closer together and laughing at the slightest opportunity, resulting in a more jolly and relaxed atmosphere. Late afternoon and about 10 miles to go before we reached Magdagach, we were really knackered, the bantering over the radio petered out during the afternoon due to tiredness and we were struggling to hold it together even though we only had a few miles to go to our destination. Earlier in the afternoon, I had to resort to taking painkillers to ease a persistent nagging pain in my groin. The road surface improved dramatically as we got closer to Magdagach. We were driving along a straight section of road in the middle of nowhere, so to speak, when I saw, set back from the road, a brightly coloured western style motel. I couldn't believe what I was seeing, realising it wasn't an illusion, I turned off the road, followed by 03 and stopped, I went inside to ask if they were open, the receptionist said that they opened for the first time that day, I secured our rooms and we settled in for the night. At the bar a little later, we reviewed the driving that day and couldn't believe our luck at finding the motel and being amongst its first customers, everything looked and smelt new. I was told that the owners planned to establish a chain of motels positioned along the new highway, I couldn't help commenting that before they can do that, the contractors have to finish it!

Friday 24th May, day 55, I awoke from a good night's sleep, feeling fully rested and ready for another day behind the wheel. I met the guys at breakfast and we ate as much as we could accommodate, thanked the motel manager and receptionist for looking after us then continued driving east to Novobureyskiy, a

334 mile, 10 hour journey. Our route brought us to within a few miles of the Russian side of China's north eastern border. The road, if you can call it that, continues to run parallel with the Russian-Chinese border all the way to Vladivostok, 1100 miles and 5 days further on. The road condition that day continued as before, requiring maximum concentration to avoid becoming a casualty and needing repairs miles from anywhere. A few days ago, Graham and Mike mentioned to me that they had a wheel wobble and mentioned it again at breakfast saying that the wheel wobble was getting worse; I said that I would get it checked at the first opportunity. I thought about the wheel wobble 03 was experiencing and wondered if it was causing them to drive slower than previously, I called 03 to ask at what speed does the wheel wobble start, "At 40 mph," came back a reply, I then said, "Have you tried to accelerate above 40 mph to see what happens?" "No," was the reply, "Give it a try," I said. I didn't know it then but 03's wheel wobble problem was to remain with us until we reached Vladivostok. At 5pm that afternoon, we came across a transport motel at the outskirts of Novobureyskiy, it looked O.K. so I signed us in. I then visited the vehicle workshop close by to ask if there was a mechanic available to check 03's steering. Graham, Mike and I hung around while the mechanic jacked the car up and shimmied under to investigate, emerging a short while after saying, "It is O.K."

"The wheels need balancing that's the problem," Graham interjected, I turned to the mechanic to ask if he could balance the wheels, he eventually understood what I meant and set to work taking the wheels off. While 03 was receiving attention, I asked the boss of the garage if he could change the rear shock absorbers on 02 at the same time. I had to show him a new shock absorber and point underneath the back of 02 before he understood. The work was completed in an hour and when I asked how much I had to pay I was told what amounted to the equivalent of $25, hardly anything compared to the amount of work he did. I was hopeful that the wheel balancing had cured 03's wobble problem. The repairs completed, we went to the café attached to the motel to see what was on offer in the way of food and settled for a bowl of something that looked like stew, a slab of bread and a beer.

Saturday 25th May, day 56, the food I ate the night before didn't agree with me causing visits to the toilet at regular intervals throughout the night. I have always had a cast iron stomach as far as food is concerned but of late, there have been occasions when just seeing some of the food we have eaten has made my stomach turn over, I also noticed that I had lost weight, causing me to take in my trouser belt a notch. It was a brilliant sunny morning, the air was clean and fresh as we fuelled and checked the vehicles, there wasn't much on offer at the café for breakfast so we settled for dried fruit, cereals and coffee from our own food stocks. The road was pretty good as we drove through Novobureyskiy but as soon as we passed the outskirts on the other side of the city, the surfaced road ended reverting to the unforgiving potholed and rutted dusty surface we had endured during the past few days. I wasn't looking forward to the journey to Khabarovsk, the thought of 02, with me sitting in it, being bounced about for the next 297 miles and 8 hours would be a nightmare. There hadn't been any radio contact from the guys in 03 so I assumed that we had overcome the wheel wobble, as I was complementing myself for another problem solved, the radio crackled into life, it was Graham telling me that the wheel wobble was still with us, I said that there was nothing we could do until we reach Khabarovsk. I said to Graham, "Have you tried driving faster?" "No," he said, "Try it if you can," I replied. I'm no expert but I have sorted out wheel balancing problems in the past. I have found that the problem is usually traced to tyres that have worn unevenly; in that case wheel balancing may be the answer. If that doesn't work it has to be that the running gear needs attention. Whatever was causing the problem probably reaches a vibration peak (when the vibration is at its worst). For example, if the wheel wobble that 03 had acquired peaks at 40 mph, you have to grit your teeth and accelerate, if it stops wobbling you have a temporary solution, if not you drive slower until you can get it fixed. Graham and Mike drove 03 all the way to Khabarovsk, 297 miles, nursing the wheel wobble so progress was slow.

The road that was leading us through the mountains was pretty bad and aggravating 03's problems. In spite of having to keep below 40 mph, we seemed to be making progress. It was midday, we stopped for fuel earlier but there was no food available, we drove on hoping to find a roadside café but nothing materialised. We passed a roadside rest area, but before you get visions of the type of roadside facility you expect to see as you drive through Europe, forget it, this was the pits! The only thing it had going for it was that the sun was shining. The tin shed tucked away to one side was a Russian version of a unisex toilet, the dirt floor interior was divided into two compartments, the automatic flushing ceramic wc pan and designer seat and lid we are familiar with was in fact two holes in the ground that generated a smell that took your breath away if you got a whiff of it.

We positioned up wind so as to avoid getting our lunch tainted and soon had a brew

A Mongolian roadside, unisex toilet – very basic!

underway. From the back of 02, we had a bowl of hot soup and bread followed by Ambrosia rice pudding straight from the tin and to finish, a cup of strong tea, what more do you want! To be fair to the guys, they went out of their way to make things work out on occasions such as this, they responded when asked, they drove long hours day after day, ate food that generally was lousy and some of the places we stayed at were pretty grim. I was a bit optimistic when planning the route that included camping most nights once we left the European comfort zone, I didn't think about the below zero temperatures at night and what effect it would have on our 70 year old bones. I also underestimated the road conditions and the daily driving time needed each day to reach our destination but as a team, we made it happen. It was a beautiful sunny evening when we arrived at the modern city of Khabarovsk. We continued to drive towards the city centre and a few minutes further on, I stopped in front of a huge shopping and small business complex that included an auto workshop and next to it, a tyre and wheel balancing company. It was an ideal opportunity to get 03's wheel wobble looked at once more so I made my way to the workshop and parked outside. 03 came to a stop as I went inside the pristine workshop to explain the situation. I was met by the owner who spoke English so I was able to explain in detail what was happening, when I finished, he gave orders for an engineer to descend into the examination pit and at the same time indicated to the guys in 03 to drive forward. The owner supervised the inspection himself, emerging from the pit 30 minutes later to tell us that he couldn't find anything wrong apart from the front wheels needing to be realigned which he attended to. I thanked him for his help and asked what the cost was, but once again I was told there would be no charge. I thanked him for his generosity. To keep Graham and Mike happy and to make sure that 03's problem was dealt with once and for all, we took 03 next door and had the wheels rebalanced and at the same time had the front wheels put on the back and the back wheels put on the front. Confident that the wobble was now history, we set about finding somewhere to stay. Not exactly knowing where we were heading, we drove through the city and eventually came to a stop facing the expanse of the mighty River Amur. I looked to my left, there was a riverside hotel, we must stay there tonight I thought to myself and hopefully we will have a view across the river. The following day was a rest day so the hotel would be an ideal base to return to after exploring the city. I secured our accommodation for two nights, the rooms were comfortably furnished, facilitating a well-earned rest. Feeling refreshed after a shower, I met the guys and we then made our way to the hotel restaurant, it looked O.K. but we decided to investigate the riverside establishments we'd noticed earlier. We settled for a bistro close to the water's edge, surprisingly the food and local beer was quite good. I don't remember the name of the place we were at, it must have been some sort of holiday centre, there were lots of people milling around and later that evening, two lines of people six or eight abreast had formed to walk along the boardwalk, one line going one way and the other going in the opposite direction.

Sunday 26th May, day 57, I had set this day aside as a rest day; believe me when I say we needed it. We all benefited from a good night's sleep and a bit of a lay in in the morning. We met for breakfast later than usual and after, we studied a street map and plotted a route that would take us to places of interest. It was a short walk to the square at the city centre and being a Sunday, there were a number of festive activities taking place. We happened to be at the square when a religious procession was about to start, from our vantage point we could see the whole of the route the procession would take and settled down to await its passing.

There were two gold coloured union topped churches, one situated on the top of a hill to our right and another situated on a hill to our left, separated by a 500 metre road that went downhill from our right and uphill to our left. It is a regular event, but for what reason I never found out. The procession forming to our right was led by a host of clergy clad in gold and white robes and head gear, nuns, a choir and church workers, police and representatives from all the other services, then last of all was the army of devout worshipers. The whole column responded from a signal from the front and jerked forward then settled down to a slow pace. The scene was spectacular as the column swayed from one side to the other, I can only describe it as a penguin shuffle and at the same time, the leader was continuously reciting prayers that everybody responded to. Religion throughout Russia has suffered from persecution over the centuries. The walkabout that day was long overdue and just what we needed, the jolly comradery and bantering over the radio kept our three man team together, enabling us to achieve the daily distances we did. However, the continuous hardship of the last 15 days had pushed our endurance threshold to its limit, so a rest day was just what we needed. We made our way around the city, stopping at places of interest, after lunch at an open air bistro, we strolled back towards our hotel and on the way we came across a flea market. The market was pretty much the same that you see at other countries around the world but the rubbish, whoops, I mean antiques and artefacts were mainly Russian. We hovered too long at one particular stall run by a husband and wife, they spoke excellent English, enabling us to talk freely about what it's like to live in Russia, when we had finished, we thanked them for talking to us. It was interesting but depressing to hear what they had to say, as we walked away I slipped my hand into my inside pocket to make sure my British passport was safely tucked away. After our chat with the Russian couple, I couldn't help thinking that maybe we take our western lifestyle for granted, I found the Russian people who I came in contact with to be very friendly and helpful but I don't think I would like to live there. That evening after dinner, we decided to take the air and joined the long line of eight people abreast walking along the boardwalk at the river edge.

Monday 27th May, day 58, feeling better after sleeping two nights in a soft bed, we were eager to be on the road and travelling south to Chkalovsk, a 287 mile, 10 hour journey, our last overnight stop before we arrive at Vladivostok and the end of stage 3 of our journey. I was excited at surviving the journey through Ukraine, Kazakhstan, Mongolia and Russia, but a little sad that stage 3 was coming to an end. We had been driving for an hour or so when I found myself thinking how much I liked my little Suzuki Jimny and how confident I was that it would complete the journey around the world. I had become accustomed to driving alone in 02 but on that occasion I had run out of things to think about so I called 03 to have a chat, Graham picked up and we spoke about general matters then I said, "By the way, how's the steering?" There was a pause then Graham replied, "It's better but still vibrating," feeling a bit deflated I said, "There's not much I can do about it until we reach Vladivostok." From then on, I decided not to mention it again, but what had started to worry me was Glyn Maher and Roger Winkworth were joining me at Vancouver for the start of stage 4, the last part of our journey around the world. I didn't like the idea of them taking over 03 if there was a fault with the steering so I decided to give it priority when I made contact with the Suzuki distributor at Vladivostok. The thought did occur to me that I had not driven 03 to test the steering for myself so decided to do that at the next opportunity. There was an improvement of the road surface, not so many potholes and cracks so we were able to maintain our cruising speed of 55 mph for the remainder of the day. The weather was getting warmer and the sun continued to shine.

The road south ran parallel with the Chinese border on our right for about 7 hours, at a guess, I would say at one point we were within 25 miles of the border. With 150 miles to go to our destination, we followed the Siniy mountain range that was some distance to our left and just before we arrived at Chkalovsk, we passed Lake Khanka to our right. The sun was low as we entered the town, we stopped at a garage to top up with fuel and at the same time I asked if there was a hotel in the town but got nowhere, I then produced my list of phrases and pointed to the one relating to accommodation and hoped for the best. The lady gave me a look that indicated that there was no hotel in the town. Not satisfied with the response from the garage, we drove further into the town and stopped at a shop. I enquired again using the same procedure as before but this time I was directed to a road close by where a motel was situated. We drove around for some time looking for something that resembled a hotel, concerned that it was getting dark, we widened the search area and eventually found what we were looking for. The place looked closed but after banging on the door, the owner appeared and welcomed us in, we were his only guests so we were soon having hot showers. We spent an enjoyable evening talking to the hotel owner and his wife who both spoke English, they asked a lot of questions about our journey so far and what happens when we reach Vladivostok the following day.

Tuesday 28th May, day 59, the couple who ran the hotel made sure we started the day with a hearty breakfast, it was the last day of stage three; we were in no hurry that morning, the journey to Vladivostok was about 187 miles and 5 hours driving time but we were excited at the prospect of arriving at Vladivostok even though at times the journey from Novosibirsk seemed to go on forever. When we departed Novosibirsk, we were three guys who had come together pretty well for the first time, three unknowns if you like. At the beginning there were clashes of personality and

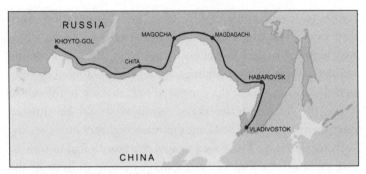

Around the top of China to Vladivostok

disagreements but they were short lived enabling us eventually to come together as a team with a determination to work together and succeed. By the time Graham and Mike arrived at Vladivostok they would have driven a total distance of 4213 miles in 18 days, averaging 234 miles a day, at times driving through some of the most inhospitable terrain in the world. Credit to both of them, when they arrived at their journey's end, they achieved what they set out to do. I still had a long way to go before I reach my personal journey's end but I will always be grateful to Graham and Mike and was sad when we went our separate ways a few days later. I had already briefed Graham and Mike about our program when we arrived at Vladivostok, but during a stop to refuel the cars with enough fuel, sufficient to reach our destination, I elaborated in more detail about what I knew was arranged for us when we were to arrive that afternoon. I had already notified the Suzuki P.R. team that we would arrive at Vladivostok on the 28th and at the dealership some time that afternoon. 02 and 03 were to be handed over to the mechanics, who had been instructed to service and overhaul both vehicles, working through the night if necessary, to prepare them ready for a press conference and photo shoot the following day. As we approached the city of Vladivostok, the road condition improved and the volume of traffic increased considerably, there was construction work underway all around us as we flowed with the traffic on a four lane highway in each direction to and from the city. Towering western style high rise buildings and brightly coloured flashing signs lined each side of the congested road making it difficult to locate the Suzuki dealer that I assumed would be situated prominently somewhere along the main highway into the city. Fortunately for us, I managed to spot the Suzuki sign in time to turn right off the highway and came to a stop in front of the showroom.

I went inside and introduced myself to the young lady at reception; the guys joined me then a few minutes later, the owner of the dealership introduced himself, speaking in broken English, then guided us to a conference room and, through an interpreter, explained to us that we were to collect the personal items we need from the vehicles so they could be taken to the workshop. We were booked into a hotel on the far side of town and their driver would take us there as soon as we'd had some refreshments. We were told that the Suzuki P.R. team would be arriving that evening to take charge of the reception the following day, scheduled to commence at 12 o'clock, we would be collected from the hotel an hour before.

Wednesday 29th May, day 60, we were collected from the hotel as promised, looking smart and smelling sweet, on the way to the reception, the guys and I talked about our first glimpse of the Sea of Japan (connected to the Pacific Ocean), after a meal the night before, we couldn't resist walking to the shoreline just to look at the sea, to think, I thought to myself, I have driven half way around the world, I couldn't believe I was actually at Vladivostok looking out over the Sea of Japan. We could see the dealership as we turned off the highway, 02 and 03 were positioned in front of the showroom either side of the glassed double doors, the cars were pristine, cleaned in and out and polished to a brilliant finish, reflecting the sun's rays, even the Cooper tyres received a coating of tyre black as a finishing touch. Surrounded by coloured gas filled balloons, 02 and 03 looked as though they had just come from the factory instead of not so long ago crossing Mongolia. The guys and I were led into the reception area and were surprised at the number of people milling around, press, T.V. cameras and journalists. It was the biggest reception so far, there had been other receptions, photo sessions and T.V. coverage during our travels but not on the scale that confronted us on this occasion. I found out from a presenter working for a T.V. company that we were featured in a local travel programme when we first entered Russia and our progress had been monitored and picked up by other T.V. stations. I realised at that point why people had been waving and sounding their car horns as we drove across Russia. The guys and I were ushered in and asked to sit at a long table clad in white linen with microphones for each person. It was indicated to me that I should sit at the centre with Graham and Mike on either side; the remainder of the seats in front were occupied by dignitaries, special guests, and the press. We were briefed as to the procedure, also that each of us would be talking through an interpreter. It was daunting looking at the people looking at us but we managed to answer the questions and give a good account of ourselves. The session went on for an hour or so and everybody seemed happy with the result of their effort. Not many people spoke English at the event but I did manage to have a chat to the workshop manager who assured me that they had thoroughly checked the steering mechanism and made any necessary adjustment, also both vehicles had been fully serviced, pressure washed and polished. Relieved that the session had come to an end and that we could make our way back to the hotel, I looked around to find Graham and Mike, as I did so I was approached by the manager of the P.R. team who asked if we would drive 02 and 03 to the local race track to continue the photo shoot, also they would like to film me driving 02 round a motorcycle scramble course, which I did to everyone's satisfaction but at the same time it made one hell of a mess of my pristine 02. I drove back to the Suzuki showroom carrying a quantity of mud with me that was deposited at their pressure washing facility after 02 had been thoroughly cleaned.

We made our way back to our hotel, sucked dry of any energy we had and decided to rest for a while then later I wanted to locate the ferry ticket office and meet personally Olga, my email contact, and pay for our tickets. That afternoon, I sat alone in my room at the hotel overlooking the Sea of Japan, thinking about the journey so far and what I had achieved. At home, when I was putting the project together, I really had no idea how it would actually turn out. Although working from my small office at home, I approached and dealt with every part of the project methodically and with my best endeavours to make it work. I was offered and pleased to receive help from the crew at various times but when it came to talking to freight companies to arrange ferry booking and shipping the vehicles from Vladivostok to Vancouver, Canada and again from Newark on the east coast of the U.S.A. to the U.K., I was promised and received help initially but thereafter I was on my own as far as getting the shipping properly organised. I made a point of being on top and in control of everything, preparation, itinerary, crew training and the journey itself. Some aspects such as accommodation, food as we travelled and time allowed between destinations didn't work out as I had hoped but with the guys' help, we managed. All things considered, I think we did pretty well for a bunch of guys in their seventies.

When working on the itinerary, the original idea was that we would make for the city of Magadan, Russia further to the north, after many emails back and forth, I found out that it was not possible to cross the Bering Strait from Magadan to Anchorage,

Canada so as an alternative, I arranged for the vehicles to be shipped from Vladivostok. The revised arrangement was that when we arrived at Vladivostok on or about the 28th May, we would, within a few days, ship the vehicles and crew by drive-on ferry to Sakaiminato, Japan via South Korea. After arriving at Japan, we would visit Suzuki's headquarters to meet the people and participate in a P.R. and publicity programme. After a few days the vehicles would then be packed into a container and shipped to Seattle on the north west coast of America ready for the start of stage 4, well that was the plan anyway but unfortunately it didn't turn out like that. What followed was a series of events that nearly brought the journey to an end. Having settled for Vladivostok as our departure port to Japan, I assumed that the problem was behind me. Throughout our journey, I kept in touch with everybody at home, especially Vi, my wife, who dealt with important phone calls and was my eyes and ears and who let me know if there was anything I needed to know about, I also spoke regularly to Maureen, who managed the project P.R., so I was informed as to what was going on at home allowing me to focus on what lay ahead. Roger, who was to join me together with Glyn for stage 4 and who was in the freight business, helped initially with the shipping information I needed to enable me to make decisions, however, the information I received was confusing and conflicting to a point where I was being told that there was no shipping service from Vladivostok to Japan and that I should consider shipping from a port on mainland China. By that time, I'd had enough. I was grateful for the help but I couldn't accept what I was being told and in the end I had to say that I would deal with it myself. Cursing because I had wasted so much time, I tapped into my laptop at home 'shipping agents at Vladivostok' and up came Links Ltd, I then drafted an email explaining who I was and went on to say that we have two vehicles and crew that need passage from Vladivostok to a port at Japan, is there a service? A reply came back saying yes there is a service departing every Wednesday, after a few more emails, I had provisionally booked the two cars and crew passage on the ferry departing 5th June and I was instructed to pay for the tickets when I arrive, another problem solved, or so I thought.

About two weeks before we arrived at Vladivostok, I had to contact Yuri Melnikov, the manager of Links Ltd, for some reason or other but before ending my email, I asked if he knew if we needed any special paperwork to enter Japan. My question was a follow up after my negative response from the Japanese embassy and other enquiries I had made before departure. There didn't seem to be any standard procedure so I was hopeful I could sort it out on arrival. I didn't get an answer from Yuri Melnikov to my question about entering Japan, if I had, it would have reminded me to enquire further if there was a problem, either way I consider that I was at fault and should have pursued the matter to clarify the situation before I departed the U.K. I already knew that we didn't need visas so I forgot about it and carried on as though everything was O.K. so when we arrived at Vladivostok, the cars were serviced and we made ourselves available for the reception as planned. That evening, we located the ferry ticket office and I handed over the money and collected our tickets.

Thursday 30th May, day 61, I arranged to meet Yuri at our hotel at 10am that morning to hand to him documentation he needed relating to the vehicles, after a late breakfast, we met face to face for the first time as planned but I noticed that he didn't look happy and I certainly wasn't prepared for what he was about to tell me. We dealt with the pleasantries he then said, "I have bad news to tell you, you cannot take your vehicles to Japan." I just looked at him as holy shhh*t slid out between my teeth. "What is the problem?" I asked. "The Japanese will not allow foreign vehicles from Russia to enter Japan," he said, it was a devastating blow. Yuri and I spent the rest of the day trying to get the problem sorted out, I spoke to Suzuki G.B. to find out if they would contact Suzuki Japan to help, Yuri had discussions with various official bodies located at Vladivostok. I argued that we would only be passing through to the docks on the east coast for shipment to the U.S.A., but irrespective of our effort, it appeared that the only way we would be allowed to take our vehicles into Japan would be on the back of a low loader or sealed in a container. After a very long and tiring day riding the 'yes we can go, no we can't' roller coaster and getting nowhere, I was beginning to think my ambitious journey around the world would end at Vladivostok, I have to say I wasn't pleased with myself at that point in time, I felt that I had let the guys and the project down. I agreed to meet Graham and Mike for dinner that evening but I didn't feel like making an effort, my mind was spinning like a top trying to find a way out, I sat alone in my room situated high up at the hotel watching the sun dropping below the horizon. After a while, I reached for the phone and dialled Yuri's office number, after a few rings Yuri picked up, I said, "Thanks for your help today," replying in English he said, "I wish I could have done more, what are you going to do now?" "It's just another problem for me to solve," I replied. "Yuri," I said, "can you ship the two vehicles direct to Vancouver, Canada?" there was a pause for a moment then he said, "Yes I can," first step forward I thought to myself then asked if he could have a quotation and departure date for me the following morning. I thanked him and put the phone back on the receiver.

I was turning over the bones of a plan in my head when I met the guys, over a beer I ran through what had happened during the day resulting in us not being able to drive the vehicles on Japanese roads. "To keep the show on the road, so to speak, I have put together an alternative plan. The proposal is that I ship the vehicles direct to Vancouver from Vladivostok bypassing Japan altogether, stage 4 will now start from Vancouver. The arrangement we have still stands, the ferry costs are paid for, also the project's stage 3 commitment to you finishes when you arrive at Japan, your own personal arrangements to stay on and tour Japan will begin." I also said, "I will not be travelling with you to Japan. I have decided to spend time making sure that there are no hidden problems waiting to present themselves during stage 4 and I need to notify Glyn Maher and Roger Winkworth of the revised plan." I don't think the guys were very happy but I was determined to make it happen.

Friday 31st May, day 62, I called Yuri before breakfast, he told me that the cost to ship the two vehicles in a container to Vancouver would be about $6131 (£4167) and a ship would be leaving on 7th June but he needed payment beforehand. "O.K.," I said, "you let me have a copy of the invoice and email me another copy with your bank details, I will give you half now and transfer the remainder within two days." "That is acceptable," Yuri said then continued, "the first thing we have to do is to decontaminate the vehicles by pressure washing, there cannot be any mud or soil on the vehicles, if on arrival at Vancouver customs find anything they may impound the vehicles. First we must wash the vehicles then transport them on a low loader and put them directly into the container." I thought that it seemed a bit extreme but I went along with it, later that morning and with the guys help, we managed to pack the very clean 02 and 03 into an allocated container and see it sealed to await shipment. Graham and Mike spent the rest of the day sightseeing, I met Yuri at the hotel to pay him as agreed and make sure our paperwork was in order to satisfy the Russian and Canadian customs. Yuri went back to his office to tie up the loose ends, I went to my room to speak to Vi and update her about what had happened and arrange for her to make the transfer of the outstanding amount. I said to Vi

Vehicles decontaminated before being loaded into a container

that I would call her later, laying back on my bed to think about
what I had to do next. There was a noise outside my room, I
opened my eyes, wondering where I was, I had been asleep for
two hours. I looked into the full length mirror and there was that
old man again. After a shower and clean clothes, I felt refreshed
and ready to take on the world once more. I remembered what I
had to do next; somehow I had got to sweet talk Olga at the ferry
office to reimburse me the cost of the ferry fares for me and the
two cars because passage to Japan was no longer required. I looked
into the mirror once again, the vision of the old man had gone
and had been replaced with a reflection of me on a good day;
I took a closer look to make sure that there was no bushy hair
protruding from my ears and nose or black bits between my teeth.
Satisfied that I was irresistible, I double dosed with cologne then
made my way to the ferry office. Stretching to make myself taller,
I explained to Olga what had happened, I could see her defences
crumbling as she listened to my story, she had no chance of
fending off my charm and charisma and it wasn't long before I

Loading the container – next stop Hong Kong

was walking back to the hotel clutching my refund. I know I elaborated a bit but Olga is a very lovely lady and, like all the Russian people, she was very helpful.

02 and 03 were securely tied down in the container and would be on their way on the 7th and I was relieved that I was able to get my money back from the ferry company, so, so far so good. On the face of it I had been able to replace a disaster with a viable alternative, surely nothing else could go wrong, but it did!

The guys were having a beer at the restaurant on the ground floor of the hotel, I joined them and we remained there for a meal before walking into the city. During the course of the evening, I brought them up to date as to what I had arranged and confirmed that I managed to get a refund for the cars and me and assured them that their booking had been confirmed and handed them a copy of the receipt as proof of payment. I sensed that Graham and Mike wanted to say something but didn't so I said no more but made a mental note to mention it again the following day. In a way, I was disappointed at not going to Japan, our itinerary included visiting Suzuki headquarters to meet the people at the top, also a visit to one of the manufacturing facilities and a film and a P.R. session, sadly I was to miss it all.

Saturday 1st June, day 63, I woke early from a troubled sleep; it was still dark as I lay thinking about what required my attention that day. The first grey fingers of dawn light penetrated my room as I reminded myself that I had to visit the bathroom twice during the night as well as taking painkillers in between to deal with a nagging pain in my groin that had become more regular. Realising I was wasting my time lying in bed, I decided to get up and go for a walk to think things through. I made myself a cup of coffee then stood in front of the mirror, drinking it as I looked at the old man looking back at me; don't let it beat you I said to myself. It wasn't long before I was walking along the water's edge towards the marina, I found an isolated spot to sit and think things through. Ever since I was a youngster I have been attracted to or never far from the sea and boats, I don't know why because there is no history or tradition in the family. I must have sat there for almost an hour, thinking everything through and committing what I had decided to paper. Pleased with myself that I had got everything into some sort of order, I walked briskly back to the hotel and had breakfast with the guys. It was a beautiful sunny day and we agreed it would be an opportunity to explore Vladivostok, I said, "I need an hour to make some phone calls and send two emails, and will meet you at the hotel reception." We spent the rest of the day visiting the city's attractions, the open air market and the submarine museum. Graham and Mike had a serious appetite for walking, pacing it out quick time to wherever we were going with me following behind. I was relieved when we found somewhere for lunch. After a meal and a short rest, the guys produced a street map and pointed to places my feet were reluctant to go so I suggested they go on without me and I returned to the hotel. I sat on my bed, resting against the headboard to complete my paperwork and bring my diary up to date but at some point I must have fallen asleep, I woke up, pen in hand, still sitting upright, it was 6 o'clock. I panicked a bit because I had promised to phone Vi. I called home, noting that Vladivostok is 10 hours ahead of the U.K., Vi picked up after a few rings, it was a real treat to hear her voice but there was none of the usual bouncy tone; Vi listened intently as I explained what I had organised, after I had finished I said I loved her to bits and missed her very much, I could sense she was upset so before the situation deteriorated further I said I would phone her the same time the following day and finished the call. I sat on the bed thinking about how upset Vi really was, I didn't intend for her to experience such emotional turmoil, I sincerely hope I haven't messed up our marriage. Graham, Mike and I met five guys of various nationalities who were about to collect their old English motorbikes that had just arrived at the docks packed in a container. They intended to ride them from Vladivostok to Europe, going west in the opposite direction from which we had come, they were a nice bunch of guys, they asked us a lot of questions about what the roads were like, they proposed to take a route through Siberia further to the north. We had planned to meet them before they left but we didn't see them again.

Sunday 2nd June, day 64, there wasn't much happening as it was a Sunday, after breakfast we sat in the hotel lounge for a while to have a chat and to decide what we would do for the rest of the day. I had already mentioned previously to Graham about the $500 or so of project funds that he and Mike were each holding for emergencies and that it needed to be returned to me before they leave for Japan. Since mentioning it, there had been no further reference so while we were seated chatting, I took the opportunity to raise the issue once again, it went a bit quiet after I mentioned it and I readied myself for what was to come, Mike then said, "I don't think we should hand back the money, we will need it to cover our expenses when we arrive at Japan." I was saddened by what Mike had said as I thought about what my reply should be. I gave a long sigh then said, "I collected Graham and yourself from Novosibirsk airport on the 9th of May and by the time you reach Sakaiminato, Japan you will have been taking part in stage three for 30 days or so, all expenses paid including ferry costs and airfares as agreed, why do you think you shouldn't hand back the money?" "I was under the impression that the journey ended on the 11th and you will be with us to pay all our costs, also we would have had use of the vehicles until then," Mike replied. I thought for a moment and accepted that Mike's argument was reasonable and that they should retain the money in question. I continued to think about the situation then turned to Graham and said, "Can I ask you to represent me and visit Suzuki headquarters on my behalf to meet the people and take pictures? It is not what I had planned but you can wave the flag and tell them why 02 and 03 are waiting on the docks at Vladivostok." It was a bit of an anti-climax sitting around doing nothing and alien to us because we were used to being under pressure and tired after driving long hours along pothole riddled roads to reach our destination on time. Keeping ourselves occupied for the next few days while we waited for the ferry to Japan to arrive wasn't as straight forward as it seemed, wandering around the city to find something to look at was becoming hard work.

Monday 3rd June, day 65, the morning routine of a walk along the water's edge, an extended breakfast and discussion about what we should do for the rest of the day had become normal procedure. I said to the guys that I didn't think I could manage another tour of the city and suggested that I would meet them later for lunch at the marina. To be truthful, I wasn't feeling too good, I had a reasonable night's sleep but I still felt tired, I don't suppose lazing around doing nothing was helping. I was confident that the guys were now happy about the arrangement for when they arrive at Japan and that I needn't give the matter further consideration. I decided to spend the remainder of the morning thinking about what I would say to Vi when I phoned her later that evening and what needed to be done before I was to meet up with Glyn Maher and Roger Winkworth and the start of stage 4. The original plan was that we start from Seattle on or about the 5th of July, it wasn't possible to be more precise until the container with 02 and 03 actually leaves the dock at Vladivostok. However, the destination of the container and the start of stage 4 had been changed to Vancouver due to not being able to take our vehicles into Japan so I had to notify Glyn and Roger of the new arrangement, which I did later that morning. I was becoming more concerned about the upset and turmoil I had inflicted on Vi, I hadn't seen her since the 17th of April (50 days) and the thought of us not seeing each other until the end of August may be too much for her to cope with, I needed to do something. I turned it over in my mind, groping for a solution, and eventually concluded that the container would take 17 days to reach Vancouver so an opportunity presented itself for me to meet Vi somewhere and spend a few days together. Relieved that I had made a decision, I decided to put my proposal to her later.

I met Graham and Mike and we spent a pleasant hour or so having our lunch and a beer overlooking the marina. That evening, I put my proposal to Vi, she became excited at the prospect of getting together and we agreed that we would meet at Lefkas, Greece on the 9th. Vi booked my flight from Vladivostok to Athens via Moscow departing on the 5th. After a few days of old couple bonding and patching things up with Vi, I would then fly from Athens direct to Vancouver to be there in good time to receive the vehicles from our shipping agent. Well that was the plan anyway, if only it was that simple!!! That evening over a beer, I outlined my proposals to Graham and Mike, I asked if there was anything further they wanted to know about the ferry, accommodation or when they arrive at Japan, they said they were satisfied with the arrangement and pleased with the way everything had come together.

Tuesday 4ᵗʰ June, day 66, I knew it would be a difficult day for Vi and myself, it started badly, I woke quite early but lay there looking up at the ceiling, reminding myself that I had to contact Yuri to ask if he knew when the container was being collected from the docks, also I had to visit the ferry office to make sure that the ferry would be on time, and not to forget to notify the hotel that we would be checking out the next day. I got out of bed and made a cup of coffee and stood by the window watching the streets come to life and at the same time remembering it was the 4ᵗʰ of June, I thought of our son who left for another place that day in 2008. Vi manages to cope with it better than I do, I know he was a pain in the arse at times but I miss him so much, I just can't help shedding a tear. After a while, I dressed and went for a walk, I needed fresh air. After breakfast, I phoned Yuri and asked if there was any news, he replied confidently, "It is being collected Friday 9ᵗʰ." Relieved after hearing the news, I thanked him for his help and said that I would monitor the container's progress via the internet. What happened later threatened to end, once more, my quest to drive around the world. Pleased that the container would be on the move soon, I gave it no further consideration. It was a warm bright sunny morning, the guys and I wandered to the ferry office at the docks, another excuse to have a chat to Olga, who confirmed that the ferry was on time and would arrive at the dock at 9.30am the following morning. Everything seemed to be working out fine, the only depressing thing left to do was to pay the hotel bill in the morning. Blissfully,

I was free of concern about how everything would turn out and spent the remainder of the day with the guys as they perused the interesting sights that they missed on their many tours of the city during our stay at Vladivostok.

It was our last night together and I was determined that we would celebrate the success of stage 3, it was decided that we would have a meal and a beer or two at the hotel restaurant. We met at the restaurant and decided to have a beer before ordering, 3 beers each and an hour later the waitress took our order, the meal was O.K. and went down with the aid of another beer. As the evening progressed, a party of Russians came into the restaurant and occupied a long table close by and immediately ordered 4 bottles of Vodka, they were already well oiled before they arrived and were soon swaying and shouting at one another, their speech slurred as they proposed a toast to everybody and everything they could think of. I guess the people on the next table had their reason to celebrate and so did we I thought. I asked the waitress for a bottle of what they were drinking and 3 glasses. The waitress, clutching the bottle, reappeared within seconds pointing at the label to emphasise the quality and value. I poured the vodka saying, "I hope you don't mind, I normally have a drink for our son, Lee, this day each year, will you join me?" Filling the glasses a second time, I said, "I also want to thank you for your support and help in achieving a successful outcome of stage 3 and apologise to you for being a bit grumpy on occasion." After the third glass, I don't remember much but ended up in bed.

Wednesday 5th June, day 67, the sun was shining into my room when I woke, I sensed that my eyes were open but all I could see was a white haze, my head was pounding as I regained enough vision to see that it was 10am, I should have vacated the room by this time and be at the reception to pay the bill. I tried to remember what happened, my mind was blank as I lifted my head off the pillow as part of the process of getting out of bed. The pounding going on inside caused me to pause and whimper with pain. I groped my way to the bathroom and fumbled for two paracetamol and a glass of water then stepped into the shower, I felt terrible, the task of dressing myself seemed to be taking ages, I looked a mess as I passed the mirror on the way out of the room and to breakfast if still open. I managed some toast and 3 cups of strong coffee before Graham and Mike joined me looking like death, enquiring if I was alright. We vacated our rooms and I paid the hotel bill, which had a sobering effect. By 11.30am, I gave Graham and Mike an affectional hug each and wished them a safe journey, got into my taxi and then I was on the way to the airport. I was relieved that I no longer had the responsibility of stage 3. I remembered that when I was dealing with the shipping arrangements, it was brought to my attention that there was a report going around at the time about pilferage from vehicles when they are unloaded from the container. Remembering this when we loaded 02 and 03 into a container at Vladivostok, I removed the filming kit, valuables and personal items from both vehicles before they were sealed into the container. The problem now was that I had to carry the 56lb (25kg) load with me wherever I went until being reunited with the vehicles at Vancouver. Looking a bit green and feeling lousy, I arrived at the check-in desk looking like a vagrant and my possessions causing the checking clerk to eye me suspiciously. Relieved of the bulk of my load, I boarded the flight to Moscow at 2 o'clock in the afternoon, I was asleep the moment we got airborne and woke up when we touched down at Moscow at 10.30am the same day, travelling back in time. I arrived at Athens airport at 11.30 the same evening, my body clock a shambles. I managed 4 hours sleep before my early morning call, sounding like church bells ringing in my room, brought me back to life. I had to be at the bus station that morning at 6.30am to catch a bus to Lefkas, another 6 hour journey. I finally arrived at my destination late that afternoon totally drained.

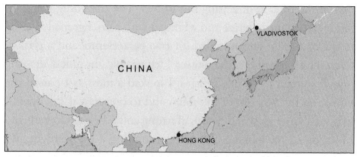

From Vladivostok the vehicles went by container ship to Hong Kong, before being re-loaded on another ship for Vancouver in Canada

Thursday 6th June, day 68, the next 2 days I isolated myself, I just wanted to sleep and recover from the mental and physical strain of the past months, the loss of 14lbs (6.5kg) in weight and looking gaunt wouldn't go unnoticed. 02 and 03 were sealed into a container and were on their 17 day voyage to Vancouver via Hong Kong. From here on, there was not much for me to do other than being reunited with Vi on the 9th and monitoring the progress of the container so I will scroll forward in time to arrive at relevant dates and what happened next.

Friday 14th June, day 76, I received an email from Roger Winkworth to say that the container was on the docks at Hong Kong awaiting the arrival of the container ship, Arthur Maersk, to uplift the container and deliver it to Vancouver, so far so good, rolling forward once again.

Thursday 20th June, day 82, the Arthur Maersk departed Hong Kong docks for Vancouver as scheduled but did not load our container. Roger, being in the freight business and with his best intentions, informed me as to the situation and said he had been in touch with Links Ltd and asked Yuri to deal direct with him in future and keep him informed of any changes to the situation.

Concerned that Roger had decided to intervene, which in my view would only confuse the situation further, I emailed Yuri relaying what Roger had said and asked if he would carry out an investigation to find out what had happened, I also said to Yuri, "I understand that Roger Winkworth has asked you to deal direct with him, I believe this will cause confusion so please be advised that I would like you to continue as before and I will keep Roger informed as and when necessary." Yuri replied saying that he was already looking into it and would get back to me. He said that he would communicate only with me as before. Sometime later, I received an email from Yuri notifying me that the shipping clerk dealing with our container allocated the wrong code number causing confusion and resulting in the container remaining on the docks, that's why it wasn't collected. Having a clearer picture of what had happened, I passed the information on to Glyn and Roger and said I would keep them informed as the situation unfolds. I then sent another email to Roger thanking him for his help and asked if he would continue monitoring the movement of our container, I then asked him not to contact Yuri direct but instead deal only with me to avoid further confusion. My frustration from not being able to do anything, also the days of toing and froing between me and Yuri, and Yuri and the shipping line was driving me crazy. Because of the mix up, we lost our container space on the Arthur Maersk, the next ship with available space would not load until 2nd July. I thought to myself, I sometimes wonder if there is someone somewhere testing my ability to cope.

Tuesday 2nd July, day 94, our container with 02 and 03 sealed inside had been waiting at the Hong Kong docks for 18 frustrating days, desperate to receive some good news, I emailed Yuri asking if there was any news, his reply confirmed that the container would be loaded that day. The tracking system did not work for a few days but eventually Roger informed me that our container was on a ship destined for Vancouver. We had lost 18 days shipping and waiting at Hong Kong docks and another possible 23 days shipping, unloading and going through customs at Vancouver, total time 41 days, the original time allowed was 27 days. The situation confronting me now was that we would start the journey from Vancouver to Anchorage, Alaska 14 days later than originally planned therefore requiring the itinerary to be adjusted to accommodate a later start date and to reschedule already booked flights for Glyn, Roger and Tomasz Malewicz, our cameraman for stage 4. If everything went according to plan, I proposed to start the journey north to Anchorage on Friday 26th July. I remained vigilant, monitoring our container's progress, when I was certain the ship would arrive as scheduled, I notified Glyn and Roger to inform them that they should reschedule flights to arrive at Vancouver Tuesday 23rd July and to let me know their flight number and arrival time. I then emailed Tomasz Malewicz to ask him if he could arrange to arrive at Vancouver on or about the 16th-17th so that we could spend time together to review the filming so far, also to discuss what filming we need to complete while we were waiting at Vancouver. Satisfied at what I had organised, I booked hotel accommodation for when the guys would arrive. As for me, I planned to arrive at Vancouver on 15th July, 11 days before departure, to meet Tomasz at the airport and also to meet Gabryelle, our contact at Astra International, our shipping agent, to deal with customs paperwork, car insurance and any unforeseen problems that may present themselves. Finally everything was in place, all I needed now was for it all to happen.

If there really was someone out there testing my ability to cope or crack under the strain, they would be very disappointed. It pretty well all came together as I had hoped. I met Tomasz on the 16th, we spent one night at the Best Western then for 6 days I was a guest of Peter and Joy, friends of Tomasz, really nice hard working people who made me welcome, they rented a house in the suburbs of Vancouver. Before Glyn and Roger arrived I was able to bring Tomasz up to date with the project so far and we managed to get a lot of filming in the bag, including footage taken from a seaplane. I met Gabryelle, our agent, for the first time and completed the customs formalities and sorted out an unforeseen problem with the vehicle paperwork that was picked up by customs. Finally, we were ready for when the vehicles arrive. I collected Glyn and Roger from the airport and booked them into the Best Western, on arrival there was a note at reception from Gabryelle asking me to contact her urgently which I did. Gabryelle told me that the container had arrived at the customs but they couldn't release the vehicles because there was yet another discrepancy with the paperwork. I said to Gabryelle that we only had two days before we leave and we must get it sorted out.

Thursday 25th July, day 117, I wasn't happy that we hadn't been able to clear the vehicles through customs and decided to phone Gabryelle regularly to monitor the situation. While we were waiting, we decided to track down the government office dealing with imported vehicle insurance, it took most of the day to find the correct office and purchase our very expensive insurance. During the day I tried to contact Gabryelle but she could not be located, I was getting very worried as I tried her office for the umpteenth time, the phone rang and she picked up. I was relieved to have made contact, "Any news?" I asked. "You have to come to the office right away, there is a problem," she said, my heart sank as I replied, "It is already after 4pm and we are still at the city centre, we will be there as quickly as possible." Glyn, Roger and I were a bit subdued as we hurried on and off trains and made the final brisk walk to get to Gabryelle's office. We turned the last corner and looked to where Gabryelle's office was located, our faces beamed with relief when we saw 02 and 03 parked outside,

Roger and Les arranging insurance so the fourth and final leg can begin

my concern over the past weeks about the wellbeing of the vehicles faded away as I entered the office and saw Gabryelle laughing her head off. When the excitement and relief subsided, I dealt with the remaining paperwork, thanked Gabryelle for her help and at the same time said, "You nearly gave me a heart attack." We said goodbye then drove to our hotel.

Back at the hotel, we checked both vehicles, they were clean and only needed the kit that I had been carrying with me from Vladivostok to be reloaded together with the food and provisions for each vehicle that I had purchased locally during the past few days. It was late but we were ready to go the following morning. Over a beer, I reviewed the route, procedures and emphasised for safety reasons that we must remain in sight of one another at all times. I went on to remind Glyn and Roger why we were driving north to Anchorage, it was because it was the original destination had we been able to secure passage from Magadan, Russia direct to Anchorage, the start of stage 4 but that wasn't to be. I dealt with everything I could think of and clarified the various points

Russian roadside place of worship.

The road bridge across the harbour at Vladivostok, the Sea of Japan to the right.

Les, Mike and Graham and the management of the Suzuki showroom press day, Vladivostok.

Vancouver floatplane terminal, Les and Tomasz took the opportunity to climb on board a float plane for a flight around the Vancouver harbour.

Les greeting Glyn and Roger at Vancouver airport, in spite of all the reorganisation, they arrived as planned.

Vancouver city and waterfront.

The guys checking 02 and 03 outside the Best Western Vancouver before the start of stage four.

The original saloon at Dawson City.

Traces of gold after panning at claim 33.

Claim 33 - learning to pan for gold, bent over the water filled troughs, washing the pay dirt in anticipation.

Mountain range viewed from the Alaska Highway.

Rush hour along the Alaska Highway.

Passing one of many logging trucks and the dust
cloud that follows, high in the mountains.

The Canadian wilderness.

Relieved to find the isolated fuel pump at the top of the world.

The endless stunning scenery as viewed from the top of the world Highway.

Tomasz at work.

Peace and tranquillity at Kluane Lake, Burwash Landing.

Bison grazing at the roadside along the Alaska Highway

A moose feeding in a lake, seen from the Alaska Highway travelling south.

One of the many breathtaking views, a fast flowing river twisting and turning its way along a valley floor.

raised and finished by saying, "Tomorrow we will start a 5000 mile, 18 day journey that will take us as far north as Anchorage then east to link up with the Taylor Highway then south via the Alaska Highway to Calgary and the U.S. border town at Carway. Tomasz, our cameraman, will be my passenger for stage 4 as I continue to drive unassisted the remainder of my journey around the world." Glyn, Roger, Tomasz and I would be in close contact with each other for the next 30 days until we reach the east coast of the U.S.A., how it would work out only time would tell.

We were as ready as we would ever be and the guys were briefed about the journey ahead of us. It only remained for Tomasz and I to stay awake to receive a call at 12.40am (just after midnight), 8.40am the same morning U.K. time from Julian Clegg, presenter of the programme Julian's People on B.B.C.Radio Solent U.K. The idea was that when I received Julian's weekly call live on the show he would be filmed at his end talking to me at Vancouver and I would be filmed simultaneously at my end talking to him. It worked out fine, everybody was happy with the way it all came together, by the time we got things wrapped up it was 1.30am Canadian time.

Friday 26th July, day 118, from here on, our itinerary was back on track. It was late by the time I got into bed and I was wide awake at 4.00am, I remained awake going over everything and only drifted into a shallow sleep when I assured myself there were no loose ends. A little later, I showered, made some notes then loaded all my kit into the back of 02, paid the hotel bill and decided to have an early breakfast, I wanted to get the show on the road. The guys joined me a few minutes later; I guess they were also eager to get going. Over breakfast I mentioned about 03's wheel wobble and the various attempts to correct it, I went on to say that Graham and Mike complained about it frequently during stage 3, I did a test drive in 03 and all I could detect was a slight vibration at 40 mph but as soon as you increase the speed above 40 mph the vibration faded. Glyn and Roger drove 7524 miles, the issue about a wheel wobble was never raised. Tomasz Malewicz, a Polish cameraman, occupied the passenger seat in 03, a real nice guy, he agreed to join us after I contacted him at the beginning of the year. Closer to the time, I emailed Tomasz to make sure he had all the information he needed, and one point in particular was that his bag containing personal kit must not weigh more than 22lb (10kg) and be small in size. When I collected Tomasz at the airport he arrived carrying a massive ridged plastic four wheeled orange case that weighed in the region of 40lb (18kg), I said light heartedly, "I don't think there is any room for that case, we are already over weight." By the time he had lightened the load by removing some items he had brought to Canada for his friends and I rearranged the interior of 02, we got the case on board. Pleased and relieved that we were rolling north at last, I started to relax; the last few weeks had been an absolute nightmare. I called 03 using the handheld radio and Glyn responded, I asked if everything was alright and were they happy to cruise at 55 mph, "No problem," I heard Roger say in the background. I said, "The road condition is excellent and it will be like this all the way until we reach the east coast of the U.S.A. The early morning mist cleared allowing the first rays of the sun to break through as we headed for Williams Lake, a 322 mile, 8 hour journey. Knowing that there would be no problem with the road condition, I was able to plan our route and timetable with a level of accuracy. As I travelled around the world, I marvelled at the scenery as I passed through individual countries, it didn't matter if the terrain was hostile or not, each country had its own version of breathtaking scenery that I was privileged to see. I have been to Canada before on business but with limited time to look around so I was excited at the prospect of driving through the wilderness and meeting English speaking people. It was sad in a way but I was privileged to be able to do something that unfortunately most people can only dream of doing. We passed the Cheakamus Indian Reserve and place names like Squamish Garibaldi and Whistler, words and names used by settlers many years ago. My first impressions were confirmed when we stopped for coffee at the roadside hamlet called Cache Creek, a store and coffee shop run by two mature ladies who when they found out where we had come from and where we were going became very interested and inquisitive, resulting in each of us receiving a slab of cake on the house.

We reached the town of Williams Lake late afternoon and found accommodation at a roadside lodge, spending the remainder of the early evening relaxing and chatting about the route north and stopping if we have time at places of interest. The exchange rate being favourable to the U.K. pound meant that medium priced accommodation was competitive and usually had its own coffee shop or restaurant which was always convenient, especially when we arrive late in the evening. I was beginning to get a good feeling about Canada.

Saturday 27th July, day 119, we breakfasted and were on our way by 8am to Smithers, a 317 mile, 9 hour journey, arriving about 6 o'clock. The roads were busy with leisure traffic, cars towing lake boats, lumbering motorhomes and born again leather clad Harley riders keen to get to their destination and enjoy the sun. We cruised along straight roads that disappeared into the distance; the ever changing panoramic scenery that presented itself on either side of the road as we passed was stunning preventing boredom gaining a foothold. 02 and 03 glided along the super smooth roads, the car windows open allowing the cooling breeze to pass through. The soothing hum from the little Jimny engine and the muffled chatter from the all-terrain tyres worked in harmony to produce a sound and feeling of total bliss. The drive along the Cariboo Highway to Prince George, our lunch stop passed so quickly, over lunch we were like school kids talking excitedly about what we had seen. We were soon going north once more, fortified by a proper beef burger and a sprinkling of chips!!! The weather collapsed during the afternoon, turning to rain later, the first rain I had seen for some time, it must have had an effect on the animals because we passed some deer grazing by the roadside as we arrived at Smithers, what a day. There was a jolly mood as we booked into the slightly up market lodge, tired but with an appetite that needed satisfying, we made ourselves comfortable in the restaurant and enjoyed some local tasty food. Everything was working out fine, the tension, worry and concern I had been harbouring as to whether it would come together as I had hoped was fading and I began to look forward enthusiastically to the next day.

Sunday 28th July, day 120, the unsettled weather had cleared and was replaced by blue sky and brilliant sunshine by the time we had checked and refuelled the vehicles. It was 8.30am when we turned north to Dease Lake, a 367 mile, 10 hour drive along the Stewart-Cassiar Highway. The road followed a natural route through the huge mountains, some capped with snow, and grazing animals gave us a cursory glance then carried on feeding. Glyn and Roger had got the hang of driving by then and frequently took the lead, easing the pressure on me, I didn't have to worry about the route, I just had to follow the car in front for a change. So as to keep us occupied, we organised a contest between 02 and 03 to see who could spot the most species of animal each day, not to be outdone, I cheated most of the time. There seemed to be plenty of deer but black bears, moose and buffaloes remained elusive. We arrived at Dease Lake, an isolated spot with only one roadside lodge and coffee shop but at least it was clean and warm.

Monday 29th July, day 121, another long day ahead of us, our journey to Whitehorse was a 388 mile, 9 hour drive, on the way passing the Cassiar Mountains, turning left at a T junction and the sign for Watson Lake then on to Whitehorse, hopefully arriving sometime about 5pm.

The single lane each way highway was monotonously straight at times and stretched as far as you could see, on other occasions the road led us through valleys, skirting crystal clear lakes and fast flowing rivers and the clear air exposing mountain ranges in every direction, I felt privileged to be able to see it. I looked forward to the regular stops for a short break from driving and a cup of coffee, there is always someone that takes an interest in us and the vehicles, where we have come from and where we are going, we have met some great characters on our travels and I lost count of how many times I posed with people for pictures, mum and the kids standing in front of the vehicles and dad behind the wheel or me and the guys leaning on the vehicles, one of us holding the baby, the rest shaking hands. We attracted more interest as we travelled south through Canada and the U.S.A. We arrived at Whitehorse as predicted and there was a wide choice of accommodation to choose from and we were soon fed, watered and bedded down for the night.

Tuesday 30th July, day 122, it was the 5th day driving on Canadian roads, the journey from Vancouver to Anchorage was rapid because I was concerned that we should arrive at Anchorage on or before 2nd August, day 125, I pencilled in 4th August as the start of our journey south, also I needed time to get to know the people I would be spending the next 4 weeks with. I managed to keep everything together so far, I didn't want anything to happen that would cause a problem that I couldn't handle. Glyn got a bit upset at Smithers but apart from that incident, Glyn and Roger seemed to have settled into the daily routine and understood the reasoning in relation to safety procedures, also checking and looking after 03. From what I had seen so far, I had struck it lucky with Tomasz, he turned out to be a very nice guy and a very good cameraman, on the face of it we seemed to be coming together as a team. The route and itinerary for Canada and the U.S.A. that I put together was different to anything previous, I highlighted places of interest also places I particularly wanted to visit, although fewer in number, it was important that we arrive at each destination as scheduled to ensure that we eventually arrive at North Bergen on the east coast of the U.S.A. on Monday 26th August to hand 02 and 03 over to our agent for shipment to the U.K., our final destination

During the lunch stop, I reminded the guys that we would be staying at the old gold mining town of Dawson City that night and I hoped to meet Duncan Spriggs who owned and ran a saloon at Dawson and is the brother of a friend of my wife and I, back at the U.K. The 321 mile, 9 hour journey to Dawson City was nothing short of spectacular, more of what we had seen so far but the vastness of it all took your breath away especially when we stopped at Good Hope Lake, the panoramic view was enough to blow your mind further. We stopped for a break and coffee at Pelly Crossing, a beautiful spot, before continuing to Dawson City and the Yukon. The road that led into the old original Dawson City was like driving back in time, the wide dusty streets, saloons, hotels and houses of ill repute with the undertaker next door if the strain was too much for the older clientele. We parked outside the undertakers and further along the wood clad sidewalk, we booked into the downtown hotel that requested we check in our guns before we went to the bar!! We got ourselves settled in and we were soon exploring the town, eventually locating the saloon we were looking for. The place was packed with well-oiled people, some having difficulty standing, and everybody was shouting to be heard, it was some sort of mad house. The peeling

Downtown Hotel at Dawson City

The crew with Duncan Spriggs (second from right) in Dawson City

Glynn preparing to sample the 'Sour Toe Cocktail'

Lowes Mortuary was conveniently situated next to the crew hotel!

Three wise monkeys: overlooking the Yukon River

paint and wallpaper, rickety tables and chairs and collapsed floor qualified the building to be listed as derelict. I managed to get to the bar and order 4 beers, the man who served me had the DTs, as he handed me the beers he was shaking so badly, the beer went in all directions splashing my face and hands.

I navigated my way to where the guys were standing, they stared at me and said, "What happened to you?" "I slipped," I replied, saving the real cause for whoever gets the next beer. I phoned Duncan earlier to let him know we had arrived and would meet him at the saloon. While we were waiting, I said, "I have never met Duncan before but the story is he came to the Klondike to prospect for gold, he didn't find much gold and found it hard work so he bought the saloon, over a period of time the drink got the better of him so I guess we are looking for a rundown man in his late 40s with a red nose." By that time, we managed to be seated at a rickety table watching the door. A young looking well-presented man walked through the door and made for the bar and exchanged a few words with the barman who in turn pointed in our direction. Side stepping the collapsed floor, Duncan came over to us and introduced himself. We sat talking for a few minutes then I asked Glyn if he would get 5 more beers, I asked Duncan what made him leave everything in England and come all the way out to Dawson to prospect for gold, at the same time keeping an eye on Glyn at the bar. Duncan said, "It's a long story, I was young and seeking adventure, I staked a claim and dug for gold, it wasn't long before I realised that I could make more money if I owned the saloon so eventually I bought it." I looked to see how Glyn was getting on and saw he was heading in our direction looking like he had chickenpox, his face and hands covered in brown beer spots, we were all laughing. Duncan said, "I see you have met the barman." Glyn handed each of us our beer as Duncan continued, "The gold rush started in 1896 when gold was found at a place which was later known as

Bonanza Creek and within a year or so there were over 100,000 people digging for gold, some found it, the remainder mostly ended up in poverty because of it." I said to Duncan, "What about the saloon?" he replied, "I had to sell it my liver couldn't take it anymore." He went on to say that he hadn't had a drink for 6 months, holding up his half empty beer glass saying, "However, this is a special occasion you have come a long way so the least I can do is have a drink with you." It was interesting to talk to Duncan, we remained chatting for another hour before we said goodbye and made our way back to the hotel, during the time we were chatting with Duncan he didn't have a second drink. Although we intended to meet once more before we moved on, we didn't manage it. It was a pity because I would have liked to have spent more time with him.

Wednesday 31st July, day 123, we were excited at the prospect of a rest day and an opportunity to go back in time and take a leisurely stroll around Dawson City old town to get a feel as to what it was like 120 years ago, visit the sights and places of interest, the old gaily painted wooden buildings and a lot more, it was magic! After lunch, and I have to say, I could hardly control my excitement because we were going to find a stream and pan for GOLD. The very thought of doing something that I had dreamed of doing since I was a kid was overwhelming, I couldn't wait. We had lunch at Klondike Kate's located at 3rd Ave. & King St. We must have looked like prospectors because the meals were jumbo size. After being properly fed and watered, we were on our way to find our gold and stake a claim. On the way to our own Eldorado, we stopped and perused old mine workings and a miners' camp before moving further along the valley and Claim 33, an old mine no longer producing commercially but kept alive by three lovely ladies, Sylvia Burkhart, Proprietor, and Partners Robyn and Ginny. There weren't any other visitors there at the time so we got their full attention. Over a cup of coffee, Robyn ran through the workings and history of the mine including the quantity and value of the gold extracted. Sylvia produced a small pot, the size that would fit into the palm of your hand, containing gold nuggets valued at $50,000 then in a serious tone said, "Gold is still out there if you want to look for it."

For $10 a head, we were issued with a pan each then taken outside to the long water filled wooden troughs and we were assured the pay dirt lining the bottom of the trough contained gold dust. Keen on the get rich quick idea, we watched intently as the ladies gave us a demonstration ending with a sliver of gold remaining at the bottom of the pan. Gripped by gold fever, we rolled up our sleeves then dived elbow deep into the trough, scooping up the pay dirt like a J.C.B. digger. Convinced that we didn't learn anything from the demonstration, the ladies dumped the contents of our over filled pans back into the trough then with one to one stage by stage tuition a sliver of fine gold particles remained at the bottom of each of our pans. "I'm rich, I'm rich," someone shouted as the ladies bagged our gold and handed it to each of us. We had a great time; the lovely ladies really looked after us. We were invited back to the office for a second cup of coffee, they asked a lot more questions about England, what we were doing and where we were going, they also asked about our charity, Heaven Can Wait I'm Busy. After a brief discussion between themselves, each of the ladies put a small nugget into a bag containing pay dirt and handed it to me saying, "It is a donation to the charity." Sylvia continued by saying, "We would also like you to keep 2 pans as a memento," fantastic people. By the time we left Claim 33, it was late afternoon so we decided to head back to town. On the way back we passed a stream set back into a wooded area, we couldn't help ourselves, no one said anything as we turned off the gravel track and parked 02 and 03. Confident that we were now qualified prospectors, we approached the edge of the stream in a blasé, cocksure manner. Eyeing up the competition, I went down on one knee and started panning, 20 minutes later, my trousers soaked through and disappointed that I still had to be nice the bank manager I threw my pan into the back of 02, looked at the guys already waiting in 03 then drove off without another word.

Back at the hotel we agreed to meet for a beer before dinner. Rested and refreshed, it wasn't long before we were in conversation with a group of people who were touring Canada on Harleys. The born again bikers told us that they hired the Harleys at Vancouver to do as much touring as they could handle then would return the Harleys back to the hire shop, it sounded like a good idea to me, all I had to do now was to convince my wife to get on the back, I may have to think again! Feeling short of energy, partly caused by eating too much food, we decided against another tour of the town and settled for a quiet half hour seated in the lounge. After a while, a few people who were on tour came into the lounge shattering the peace and quiet then a few minutes later another man came in, I thought he was a magician. Listening to what he was saying to the group of people, I became more interested and wanted to know more. After the presentation, Glyn asked me what it was all about, I said, "As far as I can make out, the man entertaining those people has a miner's frostbitten big toe, you pay him $5, he then provides a drink with the miner's toe in the glass, if you manage to down the drink without throwing up you receive a certificate to that effect." Reputed to be another tourist gimmick, we continued chatting between ourselves, however, a beer or two later, the man with the toe indicated to us that we should have a go. Being the leader of our group, I thought that I should set an example and stepped forward I paid my $5 and was handed the glass, I nearly threw up there and then. The toe was black in colour, 2 inches (50 millimetres) long, the toenail needed trimming and a bone was visible at the open end. To qualify for a certificate, I had to drink from the glass at the same time sucking the toe into my mouth and holding it there while I finish the drink then spit it back into the glass.

I looked at the toe, wondering if I really wanted a certificate and at the same time the beef I had eaten earlier was about to let me know that it was coming up, I turned to the guys hoping for a way out but everyone in the now silent room was looking at me expectantly. Realising I was trapped, I lifted the glass and strained the liquid through my teeth then opened my mouth to let the toe pass through nearly vomiting as it touched the back of my throat, the beef was on its way when I spat the toe back into the glass. The only good thing about it all was that I got my certificate and watched Glyn, Roger and Tomasz having to do the same thing, another wonderful day.

Thursday 1st August, day 124, we reluctantly departed Dawson City at 9.30am, crossed the Yukon River by ferry and started a 225 mile, 8 hour journey to Mentasta via the Top of the World Highway, crossing the Canadian-Alaskan border then on to Chicken, a roadside fuel and food stop. Along the Taylor Highway, we passed the Tetlin Indian Reservation before we arrived at Mentasta Lodge, our destination, at 6.00pm. It was hard to believe we were only 250 miles from the Arctic Circle. The lodge was a cluster of wood buildings, the rooms clean and cosy with a strong smell of pinewood. The lodge itself nestled at the bottom of Mentasta Pass which ran between high snow-capped mountains on either side. A fast flowing, crystal clear river that flowed along the side of the road provided the purest of water for the lodge, a Mecca of peace and tranquillity, a place to look at nature eat and sleep. There were about 12 other people at the bar, some travellers like us, others scratching a living locally during the day and propping up the bar at night. It wasn't long before we were like long lost friends embracing each other and swapping

Chicken, at the Top of the World Highway – population 11!

T shirts and home addresses. One of the regulars was a woman who I will for the benefit of the story call Jane (short for Calamity Jane), a lovely lady who I can best describe as looking older than her years, she was missing a few teeth, what remained were yellow, her greying strands of unkempt hair were tied to form a ponytail but the rigid strands of hair pointed backwards forcing her baseball cap to tilt forward over her eyes. Jane was a heavy smoker and beer drinker capable of drinking any man under the table, flat chested, wearing man's clothes and knee length rubber boots, she was a picture but one of the nicest people you could wish to meet. A beer or two later and the onset of double vision and slurred speech, we were talking to Jane about her cabin. Jane said her cabin was in the forest on the other side of the river and she lived there all year round, sometimes in the winter she was snowed in for 3 or 4 months. I remember someone casually asking how she manages for food, Jane replied saying that at the onset of winter she shoots a moose. "Shoots a moose," we blurted out and at the same time sprayed beer in all directions. At that point my

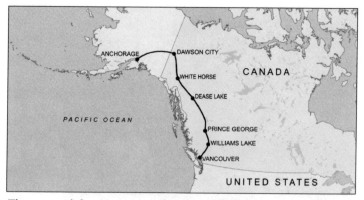

The route north from Vancouver in Canada to Anchorage, USA

memory gets a bit vague! Apparently, the guys were a bit sceptical so Jane invited us to her cabin to see for ourselves. Jane somehow managed to get us into her flat bottomed boat and rowed us to the other side of the river. By the condition of my clothes the next morning, I must have stood in water up to my knees, but I didn't remember anything of the rest of the evening. Apparently, what happened was that Jane took us to her cabin and showed us around then led us outside to a small undercover area and hanging from a beam was the remains of a moose carcass and a neat pile of bones and antlers belonging to previous victims. Somehow, Jane managed to get us safely back onto our side of the river. The following morning, I surfaced from my sleep, not feeling in prime condition, my eyes wouldn't open so I lay there trying to remember what happened, I got my eyes working and achieved a sitting position at the side of the bed. As I began to see clearly, I saw my mud caked clothes scattered all over the floor and my best boots half filled with water. Must have been very strong beer! Memories of the previous night's folly were becoming clearer. After two cups of strong coffee, a shower and clean clothes, I felt a little better and headed for the coffee shop and breakfast.

Beneath the statue of Charles Darwin in Anchorage

Friday 2nd August, day 125, the guys were already at breakfast looking really ill, there wasn't much talk at the table; I guess we were all suffering. I thought about the previous night's escapade and Dawson City and reminded myself that the guys had come together nicely as a team and had been under pressure to get to Anchorage by Friday, so I guess it was a time to relax and enjoy ourselves before we got to the serious business of driving south. We got ourselves organised in slow motion and on the road by 9.45am. The 268 mile, 7 hour journey to Anchorage would pass through the settlements of Slana, Gakona and Glennallen then continue west along the Glenn Highway to our destination. The journey was uneventful, 02 and 03 purred along all day at a steady 55 mph to arrive at Anchorage city limit at 5pm and continued to follow the traffic to the city centre. Within a few minutes of arriving at the city centre we located what looked like, from the outside, a clean and respectable motel. The practice normally when booking into low cost accommodation is that I or one of us inspect the rooms beforehand, on this occasion I didn't follow procedure and handed my card to the receptionist who immediately processed it. Realising what I had done we went to the rooms and agreed between ourselves that they were not acceptable, I returned to the reception to complain about the rooms and cancel my card payment but the Chinese manager wouldn't give me a refund, I apologised to the guys and asked them to make the best of a bad situation. We weren't happy after having a closer look at the rooms, I made light hearted jokes about the things that were wrong with the rooms but I was bitterly disappointed with myself for letting the guys down, at least the sheets were clean! After we parked 02 and 03 in front of our rooms so we could keep an eye on them, we cleaned ourselves up and looked presentable then walked to the tourist area to find a place to eat. Over the meal, the guys and I talked about Anchorage and the places of interest we could visit while we were there. I guess we still had the grubby motel on our minds because Roger mentioned that he preferred to leave the following morning rather than wasting another day at Anchorage. Glyn, Tomasz and I also agreed with Roger's suggestion, leaving

The Alaska Highway with the Ruby Mountain Range in the background

Saturday morning would mean we would be a day ahead of schedule. Walking around a city was alien to us; we were all looking forward to the official start of stage 4 and the journey south. We spent the rest of the evening seeing as much as we could but our hearts were not in it. Summer day time that far north scrambles your mental clock, walking around at 11pm at night in broad daylight is the same as 2pm in the afternoon, I found it difficult sleeping at night without waking up two or three times and that particular night was no exception.

Saturday 3rd August, day 126, we were awake early, there was no coffee shop attached to the motel so we decide to stop for breakfast outside the city limit, Tomasz told me that he had been bitten by insects but a closer inspection revealed that both arms were covered with flea bites, probably from the motel the night before, luckily we had medications included in the first aid kit for such an occasion. At last we started stage 4, the final part of the journey around the world. Departing Anchorage at 8.30am, we backtracked in an easterly direction to Tetlin Junction, our destination, a 290 mile, 9 hour journey, arriving a little after 6pm, the journey was uneventful and as before we were blown away by the scenery.

I hadn't said anything to the guys at that point as to why the following morning would be special to me so I thought the ideal time would be over a beer before dinner. We settled into a small roadside hotel and were relaxing in a cosy lounge before going into dinner so I seized the opportunity to talk to the guys. I said, "Tomorrow is special day for me and it has been ever since I became interested about travel and happened to read about the Alaska Highway, from then on I have wanted to see it touch it and above all drive on it. Why, you might say, would a road be so significant?" I continued. "The Japanese bombing of Pearl Harbour in 1941 forced the American and Canadian governments to re-evaluate the security of North America. They needed a secure supply route to transport men and materials from Dawson Creek in the south to Fairbanks in the north of Canada in the event of a Japanese invasion, a distance of 1,523 miles (2,450km) and it needed to be completed within one year, unthinkable in those days. The feat of engineering was unprecedented at that time and I believe remains the case to this day. The team was mustered together at Dawson Creek to take on the gigantic task and comprised 11,000 U.S. troops, 16,000 American and Canadian civilians and 7,000 machines used to construct the road, to build 133 bridges and create 8,000 culverts. The work was completed, believe it or not, in 8 months, 12 days but remained closed for military use until 1948 when it was opened to the public for the first time. You have got to hand it to the Americans and Canadians at that time, shocked at what happened at Pearl Harbour, they recovered and achieved what some people at the time said was unachievable." The guys listened with interest at what I had to say and I finished by suggesting that we stop at the southern city of Dawson Creek (not to be confused with Dawson City) and visit the famous cross roads and 'O' Mile starting point of the Alaska Highway, "And by the way," I said, "the Alaska Highway is right outside this hotel."

Sunday 4ᵗʰ August, day 127, we finished our lumberjack size breakfast, then moved to the garage next to the hotel, Tomasz was filming us in the process of checking and refuelling the vehicles ready to head south to Destruction Bay, a 225 mile, 7 hour journey. I felt a real sense of achievement as I stood in the middle of the Alaska Highway looking at the road snaking south into the distance. Content that I had ticked another box, I said to Glyn and Roger that from here on we would take turns at being in the lead, it seemed to work O.K. and gave me a chance to see things I miss when leading. The scenery was once again stunning but I soon realised that the long straight roads had acquired two ruts in each direction, caused by years of heavy truck use. The problem was that the distance between the wheels of 02 and 03 was narrower than the ruts in the road surface which meant that only one side of 02 was in the rut, the other two wheels ran along the part of the road in the middle. The problem with the ruts occurred mainly when driving on older sections of the road, other sections that had been resurfaced at some time seemed to be O.K. However, it became a test of my driving skills, especially in the afternoon, a time of least concentration, hardly any other traffic to consider, driving along stretches of road that extend as far as you can see, sitting comfortably, a little lethargic and over confident, looking at everything but actually seeing nothing, 02 steering itself as though it was running on rails cruising along at a steady 55 mph mile after mile, thinking about everything other than driving and a blink of an eye away from an afternoon nap at the wheel. If the road surface changes from the endless light grey coloured smooth surface to a darker shade and passes unnoticed, 02 unilaterally decides which rut to drive along and at the same time sends a warning by jerking the steering wheel one way or the other causing me to overreact and turn the wheel in the opposite direction to compensate; in so doing, 02 leaps out of one rut, only to drop in the opposite rut.

When it happens and lacking the reaction of the speed of light, I overcompensate by tugging the wheel in the opposite direction and end up relocating the rut that had just been vacated. It tends to wake you up very quickly. Fully awake and paying attention as a result of my altercation with the rutted road, I once more focused on the scenery. To my right was the southern end of the Wrangell Mountains and at its base was the breathtaking spectacle of Logan Glacier, a mass of ice constantly on the move, to my left but further in the distance, the Dawson Mountain Range, the sun from the west reflecting off its snow-capped peaks. We arrived at

Destruction Bay at about 5pm and followed a dirt road to the lake-shore edge and Burwash Landing Lodge, our accommodation for the night. The lodge was of wood construction and from the inside, there was a panoramic view of the huge Kluane Lake; in season, the lodge is a centre for fishermen, specimen fish in glass cases occupying all the available wall space. After our evening meal, I took a stroll along the shore of the lake to think through some issues that were on my mind, I recall sitting on a log that had been washed ashore, listening to the soothing sound of the lapping water and call of birds as they flew overhead. I sat there thinking that ever since day one of the journey I had thought of nothing else other than keeping everything together, dealing with the problems as they occurred, keeping an eye on crew and vehicles and, above all, keeping to our schedule and eventual successful conclusion. Deep down though, I knew that at any time it could all end. I continued to think about the journey so far, then for the first time I said to myself, I've managed to hold everything together for the last 129 days so I guess I can hang in there for another 19 days.

Monday 5th August, day 128, another day, we met for breakfast early and were soon fuelled and on our way south, the sky was grey and rain was expected later as far as I understood. Glyn and Roger in 03 had a routine where Roger drove during the morning and Glyn the afternoon, it looks like Glyn got the short straw! Our destination that day was Whitehorse, a 295 mile, 8 hour journey. The day started well enough and the agreement to alternate lead position throughout the day seemed to be working. For the first few miles, we cruised along at a comfortable 55 mph then for no apparent reason, 03 started to accelerate and disappeared in the distance. I maintained our standard cruising speed and a mile or so further on, I caught up with 03, now doing 45 mph. I looked and sounded the hooter as I passed and continued to lead. A few minutes later 03 drove past at about 65 mph and again disappeared into the distance, the yo-yo driving, as I call it, continued throughout the morning so I decided to have a word with the guys when we stopped for lunch and fuel. After consuming man sized burgers and coffee, we fuelled the vehicles and 03 was about to leave the fuel station when I asked Glyn and Roger if they could wait for a moment while I had a word with them. I politely said, "I would like to remind you why we drive in sight of one another, the rules are not set in concrete but they have served us well so far, we cruise at 55 mph because it's our best economical speed, as soon as you drive faster the fuel consumption increases dramatically. The reason we drive within sight of one another is mainly for safety reasons, in the event of an accident the unaffected vehicle will be at the scene and able to assist within minutes. The other reason we remain in sight of one another at all times is because the lead vehicle ensures that we are going in the right direction, if for some reason the lead vehicle arrives at a junction and takes a left turn and when the following vehicle arrives and for some reason turns right or continues straight on, we will be split up and out of contact. With the handheld radios out of commission it may be difficult to find each other. If we are in sight of one another and we get lost, we get lost together."

We arrived at the town of Whitehorse at 5pm and set about finding accommodation, there weren't many places but what we did find was closed or boarded up, I asked a local person for directions to a hotel and was told that there were no hotels open. I was concerned that it was almost 5.30pm and there was nowhere in the town where we could stay overnight. I looked at the map and said to the guys that the only alternative was to drive to Teslin, another 100 miles further on. By that time, we were tired and hungry and didn't feel like driving but we had no alternative. At 7.30pm, we arrived at Teslin, a holiday village, well and truly knackered, I indicated to 03 to stop and we both turned off the road and parked in front of a sign saying Takhini Hot Springs, I said to the guys that if we were to make our way to the hot springs there was bound to be accommodation close by. We located the hot springs and a small hotel but unfortunately there were no vacancies, the owner of the hotel suggested that by the time we had a swim at the springs he would have organised accommodation and somewhere to eat. There were people of all ages swimming in the mineral rich water, the tranquillity was shattered and curses muttered as we jumped in the water directly under the 'no jumping in the water' sign, it was heaven. We lulled about at the shallow end like four beached whales feeling in need of sustenance, the 30 minute soaking had worked wonders and we were soon back at the hotel to find out where we had been billeted.

Tuesday 6th August, day 129, we slept late that morning, I guess the dip in the hot springs had its effect, we consumed our syrup covered grits breakfast then we headed south to Watson Lake, a 200 mile, 7 hour journey. The morning was bright and sunny,

Roger and Glyn leaving their 'calling card' at Signpost Forest

the crisp fresh air filled our lungs as the road guided us along the valley floor of the Cassiar Mountains and at times ran parallel with the Swift and Rancheria Rivers and animals, disturbed by our appearance, ran for cover. We arrived at Watson Lake earlier than anticipated so decided to stop at a roadside coffee shop for a short rest and refreshment, we were all in a jolly mood, Glyn and Roger seemed to accept what I had said to them about staying together. I said, "The map indicates that there are hot water springs situated on the way to Fort Nelson, do you want to drive further and hopefully have a swim and stop for the night?" Considering the options, everyone was in agreement so we continued to drive further south. We drove for about a mile then stopped to take in the sight that panned out before us, thousands of metal name plates and notices of every description, some very old others more recent, nailed to upright posts buried in the ground. What started as a tourist attraction had become a must do thing with your own sign, so over the years passers-by have stopped and nailed their contribution to one of the wood posts upended into the ground for the purpose, it has expanded and covers a large area and is known as Sign Post Forest. After driving south for another 2 hours, I struggled to keep my eyes open, it was one of the rare occasions when tiredness catches up with me and I had to stop. Indicating to Glyn to stop, we turned off the road, I said that I was sorry but I needed to close my eyes for 10 minutes, Roger offered to drive 02 for a while but I thanked him and said that I was the only person who drives 02. Tomasz got out of 02 with the camera, as he did so I closed my eyes and immediately lost consciousness. I remained in a deep sleep for about 10 minutes then it's as though I had been switched back on and came back to life refreshed and batteries fully charged, I started 02 and waved to the guys to get the show back on the road. The sun was still high although it was close to 7pm in the evening, it was clear that we were not going to reach the hot water springs close to Fort Nelson and as luck would have it, we passed a sign a few minutes earlier pointing the way we were going saying Coal River Lodge.

A short distance further on, the road descended into a valley and set back from the road was the Coal River Lodge, our safe haven for the night. During our meal, we got into conversation with other guests and spent the rest of the evening putting the world right. I reminded myself that I had to make a phone call the following morning to Tracy Millwood, one of the owners of the Suzuki dealership at Edmonton, I had been in touch with her during the past year or so, with her asking me if we would take part in a P.R. and press day.

Wednesday 7th August, day 130, I awoke from a disturbed sleep at 6.30am, expecting the early sun to brighten my room but it was still dark, I looked at my watch a second time then went to the window and saw it was raining heavily and a thick blanket of mist covered the whole valley. I didn't get much sleep that night, partly because of my catnap the previous afternoon and a slight but persistent pain in the groin, sleeping only after the painkillers had an effect. I didn't feel too good as I sat sipping a cup of coffee while waiting for the guys to surface. It was a 223 mile, 7 hour journey before we would reach Fort Nelson. We were on our way at 9am, the rain was quite heavy but I was assured by the lodge owner that the weather would improve when we exit the valley. Thirty minutes later, it was as though a curtain had divided the weather, on one side rain and mist, on the other brilliant sunshine that continued for the rest of the day. Leaving the rain curtain behind us, we drove south along the Alaska Highway, a single lane each way straight flat section of road that ran for about 5 miles. Looking along the arrow straight road and away in the distance, there was a black object in the middle of the road, because of the distance between us and the object, I didn't give it further

A Wood Bison – North America's largest land animal

thought. Having an interest in the way the highway was constructed and how they managed to include very long straight flat sections, I guess the engineers decide what height a level surface should be to clear variations over a given distance, back fill and under pin, add a road surface on the top and you have a highway. The downside is that the road surface level can be as much as 12 feet (3.6 metres) above the terrain it is built on. The problem is, if you breakdown there's generally no place to stop until you reach level ground. The other and more serious issue to be considered is, if you fall asleep at the wheel you will probably be over the edge before your eyes are open. The road cut through dense forest areas high off the ground, facilitating a bird's eye view through the trees and seeing wild goats and deer grazing in the shadows. I decided to look ahead to see what the black object was and became excited when I saw what I thought was a moose standing in the middle of the road. The road was now level with the surrounding terrain and on either side of the road were many more black objects under the trees, sheltering from the sun, can't be more moose I said to myself as we got closer, and then blurted out, "Buffalo". Standing in the middle of the road was a big bull wood bison, making what traffic there was detour around at a safe distance. I was overwhelmed at seeing a wild buffalo for the first time, I had seen them at London Zoo and on the films but to be standing close to the real thing was something else; we were all elated at the experience as we continued south. After a while, Glyn and Roger, who were ahead of us in 03, drove up an incline in the road then disappeared over the top of the hill, at that point, Tomasz and I in 02 were trailing some way behind and were completely unprepared for the scene and carnage that came into view as we came over the crest of the hill. Spread out before us was a road accident, police and special teams were still in attendance but the paramedics and ambulance had already left the scene, sadly with what was left of the truck driver.

The few cars in front of us slowed to get a closer look causing a backup so before we got too close, we stopped and parked behind the emergency vehicles, I got out to have a closer look and

A reminder of what can happen

asked the constable in charge what happened. He informed me that it appeared that the driver fell asleep at the wheel and drove over the edge of the road, looking at the smashed lorry cab, I decided not to ask if the driver survived. The very long articulated lorry was fully loaded, lying on its side about 8 feet lower than the road, as the lorry rolled on its side and stopped, the forward momentum of the load continued smashing through the trailer headboard and pulverising the lorry cab and anything in it. Sickened by what we had seen, we continued on our way. I, for one, thought about the near misses and encounters I'd had and so far survived, I thought to myself, only another 16 days to go. We arrived at Fort Nelson at 5.30pm, the plan was that we would start as early as possible the following morning because of the distance to Grand Prairie, to save time we refuelled the vehicles before locating our accommodation, I was shocked by the price I had to pay for fuel. $1.70 (Canadian) a litre for Regular was the highest price so far.

Thursday 8th August, day 131, 8am, we continued to travel south on the Alaska Highway, our destination was Grand Prairie, south of Fort St John, an estimated 349 mile, 10 hour journey. The previous evening I mentioned to the guys that if we were to get an opportunity I would like to camp for a few nights as it was part of the programme; they didn't show any enthusiasm at my proposal so I didn't pursue it further at that time. The weather was overcast with heavy grey clouds that threatened rain during the morning but it never materialised. We passed another small herd of bison grazing at the roadside, a real pleasure to see such powerful majestic animals close up in the wild. It was 03's turn to lead and they passed Tomasz and I in 02 like they were driving a Ferrari and disappeared into the distance, a mile or two further along the road they would park if they could and wait until we got close then zoom off into the distance once more, the yo-yo driving was back with us again. I was disappointed that Glyn and Roger had disregarded my advice to drive within our safety guidelines and I wasn't of a mind to speak to them again about it as I wanted to avoid the issue turning into an argument, I decided not to respond and let them sort it out for themselves. I watched 03 far in the distance and noticed that they applied their brakes, probably to stop. As Tomasz and I got closer, we could see that something had happened on the other side of the road, we stopped behind a line of other cars and walked forward to where 03 was parked, "Another accident," Roger said. I could see that a car, including passengers, towing a trailer was driving in the opposite direction and somehow drove over the edge of the elevated highway, both the car and trailer ending upside down and personal belongings scattered everywhere. Passengers from the car were sitting and lying on the grass holding various parts of their body waiting to be attended to by the two paramedics and passers-by that stopped to help. Being in close proximity of two accidents in two days made me think about paying more attention when I'm driving. 03 tucked in behind 02 when we left the scene of the accident and remained there until we reached The Buckinghorse River Lodge for lunch and fuel, there wasn't much said over lunch, I guess the accident had an effect on all of us. I made a call and spoke to Tracy Millwood of Woods Suzuki Dealership at Edmonton, Tracy told me that the situation had changed and the press day had been cancelled, she offered to ask one of her salesman to organise a B.B.Q. instead the following Saturday, I thought about it then thanked her but declined her kind offer.

I was disappointed that the press day had been cancelled but I thought the day would be better spent by making a detour and visiting Banff, an exceptionally picturesque place, one of the jewels in Canada's crown. Glyn and Roger had mentioned previously that they would like to visit Banff and were pleased when I told them that we would pass through there on Saturday. Becoming tired in the afternoon happened quite often so I disciplined myself to stop for a few minutes if I had to, up until recently I had been able to drive anything up to 12 hours day after day without any problem but now I seemed to be struggling. Nevertheless, I was determined to continue to drive 02 by myself and complete the journey around the world. Late afternoon, we arrived at Dawson Creek and drove to the crossroad at the centre of town and to see the Mile O signalling the start of the Alaska Highway, I have ticked another box, I have driven the Alaska Highway. We stopped for a while to savour the experience, taking pictures and for Tomasz to film us acting like idiots in the middle of the road then continued our journey. We eventually arrived at Grand Priarie at 6.30pm, a pretty town, the sort of town you see in the films, I stopped at the first hotel we came to, it looked expensive but I thought that the team spirit had got frayed at the edges and the guys needed a bit of a lift so booked the rooms. We finished our meal in the hotel restaurant and remained at the table to have a beer, Tomasz left us to go outside to have a smoke, Glyn, Roger and I chatted about what we had seen during the day and our journey to Jasper the following day. At some point, and as both Roger and I have an interest in anything that floats, we got talking about boats and sailing, Glyn didn't contribute to the conversation so just sat at the table. Roger and I must have been talking for some time because by the look on Glyn's face, he was about to blow a fuse! I turned to Roger with the view to changing the subject to something that would interest Glyn but it was too late, the fuse had blown, "That's it," Glyn said, "I'm going home in the morning." Sick and tired of pacifying people and dealing with their problems, I looked at Glyn feeling like I wanted to scream but instead said, "Why do you want to go home?" "You two haven't spoken to me all night so I'm going home in the morning." I said, "Sorry, it wasn't intentional, Roger and I were talking about sailing, you live at Lymington, you must know something about boats or you should have asked us to talk about something else." I then said, "Go to bed and in the morning if you still want to go home, I will drive you to the nearest airport." I decided to go for a walk before going to my room; I needed to think things through. I said goodnight to the guys and stepped outside, it was still daylight, the air was warm and smelled of blossom, I needed to get the sick feeling out of my system and somehow I had got to hold it all together. It was times like this that I needed to phone Vi at home just to talk to her and ask her what she is doing and how is everybody, I somehow feel better after our little chats so I phone when I can. I also look forward to the live interviews with Julian Clegg at B.B.C. Radio Solent for the same reason.

Friday 9th August, day 132, we met for breakfast at 7.30am, Glyn didn't mention anything about going home and I wasn't about to poke a tiger with a stick, so I let it drop and carried on as normal. 02 and 03 were checked and refuelled and we were soon heading south to Jasper, a Mecca for tourists, a 313 mile, 7 hour journey. At Grande Cache, we turned right along the scenic Route 40 south to Jasper, passing through the Willmore Wilderness Provincial Park, crossing the Musket River a number of times as we made our way to the Snake Indian River arriving at 4.30pm. Jasper was full with tourists packed together on the sidewalks making it difficult to get anywhere. We parked in the only two spaces available and rubbed shoulders with the mass of people going in all directions.

We found a coffee shop and managed to secure four seats at a partly occupied table and waited a long time before we got served. I enquired at three hotels in the town seeking accommodation but they were fully booked so I suggested that we continue to drive along Route 93 towards Banff and maybe find a roadside

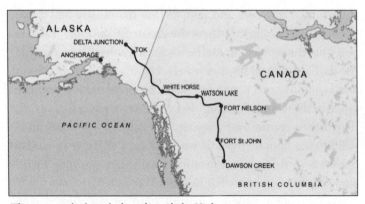

The route south along the legendary Alaska Highway

lodge. Everyone agreed so we inched our way out of town and on to Route 93. I was leading in 02 and Roger was driving 03, I was getting close to the left turn to join Route 93 that would take us towards Banff when Glyn and Roger in 03 passed Tomasz and me, driving at speed heading west along Highway 16. Sick to death at having to deal with one situation after another, I turned onto Highway 16 and chased after them to tell them they were going in the wrong direction. At about 75 mph, I couldn't close the gap, 02 was bouncing all over the road, I sounded the hooter and flashed the headlights to get Roger's attention but got no response. The Motorola handheld radios were not working due to one of them not holding the charge, to help out in an emergency, I purchased two medium power communicators from a store a week or so before, we had one with us in 02 and tried to contact 03, no response. By this time, 03 had disappeared out of sight and I was still travelling at 75 mph. I slowed to a more manageable speed; it was an hour and 60 miles later that we caught up with 03 parked at the side of the road. Tomasz remained in 02 while I went to talk to Roger who was sitting in the driving seat in 03. To say I was cross would be putting it mildly. I looked in the car at Glyn who was looking at the floor then turned to Roger and said, "What the bloody hell do you think you are doing?" "What's the problem?" he said, "I will tell you what the problem is, for the last hour you have been thrashing the daylights out of 03, I have been chasing you at over 75 mph and I couldn't catch you and to make matters worse you have been going in the wrong direction." Roger didn't have much to say after that. I then continued by saying, "It is almost 7pm now and it will be after 8pm by the time we arrive back at Jasper so our best option is to find accommodation locally, lets continue further along the road and see what happens."

As luck would have it, a few miles further along the road, we came upon the Tete Jaune Lodge situated at the base of Mount Robson, alongside the Fraser River. Ted, the owner, welcomed us and allocated our rooms, I asked if there was any food available he said there wasn't a restaurant but we could have what food he had, with what Ted had and what was in the back of 02, we managed to put a meal together with a beer or two to wash it down. When we arrived at the lodge, I noticed that a bunch of youngsters were offering white water rafting from an office next to the lodge, as soon as I had finished cleaning up after the meal, I discreetly slipped away to the white water rafting office to see what was on offer. The outcome of my meeting was that I had booked Glyn, Roger, Tomasz and myself to go white water rafting the following morning. In reality, I couldn't afford it but I needed to bring us together as a team so getting soaked in the morning might be just what we needed. The project operating funds would run out within a few days so I would be paying the bills personally from then on. The reason for the shortfall was due to using hotels every time we stopped and not camping some nights as planned. The other reason was that the operating fund total was reduced substantially at short notice, just two of the many issues I'd had to deal with as we travelled and I had no doubt there would be others before I reached journey's end.

Saturday 10th August, day 133, proper sleep alluded me once again, I had to take painkillers before managing to sleep for a few hours and took more when I woke up to pacify the nagging pain in my groin.

There was no hurry that morning so I had plenty of time to prepare breakfast from our food stock in the back of 02. It was brilliant sunshine; we sat at a table overlooking the Fraser River as we ate our cereals and drank strong coffee. None of us had experienced white water rafting before so everyone was excited and keen to have a go. We were booked to be at the riverside at 11.30am for instruction and to be kitted out and on the water 30 minutes later. As we had time, I explained to the guys that I thought friction and animosity was taking hold and we were no longer working as a team. I hoped that by taking part in white water rafting, it would enable us to put any issues there may be behind us and work as a team for the remainder of the journey.

The briefing and issuing of suits and helmets completed, we stood at the water's edge to listen to the final instructions and to be allotted a place in the raft, there was an element of fear on everyone's face but it didn't stop the comments being made to the effect that we looked like overstuffed sausages. The under size black wetsuits and yellow helmets were to protect us in the event of us being thrown out of the boat and hitting the rocks and to stop us sinking if we made our own way downriver without the boat, the thought was depressing as we waited in silence. We all suddenly became very religious as we were launched into the roaring torrent of the Frazer River; Glyn sat in front and shielded me from the full force of the water that hit him every time the boat nosedived below the surface. The young instructor was sitting at the back, dry and out of harm's way, shouting instructions, back paddle right left forward stop right back paddle left back paddle, the novelty soon wore off, our arms felt as though they had been pulled from their sockets and muscles torn to shreds. I heard curses from up front ending with, "Will someone throw the instructor overboard?" The unrelenting erratic motion of the boat showed no mercy to the spent crew. Thankfully, the instructor steered our boat to a calmer part of the river and beached it so that we could rest for a few minutes or take the opportunity to jump ship and get a taxi back to the lodge, I must admit I did consider it, especially when the instructor said, "Up to here is for boys, what lies ahead is for men." "Holy s—t," I heard someone mutter, another whimpered, "I want my mum." We launched and boarded the boat, this time I was at the front as we headed towards the deafening roaring sound coming from around the next bend, I nearly pooed myself when I saw what was making the noise, something you want to avoid doing if you are wearing a wet suit. My eyes focused on the 100 metre wide Frazer River forcing itself between two huge boulders 15 metres apart then dropping 10 feet into a cauldron of spray and froth and we were heading straight for it. "Ship oars and hang on," came from the back of the boat, I didn't need telling twice, I found a secure hand hold just before nosediving into darkness. Totally submerged, I hung on as though my life depended on it, the boat clawed itself to the surface and I was relieved to be breathing air and still attached the boat. "Back paddle," the dry man at the back shouted as we made an effort but the boat was full of water and no amount of paddling would shift it. The racing water had us in its grip ricocheting us through one soaking after another, the instructor barked orders as he steered us in the right direction. By the time Glyn, Roger, Tomasz and I emerged into calmer water, we looked like four shrunken battered old men, I don't think I achieved much team bonding that day. We thanked our instructor for looking after us on the water then returned to the lodge to change into dry clothes. The pounding I received on the water caused my annoying, but up until now tolerable, pain in my groin to become more aggressive so before we left the lodge I took two more painkillers knowing I had already taken four pills that day.

I didn't realise at the time that the pills I had been taking to help with the pain also had other side effects so I was a bit scrambled by the time we left Tete Jaune Lodge and backtracked the way we had come to Jasper. 03 led the way and it wasn't long before they disappeared into the distance. Before we left Tete Jaune Lodge, I understood that the arrangement was we would stop for a meal at a service area at Yellowhead Pass just before Jasper. An hour later, Tomasz and I stopped as planned expecting Glyn and Roger to be waiting for us. There was no sign of 03 so we waited for them to turn up at some point, after waiting for 30 minutes I decided to continue further along the highway to see if they were parked. Sure enough, a mile further on they were waiting for us, I wasn't feeling quite right as I stopped 02, got out and said to Glyn and Roger, "We have been waiting 30 minutes for you, we agreed to stop at the service area for a meal, why do you keep racing ahead so that we lose sight of one another, you know you are taking risks so why do it?" I then continued, "If you want a meal, I suggest we get ourselves back to the service area." I got back behind the wheel of 02, I really wasn't myself as I nosed 02 to the edge of the road, looking at the traffic flowing in both directions for an opportunity to negotiate a U turn. I saw a gap in the traffic and went for it, Tomasz screamed as I turned and zigzagged my way across the flowing traffic, causing cars to react violently, horns sounding and tyres skidding to avoid a collision. I don't know what made me drive like a mad man, I was lucky, I got away with it that time but it was totally out of character and something I was ashamed of doing. When I got back to the service area, I apologised to Tomasz for what I did, and when Glyn and Roger arrived they told me exactly what they thought of me, I agreed with them and apologised to them for what I did. I wasn't popular at that point in time, Roger mentioned over our meal that he would get a plane home from Calgary, but I thought to myself, wait till the morning and see what happens.

It wasn't a good time to mention it but I said to the guys, "It is getting late and we are unlikely to find any hotel accommodation so we may have to find a campsite and camp," their reaction wasn't very encouraging, I suggested that we drive towards Banff and hope for the best. We drove for another two hours towards Banff, it was about 8pm, we had no luck with finding accommodation and a campsite we passed was full, we drove on further to a campsite at the base of Mount Brazeau but once again there was a sign saying no vacancies. Desperate to find a spot to camp, we cruised around the site looking for a space, as we toured the site for a second time, I noticed a plot that was occupied by a young couple who had pitched their tent in the corner, leaving enough space for our tent. I had a chat to the young couple explaining who we were and what we were doing and asked if they could help us by letting us pitch our tent on their plot. They agreed to help providing I squared it with the ranger. The deal was done and we moved onto the plot and started to erect our tent, Tomasz was filming the event that can, at best, be described as resembling a sequence from a Keystone Cops film, the curses, huffing and puffing and other noises we made trying to erect the tent soon attracted an audience that looked at our antics as entertainment. It was dark by the time we had got the kettle on, Roger was a bit grumpy while we were getting organised and insisted he was going to bed as soon as he had pumped up his airbed, he continued grumbling and repeated that he was going home in the morning. As he got into his sleeping bag, still moaning and cursing to himself, the rest of us, including our hosts, were listening and watching Roger and couldn't help laughing.

We were all watching as Roger tried to turn over onto his side but got tangled in his sleeping bag and somehow rolled out of

A camping 'learning curve'

bed ending up in the middle of the tent, his swearing and cursing then turned to laughter, everyone was laughing, the sound echoing through the campsite. Roger changed his mind about an early night, got dressed and joined us around the campfire. We spent the rest of the evening getting to know one another all over again. Realising that I had been a fool by overdoing it with the painkillers, I decided not to take any more. We were all tucked up in our sleeping bags and sound asleep by 11.30pm.

Sunday 11ᵗʰ August, day 134, considering it was the middle of the summer, it was near freezing when I woke up at 5.30am, my biological clock telling me that I urgently needed a pee, with no time to spare, I fumbled with the door zip, stepped outside and fell as I tripped over a tent guy rope and at the same time stubbed my toe on a steel tent peg. Containing a scream caused by the excruciating throbbing from my left foot big toe, I hopped towards the nearest scrub, one hand holding my big toe and the other clutching my manhood, not bothering to acknowledge the courteous good morning offered from the early morning walkers. Relieved that I made it to the scrub and did the necessary, I hopped back to the tent wearing only my underpants as more early walkers looked at me as they passed, thinking to themselves, not a pretty sight. My thrashing about must have woken the guys because they were awake when I stepped into the tent, I soon fired up the cooker and made hot tea for everyone, I then boiled water for washing at the cold water facility close by. I washed first so that I could prepare breakfast while everyone else was washing. We finished breakfast and had everything packed up and ready to go by 8am. For letting us stay, I promised the lady ranger that we would vacate the site before her boss arrived at 8.30am, I paid the site fee and thanked our hosts for their hospitality and we were on our way. At about 10am, the sun had broken through the low cloud, increasing the temperature and allowing us to strip to T shirts and drive with the windows open. The plan that day was to leisurely drive through Banff so as to take in the scenery then make our way to Calgary, a 221 mile, 7 hour journey. We stopped at Columbia Lodge for a

Outside Columbia Lodge, with the glacier in the background

decent breakfast and sat at a table that had a breathtaking panoramic view of the Columbia Icefield, the first of many special sights we were to see that day. As we progressed south we passed Molar and Hector Glaciers, the beautiful Lake Louise and the ever present awesome backdrop of the Rocky Mountains that stretch for hundreds of miles in each direction, without doubt the most spectacular views I have ever seen. At last, we saw our first brown bear, it was sitting by the side of the road causing the traffic to back up, car owners left their cars in the middle of the road and rushed forward with their cameras to take pictures, including ourselves.

It was our best day so far, everyone was happy and sharing scenic discoveries with one another, we were all excited at what unfolded before us. We followed the Trans-Canada Highway south, bypassing Banff town, heading for the Sarcee Indian Reserve before arriving at Calgary a little after 6pm, everyone agreeing we had a wonderful day. Calgary, like most towns in southern Canada and North America, is benefiting from the oil and fracking boom so there was a lot of oil people in town and not enough accommodation to go around but after two attempts, we managed to book into a small motel with a restaurant close by. It had been a long and hectic day and we were excited at the prospect of crossing the border into the U.S.A. the following day.

We were still in a jolly mood at breakfast, chatting about what we had seen the day before, I think because everyone had enjoyed themselves so much Roger didn't mention about going home, I was glad he decided not to leave. In spite of the issues, we would have driven 4800 miles in 18 days from the time we left Vancouver and crossed the border into the U.S.A. later that day, an average of 266 miles a day.

Monday 12th August, day 135, we were late leaving Calgary, the weather had closed in and it was raining, I was a little sad to be leaving Canada, a country that had shown us so much but we had a schedule to keep to. It continued to rain all morning, at about 12 o'clock we drove past the Canadian Bomber Command Museum and displayed outside as the main exhibit was a Lancaster Bomber, I couldn't believe what I was seeing so we stopped to have a closer look. Tomasz made himself busy with the camera, filming Glyn, Roger and me wandering through the museum looking at the exhibits. Having been a qualified pilot when I was younger, I was naturally interested in the old planes on display. I found the museum curator's office and managed to talk the curator into taking part in a filmed interview during which I asked him questions about the Lancaster. It transpired that they acquired it many years ago, it was a total wreck and had since been meticulously restored to an engines running, but non flying, condition. The curator told me that they run the engines on special occasions. I would like to be there when they fire up the old girl. Wishing we could have stayed longer, we reluctantly decided it was time to go. We thanked everybody at the museum for their hospitality and for showing us around then continued along Route 2 south to Carway, the Canada-U.S.A. border crossing. There were times when I thought that I would never make it but at 4 o'clock that afternoon, we crossed the border into the United States of America, the whole process took just 10 minutes, ending with the smiling polite customs officer wishing us a pleasant stay and a safe journey. As we emerged from the border crossing, we were immediately confronted with a huge sign proclaiming that we were now entering the Blackfeet Indian Reservation and the state of Montana. We all felt elated at the prospect of driving east and arriving at North Bergen, our final destination in 11 days' time. We arrived at the Stage Stop Inn at Choteau Montana at 6.30pm; in spite of the bad weather earlier that day, everyone was happy and enjoying themselves. We drove 287 miles in a little over 8 hours so we were all tired and wanted to relax for a while before dinner. I checked us in and handed the guys their keys agreeing to meet in an hour in the hotel lounge, I sat in my room writing up my diary and counting what money I had and how much I would need to cover the costs that would be incurred up until we were to fly home. The project journey account was depleted by then but so as to be able to meet the costs, each day I made a daily phone call to Vi to have our usual chat and at the same time let her know how much money I needed, she would then make a transfer from our private account to the project card account. I wasn't happy with the situation but having come so far, I wasn't about to let anything happen that would prevent me completing the journey. I thought about the reliability of 02 and 03, the little Suzuki engines sounding as sweet then as they did when we first started, I smiled to myself when I recalled that we were still using the same set of Cooper tyres we started with and neither 02 or 03 had had a puncture, I couldn't have chosen a better vehicle to do the job. I liked my little car, it had become a part of me, throughout the journey I had been very protective in relation to both cars and proud that they had come so far without a scratch and were looking as good as the day we started.

We seemed to be working together as a team and there was a much more jovial atmosphere. At that time, I remember thinking to myself, if only I can hold it all together for a few more days and am able to tick a few more boxes before I finish the journey. I recalled it was a long time ago when I first started planning the route, I made a pact with myself then that I would visit Yellowstone, the Little Bighorn, Custer's last stand and Cody (Buffalo Bill's town), places I saw on the films as a youngster and ever since dreamed of visiting.

Tuesday 13th August day, 136, the happy mood continued when we departed the town of Choteau, excited if you like at the prospect of travelling across America. The air was warm, the skies clear, and the sun was shining as we headed south on Route 89 to

Livingston, a 233 mile, 8 hour journey. I had become used to driving with the windows open, savouring the fresh warm air as it flowed through 02. Our route south would take us to Great Falls, a medium sized town that had grown up around waterfalls fed by the famous Missouri River. A look at the falls and a cup of coffee at the same time seemed about right to me. Following the signs to the falls soon led us to a barrier across the road, preventing vehicles from going any further and a notice that visitors must park at the car park and follow the track on foot that ran parallel with the river. As we hot footed it along the river edge as instructed, I mentioned to the guys that it was quiet, I had expected to hear the roaring sound of tons of water cascading over the falls. We arrived at a clearing where the falls were supposed to be, but there was nothing! There was an official looking person close by who informed us that the Missouri water level was low preventing any flow of water over the falls. It was 85 degrees (30 centigrade) as we stood there looking at the falls with no water while we decided what to do next. "How about a cup of coffee?" someone said, followed by, "Good idea," from everyone else as we turned and made our way back to the vehicles. We got our coffee and donuts at a traditional American diner at the edge of town, the old décor and a waitress who topped up your coffee cup every time you placed it on the table brought a smile to our faces. We debated whether to have lunch as we were there but we had to keep moving. The scenery, although different to Canada, was nonetheless spectacular in its own way, particularly when we passed the Little Belt Mountains to our right and White Sulphur Springs just before entering Livingston at 6.30pm. After first inspecting the rooms available at a roadside motel, I completed the formalities and handed the keys to the guys. The town had a prosperous look about it; I noticed there were a large number of oil and gas company trucks parked at the motel, and hotel parking lots around town as Livingston is at the centre of the U.S. fracking boom.

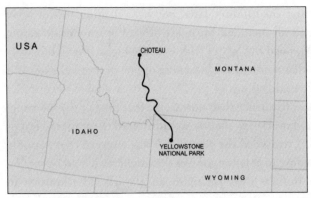

The route to Yellowstone National Park

During our meal at an Italian bistro, we got into conversation with a group of guys working a drilling rig, they told us that they drill where instructed by the owner of the land, when they find the gas they cap it and the owner of the land becomes a millionaire overnight. After we had eaten we made our way back to our motel, stopping at the Last Chance Bar to have a beer before turning in for the night. We ended up talking to some really nice local people who insisted that they bought us a beer, at the same time ending the prospect of an early night. It's fatal when someone bellows out "Are you guys from England?" "Yes," we would reply, then wait for a response that would be something like, "Do you know my brother Harry? He's working at a place called 'Birming-Ham'." When we finally came out of the bar and eventually got into bed, we were well oiled and in need of our sleep.

Wednesday 14th August, day 137, it was a special day and an opportunity to tick another box. Yellowstone National Park had always been on my must visit list when in the U.S.A., although I had visited America before, I never visited Yellowstone or the other places included in our itinerary as we drive east. Coffee was available at the motel but no breakfast, we were on the road by

8.30am and 30 minutes later, we were tucking into a serve yourself $8 all included breakfast offered at a roadside eating house. We piled our plates with eyes-are-bigger-than-your-belly portions that required the loosening of our trouser belts to get it all in. We waddled out of the Devil's Diner unable to control a touch more flatulence than normal for that time of the morning, cursing and muttering that we wouldn't need to eat for the rest of the week. I reminded the guys that it was a special day, not only were we going to Yellowstone but that night we would be staying at Cody Buffalo Bill's town, rodeo and all. The journey to Yellowstone was short, the road became more congested with campers and cars loaded with camping gear the closer we became. The road to and from Yellowstone Park itself was long and straight, terminating at a barrier with pretty girls with shoulder bags for cash and tickets, one of whom approached 02 smiling and said, "Where are you folks from today?" "England," I replied in a grumpy tone, knowing that I was about to be relieved of some money. I explained that the car behind and ourselves were together and I would pay for both. Still smiling, she said, "That will be $50 each," the bout of flatulence returned as I looked at her then said, "Is that each person or each car?" still smiling, Miss America gave me that 'you're a pain in the arse' look, "Each car Sir." Begrudgingly, I handed her the money and received our tickets followed by, "Have a nice day!" There are two viewing routes called short or long or half or full day loops, you can follow either and they are set up to take visitors past the main features, we chose the short loop because we were going to Cody later. To be truthful you need to allow two days to get value for your ticket and to see all.

Once inside the park you can pretty well stop anywhere, so just after being relieved of our money, we stopped to have a look at the map I was given so as to familiarise ourselves with the route we were to take and what exit we needed to be near when it was

Les – a moment alone at Yellowstone National Park

time to leave. You can understand why the Yellowstone Park rangers are touchy about protecting the environment; they want you to see it and touch it but not destroy it. There were park rangers everywhere to help and guide us and to explain about the history of Yellowstone. From our elevated position, the guys and I surveyed the area in all directions and we agreed that the views and scenery were absolutely stunning. Following the route selected, we passed various small animals, including elk, on the way. We stopped to follow the flow of people on foot along a wooden walkway that led us on a circuit around gushing hot sulphur springs that sprayed a rotten egg smelling mist over the unwary, we arrived at the end of the walkway, not exactly smelling of roses, we drove further along the road to the hot liquid mud geezers that surrounded a small bright turquoise coloured lake. Not far below the surface was nature's furnace, the super-heated water it produced liquefied the deep down white clay to the consistency of porridge then belched it into the air when you least expected it, the smell was diabolical. The guys

Gushing hot sulphur springs at Yellowstone

and I spoke to a ranger who told us that the Yellowstone National Park as we know it is sitting on top of a resting volcano, or 'an eruption waiting to happen' as he put it. He then went on to say that the gushers and geezers were the volcano pressure release valves. He also told us that as we climbed higher we would come to the crater rim, over thousands of years the crater has evolved as a vast fertile plateau supporting large numbers of grazing animals, including buffalo.

Bubbling over with excitement from what we had seen so far (excuse the pun, I couldn't resist it), we decided to seek food and refreshment at the service area close by before driving to the crater rim. The restaurant was crowded but after hovering for a few minutes, we joined two people already at a table, we placed our order then chatted between ourselves. It wasn't long before the couple sitting at the same table asked us if we were Australian, "No," we said, "we are English," they then asked if we were on holiday, "No," we replied, "we have been driving around the world." I explained what we had been doing and that we were heading east to North Bergen to hand our vehicles over to our shipping agent for onward shipment to the U.K. Larry and his wife, Anna, who were in their 50s sat in silence just looking at us for a moment, then said, "How old are you guys?" "In our seventies," I replied, he paused then said, "Isn't that something?" in a loud drawn out Texas accent and at the same time leaned across the table to shake each of us by the hand. I asked Larry if he was on holiday, he said Anna and himself were in the oil business and they live in Texas, they were in the area having a short break, he went on to talk about various things then he ended by saying the biggest problem they have is getting labour to do the work, at the moment he is paying an unskilled drilling rig labourer $38 an hour. I remember thinking at the time that I would pass that information around when I get back home, it sounded like a good opportunity for our young people to make something of themselves. It was a pleasure to meet and talk to Larry and Anna, they are real nice people.

At about 2 o'clock, we were making our way up to the crater rim, the higher we went the denser and slower the traffic became, there were animals all around us as we approached the crater rim. Tomasz and I in 02 and Glyn and Roger in 03 were behind a large camper so our forward vision was restricted, the camper slowed to walking pace and at the same time moved to the centre of the road. My driving position was the opposite side to the camper driver so I was able to see what had caused the detour. Standing in the road was a huge bull buffalo, unconcerned as the camera clicking people in the vehicles inched by. I eased 02 past the beast, stopping for a few seconds to gauge its size; I looked into his big brown eyes and knew he was looking at me, I wondered what he was thinking. My mind still spinning with excitement from being so close to such a majestic animal, I drove a little closer to the gap that allowed visitors to see into the crater. As the vehicles rolled to a stop, the scene that unfolded before us stunned me into

Grazing Bison in the dormant crater

silence, the heart stopping view was unbelievable. The natural cut-out in the creator rim allowed visitors a panoramic view of the crater floor, the golden coloured grass bending to the light breeze stretched for miles. Just a few hundred yards from where 02 and 03 were parked was a sight that I had always thought I was unlikely ever to see. Spread out before us was a herd of about a 1000 buffalo grazing majestically on the golden grass with the far side of the crater as a backdrop. A sight everyone should see, it was magnificent. Glyn, Roger and I stood there trying to take it all in, Tomasz was busy filming us, the surroundings and of course the buffalo. We stayed as long as we could to savour the view but reluctantly we had to move on. We saw more wonders as we made our way to the exit and a cup of coffee before heading for the town of Cody (the famous Buffalo Bill Cody's town) arriving at the town limits at 5pm. We approached from the west along a road shaded from the sunlight that followed a river along a valley floor, emerging into daylight and the real mid-west cowboy town of Cody.

It was all happening that day, first Yellowstone and now Cody all in one day. We drove towards the town centre, passing the rodeo arena on our left and close by was the Big Bear Motel, we turned off the road and stopped outside the motel office and I went inside. The motel was a family owned and run establishment, the young lady behind the desk was talking over the phone so I took the opportunity to look around. It was definitely a cowboy town with saddled horses tethered to rails, girls in crafted high heel leather boots and jeans that are put on with the aid of a vacuum packing machine, check shirts and leather waistcoats with tassels. The guys, mostly over 6 feet tall, were dressed the way cowboys do, including wide brimmed hats. I ticked another box. I completed the formalities, booking us in for two nights, our rooms were on the first level and the vehicles were parked out front but one level lower making it easy to transfer our kit from the vehicles to the rooms. We were settled and having a beer when all hell broke loose, about 12 Harleys had arrived, the black leather clad riders and passengers were nudging the tail end of their twilight years and gave the impression that they had broken out of an old people's home. Shouting so as to be heard above the roaring engines, they struggled to cock their legs over their bikes and stand unsupported. The quiet and tranquillity was re-established only when the last of the bikes was switched off.

It was an opportunity to talk to Glyn, Roger and Tomasz, they already knew that the following day was to be a rest day, also a time to have a close look at the town and visit the Buffalo Bill Museum, what I didn't mention in much detail before was that same evening, we were going to the rodeo. I then went on to say that before we were to eat tonight, I was going to the rodeo arena to talk to them about who we were and what we were doing and to ask if we could drive around the arena ring as part of the show. Later, I drove to the arena and spoke to the owner, he was a nice guy, a man mountain, over six feet, six inches tall, a very big man, he listened to what I had to say and agreed that it would be an added feature to the evening's events but he declined my proposal saying that vehicles were not allowed in the arena for various reasons. However, he said he would provide a platform at the ringside for our cameraman. I returned to where the guys were waiting and told them what was said, we then walked further along the road to a saloon that had been recommended to us as a place to eat with entertainment. The saloon was straight out of a modern western movie, the food was O.K. and the beer passable, a band played western music and there was line dancing, we had a great evening and a good beginning of our stay at Cody.

Thursday 15th August, day 138, I was awake early and soon outside breathing the morning air, I obtained a map of the town from the tourist carousel at the reception and sat down with a cup of coffee, the only beverage available, and studied the layout of the town. William F. 'Buffalo Bill' Cody, the man himself, helped establish the town in 1895; he built a ranch just south of the town, and constructed the Irma Hotel in 1902 which he called 'just the sweetest hotel that ever was'. Bill and his wife, Louisa, had four children, all girls and as we all know went on to become a legend of the west. The Irma Hotel is still there operating commercially, a Mecca for those people who like anything western. The town is divided into the old cowboy town, as I like to call it, and the more modern town that has been added to over the years. I finished ringing around the points of interest when the guys found me. We walked together to a diner a short distance along the road and consumed a breakfast each that left us fighting for breath and was big enough to feed an average family, will I ever learn?

Still fighting for breath, we started our walking tour of the old town, the saloons and old shops and, in some instances, town life a 100 years ago all received our close scrutiny. The tour of the town ended late morning at the Buffalo Bill Historical Centre, a modern museum situated in the modern part of town. Buffalo Bill was a pioneer and a hero who is recognised and acknowledged as such throughout the museum. A must visit place if you are ever in the area. It had been a fascinating and exciting morning, but we needed to find our way back to the Big Bear Motel. We had started our tour that morning with a bounce and spring in our step, plenty of chat, and distance no barrier. Retracing our steps to the motel in the sweltering sun, worn out and haggard, seized calf muscles and sore feet that didn't want to function properly was another matter. We arrived back to the motel at 2.30pm, drained of what energy we had and in need of an afternoon nap. It was 5pm when we emerged refreshed from our rest. Over a beer at the bar opposite, I outlined our itinerary for the following day, emphasising that our destination was the town of Buffalo, Wyoming but first we would be visiting Garryowen and the Little Bighorn. We were looking forward to walking the site where it all happened. At 7.30pm that evening, we made our way to the rodeo arena, managing to get Glyn, Roger and me centre front row seats; Tomasz, complete with camera and sound kit, was set up on the platform in front of us. The rodeo is a weekly family affair, Mum, Dad and the kids, popcorn and coke, the band played for a few minutes then the procession started. Everyone involved, whether management, competitor or arena safetymen, stockmen and women, clowns and anyone else involved on horseback and walking, moved around the arena all waving flags and banners. The arena wasn't quite full but those there were going crazy with excitement. For two hours there was no let up, the entertainment was continuous, roping cattle, bronco riding and those fearless competitors clinging to the back of a corkscrewing bull have my absolute admiration. Sadly, there were occasions when it went seriously wrong and the competitors on those occasions were stretchered out of the arena. It was my first rodeo and the two hours entertainment passed too quickly but I will remember that night forever. Making our way back towards our motel, someone said they were hungry so we stopped at the next diner we came to for a bite and a beer. It was a cosy place, we all ordered food we shouldn't have had that late at night, by the time we had eaten and flushed it down it was almost 12 o'clock.

Friday 16th August, day 139, we were all awake and up ready to go early, the vehicles had been checked and our kit stowed and we were having our free coffee by 8.30am. We were still full from our feast the previous night so we agreed that we would stop for breakfast later. The experience of the past two days was fresh on our minds as we headed towards Garryowen and the Little Bighorn, about a 2 hour drive. The jolly atmosphere continued, we seemed to be working together as a team so I didn't have to worry so much, allowing me to focus on the things that mattered, but I always kept an eye on what was happening around me. The pain in my groin had become less noticeable since driving on paved roads in Canada and the U.S.A. I guess the problem was aggravated by me bouncing up and down as we drove across Russia, Kazakhstan and Mongolia. At 11am, we parked at the Little Bighorn then walked the short distance to the visitor centre, it was the first time I had seen a map of the battleground, I didn't realise the battle took place over such a large area. Realising that to visit the whole site would take a full day, we agreed to spend the short time we had looking at the presentation at the centre, sit in on a lecture at the open-air auditorium and visit the sites within walking distance including 'Last Stand Hill' where Custer and 41 of his men died.

Glyn, Roger and I spent time at the visitor centre studying a large map of the battle area which also explained the sequence of events leading up to the death of Custer and the soldiers who fought alongside him. Armed with some idea of the layout of the

Cody and the world famous rodeo – Buffalo Bill's town!

battlefield and what happened, we moved on to the auditorium and a presentation that was about to start. The park ranger giving the presentation introduced himself then went on to describe what happened to a packed audience. The 45 minute presentation covered the years of persecution and harsh treatment of the Indians by the army and settlers and the coming together of the tribes to take on and annihilate the army under Lt. Col. George Armstrong Custer, 7th Cavalry Commander, at the Little Bighorn. It was a bit of an eye opener when told about the senseless orders that filtered down through the chain of command. Custer's force numbered about 600, apparently at that time he wasn't aware that the Indian strength was in the region of 7000. I have always been interested in this sort of thing, I should have thought that there was something lacking in his intelligence reporting, Custer should have known what he was up against and hightailed out of there to fight another day.

At the end of the presentation, we had a clearer mental picture of what happened and set off to walk part of the battlefield that was close by. It was a pleasant sunny day, there was a warm breeze and the sound of birds all around, but in a way it was a sombre place, so many people lost their lives that fateful time, yet it had a sort of comforting feel about it as we followed the arrows directing visitors to various parts of the battlefield. Tomasz kept himself busy filming from the moment we arrived and continued throughout the morning and was following behind, capturing

The site of Custer's Last Stand

everything as we made our way to Battle Ridge and Calhoun Hill. Glyn, Roger and I walked in silence as we each surveyed the scene and visualised the carnage that took place over two days in June 1876, there were marker stones everywhere, indicating what happened at this or that spot, and in most cases the names of the soldiers who died there, very depressing. We eventually arrived at Last Stand Hill, the place where Custer and 41 officers and men of the 7th Cavalry ended their lives, the position of those who fell that day is indicated by an inscribed stone, Custer's remains were eventually reinterred at the U.S. Military Academy at West Point, 11 officers and two civilians were transferred to cemeteries in the east, the remains of the command were buried together in a mass grave around the base of the memorial. I sat alone at the memorial for a while, thinking about what happened the day of the battle, I understand that Custer and his men had been searching for the Indians for a number of days, they were tired and hungry and in no fit state to defend themselves in battle. Based on information given to Custer at some point that an army scout had located an

Markers indicate where Custer and his men fell

Indian village, bearing in mind Custer didn't know the strength of the Indians, he divided his command into three, sending two units in different directions to attack the village. In so doing, Custer made it easy for the Indians and history was made. What I can't understand, unless I have missed something, is that ultimately, Custer was responsible, he mismanaged the situation, resulting in the death of 260 army and civilian personnel but ended up becoming a hero. Glyn, Roger, Tomasz and I remained at the memorial for a few minutes longer to have a final look around before leaving for the town of Buffalo, Wyoming, another three hour drive. The route to Buffalo cut through vast areas of hilly grassland, the traditional Indian hunting ground for thousands of years; you can understand the Indians not exactly jumping for joy when the white man arrived. Late in the afternoon, we crossed from Montana into Wyoming arriving at Buffalo and checking into the Comfort Inn on Highway 16 East at 7pm.

It was another long day, after our meal we were content to sit for a while in the reception area reviewing what we had achieved over the previous few days. I was personally pleased with myself as to the outcome bearing in mind I put the itinerary together during the winter nights at home in the U.K. hoping everything would turn out O.K.

Saturday 17th August, day 140, the sun, nature's alarm clock, was shining through the window of my room when I opened my eyes, the start of another day, I lay in bed thinking to myself, only 7 more days to go before we deliver 02 and 03 to our shipping agent at North Bergen. Apart from the few miles I will have to drive from when I collect the vehicles from the U.K. port of entry to my home, I will, near as damn it, have driven around the world when I reach North Bergen on the eastern seaboard of the U.S.A., the very thought of it made me smile. The plan that day was to drive as far as Murdo in the state of Dakota, about a 332 mile, 9 hour journey, arriving at 6.30pm Buffalo time plus an hour Murdo time so it would be 7.30pm real time when we arrive. Throughout the journey, the crew and I had to adjust to the time zones' variation as we travelled around the world, travelling in an easterly direction means that you add time when you cross a time zone, on occasion this could be twice a day, it's mind blowing, you lose track of time and sometimes you don't know what day it is. We finished our breakfast, checked and fuelled the vehicles and were on the road driving east by 9am, it was a pleasant morning, a cloudless sky and brilliant sunshine, the making of a perfect day. Unfortunately, that wasn't to be. After driving an hour or so along the highway, 03 slipped back into the 'yo-yo' mode and drove past Tomasz and I in 02 and disappeared into the distance, I wasn't too happy about it, I just watched as they dropped out of sight behind a hill. I was uneasy when Glyn and Roger drove off in the distance the way they did, I had already asked them not to do it for the reasons previously stated, I didn't want to pull rank on them at this stage and maybe spoil the remainder of the journey for them so I let them get on with it hoping they didn't have an accident. The route was pretty straight forward and with luck they would wait at a service area for Tomasz and me to catch up. Over the last day or so, 02 had developed a slight vibration that travelled up to the steering wheel, it was manageable but I thought that when we were to stop for lunch and if there was a garage close by I would change the wheels around to see if that cured the problem. It was lunch time as we entered the town of Sturgis, a famous place for Harley Davison owners, once a year the town is host to one of the largest Harley conventions in the world and it took place a few days before we arrived so the town was still buzzing. We stopped at a shopping area that included a diner, I said to the guys that they should go ahead and order their food at the diner while I visited the motorcycle dealership at the end of the complex to ask if there was a tyre and wheel balancing shop close by. I entered the motorcycle showroom and made my way to the back and a man who turned out to be the manager; a salesman sitting at another desk nodded in recognition. I introduced myself to the manager and asked if he could direct me to a tyre shop, explaining that I wanted to change the wheels around on 02, he informed me that it was after 1pm and the workshops were closed, I asked why the shops were closed and he replied saying that it was Saturday, most auto shops close at 1pm, scratching my head, I said that I didn't know it was Saturday.

I thanked the man, turned and walked past the lines of sparkling new motorcycles as I made my way to the showroom entrance, as I did, I automatically scanned the bikes on display and noticed a headlamp of a bike tucked away at the back that looked familiar.

At that point I should have continued to walk out of the showroom, but I didn't, bloody fool! I squeezed my way through the tightly packed bikes on display to the one I had my eye on, becoming excited like a sixteen year-old getting his first bike.

When I had a closer look it was a 1979 Triumph Bonneville 750, sparkling like a diamond. When I was a youngster, and again when I was sixty still thinking I was a youngster, I owned at one time or another 13 bikes but never managed to acquire a Bonneville. I was mentally reminiscing about my old motorcycle days and cooing like a baby as the salesman, seeing my interest, vaulted over his desk and slid up alongside me like a snake about to hypnotise its prey. He said, "Can I help you sssss-sir?" (for the purpose of describing what happened next, I will refer to hissing Sid the salesman as Sid), "Just looking," I replied, then he went on to say that the bike was for sale on behalf of a private owner, and would ssssss-sir like to sit on the bike and try it for size, Sid was a sharp salesman but I had the measure of him, I thought to myself as Sid cleared a path and pushed the Bonneville through the showroom doors, parked it on its stand and started it. The roar of the engine was like music to my ears and made my bottom lip quiver, Sid had me hooked and was reeling me in. The two voices fighting each other in my head, the excited one saying treat yourself, you only live once, and the other, sounding a bit like my bank manager saying, your wife will murder you when she finds out. In an effort to break the hypnotic hold Sid had over me and come to my senses, I made an offer confident that it would be rejected and I could go on my way. A few minutes later Sid came back sporting a grin from ear to ear, "Your offer has been accepted," don't do it the voice in my head repeated. The next thing I remember is standing outside the showroom clutching a receipt for a $1000 removed from my wife's and my joint account via my debit card and wondering how I was going to tell her what I had done, even worse, I had more to pay, I was up to my neck in it this time.

I was sitting on the bike outside the showroom when the guys, concerned that I didn't follow them to the diner come looking for me, Tomasz must have had some idea that I had been up to no good because he came with the guys carrying the camera and immediately started filming, Roger boomed out as he walked towards me, "Don't tell me you have bought that bike," "Yes," I said with a sickly grin on my face. I told the guys what happened, they looked at me and said, "Wait till Vi finds out." I had a final word with the showroom manager saying that I would contact him in a day or so to confirm the shipping arrangements and transfer the remaining payment of the purchase price, then joined the guys at the diner. We arrived at Murdo at 7.30pm as predicted and after looking at the rooms, we checked into a tidy looking motel, after placing our kit into our rooms we went to a bar attached to the motel to have a beer before dinner, I wasn't looking forward to telling Vi what I had done, if I didn't phone she would get worried so I decided to bite the bullet and hope for the best. The guys and I were sitting at a table with our beers and chatting, I stood up holding my iPad and walked to the far end of the bar to make my call using Skype, while I was waiting a few seconds to be connected, I noticed that the guys and everyone else in the bar had stopped talking, it was deadly quiet apart from the loud ringing tone coming from my iPad. Vi answered, her voice and picture loud and clear bouncing of the walls like a sound system at a football stadium, "Hello dear," I whispered, trying to keep my voice as quiet as possible, "Why are you whispering?" came bellowing back for everyone to hear, "I am in a bar," I replied. We dealt with the normal things we talk about and then I told her I loved and missed her, with kissy kissy to soften her up a bit, before I mentioned the bike. Still whispering I said, "By the way, I bought a Triumph Bonneville."

Vi didn't respond immediately but when she did my normally placid and accommodating love of my life exploded and unloaded verbally. What Vi didn't call me isn't worth mentioning, the flow and general tone of our one way conversation travelled the length of the bar, I just sat there with a hard done by look on my face waiting for her to finish. When Vi finally stopped, we just looked at one another in silence. Not knowing what else to say, I swallowed to moisten my throat and then said, "I take it you are not too happy about me buying the bike," at that point the screen went blank. It took three days and many sweet talking phone calls before things got back to somewhere near normal. The repatriation of the Bonny back to the U.K. was another matter, what would normally be a straightforward logistical operation turned into a nightmare caused by our agent in Canada that resulted in additional cost and shipping delay, the bike finally arrived back into the U.K. just before Christmas but that's another story. It had been a memorable day; I remember driving that afternoon trying to work out how the hell I ended up buying a motorbike and it being the cause of upsetting Vi once more. It concerned me very much but what was done was done, I needed to focus my attention on the last few days of the journey. We continued to drive along Route 90 to Murdo, passing Mount Rushmore National Memorial, the Pine Ridge Indian Reservation and the Wounded Knee Battlefield, arriving at the town of Murdo, South Dakota, at 7.30pm local time, after adding an hour. We selected and checked into a motel and took the opportunity to relax for a while. I decided to have a closer look at 02's tyres and have a general poke around to see if I could find what was causing the steering to vibrate, it was irritating but not critical. I had a shower but struggled to make myself presentable due to not having any clean clothes, I turned my travelling bag out on the bed and said to myself, it's no good, I can't put it off any longer, I will have to wash my clothes and for the first time in my life use a washing machine!

There was a notice pinned to the wall of my room stating that there was a washing and ironing facility at the motel and to enquire at the desk, I collected up my dirty washing and headed for the reception, as luck would have it, a small bus load of people beat me to the reception so I had to wait in line clutching my bag of dirty washing that, having been disturbed, was now discharging an unwelcome smell causing some of the people in the queue to sniff under their armpits. Embarrassed that the people at reception had traced the offending smell to my washing bag, I hurriedly purchased powder and a token and was directed to a room at the back of the building. The room was already occupied by a number of women tending to their machines, I passed through the partially open door, trying not to be noticed and avoiding eye contact as I made my way to the only machine vacant and sat down on a bench opposite. I looked at the dated and well-worn machine that confronted me; the self-adhesive panel containing the instructions for its use had faded long ago and was unreadable. The panel containing the cluster of dials, knobs and buttons to press, although limited in number, carried no indication as to their function. As I focused on the panel to get some idea how it worked, my mind drifted back to the time when I sat for the first time in the co-pilot seat of a Bell 47 3B1 helicopter (the type with a plastic bubble at the front), it was my first lesson and I listened intently as my instructor explained the function of the instruments, I smiled to myself when I recalled the day I qualified. I was tired, it had been a long and eventful day, I started to consider dumping my washing and buying what I needed to see me through the remainder of the journey, at that moment a pleasant, round faced, kind of cuddly lady tapped me on the shoulder and at the same time said, "Do you need some help honey?"

I explained that I had never used a washing machine before, the smiling angel took control, she prepped the machine for me then said, "Put your load in, shut the door and press the button," she indicated to the button. I emptied my dirty washing on the floor to check that there were no paper handkerchiefs in any of the pockets, I had seen my wife do that, loaded the washing machine, closed the door and pressed the button then sat back to wait. I must have fallen asleep, I woke an hour later, the room empty and silent, I noticed that my machine had stopped so decided to retrieve my laundry, I tried to prise open the handle-less door but it wouldn't budge. I then turned my attention to the array of buttons pressing each one independently expecting the door to pop open but no luck; I finally came to the conclusion that I had to push the door. I lightly pushed the glass panel and the door clicked open. Beaming like a Cheshire Cat, pleased that I had mastered the contraption, I went about retrieving my clean washing piece by piece, folding each item neatly as I piled it up on the bench. I was half way through the folding process when I realised that all the white clothes had turned a shade of grey, my lovely white 'Heaven Can Wait I'm Busy' T shirts didn't have the same effect in grey thanks to the offending black socks I included in the wash. It was one of those days.

Sunday 18th August, day 141, I still had a lot on my mind but managed to get a night's sleep, waking early ready to take on another day. I swung my legs over the side of my bed then sat there for a minute or two, had a good scratch and at the same time chuckled to myself when I remembered the day before. I bought the Bonny without telling Vi beforehand, reminding myself that I still had to square things with her, and just to round the day off I made a mess of my washing, not the sort of day I wanted too often. I joined Glyn, Roger and Tomasz for breakfast, the route that day was straightforward, we were to remain on Route 90 to the town of Albert Lea, our stopover that evening, a 375 mile, 9 hour drive, expecting to arrive at about 6pm. We checked and fuelled the vehicles and were soon on our way, the weather remained kind to us as we joined Route 90 east and blended in with the flow of Sunday morning holiday traffic. It was like a mass exodus in both directions, boats of all sizes and descriptions, small planes with folded back wings, gliders, dirt bikes and polished aluminium caravans, some being towed by huge motorhomes packed with the kids, Mother in-law and the family dog. Driving that day was uneventful; we stopped for lunch close to the town of Sioux Falls. I noticed that the further east we went the more commercial the surroundings became, to our right was the state of Nebraska, Sioux City and a little further south Kansas City, names so familiar. Thankful that we finished the day's driving without any problems and arrived at Albert Lea as predicted, we checked into the local hotel and decided to find somewhere to eat and relax for the rest of the evening. The only place in town that offered food was owned and run by a Mormon family, there was no menu, they only had one main course and pie for afters, to drink you could have water or lemonade, a strange place.

Monday 19th August, day 142, we were disappointed with Albert Lea, the part of the town where the hotel was situated had no street lighting so when daylight faded, the town was in pitch black darkness. The only light available, apart from the odd windows of an occupied house, was from passing cars, it had a sort of eerie feeling about the place. I was glad to be out of there and back on the road heading to Davenport, a 268 mile, 8 hour drive. The route took us south to the town of Des Moines then east again to Davenport, our stop for that night.

We entered the town from the west heading for the centre, almost immediately we came across the La Quinta Inn set back from the highway, it looked too inviting to pass by. There were already a lot of cars in the car park, nevertheless, we managed to park the vehicles and I went inside to see if there were any vacancies. As I approached the reception, I could see that there were three ladies of average height plus a taller person who I suspected couldn't make its mind up as to whether it's a him or a her, it's something that tends to unsettle me when I am confronted

Overnight stop at the town of La Quinta

with it, that to one side, I was welcomed with enthusiasm by all the ladies! Questions were asked about my 'Heaven Can Wait I'm Busy' T shirt, I went on to explain who we were, what we had been doing and where we were going, that did the trick, they boiled over with excitement prompting Kelly, the general manager, to ask me if she could take some pictures of her staff and ourselves standing by the vehicles. I thought for a moment then replied, "I have a better idea, I will give each of you ladies a new T shirt if you will wear them for the pictures and give me the best deal you can for two double bedrooms for one night," the ladies faced each other muttering a few words then Kelly turned and said, "Yes," to the T shirts then lent forward, at the same time looking to make sure we were not overheard and whispered into my ear, "One room at trade rate, the other free, call it a donation to the charity on behalf of La Quinta Inns." I arranged with Kelly to meet for the photo session later that evening then went outside to tell the guys what happened, on the way I reminded myself that I hadn't inspected the rooms then looked at the opulence of

Fishing for Salmon.

Living fifty miles from a supermarket, so a small plane parked in the driveway is more practical for collecting the groceries.

Takhini natural hot springs.

Driving along the lakeshore to the entrance to Yellowstone National Park.

A view of the Frazer River from the Tete Jaune Lodge, our overnight stop and white water rafting the following morning.

Breath-taking views across a valley and Glazier in the background.

A black bear chewing roots by the side of the road, seen as we drove south.

The guys cursing and hanging on for dear life as they take on the Frazer river.

Such enormity, a valley and flowing river, on the far side and a Goods train a half a mile long.

At every turn another breath-taking view.

Dawson Creek Mile Zero, the traffic island marks the start of the Alaska Highway going north.

A traditional Indian teepee being inspected during a short break at a roadside lodge.

Canadian Bomber command museum and German fighter project.

At last, crossing the Canadian-US border into the Blackfeet Indian Nation territory.

Driving through the centre of New York City and the end of our journey.

Roger and Glyn tucking into man-sized burgers in New York.

02 and 03 on display at the Novotel Southampton Journey's end reception.

Les receiving congratulations from Alun Parry of Suzuki GB at the journey's end reception.

the hotel décor and didn't give it another thought, as it turned out our rooms were as good as they get and a basis for a good night's sleep. Relieved that I was one day closer to completing the task I had set myself and pleased that the guys were still in one piece also that the vehicles were undamaged, I thought for a moment wondering how I would feel when we finally arrive at journey's end and I am relieved of the day to day pressure of driving the project forward.

The guys and I arranged to meet at the hotel bar at a little after 7pm, freshened up and wearing the new T shirts issued from the stock I carried in 02, we all arrived together looking clean and tidy for the pictures and smelling like roses for the ladies. Over a beer, I wanted to make sure that everyone knew the route for the following day and to mention that from here on, the traffic would increase considerably each day the further east we go and it would be easier to get separated so please stay together. We finished our beer then moved 02 and 03 into position in front of the hotel; I then went inside to tell the ladies we were ready. Wearing our T shirts, they were busy booking in guests when I arrived at the reception, Kelly saw me approaching then said, so that those guests waiting to be attended to could hear, "These English guys staying with us have driven around the world, isn't that something?" A few minutes later, the four ladies behind reception, and another six hotel staff who appeared, joined us in a group photo that included Glyn, Roger and me. Tomasz had already set up the film camera and left it running to capture the event, then became photographer, having been given an assortment of cameras from people who wanted pictures. Although the photo session was brief, the guys and the hotel staff made a jolly time of it and made us most welcome.

Tuesday 20th August, day 143, we tucked into a hot breakfast provided by the hotel, thanked the staff for looking after us, said our goodbyes and were driving out of the car park by 8.45am and heading along the 80 east to the town of Coldwater, a 310 mile, 8 hour drive. We needed to be in the Coldwater area by that evening because Roger arranged for us to meet and stay with Steve and Diane, members of Roger's family who live in America, their house is at the residential town of Rochester Hills, just north of Detroit, a morning's drive from Coldwater. There was no mistaking the signs indicating the manufacturing might of America as we drove east, the sheer volume of commercial traffic on the roads heading in both directions was unbelievable. We seemed to be part of an orderly conveyer belt of vehicles that travelled at a steady 55 mph that twisted and turned its way into the distance, we passed vast areas of farm land under cultivation that sometimes seemed to go on forever but when we passed industrial areas, the manufacturing facilities generally were huge and modern in appearance. There were also the closures and run down areas but I couldn't help feeling that the whole eastern side of America is one giant factory. I have seen it before when driving through Russia, there were big industrial complexes there also but from what I saw it was generally old and rundown. There were closed and derelict factories everywhere and pollution unchecked. I have to say though, the Russian people I had the privilege to meet and who lived and worked in that environment were among some of the nicest people I have ever met. My memory of those people with little hope of a prosperous future will remain with me forever.

We stopped for coffee and a short break mid-morning, while we had a few moments to spare I opened out my working map of the U.S.A. to show the guys where we were and indicated the adjustments we needed to make later to arrive at Coldwater. After topping up our tanks, we were back on the road and pointing east and were soon passing, on our left side, Chicago the Windy City, Milwaukee, the state of Wisconsin, Lake Michigan, and Lake

Superior further north and to our right Springfield, St Louis, Indianapolis and Cincinnati, all within easy reach should we decide to turn off the highway. There was a noticeable change as we passed Chicago, the safety of the orderly flow of traffic ended and was replaced by a time is money, more aggressive attitude, the flow of traffic became faster and irregular, the sound of horns more noticeable as trucks raced to overtake each other, suddenly we were very vulnerable and I was eager to get clear of the hostile situation as soon as possible. At last, the turn-off to Coldwater presented itself and we were able to turn off the highway. It was a short distance to the town of Coldwater and we arrived at 5pm, a little earlier than estimated, after inspecting two motels we finally found one with rooms that were acceptable to the guys and we settled in. Roger contacted Steve and Diane to let them know where we were and that we expected to be at Rochester Hills at about 1.30pm the following day. Roger told us that Steve had organised a barbecue and had something very special to show us, so we were looking forward to our visit. There wasn't much of interest that I recall about Coldwater other than the town looking a bit tired and the people I came across didn't seem to have much interest in what was happening around them. We managed to get something decent to eat and afterwards I told the guys that I was going to my room to update my diary but to be truthful I was knackered and the slight pain in my groin that I had been nursing had been active all day and I needed to take a couple of painkillers. The guys decided to walk to the centre of town and said they would see me later; I finished what I had to do and was about to get into bed when my iPad fired up with a call from Vi, just what the doctor ordered I thought.

It was about 4am in the morning at home, Vi said she couldn't sleep, we chatted for half an hour, I said, "With luck I will be back into the U.K. on the 29th," also that I missed her very much. We talked a few more minutes then she said, "I paid the rest of the bike money, that will cheer you up," it did but I didn't dare tell her about the problem caused by our shipping agent at Canada as far as shipping the Bonny to the U.K., I arranged with our east coast shipping company to handle the shipping. Our agent in Canada insisted they could do it cheaper and quicker so I transferred the shipping to them. The complicated shipping mess that transpired resulted in the Bonny costing three times as much to ship and three months before it arrived at the U.K. Will I ever learn?

Wednesday 21st August, day 144, it was a beautiful sunny morning as we made our way to Rochester Hills, just north of Detroit. We planned the short journey to include driving through the centre of the famous city of Detroit but we weren't prepared for what we saw when we got there. The once thriving centre of the U.S. auto industry was wallowing in the aftermath of a serious industrial melt-down. As we approached the city, I expected to see prosperous middle class housing and all American families going about their business, but instead what I saw was street after street of run down, unoccupied and derelict houses and property of one type or another that continued until we got close to the city. As we cruised towards the centre, we passed groups of people hanging around at street corners who looked at us suspiciously. The city centre had a more prosperous look about it and from what Steve told me later that day, the whole of Detroit was being revitalised on the back of the recently successful and expanding auto industry. We arrived at Rochester Hills at 1pm without a hitch but finding the house required some backtracking and two phone calls between Roger and Steve before we finally arrived and boy were we in for a surprise when we got there. As we drew up to the house that was situated in a smart wooded urban part of town, we were greeted by Steve but parked on his driveway was what looked like a Chevy Corvette, after closer inspection and Steve's explanation it transpired that we were looking at something really special.

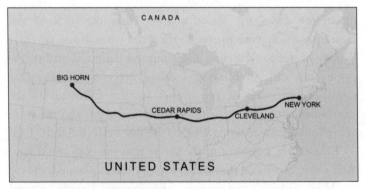

Last stage of our journey to New York

Reluctantly, I was dragged away from the supercar to be shown where I would sleep and we were to reassemble back at the car within a few minutes so that Steve could tell us why the car was parked on his driveway! As soon as we were assembled around the car, Steve told us he has worked in the U.S. for close on 20 years and was now a senior member of the design team responsible for producing the new Corvette Stingray and what was parked on his driveway was one of a number of pre-production cars that were being road tested throughout the U.S.A. This particular car, he said, he uses on a daily basis and believes that it will be one of the best and most technically advanced cars General Motors have ever produced, he then went on to say that this model is the top of the range, the specification included HUD (head up display), something I was familiar with from the helicopter days, the basic instruments are also displayed along the bottom of the windscreen on the driver's side so you can see what is happening without taking your eyes off the road in front of you, comes in handy for night driving. The car was loaded with state of the art kit and gizmos neatly packed into a body styling second to none in the world, in my opinion. With Steve's permission I was first to sit in the driver seat and press the starter button to bring the snarling V8 to life, I couldn't take it on the road but I could wind the engine up in the drive, the sound coming from the back of this masterpiece was pure magic. For a short while I just sat there looking at the panel styling and admiring the build quality, the engine was still rumbling as I closed my eyes to savour the unmistakable smell of the leather interior followed by the unavoidable onset of an I-must-have-one tantrum and the voice of my bank manager saying DON'T EVEN THINK ABOUT IT.

Reluctantly, I got out of the car so that the guys could have their turns. Steve said that if everything went as planned, the car would be available some time the following year, I made a mental note to watch out for it when it goes on sale in the U.K., I will be too old by then to ride the Bonny but I should be able to manage a Corvette Stingray! By early evening everyone had a chance to sit in and poke around the Stingray, we were all still buzzing with excitement when Steve and Diane, our hosts, invited us for drinks on a balcony at the back of the house overlooking a wooded area. Steve and Diane, a lovely couple, made us very welcome expressing interested in and asking a lot of questions about the journey around the world. From inside the house, Steve called out, "It's time to start the barbecue," and at the same time appeared with six of the biggest steaks I had ever seen piled on a platter with a heap of proper beef burgers, real food at last, what a feast. We all had a fabulous evening, we were thoroughly fed and watered and it was time to say thank you and goodnight to our hosts.

Thursday 22ⁿᵈ August, day 145, I awoke from another good night's sleep feeling refreshed and full of energy, I don't know whether it was because I was exhausted and needed the sleep, or that last gin and tonic, whatever it was it worked. Steve and Diane are working people so we couldn't hang around, we were up, breakfasted and after thanking our hosts for their special hospitality, we left to make our way to the town of Youngstown Pennsylvania, a 280 mile, 8 hour journey.

Sitting behind the wheel of 02 driving south, passing Detroit once more, heading towards Toledo, Ohio then a left turn to continue driving east on the 80 towards Youngstown, our planned overnight stop, I couldn't help thinking as 02 and 03 merged with the traffic flow, just two more days and with luck we will arrive at journey's end. I had mixed feelings now that the journey was coming to an end, elated that I would achieve what I set out to do, looking forward to being reunited with Vi, we had been apart for a long time so I desperately wanted to give her a good cuddle, I missed her very much, and I had some patching up to do with the rest of the family. On the other hand, part of me wanted to keep going, suddenly all the hardship and problems that I had to deal with were fading into insignificance. Later that morning, we stopped for coffee and to refuel, Glyn, Roger, Tomasz and I all agreed that we had a wonderful time staying with Steve and Diane and an opportunity to experience American hospitality, just one of the many pleasant experiences we had as we travelled through Canada and across America. After the break, we were back on the 80 driving east, to our left the city of Cleveland situated on the shore of Lake Erie, a little further north Niagara falls and Toronto across the Canadian Border all less than a day's drive away. We approached Youngstown later than expected, as we did we came across a sign that said 'London' pointing in the direction we were going, we stopped to take some pictures standing under the sign and Tomasz filmed Glyn, Roger and me under the sign pointing in the direction of London. It wasn't long before we arrived at the town of London and occupying a position at the cross road at the centre of town was the Elephant and Castle Pub and Hotel. I turned into the car park followed by Glyn driving 03, I suggested that this place was probably as good as any as it was getting late so Glyn and I went to the reception to ask if they had two twin bedrooms, if so, could we have a look at one of them.

The receptionist handed a key to Glyn while I remained talking to the young lady to find out why the pub and hotel has the same name as The Elephant and Castle, the famous South London pub in the U.K., smiling as though she had done this before, she explained that settlers established a village that had various names at one time or another until they eventually settled for the name of London. Over time, it expanded and became a large town and a place where U.K. immigrants settled, so it was natural that there were a lot of places in the area that have London or English names. Glyn hadn't returned at that point so I explained to the receptionist who we were and what we had been doing then asked if we qualified for a discount, she didn't respond to my suggestion, instead she said that the owner of the hotel was there that evening and was sure he would like to meet us all. Glancing at the computer screen then turning to look at the few remaining room keys hanging on their hooks, she said, "You can have two of our best rooms at a special low price." As though on cue, Glyn emerged giving me the thumbs up, I thanked the lady behind the desk and handed Glyn his and Roger's key then walked outside to tell the guys that we were booked in and to collect our kit and take it to our rooms. Thirty minutes later, we met at the bar to sample the pub's advertised offering of a pint of real English beer, when it arrived it was dark in colour and what we call flat (no head on the beer) and to make matters worse, it was warm. We then tried the real pub grub available at the restaurant and tucked into an American version of an English Sunday lunch, it wasn't what I expected but it tasted O.K., however, they needed to do some more development work on the Yorkshire pudding, it was as tough as old boots. I spotted apple pie and custard on the specials board and decided to try it, when the waitress came to take our order the guys couldn't resist the temptation so four portions were ordered. While we were waiting for the apple pie to arrive, I noticed a well-dressed middle aged man making himself busy behind the bar and in and out of the kitchen talking to the staff, and occasionally looking in our direction, eventually he came to our table and introduced himself as the owner. We chatted for a few minutes but you could see he wasn't with us; his eyes were darting about all over the place watching what was going on around him. He focused on us long enough to wish us well and a safe journey then turned to deal with something that needed his attention, we just looked at each other and burst out laughing. Expecting the worst, we sat in silence as the waitress weaved her way towards us with our apple pie, she put the heavy tray on the table and placed a plateful of apple pie and custard in front of each of us, we just looked at it, each of the dinner sized plates had a six inch square by two inch thick slab of pie crammed full with apples and laced with a generous covering of freshly made custard, we cautiously sampled the first spoonful, it was perfect. We remained at the table long enough to let our meal go down, it also gave me an opportunity to mention that time was running out so sometime the following day I would like Tomasz to film us erecting our tent and camping in daylight, although we had already camped it was late in the evening making filming difficult.

Friday 23rd August, day 146, we met for breakfast at 8am, there was no rush due to the journey being shorter than usual, we all mentioned the noise throughout the night, music from the bar and cars arriving and leaving the car park, I guess that is the downside of staying at a pub. I reminded the guys that in another two days we would reach North Bergen and journey's end, I also reminded Glyn and Roger to stop if they saw a campsite where we could film.

We checked 02 and 03 to make sure that the kit was secure then after a few minutes' driving, stopped at the first gas station we came to and filled the tanks. While I was filling 02, Glyn opened the driver side door and wrote down how many miles

I had driven from the last time we stopped for fuel, then made a note of how many litres at the pump of the fuel I needed to fill 02's tank, a simple calculation reveals how many miles I get from a litre or a tank full of fuel. It's a procedure Glyn and Roger adopted some time ago after I asked them to drive at a steady speed to conserve fuel, I explained that the yo-yoing and dashing about was only wasting fuel, 02 is 100 kilos or so heavier than 03 and my best fuel efficiency speed was 55 mph, that's why we drive at that speed. Their argument was that they use the same amount of fuel as 02, I gave up trying to explain that if 03 was driven at the same speed as 02 their fuel consumption would be less and by travelling together we would eliminate the possibility of getting separated and one of us would be on hand in the event of an accident. Checking my fuel usage had gone on long enough, on that occasion I wasn't too happy as I watched Glyn making a note of my mileage so I decided to bring it to an end by telling Glyn to p—s off, but I reminded myself that I only had two days to go and not to make an issue of it. We continued along the 80 east to Bloomsburg, a 218 mile, 9 hour journey. We hadn't been driving long before Roger, driving 03, passed Tomasz and me and disappeared into the distance, I watched 03 far ahead of me as I wondered if there was more to the fuel issue, perhaps there was some underlying incompatibility between Glyn, Roger and myself that I hadn't detected. I thought for a moment, on reflection there had been times when I locked horns with Roger over one thing or another but nothing that I didn't get sorted out amicably, or so I thought. The yo-yoing continued pretty well until we reached North Bergen the following day, during that time, my hope was that we didn't lose contact or one of us had an accident.

The highway traffic continued to flow in an orderly fashion so I was able to maintain 55 mph, mid-morning the highway crossed the Allegheny Plateau and ahead of us and to our right were the Blue Mountains and the city of Philadelphia further on in a south easterly direction. Our lunch and fuel stop was brief, up until then our search for a suitable campsite for filming revealed nothing so I was getting concerned as we continued our journey. During the afternoon, we arrived at the town of Milton and historic site of Fort Boone. The road continued over a wide bridge that stretched across the Susquehanna River and to our right at the river's edge was a caravan and camping site, as luck would have it, I was leading in 02 and 03 was close behind, I sounded my horn to attract the attention of whoever was driving 03 and pointed at the site to indicate to them to follow me, which they did. I turned right at the first opportunity and backtracked until eventually we located the site. I drove into what looked like a main entrance and was confronted with a muddy road and discarded vehicles half hidden in the undergrowth, I was about to turn and go back the way we had come when a man came out of what I assumed to be a derelict caravan and politely asked if I needed any help. I asked, "Is there a site office or someone I can talk to?" "Sure is," he replied, at the same time directing me further along the muddy track. At that point in time the guys sitting in 03 weren't expressing much enthusiasm as I continued as instructed. We came to a clearing occupied by an old run down jumbo sized motorhome and on a rickety timber porch squatting in rocking chairs was at best described as looking like hillbillies, two elderly men and a lady. Surrounded by mud, I remained in 02 for a few seconds hoping that one of the three people would enquire as to what I wanted, there was no movement on the porch so, reluctantly, I tiptoed through the mud to the porch then one of the men said, "What can I do for yer?"

I explained who we were and what we had been doing and then asked if there was a place I could rent for two hours so that we could film us erecting our tents and going about the business of camping for the benefit of the film we were making about our journey around the world. The man sitting next to the lady looked at me, his eyes were shaded by the rim of a straw hat but I could see that they were armour piercing light blue and he was looking at me as though he was reading my mind. He blinked, "You need good light," as though he was talking to himself then said to me, "Take that track," I looked in the direction he was pointing, "it will take you to the river," he said, "the grass area by the water's edge is what you are looking for," I thanked him for his help and asked about payment, he said, "Come and see me before you leave."

The grass area allocated to us was perfect for what we wanted to do; Tomasz took charge of the situation, his professionalism taking over, asking us to remain seated in the vehicles while he set up the filming equipment. When ready, Tomasz told us that he had set the camera to film continuously from the time we arrived, erecting the tents and setting up camp, ending with Glyn, Roger and me sitting at a table having a beer as the sun goes down. We started by reversing out of sight of the camera and at Tomasz's signal, we drove forward and came to a stop at the position Tomasz indicated beforehand then we went about the business of three guys setting up camp. When you consider that the guys and I were a day's journey away from driving around the world, overcoming all the obstacles and dealing with all the problems, you would have thought putting up two tents was well within our capability, not so. From the time we started our training, we managed everything until the winter of 2012 when we had to practise erecting the tents, every time we attempted it we got it wrong one way or another, out of shape, the support poles in the wrong place and worst of all there was always a part left over. It was the same when we camped for one night after the white water rafting and it was about to become a fiasco in front of the camera on that occasion. By the time we had unloaded the kit we needed and laid it out, a group of people had formed, attracted by the camera and the antics of three old guys in their seventies. The dreaded tents were unpacked including the bendy poles, pegs and

Benefiting from the 'camping learning curve': the crew at rest alongside the Susquehann River, Fort Boon

other various bits and pieces, within twenty minutes the tent was supporting itself, we then went about opening it out and hammering the pegs into the ground, by the time I realised that we shouldn't be doing that in case we had to move them it was too late. After cursing and uttering unprintable language most of the pegs were extracted and repositioned. It was another fifteen minutes before the first tent looked presentable, concerned about our rate of progress, I mentioned to Glyn and Roger that we only needed one tent and if they would get the table and chairs set up, I would discreetly make the second tent disappear. The bystanders had increased in numbers, some arriving by small trucks with gun racks in their cabs and rigged fishing rods strapped behind pointing to the sky, most of the onlookers had a hillbilly appearance about them, tatty clothes, long beards, and hair that had grown out of control. Everything was eventually in place to simulate overnight camp, Glyn, Roger and I sat at the table for a well-earned beer watching the river flow past and the occasional fish breaking the surface of the water, a perfect location. After a few minutes, Tomasz indicated that he had stopped filming and would join us for a beer, at that point the onlookers, seeing that Tomasz had finished filming, moved in closer and started asking us questions about who we were and why we were filming, they turned out to be a great bunch of friendly people.

I mentioned to the guys as we finished our beer that as we had erected a tent, why didn't we stay the night? I didn't receive a response so I didn't pursue it further. Without further comment, we dismantled the camp, packed it in the back of the vehicles and were on our way out of the site in next to no time, I asked one of the people who had been watching us if he knew the name of the site owner, he replied saying, "Ask for Russell, the one with blue eyes." I stopped at the office as requested, the three people were still sitting in their rocking chairs and were unmoved as I tiptoed once more through the mud, "Thank you for the use of the site," I said, "we filmed what we wanted, how much do I owe you?" Without answering my question, Russell with the blue eyes asked me what we were involved in, I explained as briefly as I could what we had been doing and as soon as I mentioned that we were all in our seventies, they shifted in their seats and nodded approval to one another. Russell's expressionless face adopted a grin from the nose down then he said, "You guys have come a long way the least we can do is help with the filming so there's no charge." I thanked Russell for his courteous gesture, at the same time nodding acknowledgment to, who I presumed to be, Mar and the boy sitting beside him, I waved goodbye and drove out of the gate hoping I could find my way back to the highway; kindness followed us wherever we went, such nice people.

It was a little after 6.30pm, the sun was still high and being Friday evening, the roads were busy with weekend holiday traffic, 02 and 03 joined the flow together, continuing in an easterly direction for the remaining 40 miles to the town of Bloomsburg, our overnight stop. The town was buzzing with activity when we arrived and accommodation was in short supply due to The Junior Baseball Championship taking place in the town and to aggravate the situation further, President Obama was in the area. It was quite late by the time we acquired two rooms and a rush meal at the local diner, it was close to 11pm when we decided to call it a day and go to our rooms. I was bodily tired and worn out, but not mentally tired enough to sleep. I kept thinking to myself, just one more day and we will arrive at our shippers at North Bergen, situated at the eastern seaboard of the U.S.A., apart from shipping the vehicles to the U.K., I will have completed my journey around the world.

Saturday 24th August, day 147, sleep eluded me until the very early hours, the mixed feelings of the joy of success and sadness that the journey was about to end occupied my mind together with intermediate flashes of concern about whether I could hold it all together for one more day. Not feeling too good that morning from the lack of sleep, I made my way to breakfast, Glyn, Roger and Tomasz had already eaten and were on their second coffee when I arrived at the table, "Last day," someone said, you needn't remind me I thought to myself. I didn't eat much but two cups of strong coffee brought me back with the living, I felt much better. While we were all together, I reminded everyone that we should try and find accommodation close to the shipping company so that we would be close by ready for Monday morning when we deliver 02 and 03 to the shippers. The 154 mile journey to North Bergen went without incident, arriving in the area at about 2pm, we drove directly to the shipper's address so that we would know where it was when we delivered the vehicles the following Monday and close by was a tidy looking Holiday Inn. We stopped in the car park while I asked the guys if they wanted to stay at the Holiday Inn, we were all in agreement and I went inside to see if they had two rooms available, which they had.

Glyn collected a key from the young lady behind reception to inspect the room while I enquired if there was a bus service to New York centre. Roger remained outside talking on the phone to someone. Glyn returned to tell me the rooms were O.K. then he went outside to tell Roger the same as I negotiated the best price I could get then booked us in. Half way through dealing with the booking-in process, Roger pushed the doors aggressively as he came in to the foyer from the outside, I was talking to the young lady at the reception when he said to me in a loud tone, "I want a word with you, you have upset my wife." I heard what Roger had said but I ignored it to focus on finishing my conversation and concluding the paperwork with the young lady, who had flushed with embarrassment. My business at reception completed, I then turned to Roger and said, "What's the problem?" "You have upset my wife," he repeated. I looked at him bewildered, and then said, "How have I upset your wife?" "She said you wrote an article for the blog stating that you and I have had a serious falling out." I just looked at Roger for a moment, trying to work out what had happened then said, "I don't know what you are talking about, I haven't written anything for the blog and suggest you get your facts right before you make accusations." A few minutes later, Roger approached me smiling saying, "I'm sorry, they have got it wrong, I owe you an apology." I just looked at Roger, weighing up in my mind whether to say something or just rise above it all and ignore it, which I did. I made it easy for Roger when we met later for a beer by having a conversation with him about sightseeing at New York the following day; neither of us mentioned the incident again. However, I received an email from Maureen, who managed our press and P.R., to say that Roger had written a very complementary note to be published on the project website to the effect of how much he enjoyed taking part and praising me for what the whole team had achieved. It wasn't necessary but a nice gesture that I appreciated.

Arrival at New York, final destination!

Sunday 25ᵗʰ August, day 148, it was a rest day, just as well, I wasn't feeling too good and by the time I arrived at the breakfast table, the guys had eaten. I managed a bowl of cereal and strong coffee and started to feel better; I didn't feel like doing much so sitting by the pool writing up my notes would have suited me, but that wasn't to be. I didn't want to let the guys down, the day before, we had agreed to drive the vehicles through the centre of New York City, and for me to not go as planned would have meant someone else driving 02. I had been the only one to drive 02 since I crossed the line the day we started and coaxed my little car all the way around the world until eventually we ended up at our final destination. So irrespective of how I felt, I wasn't about to let anyone else get their hands on 02, even for a few miles. Having resigned myself to take part, we made sure that 02 and 03 were looking clean and tidy and headed for the New York silhouette in the distance, most of the traffic was going in that direction so we tagged along and eventually found ourselves driving through the centre of New York. Being a Sunday, I guess

Roger tackling a huge steak

the traffic was light compared to a weekday but nevertheless, we could not find a place to park, every space was occupied or reserved for some reason or another.

I spoke to a taxi driver who advised that we stop if we find a space and stay until we are moved on; armed with a bit of inside knowledge, we slowly drove through the centre for a second time until we came across a stationary mounted police woman.

We parked in a gap close by and I walked up to the officer and told her that we had just completed a journey around the world, and at the same time pointed at the vehicles, I then asked if it would be possible for us to take some pictures of her and the horse standing by our vehicles. "Sure," the officer replied as she nudged old Silver the horse in our direction. Tomasz managed to film what was happening and at the same time took pictures with our cameras. A traffic cop appeared as though by magic with his violation book at the ready, but I beat him to it by stepping forward to ask him if he would have his picture taken with us standing in front of our vehicles. He looked at us individually

Chatting with mounted police, New York

then at the vehicles, then smiled, slipping the violation book inside his jacket and saying, "Why not, you guys from Australia?" We did what sightseeing we could bearing in mind we couldn't leave the vehicles unattended but because there was much more that we wanted to see, we decided to return to the city to do a walking tour the following Tuesday. It was hot as we made our way back to the hotel for a swim and afternoon tea by the pool; also we needed to allow some time to prepare 02 and 03 for when we deliver them to the shipping agent the following morning. As a precaution, I planned to remove the filming equipment, satellite phone, tracker and GPS from both vehicles together with any other high value items that I would pack individually and divide them between Glyn, Roger and myself as carry-on hand luggage when we were to fly back to the U.K.

I sat by the pool for the remainder of the afternoon updating my diary and making a list of things that needed my attention before we were due to leave for the U.K. the following Wednesday. The guys had finished their swim and had gone to their rooms, I felt relaxed as my eyes drifted towards the car park, settling on 02 and 03 motionless, looking pristine like they were about to start a journey around the world, rather than have completed it. The sun's rays reflecting off the blue and white graphics that told those who care to look that they had completed a circumnavigation of the world. Still focusing on the vehicles, my mind drifted back to the time when I first decided to drive around the world and the enormity of the task I had taken on, in the beginning I looked at everything through rose coloured glasses, it wasn't long before that all changed and the reality of what I was going to do revealed itself. There were plenty of people who tried to lecture me about the folly of such an undertaking and that I was sure to come a cropper but I wasn't about to give them the satisfaction of saying I told you so, it just made me more determined to succeed. The insurmountable problems I had to overcome to get to the start date, and my decision to go, even though I had been informed by my doctor a few weeks before that I had prostate cancer. Nobody knew of my predicament, the occasional slight pain was a constant reminder of the price I would have to pay when I arrive back into the U.K. I smiled when I remembered driving through Europe, the Nurburgring and meeting Lech Walesa and the laugh a minute as I travelled with Roland Spencer and Keith Twyford, it was just what I needed at that time, they were great fun. Travelling through the Ukraine, Russia, and Mongolia, the issues I had to deal with to hold the project together, the days and weeks driving 02 alone for anything up to 12 hours a day, not being able to stop to rest and the sleepless nights for one reason or another. The disappointment of not being able to drive through Japan as I hoped, the issue relating to 02 and 03 arriving at Vancouver weeks later than planned causing me to reschedule the remaining itinerary and the relief when they finally arrived at Vancouver.

The journey north to Dawson City, panning for gold at Claim 33, my memory of the journey south along the legendary Alaska

Highway, the scenery, animals and helpful people will remain with me forever, Canada is a wonderful place. I recalled the day we crossed the border from Canada to the U.S.A., I remember standing on the U.S. side looking up at a huge sign proclaiming that we were now entering Blackfeet Indian territory, quietly relieved that I had managed to get us that far and mentioning to myself that I only needed to hold everything together for another twelve days. To have visited real Indian reservations, Cody (Buffalo Bill's town), Garryowen, Montana, the Little Bighorn and Custer's Last Stand, and many more towns we passed through with names I remembered from watching cowboy films at the Saturday morning pictures when I was a lad, I looked at 02 and 03 wondering what would become of them. I must have been thinking about the journey for some time, I looked around and realised that I was the only one remaining at the pool, I sat there a little longer, thinking about various things then remembered with sadness that I would be handing the vehicles over to our shipping agent in the morning. I sat back in the chair and gave a long sigh as I glanced once more at 02 and 03 wondering to myself, is this the end, or could it be the beginning!

Monday 26th August, day 149, we arrived at the shipping agent's loading facility at 10am as arranged, the manager and his team allowed us into the restricted area so that Tomasz could film the vehicles being loaded and secured inside the container. The batteries were disconnected and each vehicle had enough fuel in its tank sufficient only to manoeuvre in and out of the container and, with luck, get to a garage after clearing customs back into the U.K. The guys dealing with the loading were professional people, giving and receiving orders in a strong New York drawl, I was confident that 02 and 03 would be looked after. The team completed their work then closed and sealed the container. Ever since the first day when I took delivery of 02 and 03 I had been

Loading the vehicles in the container bound for the UK

like a mother hen watching over her chicks, I guess seeing the door close on them signalled a further winding down and a step closer to when what we did would only be a memory.

Tuesday 27ᵗʰ August, day 150, we boarded the local shuttle that took us to New York city centre and spent the day doing what tourists do, visiting and seeing as much as we could. There was one exhibit we came across as we walked through the city centre, ahead of us was a small crowd of people and two mounted police, everybody was looking at three men and three woman standing motionless, stark naked and painted white, protesting about something or other, I asked a man close to me what it was all about he replied, "Your guess is as good as mine buddy," strange people! By the time we had completed our tour of New York City and seen what we wanted to see, it was close to 5pm and time to ride the shuttle back to the hotel and a celebratory dinner that evening to mark the end of The Ultimate Challenge, a 150 day journey around the world. The following day, Wednesday 28ᵗʰ

Les gives a final interview for the Ultimate Challenge TV series, after nearly 19,000 miles behind the wheel!

August, Glyn, Roger, and myself flew back to the U.K. 02 and 03, secured in their container, would arrive at Southampton docks U.K., by the end of September. I was happy that I had completed the task I had set myself so long ago, but at the same time sad that it had come to an end. We were a bit subdued as we travelled home, we didn't say much to each other, I guess it was a bit of an anti-climax when you consider we had been driving together for long hours, day after day, adhering to a strict schedule so as to arrive at the east coast of the U.S.A. and journey's end on time. Sitting in the darkened aircraft unable to sleep, reflecting on what lay ahead, I knew from here on my life would never be the same.

Epilogue

I sincerely hope you have enjoyed reading Heaven Can Wait I'm Busy, The Ultimate Challenge as much as I have enjoyed writing it, I have to say though, there were times when I felt like throwing it up in the air and saying sod it. Fortunately, I persevered and two years nine months later, I finished the book. On reflection, from the time I decided to turn an idea into reality, and the time I completed the book was a little over five years, I started when I was seventy and finished when I was seventy-five. Some would say was it worth all the hassle? I believe it was; would I do it again? Well I would need to think about it, but I probably would, providing I could do it without my lovely Vi finding out. I wanted to prove to myself that I could drive around the world and in spite of all the problems I had to overcome, that's what I did.

As to what happened when I got back to the U.K. and had to come clean about my prostate cancer, the first thing I did was to visit my doctor to let him know I was back and that I wanted to see a specialist to find out how serious my predicament was. It was a month or so of going backwards and forwards to one hospital department or another, there was some reluctance as far as getting someone to tell me how bad it was and I was getting the feeling that I was going to pay dearly for my folly, I eventually told Vi that I knew I had prostate cancer before I left, she didn't exactly jump for joy when I told her, more like a sort of numbness knowing that I had kept it to myself for such a long time. Eventually the day came to hear what the consultant had to say. He showed no emotion when he told me that he would have to remove my prostate and a few other bits and pieces, then as an afterthought mentioned that I would no longer function as well in that department as I have done in the past. Oh well, it was good while it lasted; I guess I got off lightly all things considered. At the time of finishing the book I am breathing and upright, I have a few more aches and pains and I am doing a little more than just thinking about what I should do next!

I hope after reading my account of our journey some of you may consider following in my footsteps, if so, the following pages may well be of interest. Initially what I was proposing to do appeared complicated and demanding, and in many ways it was. There were times when I thought that I couldn't go on but the determination to succeed won the day on each occasion. The plus side to all this as we travelled was that I gained experience and was able to identify things we did that we needn't have done, and the equipment we carried but didn't use. Of course it is easy to say this after the event but when I started putting the project together I decided to cover almost all eventualities resulting in being over-equipped for the journey, you know the saying, you are dammed if you do or dammed if you don't, there is a compromise though in most cases. The journey around the world I brought together was complicated and costly, and needed a lot of planning and organisation, which ultimately required two vehicles and a strict itinerary and schedule to make sure we met the crew at various locations around the world as planned. The successful outcome of our adventure is a credit to all those people who helped me in one way or another, particularly the crew, when I was bringing the project together at the beginning and the journey itself. Research, planning, and to some degree luck played an important part. It was no mean achievement what we did; bearing in mind we were a bunch of old guys who had no previous experience, but we were lucky and got away with it. I was asked and answered the question, would I do it again, and I said I would, but I would do it very differently as a result of the experience I gained from being project director of The Ultimate Challenge. However, before I go into detail about how I would drive around the world a second time given the opportunity, I have put together some information that might be of interest to those who may follow.

Appendix

The following information is compiled from data supplied from one vehicle, LCO2SUZ, driven the whole distance by myself. The second vehicle, LCO3SUZ, was driven the same overall distance but each of the four stages were driven by two of the road crew on a shared driving basis. The only modifications carried out to the vehicles related to increasing ground clearance, fitting oversized wheels and tyres, and protection for the bodywork and vital parts. The journey started Sunday 31st March and finished Saturday 24th August 2013, we flew from the east coast of America to the U.K. on Wednesday 28th August. As already mentioned, the following data I have listed has been extracted from my diary and records I kept as we travelled and is correct to the best of my knowledge. I chose to drive around the world in an easterly direction, the logic being that although the route was decided before we started, each day we knew that if the sun was on our faces as we travelled during the morning we were generally heading in the right direction, likewise if it was on our back in the afternoon we would be heading in the right direction.

The aim of The Ultimate Challenge was to prove that a bunch of old guys could drive two standard Suzuki Jimnys around the world and arrive back safely, the crew unharmed and the vehicles undamaged. It was never envisaged that it would be a jolly for the boys, more a test of our ability to do something people half our age would find demanding. Our route, therefore, around the world was as straight and direct as I could make it. The days we didn't travel, for whatever reason, I have called rest days. The pronunciation and spelling of names and places described on various road maps I used varied so there might be some head scratching if you trace the route we followed!

The distance calculation I used was 1.6090 kilometres to 1 mile.

The miles travelled each day and the total miles from Southampton to Vladivostok:

Day 1	Southampton via the channel tunnel to Bruxelles, Belgium	251 miles
Day 2	Bruxelles to Cochin, the Moselle Valley, Germany	229 miles
Day 3	Cochin to Bingen on the Rhine	193 miles
Day 4	Bingen to Leipzig	319 miles
Day 5	Leipzig to Gdansk, Poland	670 miles
Day 6	Gdansk rest day	
Day 7	Gdansk to Poznan	189 miles
Day 8	Poznan to Katowice	303 miles
Day 9	Katowice rest day	
Day 10	Katowice to Bratislava, Slovakia	225 miles
Day 11	Bratislava rest day	
Day 12	Bratislava to Budapest, Hungary	100 miles
Day 13	Budapest to Magyar	70 miles
Day 14	Budapest rest day	
Day 15	Budapest rest day	
Day 16	Budapest rest day	
Day 17	Budapest to Nyiregyhaza	147 miles
Day 18	Nyiregyhaza to Auschwitz, Poland	262 miles
Day 19	Auschwitz rest day	
Day 20	Auschwitz to Warszawa	183 miles
Day 21	Warszawa rest day	
Day 22	Warszawa rest day	
Day 23	Warszawa rest day	
Day 24	Warszawa to Chelm, Poland-Russia border	146 miles
Day 25	Chelm to Kyiv	324 miles
Day 26	Kyiv to Kharkiv	292 miles

Day 27	Kharkiv to Luhansk	274 miles
Day 28	Luhansk to Volgograd,	
	Ukraine-Russia border	222 miles
Day 29	Volgograd to Saratov	232 miles
Day 30	Saratov to Samara	257 miles
Day 31	Samara to Sukhodoi	72 miles
Day 32	Sukhodoi to Zlatoust,	
	Russia-Kazakhstan border	152 miles
Day 33	Zlatoust to Qostanay	256 miles
Day 34	Qostanay to Astana	420 miles
Day 35	Astana to Pavlodar	308 miles
Day 36	Pavlodar to Semey	216 miles
Day 37	Semey to Barnaul,	
	Kazakhstan-Russia border	272 miles
Day 38	Barnaul to Novosibirsk	170 miles
Day 39	Novosibirsk rest day	
Day 40	Novosibirsk rest day	
Day 41	Novosibirsk to Biysk	213 miles
Day 42	Biysk to Kosh-Agach	328 miles
Day 43	Kosh-Agach rest day	
	(Tashanta) border closed	65 miles
Day 44	Kosh-Agach to Ulgit,	
	Russia-Mongolia border	237 miles
Day 45	Ulgij to Khovd	145 miles
Day 46	Khovd to Altai	226 miles
Day 47	Altai to Bajanchongor	234 miles
Day 48	Bajanchongor to Ulaanbaatar	403 miles
Day 49	Ulaanbaatar rest day	
Day 50	Ulaanbaatar to Darkhan	135 miles
Day 51	Darkhan to Ulan-Ude,	
	Mongolia-Russia border	222 miles
Day 52	Ulan-Ude to Chita	411 miles
Day 53	Chita to Mogocha	370 miles

Day 54	Mogocha to Magdagash	296 miles
Day 55	Magdagash to Novobureyskiy	334 miles
Day 56	Novobureyskiy to Khabarovsk	297 miles
Day 57	Khabarovsk rest day	
Day 58	Khabarosvsk to Chkalovsk	287 miles
Day 59	Chkalovsk to Vladivostok	187 miles

Total 11144 miles

Tuesday 28th May, day 59, we arrived at the city of Vladivostok to rest and to decontaminate and prepare the vehicles ready to be shipped to Japan. However, having secured passage for the crew and vehicles on the ferry I was notified by Links Ltd, our shippers based at Vladivostok, that the Japanese customs had denied us entry and no amount of discussion with officials would get them to change their minds. Apparently, vehicles crossing from Russia to Japan need special paperwork; this was not known to our shippers at the time. Because of the situation, I arranged through Links Ltd to ship the vehicles direct to Vancouver, Canada. From 28th May, day 59 through to Monday 22nd July, day 114 the vehicles were subjected to various delays at Vladivostok and Hong Kong and as a result of shipping time. During that time, no mileage was accumulated. Our journey finally continued from Vancouver, Canada on Friday 26th July 2013.

The miles travelled each day and the total miles from Vancouver, Canada to North Bergen, U.S.A.

Day 118	Vancouver Canada to Williams Lake	322 miles
Day 119	Williams Lake to Smithers	317 miles
Day 120	Smithers to Dease Lake	367 miles
Day 121	Dease Lake to Whitehorse	388 miles
Day 122	Whitehorse to Dawson City	321 miles
Day 123	Dawson City rest day	
Day 124	Dawson City to Mentasta Pass	225 miles

Day 125	Mentasta Pass to Anchorage, Alaska	268 miles
Day 126	Anchorage to Tetlin, Canada	291 miles
Day 127	Tetlin to Desruction Bay	225 miles
Day 128	Destruction Bay to Teslin	295 miles
Day 129	Teslin to Coal River Lodge	251 miles
Day 130	Coal River Lodge to Fort Nelson	223 miles
Day 131	Fort Nelson to Grand Prairie	349 miles
Day 132	Grand Prairie to Tete Jaune	313 miles
Day 133	Tete Jaune to Mount Brazeau	97 miles
Day 134	Mount Brazeau to Calgary	221 miles
Day 135	Calgary to Choteau, Canada-U.S. border	287 miles
Day 136	Choteau to Livingston	233 miles
Day 137	Livingston to Cody	180 miles
Day 138	Cody rest day	
Day 139	Cody to Buffalo	283 miles
Day 140	Buffalo to Murdo	332 miles
Day 141	Murdo to Albert Lea	375 miles
Day 142	Albert Lea to Davenport	268 miles
Day 143	Davenport to Coldwater	310 miles
Day 144	Coldwater to Rochester Hills	131 miles
Day 145	Rochester Hills to London, Pennsylvania	280 miles
Day 146	London to Bloomsburg	218 miles
Day 147	Bloomsburg to North Bergen, east coast container terminal	154 miles

Total miles 7524

Grand total miles driven on land 18668

Total miles driven
18668 miles

Total vehicle miles
including sea time approximately
29684 miles

Overall journey duration
150 days

Number of road crew
taking part at various stages
7

The amount fuel purchased for each vehicle
2899 litres
(at 6.44 miles a litre) or 29 mpg

Number of refuelling stops
118

Number of countries transitted
14

Road border crossings
12

Time zone crossings
12

Continents crossed
3

Number of bottles of beer consumed
Sufficient!

Crew training schedule before departure

1   Vehicle familiarisation and equipment check.

2   Advanced driving, examination and assessment.

3   Off road driving and vehicle recovery.

4   Emergency vehicle repair, servicing and maintenance.

5   Emergency road accident procedure and roadside first aid treatment.

6   General first aid instruction and crew medication.

7   Map reading, GPS, satellite phone, and inter-vehicle communication equipment familiarisation.

8   Field training, tent erecting and galley equipment familiarisation.

9   Itinerary and route documentation.

10   Fitness training.

In addition to the above each crew member needed to be conversant with vehicle documentation, passport visas required and receive inoculations relevant to the countries they would pass through.

The question was raised earlier, would I do it again, yes I would, given the right circumstances. Since then I have had time to think about it and reflect on the wonderful things I saw and people I met as I travelled, If only I had more time to take it all in. Now that the journey is but a memory, and when I find myself thinking back to that time, I usually remember the good times, the things that made me laugh or feel good. On occasion, I thought of the never ending problems I had to deal with that nearly brought the project to an end, I sometimes wondered how I managed it. The Ultimate Challenge is behind us now, but at the time, I gained a lot of experience, putting it together ready for departure, and eventually driving around the world. On reflection, I think it worked out O.K. but it doesn't mean I couldn't do better next time.

If I decided to drive around the world a second time I would revert to my original thinking and drive at a more leisurely pace, a husband and wife team sharing one vehicle. It would of course depend on how well you get on with your wife! Two people, one vehicle is about the right combination, you only have yourselves to worry about and cost is kept to a minimum. What type of vehicle would I use? The choice is endless, heavy or light, with or without all the gizmos and how much money you have to spend. For two people the vehicle needs to be at a price you can afford, light in weight, and a standard basic specification that is repairable anywhere in the world should the need arise. I used Suzuki Jimnys for The Ultimate Challenge, a choice I made and have never regretted, based on the reputation it already had at the time, they lived up to that reputation. The Suzuki Jimny has lots of advantages - light in weight, reasonably good fuel economy, a short wheel base and, with the rear seats removed, ample space is provided for your kit and equipment. If on occasion you want to sleep under the stars it is possible to install a lightweight demountable sleeping pod on the roof. The Jimny also has a very good accessories and equipment market that can supply upgrades to wheels tyres, springs and shock absorbers and pretty well anything else you want to fit. I guess you can say I am a bit biased, but unless there is a better alternative, I would use a Jimny. Whatever car you use, fit an alarm.

Having decided on my driving partner and vehicle, and bearing in mind I was the wrong side of 75 years old, camping overnight was considered as a last resort if there was no accommodation available. Surprisingly, when driving The Ultimate Challenge, we generally found places to eat and accommodation, although some places in Kazakhstan, Russia and Mongolia were, on occasion, a bit rough but cheap, the roof didn't leak and the (usually) three beds in one room was warm. However, there is noticeable change underway, in Kazakhstan, Russia and Mongolia, there are new wide roads, modern roadside service areas and roadside accommodation, providing you don't stray far from the beaten track you should be O.K. The remainder of the route you take around the world should not be a problem to you, food and accommodation is generally available. You have your driving partner, you have your vehicle, and you know where you would like to go, what about your documentation? You need to get this right. You will need to take with you the original vehicle purchase invoice and four copies stating that you are the purchaser and owner and that it is paid in full. The information on the vehicle purchase invoice must include the vehicle identification number (VIN No.) if the vehicle you are using has a U.K. registration paper (the old log book), the VIN No. is printed there. You need to take with you the original log book plus six colour copies. Don't forget to mark the original copy so you don't let it go by mistake, and only produce it at customs if they specifically ask for it.

Valid insurance cover throughout Europe you will have already, but once out of Europe you will need to purchase insurance at the border of the country you are entering. Don't worry about this, it's standard procedure, if they ask for your insurance at the border, tell them you will buy it from the insurance office on the other side. You will need your passport and driving licence in its original form plus six photocopies, also mini plastic versions of both, handy for when you are asked for ID.

Visas, if you propose to apply for them yourself, allow a lot of time, in the past it has been known to take many months to complete, especially when you are applying to have a number of visas on one passport. There are specialist passport agencies around the country that will do it for you. You will have to pay for this service but it's well worth it, if you can afford it, send a list of the countries you wish to visit to the agent acting for you, stating when you intend to go and how long you will be there, and ask if they could let you know the cost before committing yourself. When applying for the visas, allow plenty of time either side of the time you are likely to be in a country, you never know you might want to stay longer.

Apart from fuel and accommodation, if purchased in or close to main towns or cities, which can be paid by credit card, all other transactions including car insurance are cash and preferably U.S. dollars. Buy only the currency you are likely to need for each country but carry as much in dollars as security will allow, avoid carrying large amounts of money with you at any one time. If you are planning to be away for some time, get into the habit of using the hotel safe and what money you carry with you spread around in small amounts, some in each pocket,

Everything is coming together nicely, but you have been putting off dealing with the injections you will need, visit your doctor early to allow plenty of time to deal with any problems that need to be sorted out, tell him what you are planning, he will probably be a bit disappointed that he's not going with you, and when he has stopped secretly hating you, tell him what you are planning and whether the injection you are likely to need will clash with the medication you may already be taking. If you get over the first hurdle, he will probably direct you to the in-house nurse, or department elsewhere specialising in tropical diseases. Go through the motions as before and with luck you will be issued with a personal injection log book identifying you as the person referred to, the injections you have received, and where you received them. On occasion when crossing borders you may be asked to produce your injection log book.

Preparation is most important, think and plan ahead, nothing is set in stone so change it if you are not happy with it, or seek advice, but above all, take all the time you need to get it right. Plan your route and itinerary, talk to people who have travelled the route before, if there are specific places you want to go and things you want to see, source the information you are looking for with the help of the internet. If you have a hankering to meet famous people along the way just to say hello, send them an email, who knows, you might get a favourable reply.

So far it has been hard work but pretty straight forward, working a year or so on the preparation for your journey, you have packed and unpacked your vehicle so many times you can do it blindfolded, each time you pack what you will need, what you think you might need, and a lot more you probably won't need. Your start date is rapidly approaching. Concerned that you may have overlooked something, you start to worry. You are as ready as you are going to be, avoid thinking about what might happen and concentrate on the here and now. If you have got it right, everything you need is packed in the back of the vehicle, if not, you can buy almost anything if, for some reason, it has been overlooked or mislaid. The one thing you can't replace is the bag containing your documents, passports and bits of paper you need to cross borders. Remove one set of copies of everything from the pack and keep separately in a safe place for emergencies, always keep the remainder with you or know that they are in a safe place.

There may be times when you need help or assistance, never be afraid to ask the local people for help, irrespective of where you are or whether they speak English or not. Your phrase book and a little theatrical posturing usually do the trick. Whenever possible, park your vehicle where you can see it, and plan the daily mileage so you spend the night in a town or city, there's probably accommodation with secure parking.

I almost overlooked this one; you would have read about my encounter with the Kazakhstan traffic police. I lectured Mariusz and Gary about being careful not to get caught for speeding by the traffic police, they of course didn't get stopped, but I did, twice in one day. The police in poorer countries supplement their income by stopping westerners and relieving them of their dollars so take extra care.

I sometimes wonder why I didn't listen to my own advice!

Les Carvall, Project Director, The Ultimate Challenge.

Acknowledgements

Very special thanks to:

Vi, Carole, Simon, Hayley, Jordan, Hannah, Abigail.
My friends at home in the U.K. and Greece.
The guys: Alan Butler, Charles Scott, Glyn Maher, Roger Winkworth, Graham Higgins, Mike Bailey, Roland Spencer, Keith Twyford, Gary Scott, Mariusz Rewed, Tomasz Malewicz.
Keith and Penny Rimmer.
David Ellery, Viewpoint Productions.
Maureen Wycherly.
Kati Morrish.
Alun Parry, Head of Press & P.R., Automobile Division Suzuki GB PLC.
Guy Foster, Managing Director, and Simon Whitley, General Manager, Newmans Suzuki Southampton.
Robert Rickman, Managing Director, Precise Sheet Metal Engineering Ltd.
Novotel Hotels.
ANU Overseas.
Castrol.
Cooper Tyres USA.
Yuri Melnikov, Links Ltd.
Brian Shersby, Ideal Forms.
N.Y.K. Ltd.
Red 5.
Alan Rollett, Tess Garage Services Ltd.
Towsure Ltd.
K.A.P Jimny Parts.
Richard Austin Alloys.
Endurance Rally Association.
First Choice Spinnings.

Heaven Can Wait I'm Busy

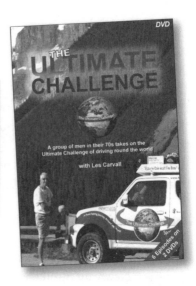

Follow the team as they travel around the world. A film of the journey is available as a six part DVD Series that places you with them.

The book accompanies a 6-part series produced for television that followed the Ultimate Challenge from conception, through its preparation and the journey itself, concluding with their triumphant arrival at New York. The footage captures the crew as they dealt with the highs and lows the disappointments, and on occasion clashes of personality. The in-depth Interviews with those taking part makes compelling viewing for everyone with a taste of adventure and travel.

TO FIND OUT MORE about "Heaven can wait I'm busy" or The Ultimate Challenge, to purchase the DVD set (or link to watch it on line) news update or to find out what we are doing next visit:

www.heavencanwaitimbusy.org